WORLD ATLAS OF
RAILWAYS

© Copyright 1978 by Intercontinental
Book Productions, Rand McNally &
Company, Chris Milsome Limited and
QED Limited

© Copyright 1978 Maps in Atlas Section
on pages 130–173 by Rand McNally &
Company

Produced for Mayflower Books, Inc., by
Intercontinental Book Productions,
Berkshire House, Queen Street,
Maidenhead, Berkshire, England.

Library of Congress
Cataloging in Publication Data
Nock, O.S.
World Atlas of Railways

ISBN 0 8317 9500 X

Printed in Italy

FIRST AMERICAN EDITION

Planning, Project co-ordination
Research and Editorial by
Chris Milsome Ltd.

Editorial Director
Chris Milsome

Editor
Chris Fayers

Contributing authors
O. S. Nock
John Bennett
Rory McPherson
Kenneth Cantlie

Text editor
Jeff Groman

Editorial assistant
Patricia Hayne

Research
Karen Gunnel
Pamela George

Concept, Design and Illustration by
QED Ltd.

Art Director
Roger Pring

Designers and artists
Alastair Campbell
Nicholas Farmer
Robin Gibbons
Elaine Keenan
Abdul Aziz Khan
Edward Kinsey
David Mallott
David Staples

Contributing artists
Moira Clinch
Sally Launder
Geoff Nicholson
Nigel Osborne
Jim Robins
David Worth

Atlas Section
Rand McNally & Company

WORLD ATLAS OF
RAILWAYS

O S NOCK

MAYFLOWER BOOKS, INC
575 LEXINGTON AVENUE,
NEW YORK CITY 10022.

Contents

Great expresses

Atlas

Railway systems

Reference

Introduction

Not so many years ago it was a widely held opinion in most parts of the world that railways were relics of the past. For medium-distance travel, the passenger train had been outstripped both in speed and general convenience by the private automobile; in commuter travel, city workers were beginning to prefer road congestion and the difficulties of parking to the gross discomfort, overcrowding and occasional breakdowns in local train services; while for long-distance travel the airplane showed an immense superiority in speed. Above all, in popular opinion rail travel was being outmoded. In the carrying of small individual consignments of freight, struggling amid antiquated facilities and outworn legal regulations, railways could not match the rapidly developing road service provided by fast trucks. Only the handling of heavy freight and minerals in bulk remained with the railways, and that mainly because no one else wanted it. To outward appearances the picture was gloomy, and it would have become so in actuality had not far-sighted men begun to stress and develop the railways' priceless asset: speed for mass conveyance – both of vast numbers of passengers, and of vast tonnages of freight.

The influence of geography
So there has come in Great Britain, France and Japan a great renaissance in railway activity. In the USA the development has been almost entirely in freight, and elsewhere in specialized traffic. Because it was the predominating influence of geography that led to the growth of railways in the first place, so, in this critical phase when so many outside influences are beginning to highlight the importance of railways in modern society, it is fascinating and immensely worthwhile to study the situation anew, on a worldwide basis, with the aid of maps. Going back to the earliest days, two of the first public railways in the world, the Stockton and Darlington, and the Baltimore and Ohio, were built to convey minerals from inland areas down to the sea for shipment. When the merchants of large industrial centers wanted quicker connection with their interests elsewhere, routes were chosen where geography made the going easiest and cheapest from the constructional point of view, and gave prospects of fast transit on a minimum of running costs.

Thus the broad conception of this book has developed, showing how geography as much as sociology and industry has dictated railway evolution. But it must not be imagined that geography was always on the side of the railway entrepreneurs and engineers. After the first modest beginnings, often with phenomenal financial success, business interests demanded the execution of bolder projects, and more direct connections. Contentment with roundabout itineraries following the contours of river valleys or coast-lines (to find easy grades), and with low initial costs, began to evaporate, and engineers were faced with calls to cross mountain ranges, to span rivers, and to traverse wide tracts of level, though unstable, marshland. This last-mentioned geographical hazard had been encountered earlier on one of the first railways, the Liverpool and Manchester, in crossing the notorious Chat Moss peat bog. The methods by which George Stephenson finally conquered this obstacle became the pattern for dealing with similar difficulties in many parts of the world.

Many of the engineering problems were entirely new. The established professional men had built harbors, lighthouses, roads and canals, but the introduction of the steam locomotive brought new parameters. There was a limit to the steepness of the grades it could climb, for while

LNER *Flying Scotsman*, restored in 1938.

a military road for foot soldiers, pack horses, or even elephants would be taken up steep mountain sides, such a route was impossible for locomotives. The surveys to obtain a practicable grade often had to be made in physical conditions of extreme difficulty: in the hill country at the foot of mountain ranges or in dense forests where there were few opportunities for obtaining long sights ahead, or for taking levels. Nor could established concepts like the suspension bridge be used in the crossing of broad valleys or tidal waterways. New ideas for long-span bridges had to be formed.

The development of techniques
It is an absorbing study to trace how the great principles of construction and early operation which developed in Great Britain, the USA and Europe were gradually extended and adapted to geographical and other conditions elsewhere in the world. British conditions and prospects for expansion called for massively built, relatively straight and level railways and there was plenty of capital ready to be invested in such enterprises. In the USA, by contrast, railways were needed to open up the virgin country. There was little money available; tracks had to be built as cheaply as possible with indigenous materials. Heavy industry was just setting up and could hardly afford large-scale imports. One outcome was the evolution of those masterworks of light civil engineering, the timber trestle bridges, so skillfully erected across many a deep valley or mountain torrent. Similarly, because of the infrequency of train services and the need to avoid high capital expenditure, engineers developed the system of regulating traffic by telegraphic "train order," in contrast to the more comprehensive system of signaling and interlocking that was found essential on the much busier routes of Great Britain, France and other countries in western Europe.

As the railway networks spread so the natural geographical resources of the world became integrated with the overall picture. Conveyance of coal was the first task of railways in Great Britain and France, and although horses did much of the hauling in the very earliest days, coal was the locomotive fuel. In the USA, although there were great discoveries of coal in certain areas, the vastness of the country made its transport to other parts uneconomic, and the great majority of early American locomotives burned the indigenous fuel of the forests – wood. Thus environmental considerations were in evidence from the earliest days. The voluble reactionaries in Great Britain who opposed railways on principle secured the insertion of clauses in Acts of Parliament prohibiting the emission of smoke by steam locomotives, and to comply with this, coke had to be used in place of coal.

Keeping pace with the times
Out of this deeply interesting historical foundation there emerges the majestic edifice of steady technical development, the evolution of codes of practice to ensure the safe running of trains at speeds that even our own grandfathers would not have dreamed of. The replacement of steam by diesel and electric power is inevitable in the modern age. In recording it, and in recalling some of the grandest moments of the steam era, tribute is paid to one of the most wonderful and most human machines ever devised and used by man.

While highlighting great passenger trains of past and present this book also shows how modern railways in major mining areas – Hammersley, in northwestern Australia, Roberts Bank in British Columbia, and Richards Bay in Africa – act as mighty belt conveyors in a single-product industry. These indeed are portents for the future, but equally so are the projects now under construction: for superspeed passenger lines in France, following the Japanese *Shinkansen*, and the running of the ingenious Advanced Passenger Train at high speed over the existing tracks of the British rail network. Today railways everywhere in the world are once again a very important feature on the map.

Evening Star, the last steam locomotive produced by British Railways.

The Development of Railways

The iron road

Although there had been railways of a kind in many countries to assist in the transport of horse-drawn wagons loaded with merchandise, even before the astonishing developments of the nineteenth century, it was the invention of the steam locomotive and its successful use on the first *public* railway in the world, the Stockton and Darlington, that provided the catalyst in the development of world transport. British engineers were to the fore in every facet of early railway pioneering: in the evolution of track, in tunneling and railway bridge building as well as in locomotive experimentation and operation. A study of railway developments all over the world in the momentous decade following the opening of the second great English pioneer work – the Liverpool and Manchester Railway, in 1830 – shows that in most of them British engineers were consultants, contractors, or manufacturers of locomotives. In Europe alone railways were established in Austria, Belgium, France, Germany, the Netherlands and Russia before 1840; in the same decade railways in Canada and the USA were expanding rapidly, and there had been a start in Cuba. It is remarkable to see the subsequent steady

Three factors helped to spread the railway world-wide: British enterprise (many foreign lines were built by British contractors); American enthusiasm for the new idea; and colonial possessions – the first colonial railway was opened in Jamaica in 1848.

The railway era really began with the commercial success of the Stockton and Darlington Railway, opened in 1825. A railway was inaugurated shortly afterward in France, and Europe as a whole continued to lead the field in the introduction of railways. Although political upheavals prevented the satisfactory development of certain railway networks, specifically those in Poland, Germany and Austria, by 1869 every country in modern Europe had built the beginnings of a railway system.

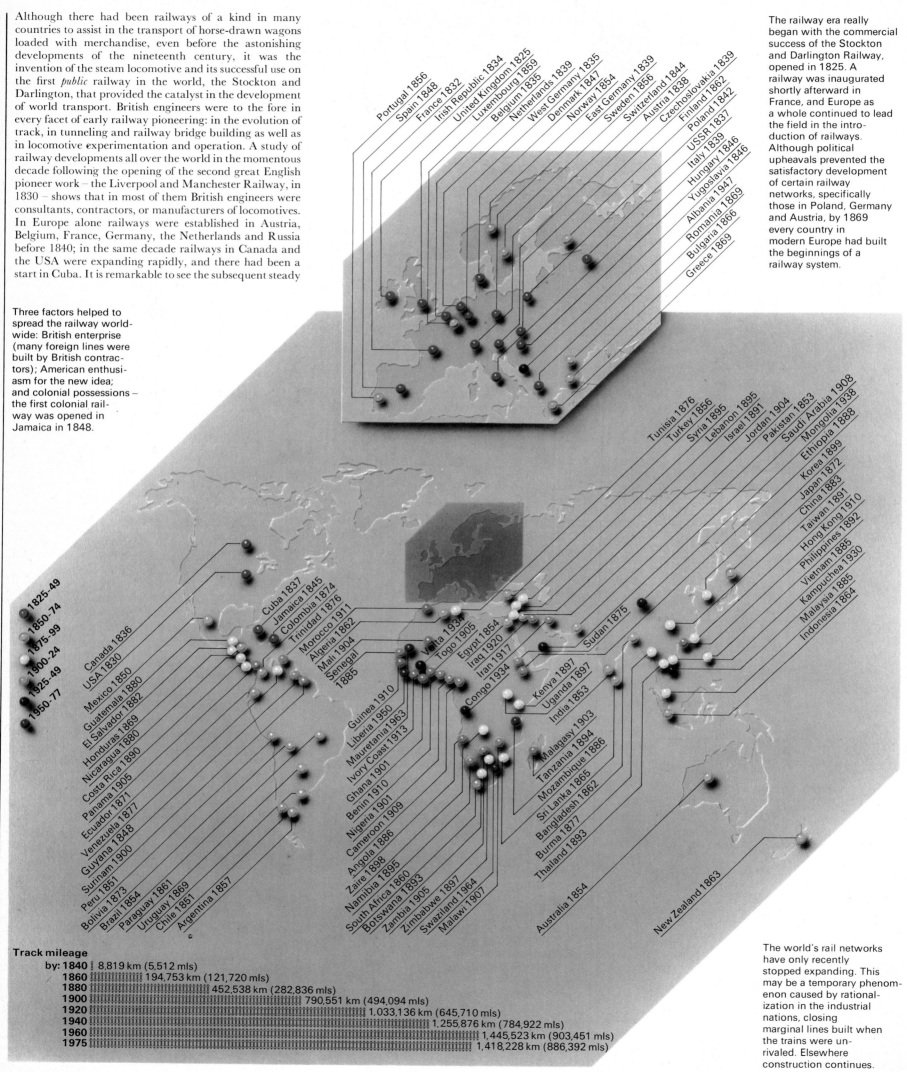

The world's rail networks have only recently stopped expanding. This may be a temporary phenomenon caused by rationalization in the industrial nations, closing marginal lines built when the trains were unrivaled. Elsewhere construction continues.

Track mileage

by:		
1840		8,819 km (5,512 mls)
1860		194,753 km (121,720 mls)
1880		452,538 km (282,836 mls)
1900		790,551 km (494,094 mls)
1920		1,033,136 km (645,710 mls)
1940		1,255,876 km (784,922 mls)
1960		1,445,523 km (903,451 mls)
1975		1,418,228 km (886,392 mls)

A cavalcade of rail: the *Rocket* of 1829; the broad gauge *Lord of the Isles*; an 1850s American 4-4-0; de Glehn's compound circa 1900; the 1937 LMS streamliner *Coronation Scot*; a 1941 GM diesel; Britain's new Advanced Passenger Train.

increase in the extent of the world's railways, with regular increments of some 200,000 km (125,000 miles) every 20 years until 1960.

The rate of increase was of course not uniform in all countries, nor were the advances in technology, speed, or quality of service. The earliest and almost phenomenal increases in extent came in the nineteenth century in the industrialized countries, of which Great Britain was foremost as an exporter of machinery, minerals and manufactured goods of all kinds to the whole world. The USA was only just emerging as a great industrial nation, while in Europe, France, Germany and Italy had all been torn by political and military upheavals. In all of them, however, railways came to play a great part in the subsequent consolidation. In the USA free enterprise and unbridled competition led to an enormous increase in railway activity in the last years of the nineteenth century. At the same time colonizing activities by the great nations of Europe led to the building of railways in many hitherto remote areas, quite apart from major, carefully planned projects like the building up of the Indian railway network,

or the great imperial ambitions of Cecil Rhodes in southern Africa. Railways were initiated before 1900, mostly on a modest scale, in Tunisia, in what is now Vietnam, Angola, Mozambique and Indonesia, while in the South American states there were railways flourishing long before 1900.

Success bred success. The provision of improved transport opened up the more remote communities and made their agricultural produce or mineral wealth available to wider and hitherto unopened markets. This in turn demanded improved railway facilities, larger locomotives and better means of traffic regulation. There was more work for the manufacturers in Great Britain and elsewhere. Overseas railways needed coal to fire their locomotives. British-owned railways in South America purchased their coal from South Wales; at least one French railway had its own fleet of colliers to collect for itself at Cardiff the choice grades of Welsh steam coal that it favored. New railways were built in South Wales to convey coal from the valleys to new ports, for shipment overseas. It was a booming reciprocal trade in some cases. Coal for

locomotives was exported from English east coast ports to the Baltic states in exchange for timber; Baltic pine was judged the finest material for railway ties. The expansion in world trade, which fostered the building of more railways, was aided to no small extent by the ability of railways to convey mail quicker than ever before. Where ocean travel was concerned, as in the vital case of Anglo-American mail, it was sometimes quicker to put eastbound mail ashore at Queenstown (Cobh) in the south of Ireland, take it by train to Kingstown (Dun Laoghaire) on Dublin Bay, ship it across to Holyhead and thence by train to London rather than wait for the steamer to make her way into the Mersey and dock at Liverpool. Even though the upheavals and reorientation of world trade after the First World War profoundly affected railway operations in many countries, expansion still continued elsewhere, as the route graph opposite so vividly shows; it is only after 1960 that the opposite trend begins to show. Nevertheless, to balance contraction in Great Britain and other highly industrialized areas, there are magnificent new projects in remote areas of Canada, Australia and South Africa.

Horse trains and iron rails

Railway development 1700–1824

1700 The origin of railways for the exclusive use of vehicles with flanged wheels can be traced back to mining practice in medieval Germany; but the development of railways as a public means of transport took place entirely in Great Britain. In using the word public, however, and applying it to the transport of goods and minerals, activity has been recorded in both the sixteenth and seventeenth centuries. The influence of this development is evident from reference to a system in the Ruhr coalfields of Germany as an *englischer Kohlenweg*. The rails were of wood, and laid exactly straight, and towards the end of the seventeenth century one reads that bulky carts were made with four so-called "rowlets" fitting the rails. These rowlets are taken to imply some form of flanged wheel, because it was claimed that their use made movement so easy that one horse could draw four or five of these bulky carts laden with coal. No less celebrated a writer than Daniel Defoe told of coal being loaded 'into a great machine called a Waggon,' and run on an artificial road called a "waggon-way."

Right This early colliery tramway in the north of England in 1773, shows a design of car that was still current 50 years later. The loaded car is relying upon gravity to propel it to the pier: the horse is there to pull the empty car back uphill to the mine.

Left Mine car Agricola, 1556. *Below* Prior Park, 1750, near Bath, the family seat of Ralph Allen, Esq, with the tramway which it is claimed by many was the first railway.

1726 Early in the eighteenth century mining interests in northeastern England led to the great coalition known as the "Grand Allies," consisting of three hitherto independent groups of colliery owners. These were the Liddell family, of Ravensworth; the Montagu family and Thomas Ord, of Newcastle; and George Bowes. In 1726 they made an agreement to bring their interests together, and the arrangements concluded also involved linking up some of their collieries by wagon-ways to rationalize movement. The result was a remarkable development, including the construction of what was termed a "main line" from the River Tyne where the coals were shipped for a distance of 13 km (8 miles) inland. Traffic was so heavy that the "main line" was laid with a double track so that loaded and empty "trains" would not interfere with one another. The country through which the lines of the Grand Allies ran is hilly, and some engineering works of considerable magnitude were undertaken to provide an even gradient. An embankment was built at Tanfield 30 m (100 ft) high, having a transverse width of 91 m (300 ft) at the base; but perhaps the most historic construction was the Causey Arch – the first bridge ever built for the exclusive purpose of carrying a railway. It was a single arch stone bridge built in 1727, 31 m (103 ft) long and 7 m (22 ft) wide, carrying two tracks of 1,219 mm (4 ft) gauge side by side.

Because these railways ran from inland regions to the banks of a navigable river it was possible to arrange the routes on a slightly falling grade, so as to make the task of a horse easier when pulling loaded wagons. At that time it was considered necessary to keep the load horizontal when descending a grade, and to do this the quaint expedient was adopted of making the leading wheels of the wagon of larger diameter than the trailing ones. Furthermore, in some wagons the leading wheels were spoked while the trailing ones were of solid wood. Flanges 2.5 cm (1 in) or 4 cm (1.5 in) deep were fixed to the inner faces of the wheels to provide an appropriate guiding effect. The wagons used in Durham and Northumberland had a primitive form of lever brake acting upon the rear pair of wheels. On the rail tracks running down to the rivers Tyne and Wear there was usually one horse to a wagon. Trains of wagons were not run.

There were places where the direction of the line had to be changed fairly abruptly and, because of the additional haulage effort that would have been necessary in pulling loaded wagons around a sharp curve, turntables were adopted, consisting of circular tables that swiveled around a central vertical axis. These were the exact prototype of turntables that came to be used in countless British passenger stations for transferring the small four-wheeled cars of the mid-nineteenth century from one track to another. On the early colliery wagon-ways there were places where the loaded vehicles would run by gravity. There the man in charge of the horse would transfer from front to rear, hitch a ride on the wagon, controlling the speed with the hand brake while the horse ran behind. At a later date in localities where horses pulled a train of three or more wagons, a special "dandy car" was provided for the horse to ride in while at the same time the train was running downhill by gravity.

1750 An important development in the 1750s was the substitution of iron rails for wooden ones. Although there were other early and experimental uses of iron rails, one of the most important was that made on the wagon-ways of the Coalbrookdale Ironworks in Shropshire. These tracks were originally laid with fine quality oak rails, but then, not only to improve their wearing quality, but also to use the products of their own furnaces, they covered the surfaces of these rails with cast iron. It is recorded that in the years 1768 to 1771 some 800 tons of strap rails were produced at Coalbrookdale. A contemporary development in the Sheffield area made use of iron plate rails with flanges on both sides. This enabled wagons with unflanged wheels to be used. It seems that the intention was to use wagons that were sometimes hauled along rail tracks and at others on ordinary road or dirt tracks, and arrangements were made at certain places where the transfer from one to the other could be made. These plateways, as they were called, became very popular in South Wales.

Cast iron edge-rail near Belvoir Castle, England, still in use around 1900.

1789 The true turning point in the early development of railway track was the invention, in 1789, of William Jessop's edge-rail, which was cast in 914 mm (3 ft) lengths. It was a beautifully conceived design on scientific principles; at the ends the base was flat where it rested on the track support, while in between the web portion below was deepened gradually to provide strength exactly in proportion to the distribution of stress caused by a load rolling along the upper surface. Instead of wooden cross ties the ends were supported on massive stone blocks sunk into the ground. Although so carefully and so correctly proportioned on theoretical grounds, Jessop's rail was inconvenient in that it could be manufactured only in short lengths, and in Scotland about the end of the eighteenth century the first steps were taken toward the production of wrought iron rails that could be rolled in much longer lengths. But many manufacturing difficulties had yet to be overcome, and the rails that supported the earliest steam locomotives in northeastern England were mostly manufactured in local foundries from cast iron and were in short lengths.

While the edge-rail first patented by Jessop was ideal for hauling short trains of coal wagons by horse, the adventures of Trevithick with his first locomotive on the Penydarran plateway suggested to other pioneers that contact between a smooth wheel and a smooth rail would not give sufficient grip to enable a locomotive to haul a heavy load. On the Middleton colliery railway, near Leeds, a form of rail with projecting teeth at the side was installed to carry locomotives with a toothed wheel. The weight of the locomotive was taken on the head of the rail as in Jessop's arrangement, but the engagement of tooth with tooth prevented any slipping due to lack of adhesion on the rail surface. This ingenious design by John Blenkinsop in 1812 was, however, expensive to make, and was suitable only for slow-moving trains. Of course at that time there was not yet any thought of speed on railways, and it was soon to be shown that this toothed wheel device was not necessary for heavy load haulage. It deserves to be credited, however, as a fine example of contemporary inventiveness.

1813 In 1813 at Wylam Colliery, Northumberland, William Hedley produced the first locomotive to work satisfactorily on a smooth rail, the *Puffing Billy*. At that time George Stephenson was engine builder at the neighboring colliery of Killingworth, and in 1814 he built his first locomotive. But Stephenson was far more than a clever engine mechanic, and he had the vision of a nationwide railway system. One thing that was causing endless trouble to these early pioneers was the track. Jessop's edge-rail was excellent in theory, but in practice there were many difficulties. The joints between successive sections of rail, whether resting on stone blocks or transverse ties of timber, became uneven; the stone blocks sank into the ground, some deeper than others.

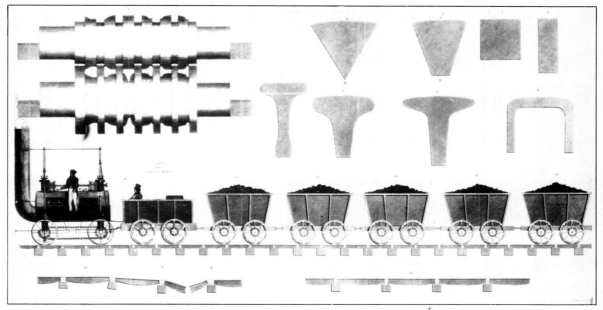

Stephenson/Losh locomotive, 1816, and Birkenshaw's patented malleable iron rails, 1820.

Therefore Stephenson with his friend William Losh patented a method of joining the rails by means of a scarfed, or overlapping, joint whereby the ends of adjacent rails were secured together. This was patented in 1816, and solved the problem, so far as slow-running colliery railways were concerned. Then in 1820, at the Bedlington Ironworks, Northumberland, John Birkinshaw produced the first really successful wrought iron rail, rolled through a mill to the required shape. This rail was not only much stronger, and less liable to fracture than cast iron lengths, but it could be made much longer – up to 5.5 m (18 ft). Although Stephenson himself had a patent for another type of rail, he specified Birkinshaw's for the Stockton and Darlington Railway in 1825.

Richard Trevithick was a pumping engines designer for mines, but he also built the first locomotive to run on rails, at Pen-y-Darren, Wales, in 1804. He built 4 locomotives,

all ahead of their time, being too heavy for the early rails, and suffering neglect from a public which failed to recognize their significance.

Richard Trevithick's Catch-me-who-can locomotive display in 1809. This was on a site which is near the present junction of Gower Street and Euston Road in London, and which is now occupied by the building of the National Union of Railwaymen. The exhibition was a financial failure and came to an abrupt end when the "train" fell off the rails.

Steam wins the day

Railway development 1825–1830

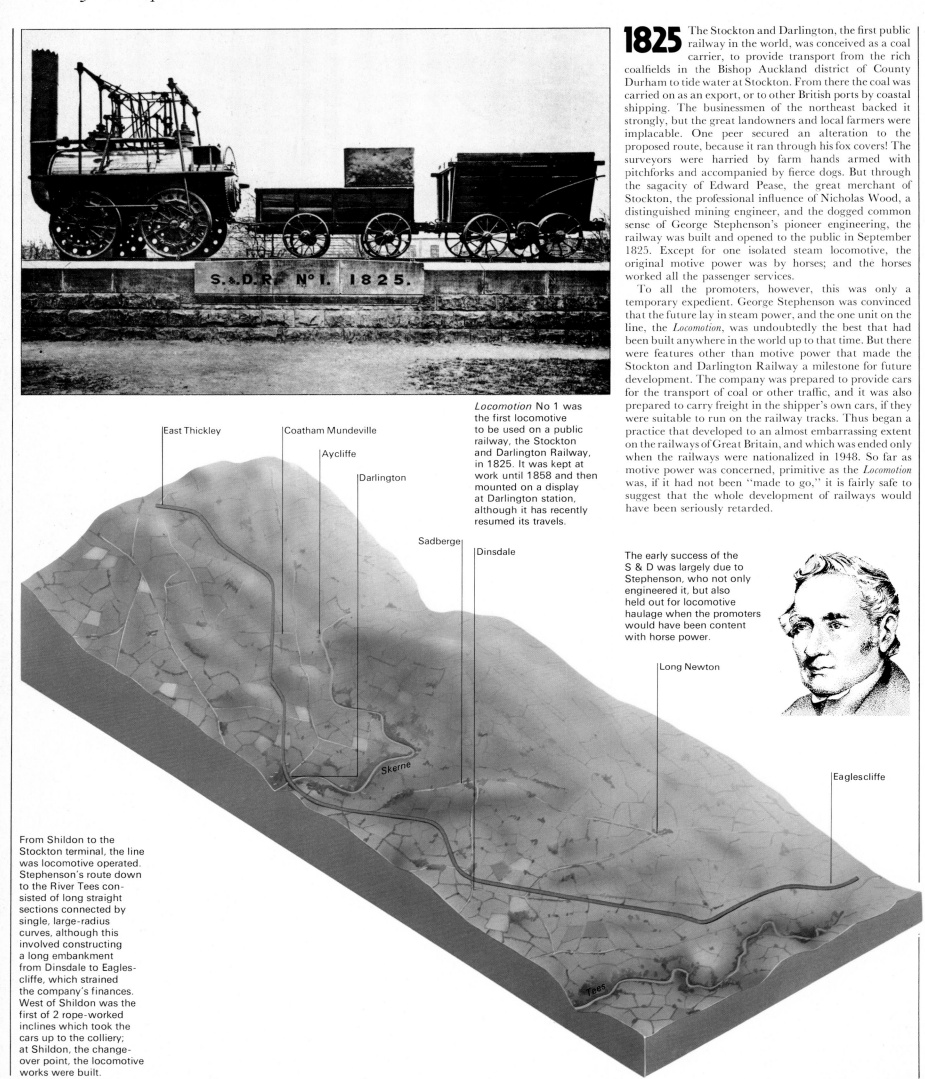

1825 The Stockton and Darlington, the first public railway in the world, was conceived as a coal carrier, to provide transport from the rich coalfields in the Bishop Auckland district of County Durham to tide water at Stockton. From there the coal was carried on as an export, or to other British ports by coastal shipping. The businessmen of the northeast backed it strongly, but the great landowners and local farmers were implacable. One peer secured an alteration to the proposed route, because it ran through his fox covers! The surveyors were harried by farm hands armed with pitchforks and accompanied by fierce dogs. But through the sagacity of Edward Pease, the great merchant of Stockton, the professional influence of Nicholas Wood, a distinguished mining engineer, and the dogged common sense of George Stephenson's pioneer engineering, the railway was built and opened to the public in September 1825. Except for one isolated steam locomotive, the original motive power was by horses; and the horses worked all the passenger services.

To all the promoters, however, this was only a temporary expedient. George Stephenson was convinced that the future lay in steam power, and the one unit on the line, the *Locomotion*, was undoubtedly the best that had been built anywhere in the world up to that time. But there were features other than motive power that made the Stockton and Darlington Railway a milestone for future development. The company was prepared to provide cars for the transport of coal or other traffic, and it was also prepared to carry freight in the shipper's own cars, if they were suitable to run on the railway tracks. Thus began a practice that developed to an almost embarrassing extent on the railways of Great Britain, and which was ended only when the railways were nationalized in 1948. So far as motive power was concerned, primitive as the *Locomotion* was, if it had not been "made to go," it is fairly safe to suggest that the whole development of railways would have been seriously retarded.

Locomotion No 1 was the first locomotive to be used on a public railway, the Stockton and Darlington Railway, in 1825. It was kept at work until 1858 and then mounted on a display at Darlington station, although it has recently resumed its travels.

The early success of the S & D was largely due to Stephenson, who not only engineered it, but also held out for locomotive haulage when the promoters would have been content with horse power.

From Shildon to the Stockton terminal, the line was locomotive operated. Stephenson's route down to the River Tees consisted of long straight sections connected by single, large-radius curves, although this involved constructing a long embankment from Dinsdale to Eaglescliffe, which strained the company's finances. West of Shildon was the first of 2 rope-worked inclines which took the cars up to the colliery; at Shildon, the changeover point, the locomotive works were built.

East Thickley

Coatham Mundeville

Aycliffe

Darlington

Sadberge

Dinsdale

Skerne

Long Newton

Eaglescliffe

Tees

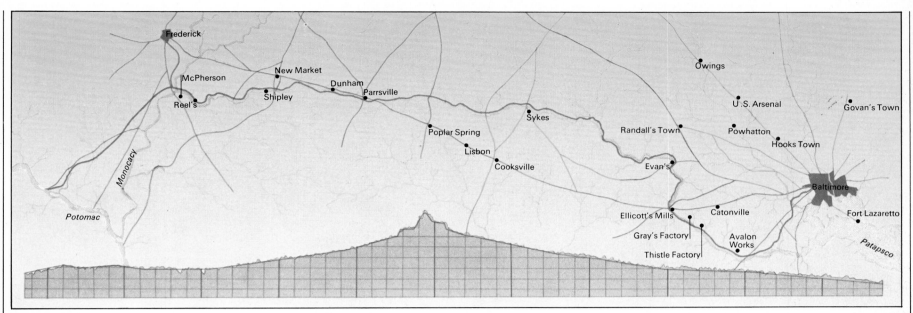

1827 In the USA in the 1820s there was need for good communication between the developing lands west of the Allegheny mountains and the seaports of New York, Philadelphia, Washington and Baltimore. The first three cities opted for canals, and indeed the successful Erie Canal between Buffalo and New York was intended to draw trade away from the others. Baltimore alone determined upon a railway, and no minor project at that. It was to be a double track right through from the city to the Ohio River at Wheeling, and in 1827 an application was made to the Legislature of Maryland for an Act incorporating the Baltimore and Ohio Railway Company. It is interesting that the term "railway" rather than "railroad" was adopted; today in the USA, of the

The railway followed the course of the rivers where it could, to make the grades as easy as possible. It was not until May 1830 that the line was opened for passenger traffic over the first 42 km (26 miles) from Baltimore to Ellicotts' Mills. The motive power was by horses. The sharp curves made necessary by the rugged country in the valley of the Patapsco River suggested that steam locomotives would be impracticable. But Peter Cooper, an industrialist and inventor from New York, had made a large investment in Baltimore land, and it was important to him that the railway should succeed. That to him meant "speed" with the use of steam power. He built a locomotive, the *Tom Thumb*, and in the summer of 1830

The first line in America was the Baltimore and Ohio, begun in 1828. For a "first," it was on a grand scale: 608 km (380 miles) long, double track throughout, the Allegheny mountains to be crossed. The first 42 km (26 miles) were opened to traffic in May 1830.

The famous race between a horse and the *Tom Thumb* locomotive on the Baltimore & Ohio Railway.

many great, and still independent companies, some are styled "railways" and others "railroads." Still more interesting is that the name "Baltimore and Ohio" survives today, because the B & O is one of the three great railway lines which are incorporated in the present "Chessie System."

Unlike the earliest railways in Great Britain and in parts of Europe, the incorporation of the Baltimore and Ohio was acclaimed by virtually universal rejoicing in Baltimore itself and in the country through which it would run. It was regarded as a great popular venture, but a plunge into the unknown nevertheless. In 1827 no one knew whether the primitive locomotives, tracks and rolling stock then used on the earliest English railways would withstand the onslaught of the severe American winters and the still more furious spring floods that followed the thawing of the snows. Still the merchants of Baltimore pressed on. It was perhaps indicative of their iron resolve that one of the first directors of the B & O was Charles Carroll, who in 1827 was the sole surviving signer of the Declaration of Independence. He was then more than 90 years of age, but in February 1828 was fit enough to turn the first spadeful of earth, with a silver spade, and to lay the symbolic foundation stone of the railway. Following the ceremony he said, "I consider this among the most important acts of my life, second only to my signing the Declaration of Independence, if even it be second to that."

took the directors for a ride down the line as far as Carrollton, the home of Charles Carroll. The 21 km (13 miles) were covered in 57 minutes.

The more conservative among the railway supporters were still skeptical of the success of locomotives, and a race was organized and run on August 28, 1830 between the *Tom Thumb* and a horse. It was a close-run thing – neck and neck for most of the way – until the drive-belt slipped from the drum and, with the blower inoperative, steam pressure dropped, and the horse forged ahead to victory. But though this victory was gained through a mishap to the machinery of the locomotive, the moral victory was with Peter Cooper.

In France, the first railway, the St Étienne and Andrézieux, built in 1828, was also primarily a coal carrier, and was at first worked entirely by horses. Two, in tandem, were used to haul trains of six or seven wagons loaded with coal. But the provision made for passenger service was more elaborate than on the Stockton and Darlington. They were quite commodious cars after the fashion of a stage-coach, covered over and with three separate compartments. But an even more elaborate affair was a double-decker. The lower deck had open sides to all three compartments, but with curtains that could be drawn to give protection against the weather. The upper deck was completely open to the elements.

The first locomotive built in the USA, *Best Friend of Charleston*, was constructed for the South Carolina Railroad in 1830.

Worldwide expansion begins

Railway development 1831–1850

Derby North Midland station, an artist's impression, *circa* 1840.

1831 It was the opening and the instant subsequent success of the Liverpool and Manchester Railway and the immense prestige gained by George Stephenson with locomotives, and by his son Robert in civil engineering, that prompted the building of railways in many parts of the world. Though the Liverpool and Manchester was a relatively small project, even beside some of the railways engineered within the very next decade, the experience gained had been profound, particularly in surmounting the unexpected and severe difficulties of crossing Chat Moss, a desolate bog land, untouched and untraversed for centuries. There the problem had been to secure a stable foundation to carry the railway; tipping stones and gravel to form an embankment proved useless, for the filling just slipped away. The solution was found by building layers of brushwood and hurdles to form a core around which the orthodox filling could accumulate and set.

When it came to building the first line between Amsterdam and Rotterdam in the Netherlands, F. W. Conrad, the engineer, was faced with a similar problem to that on Chat Moss, except that it extended for the greater part of the entire route. Practically all of the country to be traversed by the new railway lay below sea level, and was protected from complete inundation by the wonderful system of dikes or embankments; and the ground was everywhere soft and spongy. Conrad used the same technique as that of George Stephenson, except that in most places he had to use many more layers of hurdles and brushwood before he could get a reasonably firm foundation. Conrad had the first section of his line, from Amsterdam to Haarlem, opened in 1839.

In 1834 Ludwig I of Bavaria gave his assent to the construction of the first railway to be built in any of the German states. It was named after the king himself, the *Ludwigsbahn*, and ran from Nürnberg to Fürth. This name set a fashion that has been followed ever since in countries where the language is German, or a dialect of it: simply *bahn*, "road," without any qualification. The opening date, by royal desire, had apparently been fixed long before the line was finished or even the equipment ordered. A German manufacturer, asked to supply the first locomotive, could not meet the delivery date required, and so the order was placed with the Stephensons. It was the first steam locomotive to run in Germany.

The first railway tunnels were excavated with very unsophisticated equipment. Brunel's Box Tunnel on the Great Western Railway was started in 1836 and finished in June 1841. It was 3,000 m (3,280 yd) long, and up to 4,000 men and 300 horses were at work simultaneously. Weekly, one ton of gunpowder, and one of candles, was used. The methods of tunneling, illustrated *below*, had been established by the canal builders and by Brunel's father, who built the first tunnel under the River Thames.

Brunel, the most revolutionary of the early rail engineers, enraged others by adopting a nonstandard gauge of 2,133 mm (7 ft) for the Great Western Railway.

1837 In France railways had begun, as in England, with purely mineral lines in the St Étienne district, but the first to be a public common carrier was that opened in 1837 between Paris and St Germain, a distance of 21 km (13 miles). From the outset it was intended to be steam powered, but the locomotives were not entirely reliable. Like the *Ludwigsbahn* in Bavaria this line enjoyed royal patronage, and was formally opened by Queen Marie-Amélie. The event was regarded more as a fashionable social occasion rather than the beginning of a new epoch in industrial development, and the venturesome action of the 55-year-old queen was looked upon with much disfavor. The conservative attitude of the day regarded the line as something of a plaything.

In the same year as the Paris–St Germain railway was opened came the first railway in Russia, again strongly influenced by British pioneer work and again under royal patronage. The Tsar of Russia had been to England and visited some of the colliery lines in the north; impressed with what he had seen he readily granted a concession to a company formed to build a railway over the 24 km (15 miles) from St Petersburg to Pavlovsk, where a new entertainment center had been set up. The first locomotives were obtained from England, one from Robert Stephenson and one from Timothy Hackworth, and in the depths of winter they had to be landed at the nearest port that was open on the Baltic, and then taken by sleigh across the ice. The Tsar himself was present at the first steaming of the Hackworth locomotive in November 1836, and the engine was put through a baptismal ceremony according to the rites of the Greek Orthodox Church.

This first Russian railway was built to a rail gauge of 1,828 mm (6 ft), instead of that which was already becoming looked upon as something of a standard; but in England, in building the Great Western Railway, I. K. Brunel carried the question of gauge to a major confrontation by adopting no less than 2,123 mm (7 ft). He felt that once the advantages of such a wide gauge had been demonstrated – its possibilities for speed, mass transport of freight, and roominess of accommodation for passengers – all existing railways in Great Britain would be converted. But it did not work out that way. The Stephensons and their friends stood out firmly against any change, and the difficulties became so intense at places like Gloucester, where transfer from one gauge to the other had to be made, that a Royal Commission was set up, and in due course its recommendations went against the broad gauge of Brunel. But for his broad gauge lines Brunel built some magnificent engineering works, notably the great tunnel under Box Hill, Wiltshire.

1846 Despite the difficulties that had arisen in England from a diversity of rail gauges, in North America many lines were built in the early days with different gauges both in Canada and in the USA. In the latter the situation was not finally resolved until after the end of the Civil War, when some lines in the southern states were converted to the European and North American standard of 1,435 mm (4 ft 8½ in). Some of the most interesting and picturesque work in the early days of American railroading was not over disagreements about gauges but in crossing the mountain ranges that lay between the eastern seaboard and the Ohio River. The ranges of the Alleghenies and the Appalachians have none of the rugged, desolate and forbidding character of the Rockies. Indeed, to see them from the air, densely covered with thousands of acres of continuous forest land, it is difficult to appreciate that they do form a natural barrier that posed many problems for the pioneer railway engineers.

The Baltimore and Ohio, the first ever American railway, made its way beside the Potomac River to Cumberland, Maryland, amid a beautiful but often difficult terrain, and thence over the watershed to reach the Ohio River valley. At first however, the main range of the Allegheny mountains was considered impossible for a railway, but on the advice of William Strickland an extraordinary chain of communication was developed between Philadelphia and Pittsburgh, and brought into service in 1832. It was in some ways a primitive forerunner of the modern American piggyback principle, in that the whole journey was made in canal boats. These were constructed in halves, and it was in halves that they were hauled on rail-borne cars over the first 132 km (82 miles) from Philadelphia to Columbia, on the Susquehanna River. Then the two halves were joined and proceeded by canal into the very heart of the mountains to Hollidaysburg. Then they were transferred once again to rail cars for movement over the crest of the mountains and down the far side to Johnstown. After that they reverted to canal for the rest of the journey to Pittsburgh.

It was a slow and cumbersome means of transit, and the all-rail route of the Baltimore and Ohio, although serving Pittsburgh directly, and then only by a roundabout route, was much quicker. So in 1846 the Pennsylvania Railroad Company was formed, following for much of the distance from Pittsburgh to Philadelphia this older composite transport system. But the crossing of the Alleghenies involved some spectacular engineering, especially in descending the eastern slopes by the great horseshoe curve below the Gallitzin summit, and it was not until 1852 that this great artery of modern railway traffic was first brought into use. American developments farther west came later.

1850 Meanwhile the rail network in Great Britain was spreading rapidly. By the year 1850 one could travel from London to Edinburgh by train, although the present direct line from Peterborough to Doncaster was not yet completed. At first trains to the north traveled via Sleaford and Lincoln. There was already a rival route to Scotland, up the west coast. A great lengthwise merger of 1847 had produced the London and North Western Railway, which with its allies, the Lancaster and Carlisle and the Caledonian, made up a continuous line from London to Glasgow, with a northern offshoot into Edinburgh. The great central combination which produced the Midland Railway in 1844 had not yet secured an independent outlet to the south and reached London by the Great Northern's line into King's Cross.

During the 1840s, England was infected by "Railway Mania" which established most of the major routes.

Aberdeen

Dundee

Network open by 1842

Additional track by 1852

Glasgow

Edinburgh

Newcastle

Carlisle

Leeds

Sheffield

Manchester

Liverpool

York

Hull

Nottingham

Crewe

Derby

Birmingham

Swansea

Swindon

Cardiff

Bristol

Plymouth

London

Southampton

Opening up the West

Railway development 1851–1880

1854 Just as the Ohio River had been the goal of railways building westward from the Atlantic, so the Mississippi proved the great obstacle to those building the lines westward from Chicago. The mid-1850s were exciting days in the race to reach out to the West. The first line to reach the river was the Chicago and Rock Island, in 1854, followed in 1855 by the Illinois Central and the Chicago and Alton; in the following year the Chicago, Burlington and Quincy reached the left bank. All this railway activity was looked upon with the greatest distrust by the steamboat men, who operated a profitable traffic on the great river. And distrust changed to violent action when the railway companies began to build bridges across the river. The Rock Island was the first to do this, from the city of that name to Davenport, Iowa, and the bridge was opened in April 1856. The steamboat men tried to serve court injunctions claiming that the bridges were a danger to navigation, and when these failed they used more subtle and dangerous methods. In May 1856 a paddle steamboat appeared suspiciously to go "accidentally" out of control, crashed

Above left Snow drift on the Union Pacific. *Above right* Dale creek bridge on the Union Pacific.

into one of the piers bringing down the span, and caught fire. The steamboat, called the *Effie Afton*, sank, and the owners claimed, and were granted, compensation. But the steamboat men were fighting a hopeless battle.

At this same time the first railways were being built out in the West – nothing except a few local lines at the start; but in 1861 the Central Pacific Railway of California had been incorporated, with the aim of building eastward to forge a link with the eastern states. Then came the Civil War, and little could be done. But in 1862 Congress had launched the great scheme for building the Union Pacific Railroad, westward from the Mississippi. This great line, a vital artery of heavy east-west freight traffic, stands today as one of the very few railways anywhere in the world that has always been privately owned and yet was inaugurated by direct government action. During the war President Lincoln became most anxious about the isolated and undefended situation of the states on the Pacific coast. World opinion was sharply divided in its sympathies with the opposing sides in the war, and those who favored the southern states feared outside intervention in California. So the most urgent encouragement was given to the construction of the Union Pacific Railroad. It was not until 1865, however, that the first rail was laid, in the Missouri valley. With this incentive work by the Central Pacific began in earnest from the western end. It became a race, because the fares and freight rates on this transcontinental route would be proportioned according to the mileage owned by each company.

1869 The construction of the line became one of the great epics of world railway building. Out on the prairies in wild undeveloped country, where the white man had scarcely penetrated, the survey parties and work trains were attacked by bands of Indians. The Union Pacific certainly had its fill of this kind of trouble, while the Central Pacific, forging its way through tough country in the Sierra Nevada range, had the great handicap of having to obtain supplies by sea. There was no Panama Canal at that time, and everything had to be shipped to San Francisco around the tip of South America – a voyage from Baltimore, or Philadelphia, of about 24,000 km (15,000 miles). The race to link up with the advancing construction gangs of the Union Pacific went on for four years, and eventually on May 10, 1869 at Promontory, Utah, the last spike was driven. The present main line takes what is called the "Lucin cut-off," and bypasses Promontory, but the place of the link up is a popular tourist spot, with two locomotives in period paint schemes facing each other.

The construction of the Central Pacific and the Union Pacific provided the first east-west link from coast to coast in the USA, and although it was quickly followed by further developments this marked the first step in an important era in the development of the country as a whole.

One of the most spectacular terminal stations in London is St Pancras, *right*, built by the Midland Railway from 1868 to 1875. It is a monument to the Victorians' pride in the steam railway, and an indication also of the importance of railways in the Victorian economy: London's main stations were, when built, the largest buildings to have been erected since the cathedrals. Two of Victorian England's foremost architects designed it. The train shed is by William Barlow, with a clear span of 73.2 m (240 ft), the largest of its kind in Britain; the hotel fronting it is one of Sir Gilbert Scott's masterpieces.

1879 Along the deeply indented east coast of Scotland the firths of Forth and Tay presented serious obstacles to the path of any direct rail line from Edinburgh to Aberdeen. The first step was the building of a great viaduct across the Firth of Tay, opposite Dundee. Thomas Bouch was the engineer, a man whose work was inclined to be venturesome, unlike the solid, perhaps oversolid, reliability of the Stephensons and Joseph Locke. On the Firth of Tay, unfortunately, Bouch greatly underestimated the effect of the gale-force winds frequently experienced in that exposed area; not only that, but certain features of the detailed design were of highly questionable integrity – such as putting cast iron members into tension. Nor was the work inspected in progress.

British engineering has an enviable reputation for soundness of workmanship and a high sense of discipline. But in this one tragic instance, not only had the basic design been a little incautious, but its execution was atrocious. The main columns were badly cast, having an uneven thickness of metal; the lugs, to which the tension members were attached, fell off during casting and were

The Tay Bridge disaster in 1879, one of the many artists' impressions of the scene.

reattached by the process of "burning on." In the circumstances, it was nothing short of a marvel that the bridge lasted as long as it did. It was opened to traffic in May 1878, carrying a single line of railway. The end came on the evening of December 28, 1879 when a great gale was sweeping in from the North Sea and a passenger train from Burntisland to Dundee entered upon the bridge. It reached the high girders carrying the line over the navigable part of the Firth, and then the bridge collapsed, taking the train and all its passengers down into the deep water. There were no survivors. At the time Bouch had been commissioned to design a bridge for the crossing of the Forth, but his reputation was shattered.

Achievements and disasters

Railway development 1881–1913

1885 The construction of the Canadian Pacific Railway – undertaken to honor a pledge made to the provinces of British Columbia and Vancouver Island that in return for their joining in the federation to form the Dominion of Canada a transcontinental railway would be built – proved to be one of the greatest individual tasks ever undertaken by a single railway company. Although the project was initiated by the government the company was privately owned, though often the financial situation was so desperate that appeals for government aid had to be repeated several times. J. J. Hill, one of the original syndicate, had large interests in the USA, and to link up readily with these he urged that the line be carried to the south of Lake Superior and so through United States territory. But the general manager whom he himself had introduced, W. C. Van Horne, was implacably opposed to this, and he was supported by the two Scots tycoons who made up the rest of the syndicate, George Stephen and Donald A. Smith. Hill resigned and immediately set to work to promote a

1889 On June 12, 1889 there was a terrible accident near Armagh, on the Great Northern Railway of Ireland. It was an accident that highlighted two fundamental weaknesses in operation on the railways of the United Kingdom at that time. Both these weaknesses were appreciated, and many of the railway companies had already begun to take the necessary safeguards against them; but disaster struck on a line that was not so equipped. The first point concerned signaling. Earlier practice was to work trains on a time interval basis, allowing a second train to go forward a specified number of minutes after the preceding one had passed. This system was subject to misjudgment and misunderstanding, and the principle of "absolute block" working was being substituted. In this a second train was not allowed to proceed until positive advice by telegraphic bell signal had been received from the next block post that the preceding train had passed clear.

The second point concerned the brakes. While brakes were operated on all vehicles by a valve on the locomotive,

an earlier type left the rear part of the train unbraked if it should in any circumstances become detached from the part coupled to the locomotive. From Armagh a very heavy excursion train was dispatched for Warrenpoint. It had to climb a steep grade, and the small engine could not make it and stalled. It was decided to divide the train, take the first half up to the top of the grade, and then come back for the rest. But the hand brake on the caboose could not hold the detached portion on the grade. That detached portion began to run back downhill. Meanwhile a second train, starting 20 minutes after the excursion, was climbing the grade. The runaway gathered speed, and at 64 km/h (40 mph) came into a frightful collision with the second train. Seventy-eight passengers were killed and 250 injured. Shocked by this terrible occurrence, Parliament rushed through a Regulation of Railways Bill making the absolute block system compulsory on all passenger lines in the UK, as well as the installation of automatic continuous braking systems which in the event of a train division applied brakes to both sections.

The Canadian Pacific route represented the first direct link across Canada from east to west. Services started on June 28, 1886.

The east and west sections linking Port Moody to Montreal were joined at Craigellachie in Eagle Pass, British Columbia, on November 7, 1885.

Completion of the line within ten years was a condition of British Columbia entering the Confederation on July 20, 1871.

First ground was broken at Fort William on June 1, 1875. 1,126 km (700 miles) was under construction by October 1880.

From Montreal to Vancouver, 4,633 km (2,879 miles) the journey today takes three days, half the journey time in 1886.

For his part in the completion of the CPR, Queen Victoria made Van Horne a Knight Commander of the Order of St Michael and St George, in 1894.

rival transcontinental line in the USA from St Paul to Seattle, which became the Great Northern.

The all-Canadian route around the northern shores of Lake Superior involved some exceedingly difficult engineering, and although Van Horne, frequently taking command, as it were, in the field, pressed the construction work forward at an unprecedented rate across the open prairies west of Winnipeg, the continuation of the line through the Rockies involved further tremendous difficulties. The first surveys had been made by the great veteran engineer Sandford Fleming, and to avoid unduly steep grades and high constructional costs he had proposed going through the mountains by the Yellowhead Pass, a fairly long detour to the north. But Van Horne felt that such a route would leave a considerable stretch of Canadian territory near to the United States border open to rival railway infiltrations, and he instructed his engineers to find a way through as near as possible due west from Calgary. So the line was taken across The Great Divide near Lake Louise, then called Emerald Lake, and down the Kicking Horse Pass. Engineering difficulties were not ended when Field was reached, because finding a way through the tremendous barrier of the Selkirk Mountains was even more difficult. Operationally the ascent from Beavermouth to the Rogers Pass – named after the dynamic American engineer who found it – is the worst on the whole line, and today requires the use of up to 13 diesel locomotives to haul the heaviest ore trains up the incline.

When competitive lines to the Canadian Pacific were surveyed and plans made for further routes to the west coast, the Yellowhead Pass route was adopted, and the Canadian National Railways operates a transcontinental service that way. The two routes come abreast of each other at Kamloops and then run on opposite sides of the Fraser River for the rest of the way to Vancouver. At first when they are running through canyon country the scene is most dramatic, with rival trains passing along ledges cut in the rock walls, but they pass out of sight of each other as Vancouver is neared.

Left The interior of the signal box of the South Eastern Railway at London Bridge station in 1886. *Below* The accident at Armagh in 1889. The caption reads: "Wreck of train on side of embankment 70 ft high at Armagh". The rear half of an excursion train slipped on the grade and collided with the following train, killing 78 passengers.

1892 The findings of the Royal Commission on railway gauges in Great Britain, unfavorable to Brunel's 2,133 mm (7 ft) gauge, were somewhat watered down by the subsequent parliamentary legislation, which, while discouraging its use did not preclude any further extensions. But after the death of Brunel in 1859 and the retirement as locomotive superintendent of Daniel Gooch, Great Western enchantment with the broad gauge began to diminish rapidly. Mixed gauge was laid in on many important routes so that both broad and narrow gauge trains could run, and other lines were converted. By the beginning of the year 1892 the only part of the line remaining wholly broad gauge was that from Exeter to Truro – 160 km (100 miles) on the main line and about 114 km (71 miles) on various branch lines, such as from Newton Abbot to Kingswear, and from Truro to Falmouth. The remarkable decision was taken to convert the whole of this extensive area in a single weekend. All broad gauge locomotives and rolling stock had to be evacuated from the area and worked to Exeter or beyond, where there was mixed gauge track, and then a work force of 4,200 men moved down to Devon and Cornwall. The men were in gangs of 20, and each gang had 1.6 km (1 mile) of plain line to convert. The business of moving the men and all their heavy tools and equipment was complicated by all trains from the further ends of the line being standard gauge, and the men had to change to broad gauge trains at Exeter. It all needed tremendously detailed organization, because once the men had been conveyed to their places of work the broad gauge cars had to be evacuated from the western areas – otherwise they would have been trapped and immovable. No time could be wasted in moving men about from place to place during the operation and accommodation was arranged adjacent to the job to be done. Sleeping arrangements were organized in freight sheds and station buildings; and where nothing else existed tents were pitched beside the line. The whole operation went very smoothly. Fortunately the weather was fine; the last through broad gauge train left Paddington for Penzance on Friday May 20, and on Monday May 23, the full service was restored with standard gauge trains.

1900 The technique of spiral tunneling, which needed consummate skill and precision in the preliminary and final surveys, was used to remarkable effect in easing the grades on the Canadian Pacific main line in the Rocky Mountains – climbing the Kicking Horse Pass in British Columbia – and was used again spectacularly in Switzerland on the Bern-Lötschberg-Simplon line at Blausee-Mitholz, in climbing from Frutigen to Kandersteg on the great line opened in July 1913.

Despite the speed and efficiency of spiral tunneling, the endeavor was often extremely hazardous. For example, in the building of the Lötschberg Tunnel, which began in 1906, over 3,000 workers were involved. In 1908, 30 men were killed when a workers' hostel was destroyed in an avalanche; and only four months later, 25 men were drowned when water burst into a section of the tunnel blocking over 1 km (0.6 mile) of its length and causing its course to be diverted, resulting in a total increase of over 800 m (2,625 ft). Where the disaster had taken place, a wall 10 m (33 ft) thick was built to seal it off. Rock temperatures of up to 34°C (93°F) were encountered during the tunneling.

The world precedent for spiral tunneling had been set by Louis Favre, engineering the Gotthard line. It was conceived as a major international main line on the highway from Germany through Switzerland and into Italy. The St Gotthard Pass had been a highway for centuries, albeit impassable in the winter snows; but the task of building a major railway over the same route set a number of unprecedented problems. It was not so much the driving of a great tunnel under the pass itself, from Göschenen to Airolo, but the exceptional steepness of the approach valley to north and south. On both sides of the deep valley up which the railway had to be carried were high mountains and into these Favre took the line on a series of spiral locations to gain height. The actual grade of the railway is about 2.5 percent and this was achieved by having no fewer than three spiral tunnels on the ascent from Erstfeld to Göschenen.

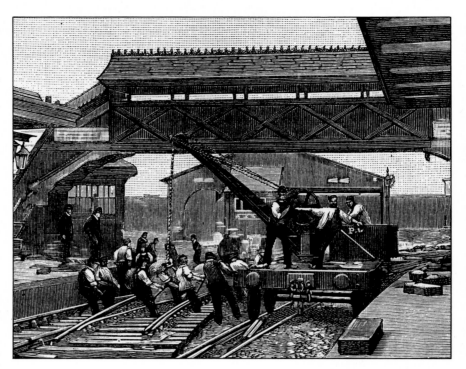

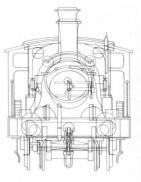

Above An 1870s standard gauge locomotive, superimposed upon a broad gauge locomotive and car, shows the two advantages Brunel claimed for his Great Western Railway: greater space, and stability, enabling higher speeds.

Left Replacing the broad gauge track with standard gauge in Devonport station.

Rhodes never envisaged the Cape-to-Cairo as only a rail line: river navigation was also to form a part. He proposed a route west of Lake Tanganyika, using the Congo and Nile. Today it is possible to travel from Cape Town to Zaire in this way. Since the opening of the Tazara line (see p 200), an alternative route via East Africa is possible, though either way there is a gap in the through route, there being no railways out of Sudan into Zaire or Uganda.

Cairo
EGYPT
Luxor
Aswān
Wadi Halfā
Atbarah
Khartoum
SUDAN
Kosti
Wau
Bondo
UGANDA
Mungbere
Tororo
KENYA
Aketi
Kisangani
Congo
Ubundi
Kindu
Nairobi
Moshi
Voi
ZAIRE
Kongolo
Lualaba
TANZANIA
Dar es Salaam
Bukama
Tenke
ZAMBIA
Lusaka
RHODESIA
Livingstone
Bulawayo
BOTSWANA
Gaborone
Mafeking
SOUTH AFRICA
Kimberley
Beaufort West
Cape Town
•••• Navigable river

1910 In the lengthy ranges of the Andes, extending high and continuously from north to south of the South American continent, with their crests little more than 160 km (100 miles) from the Pacific Ocean, are to be found the highest railway summits in the world. The highest of all, the Antofagasta (Chile) and Bolivia, was one of the first. It was a British enterprise, and is still British owned today. It reaches the remarkable altitude of 4,826 m (15,835 ft) on its Collahuasi branch. The company was formed in 1888 to take over certain concessions granted by the two governments. The line was built on the 762 mm (2 ft 6 in) gauge and continued thus with a productive length of 1,230 km (769 miles) through its period of greatest prosperity in the early 1900s. Initially its traffic was nitrates from Bolivia down to the sea at Antofagasta, but in later years traffic has been in tin and copper. By 1928 the line was converted to meter gauge and powerful articulated locomotives of the Beyer-Garratt type purchased to operate mineral trains on the heavy gradients. At the time of the conversion of the gauge a third rail was laid on many sections, but the final conversion, which involved some 320 km (200 miles) of line, mostly in waterless, desolate country, took no more than six days.

Farther north, the Central Railway of Peru has been claimed as the most spectacular in the world, reaching 4,829 m (15,845 ft) on the European standard gauge throughout. The choice of this gauge in Peru was remarkable, because generally the broad gauge standard in South America is 1,676 mm (5 ft 6 in) with meter gauge for the feeder lines. The climbing of the main range of the Andes begins at Chosica when the railway is 53 km (33 miles) inland from Callao and has already attained a height of 860 m (2,820 ft). Then comes a tremendous ascent to the summit of the line in the Galera tunnel. This point is only about 64 km (40 miles) from Chosica, but with a difference in altitude of 3,923 m (12,870 ft), the average inclination would be 1 in 16.5 but for the ingenious and spectacular engineering that intervenes. The actual gradient presented to the locomotives is about 1 in 25, but height is gained here not by spiral tunneling but by a series of zigzags up the side wall of the valley.

The trans-Andine railway, which forms part of a continuous line of communication between Buenos Aires and Valparaiso, formerly had separate Chilean and Argentinian sections, but between 1923 and 1939 it was operated first by a joint administration and then by the British-owned Buenos Aires and Pacific Railway. It is meter gauge, and includes some rack sections in climbing to its summit level of 3,186 m (10,453 ft) near Las Cuevas. If the weather is fine there is a sight from here of the highest mountain in all the Americas, the 6,959 m (22,834 ft) Aconcagua. The trans-Andine passenger train takes about 12 hr to cover the 386 km (240 miles) from Valparaiso to Mendoza, the railhead of the Argentine line.

Networks in the Great War
Railway development 1914–1922

1914 Until 1914 railways had played a small, but significant, part in warfare – in the confused campaigns in the Mississippi basin during the Civil War, and in the working of patrols with armored trains in the later stages of the Boer War. But in 1914 much of the normal pattern of international travel on the continent of Europe had been disrupted. The important chain of communication between England and Germany was necessarily severed, never again to be restored in its old form. Tracks were destroyed to hinder troop movements, bridges were blown up, particularly in Belgium during the first weeks of the campaign in the west, and locomotives and rolling stock were hurriedly withdrawn to avoid their falling into enemy hands. Then, with the overrunning of much of the industrial areas of northeastern France and the total loss of manufacturing facilities in Belgium, the French and British governments were faced with difficulties in providing replacement in time for consumable spare parts on rolling stock that had been withdrawn. The heavy industries in both countries were rapidly switched to direct production of armaments, and

Germans rebuilding a railway bridge in Northern France, maintaining vital rail links with the Front.

First World War, German troops leaving home.

the railways found great difficulty in obtaining raw materials to manufacture, in their own works, the spares that were needed. A British purchasing mission went to the USA and arranged for large quantities of steel plate, bars, ingots, and other material, to be shipped to the United Kingdom. The formation of a Railway Operating Division in the British Army proved invaluable in getting reinforcements and munitions to the forward zones in the battle areas. Track was lifted from sections of the home railways made temporarily redundant by the suspension of tourist and other peacetime activities. Many British locomotives were sent abroad for use with the Railway Operating Division. The neutrality of Switzerland made it a place where the repatriation of prisoners-of-war could be arranged and Constance, on the German-Swiss frontier, was a center through which much of this unusual traffic passed. In the campaigns in the Middle East much of the guerrilla activity against the Turkish armies, so dashingly organized and led by T. E. Lawrence, centered upon disruption of the Hedjaz Railway and the destruction of troop trains. Among the Arabs Lawrence became known as "Destroyer of Engines."

Below A mammoth French Mle 93-06 rail gun weighing 178 tons, and with a firing elevation of 40°. Horizontal traverse was not possible except by moving the gun around a curve in the rail track. It was capable of firing a shell of 348 kg (766.5 lb) over 27.500 m (29.965 yd).

Railways in the western battle areas

Although the Allied battle line from the North Sea to the Swiss frontier swayed backward and forward to some extent during the four years of the war, despite the numerous and terribly costly offensives the line remained stable enough for the pattern of railway operation to assume a fairly constant form. Two major routes of the Northern Railway of France were completely severed, namely that to Arras and Lille, and that leading into Belgium. The Eastern main line toward Nancy and Strasbourg was purely a route furnishing reinforcements and munitions for the French line of battle. The Northern main line to Boulogne and Calais became almost entirely a British Army supply route. In Great Britain the establishment of the main base of the Grand Fleet at Scapa Flow in the Orkneys imposed a severe task on the railways. Huge battleships then were coal fired, and because best quality steam coal was needed, this had to be hauled from South Wales, via Crewe, Carlisle, Perth and Inverness to the most northerly railhead at Thurso. It was a tremendous operation needing the redeployment of many

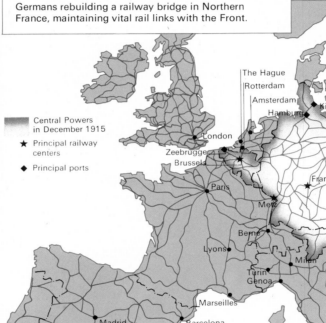

Central Powers in December 1915
★ Principal railway centers
♦ Principal ports

locomotives. A considerable number of new locomotives for the French railway system were manufactured in Scotland. The British Railways Operating Division had built up a total manpower of over 18,000 by the end of the war, covering a rail network of over 1,300 km (800 miles).

1916 The early conquests of the German and Austrian armies in the First World War, which put Serbia, Romania and most of Belgium into the hands of the so-called Central Powers, provided a remarkably complete railway network that was generally immune from attack from the Allied forces. Aerial attack at that time was almost nonexistent. The map shows how the overrunning of Belgium in the early stages of the war provided an additional outlet to the North Sea at Zeebrugge, while similar action against Serbia opened a direct line to Bulgaria and Turkey. The network itself was entirely of prewar construction but, when linked together under a largely unified wartime command, was ideally suited for the movement of troops and supplies, both from the central areas to the battlefronts and from one front to another if necessary. In the early stages of the war, the Russian forces were still in existence on the Eastern Front; but their collapse in the autumn of 1916 relieved the Central Powers of much railway movement through Poland and eastern Hungary, though the war in the Balkans was increasing.

1919

The peace conference of 1919 and the treaties that ratified its recommendations not only redrew much of the map of Europe, but they led to a regrouping of many of the old-established railway facilities. The total dismembering of the former Austro-Hungarian Empire had the most profound results of any, with the great reduction of the extent of Austria itself, and the formation of the new autonomous states of Czechoslovakia and Yugoslavia. To the north Poland gained independence. The existing railways did not suit the new countries and many new lines were needed to assist in the building up of new national unities. In Germany the railways were nationalized, and from 1923 it was only in France, with the restoration of the Alsace-Lorraine lines, that the administrative situation remained unchanged.

In Great Britain the coalition government returned to power with a huge majority in the so-called "Khaki election" of 1918 and imposed legislation upon the former private railways, forming them into four large groups.

The reasons for the British grouping arose directly from circumstances arising during the war. From its outbreak in 1914 the entire network of Great Britain and Ireland had been put under government control and was administered by the Railway Executive Committee, formed of a consortium of general managers of the leading railways. The interests of individual rail companies were subjugated to the national interest, but the interests of the owners – the shareholders – were safeguarded at the outset by a guarantee of a continuance, for the duration of the war, of dividend payments equal to those of the year 1913. During the war, however, strong representations were made by labor interests for uniformity of wage rates, which had previously been negotiated on a company rather than a national scale, and there had been great disparity, for example, between English and Scottish rates. New national scales were negotiated and paid in the later stages of the war; but it was realized that these could not be sustained by certain companies when the railways were decontrolled and handed back to their owners. The solution seemed to be to group the "rich with the poor," at the same time aiming at the continuance of some aspects of equalized working conditions that had been found advantageous during the war.

The British postwar situation, with a government-imposed merger under private ownership, and with nothing in the way of subsidies, was therefore notably different from that in all the former belligerent countries where reorganization immediately brought national ownership. After the brief postwar boom the new era was to lead the railways of Britain into a time of acute financial difficulty. The years immediately following the consolidation, in 1923, witnessed much confusion and frustration, while companies that had previously been rivals, tried to settle down together.

Above Serbian prisoners arrive at their destination in Hungary. *Below* Russian prisoners cross a bridge on the German strategic railway after the Battle of Tannenberg. *Right* Picture taken at Rethondes after the signing of the Armistice in 1918.

The fantastic streamliners

Railway development 1923–1945

1923 The grouping of the former British main line railways into four large companies, still privately owned and entirely self-supporting, taking effect from January 1, 1923, was in many ways typical of the worldwide attitude toward railways in the period of reconstruction after the First World War. The outlook was toward greater comfort for the passenger, greater safety, and improved standards of punctuality. At first there was little thought of doing more than fully restoring prewar standards of speed. Although this was done in Great Britain by 1923–4, on the Continent of Europe, after the ravages of war, most countries were still lagging behind. But what railway managements all over the world did not seem to foresee, still less to plan to combat, was the extent and seriousness of the growing competition from highway transport, both for passengers and freight. Around the great cities with their rapidly increasing populations attention was given to rail commuter traffic. The most careful studies were made of traffic flows in relation to the capacity of the lines, and around London in particular certain junction layouts were changed in order to avoid delay from conflicting movements. While electrification was envisaged, in many areas some extremely ingenious replanning of commuter services was accomplished successfully while retaining steam – notably in and out of Liverpool Street in London, terminus of the former Great Eastern Railway. On those services passenger accommodation remained in three classes, while the former "second-class" had largely disappeared in other regions of Great Britain.

A most important trend, that could be seen in countries all over the world, was the beginning of a move away from coal as a steam locomotive fuel; while elsewhere the attention of locomotive engineers was drawn to the need for firing with coal of quality much below the choicest steam grades. This trend originated during the First World War, with the cutting off, by hostile naval action, of British exports of coal. The South American railways, then mostly British owned, were hit particularly hard, and had to improvise. Then, when restoration was in hand after the war there came the disastrous coal strike of 1926, which again cut off supplies. After that second experience the changeover to oil firing became permanent. In the USA the change was equally definite, on railways serving the Midwest and western states that were adjacent to large indigenous supplies of oil. In the USA certain heavily graded mineral lines had been electrified, but there was considerable difference of opinion as to the best power system to adopt. Except in the newly developing countries there was not a great deal of new railway length built. The "grouping" in Great Britain produced some elimination of routes and short connections to facilitate inter-running between what had been separate company lines; but some of the most significant works in developing the world's railway network were in Australia. Connection between states of New South Wales and Queensland had been made in 1888, by a roundabout route that involved a change of gauge at the border station of Wallangarra. In 1930, however, the North Coast Line of the New South Wales Railways was completed on the standard gauge throughout and running through 113 km (70 miles) of Queensland territory to a terminus in South Brisbane. Even in 1925 the journey between Sydney and Brisbane took 25 hr, whereas after the completion of the new line the time was brought down to 15 hr 30 min. During this period much electrification was carried out.

Above This view of one of the Rio Grande Western's 4-6-6-4 locomotives shows both the size, and frequent ugliness, of American steam engines.

Below The first Southern Railway high-speed engines were the King Arthur class 4-6-0s. One of the new engines leaves Waterloo, July 1926.

Left Two years after the Grouping a former North Eastern Railway Z class Atlantic leaves Darlington.

Below 1927, a party of Germans view the hump in the mechanized switching yard at Wath (LNER).

1930 While electrification was being hailed as the motive power of the future, and committees in Great Britain and elsewhere were trying to establish the standard systems to be adopted, there was much important development in steam locomotive design, particularly in France, Great Britain and the USA. While speeds were gradually creeping up, the aim of locomotive engineers generally was to increase thermal efficiency to convey heavier loads without a proportionate increase in fuel consumption, especially on railways still entirely dependent on coal. There was also a move, noticeably strong in the USA, to increase the speed of through freight trains, aided by the development of the huge articulated locomotives from the Mallet compound type, by improved suspension, into units capable of sustained fast running. But when the worldwide depression of the 1930s began to affect, most seriously, railways in the advanced countries of the world, effective competition with the road haulers was found to be seriously handicapped. This was evident particularly in Great Britain, because of legislation framed in economic, political and international conditions totally different from those of the 1930s. The railways of Britain were common carriers, and they found that all the choicest and most remunerative traffic was being taken by the new competitors, leaving them with business that no one wanted. Appeals for revised legislation fell on stony ground. Public sympathy was with the road haulers while, in rural passenger transport, the convenient, friendly motor bus making its way into the heart of village communities, took the bulk of the business from the country branch lines, which were coming to be considered old fashioned and whose services were often inconvenient.

The publicity departments of railways worked hard. The speed of a few prestige trains in Great Britain, France, Germany and the USA was pushed upward, and for a time the honour of having the fastest start-to-stop run anywhere in the world was held by the Canadian Pacific, which was then waging intense, but highly unprofitable, competition with the Canadian National Railways for the intercity traffic between Montreal and Toronto. In Great Britain there was mild competition, at no more than moderate speeds, for the maximum length of nonstop run on the Anglo-Scottish services; and while the London Midland and Scottish had a daily run, made all the year round, of 478.8 km (299.25 miles) between Carlisle and London (Euston), the London and North Eastern, during the summer tourist season ran the Flying Scotsman nonstop in both directions over the 628.4 km (392.75 miles) between London (King's Cross) and Edinburgh. The Great Western scheduled the lightly loaded Cheltenham Flyer over the favorable 123.6 km (77.25 miles) from Swindon to Paddington in 65 min. But while this average from start-to-stop of 114.2 km/h (71.4 mph) was not representative of the service provided as a whole over that route, it was a splendid publicity boost, especially when, as one special feat, the journey time was cut down to $56\frac{3}{4}$ min, an average speed of 130.72 km/h (81.7 mph). By the early 1930s however, despite the prevailing depression, the supremacy of steam as a rail motive power was being challenged, not by electricity but by the diesel engine, of which one of the earliest successful examples in railway use was on the Buenos Aires Great Southern Railway. The use of diesel power on the railways soon spread throughout the world.

An American development that became of strategic importance in the Second World War lay in the mechanization of freight yards. Means for the efficient sorting and resorting of the freight trains had been developed early in Great Britain, notably on the London and North Western Railway at Edge Hill, Liverpool, and arrangements for centralizing and power operation of the switches had been adopted subsequently. But it was the Americans who eliminated the need for hand-operated brakes, by introduction of the so-called "retarders," or rail brakes. Some large yards were so equipped in the early 1920s, and in Germany the great yards at Hamm were similarly furnished, later to become a familiar and frequent target in the Second World War. British yards at March (Cambridgeshire) and Hull were also equipped, enabling these important centers of traffic to be operated with a greatly reduced workforce.

Although the weekly distance involved, and the resultant revenue, were quite small, it was undoubtedly the introduction of high-speed streamlined trains in the 1930s that helped to keep railways in the public eye, even though it did not help the overall financial position. The German Railways' Flying Hamburger, a two-car diesel railcar train running to and from Berlin, was one of the first, but criticized somewhat for the cramped nature of the passenger accommodation. In the USA a series of Zephyr services, with streamlined trains, were introduced between Chicago and cities in the Midwest, in competition with which were a series of Rockets on the Chicago, Rock Island and Pacific Railroad. In Great Britain the response to this movement was entirely with steam and principally on the London and North Eastern Railway with the Silver Jubilee in 1935 and the Coronation in 1937. These trains provided start-to-stop average speeds slightly over 113 km/h (70 mph) but brought immense publicity and prestige by their high speeds, which on one special test produced the highest speed ever attained by a steam locomotive, namely 203 km/h (126 mph). This was achieved by the famous *Mallard* locomotive of the LNER, on July 3, 1938, on a run between Grantham and Peterborough.

at the outbreak of the Second World War. In Great Britain and France passenger facilities were immediately reduced and schedules greatly decelerated, and as the aerial war developed there was sustained and relentless bombing of railway targets in Germany. Classification yards naturally came in for much attention, but in Germany as elsewhere the organization for repair was highly efficient, and this offensive, though cumulatively serious, did not have so crippling an effect on railway movement as the strategic bombing of the French railways immediately prior to the Allied invasions of 1944, in which a great number of viaducts were destroyed, thus very seriously hindering the forwarding of supplies to the battle areas. In the USA wartime traffic threw an immense burden upon the lines leading to the west coast and, to assist in carrying a far greater number of trains than that for which they were equipped, the technology of modern signaling in the form of Centralized Traffic Control (CTC) was applied to great advantage. Although large-scale production of diesel-electric locomotives had begun, steam carried the main burden of wartime traffic in the USA, with passenger train speeds little reduced from those achieved in peacetime.

Right Many spectacular photographs were taken of bomb damage to Britain's railways. Most of it was superficial, as shown in this picture of Liverpool Street station. *Above* A crash could be more devastating, causing much damage.

1939 In the last years before the Second World War there was a great worldwide improvement in passenger train services. It was not so much the spectacular few streamlined trains, but the general average. This was particularly true on the great American railways running east from Chicago, like the Pennsylvania and the New York Central, whose fast running with start-to-stop speeds of 105–113 km/h (65–70 mph) were made with heavy overnight sleeping car expresses. In France the standards were equally high, again with heavy trains, while in Great Britain the number of trains maintaining average speeds of 96 km/h (60 mph) or more was exceptionally high in relation to the size of the country. Despite their financial difficulties, which in Great Britain meant low or nonexistent dividends for the shareholders, railways were in excellent physical condition and everywhere proved an invaluable tool of basic strategy

The new age of railways

Railway development 1946 and after

1950 The first ten years after the end of the Second World War saw great changes on the railways of the world. Much of it was in the unwelcome form of retraction of facilities and reduction of worked track in face of a rapidly worsening economic situation. Yet in many countries there were notable advances in technology. Apart from the USA, whose land had not been invaded, nor her cities subjected to aerial attack, the railways of Great Britain were practically alone among those of the most heavily involved belligerent nations in having their tracks and workshops intact at the end of the war. Damage had been repaired, although the standards of maintenance of track and rolling stock had, by *force majeure*, been very much reduced. But the fact that the railways of Britain were still operating meant that they received nothing in the way of financial aid towards recovery, such as that made available to those on the continent of Europe, and elsewhere through the "Lend-Lease" Act and so on, which enabled the rapid restoration of services to be made.

In Great Britain, because of circumstances that were not very widely understood, the prestige of railways had sunk very low, and nationalization was hailed by many people as the panacea for all ills. Then when the necessary legislation had been passed by Parliament, and the situation deteriorated rather than improved, the blame for the worsening financial position was shifted on to the steam locomotive. At the beginning of the 1950s, however, no funds were available to permit a change to electric or diesel power on a big scale, and apart from commuter routes the railways of Britain remained steam powered.

Ironically, railways in the USA itself were soon facing an unexpected and unprecedented situation. All over the country commercial air services were being introduced,

while there was a great increase in the operation of large trucks on the highways. Businessmen began to transfer their patronage from the long-distance luxury express trains to air services which, even with the airplanes available in the 1950s, were immeasurably quicker than the fastest trains.

1963 In Britain it was very different. The ever growing deficit on railway operation was a charge on the national exchequer. In 1955, to try to halt and reverse the process, Parliament voted funds for a large-scale modernization plan, of which one of the principal features was the elimination of steam power. Large sums were spent on new rolling stock, improved signaling and construction of huge classification yards. The existing electrified lines were extended, and work commenced on electrifying the main line from London to Birmingham, Liverpool and Manchester. Contracts were placed for many hundreds of diesel locomotives, as a first step toward the replacement of some 18,000 steam locomotives. But still the adverse financial trend was not halted. In 1961 a distinguished industrialist, Dr. Richard Beeching, was appointed Chairman of the British Transport Commission, later reconstituted as the British Railways Board, and he subjected the entire network to ruthless analysis as to which routes and which facilities were profitable, with a view to closing altogether the unremunerative lines and developing others. The plan, although highly controversial, was actually carried through, from 1963.

1976 Altogether contrasting was the situation in Japan where the great prewar plan of a new high-speed national network was finally consummated, in its first phase, by the opening of the New Tokaido line in 1964. In the USA the railway situation deteriorated alarmingly. The privately owned railways were hamstrung with outdated legislation, which the Federal government persistently refused to revise. Most railways cut their passenger services to the minimum that legislation would permit, and would have abandoned them altogether, if they had been allowed to. To relieve the railways themselves of the responsibility of operating passenger services the National Railroad Passenger Corporation (Amtrak) was set up by Act of Congress in 1970 and a network of long-distance passenger routes chosen for development. These included all except two of the remaining passenger routes in the USA. In the meantime, by the application of modern technology, great and successful efforts were made to win back some of the freight traffic lost to long-distance trucking enterprises. In Great Britain, in 1976, a massive program of accelerated service was introduced between London (Paddington) and Swansea, and between Paddington, Bristol and Weston-super-Mare, with a large new fleet of diesel-powered High Speed Train sets (HST), having 4,400 engine horsepower and scheduled to run at 200 km/h (125 mph) over lengthy stretches of both routes. The important feature of these new services is their uniformity of high speed throughout the day and the frequent intervals at which they run.

There is a maximum distance for the route length of intercity passenger services (*below left*). Beyond 600 km, (370 miles) it is quicker for the passenger to fly. In the USA, air travel (blue) shows a continuing supremacy over rail (green). However, many European cities are close and intercity trains still perform an important function.

Railways are occasionally branded as an outmoded transportation concept, fit only for a museum of industrial archaeology, but the figures belie this. The diagram, *below*, shows how the total amount of traffic, world-wide, has increased in the 30 years since 1948: freight traffic has multiplied almost 4 times, and passenger traffic has more than doubled.

1976	16 *10*	241 *151*
1974	17 *10*	217 *141*
1972	14 *9*	198 *124*
1970	17 *10*	172 *107*
1968	21 *13*	157 *98*
1966	27 *17*	109 *68*
1964	29 *18*	80 *50*
1962	32 *20*	54 *34*
1960	34 *21*	49 *31*
1958	37 *23*	41 *26*
1956	26 *16*	45 *28*
1954	27 *17*	47 *29*
1952	20 *13*	55 *34*
1950	15 *10*	51 *32*
1948	11 *7*	66 *41*

figures in thousand million passenger kilometers
passenger mile equivalents in italics

640 *398*
707 *439*
784 *487*
866 *538*
959 *596*
1,069 *664*
1,184 *736*
1,447 *899*

figures in thousand million
passenger kilometers
*passenger mile
equivalents in italics*

1,804 *1,121*
2,258 *1,403*
2,823 *1,754*
3,338 *2,074*
4,008 *2,490*
4,642 *2,884*
5,400 *3,355*
6,608 *4,106*

figures in thousand million
net ton kilometers
net ton mile equivalents in italics

Above Ex-LNER *Sir Nigel Gresley* preserved. *Left* Modern Amtrak cars, USA. *Below left* Interior, Bern station, Switzerland.

Right A night express leaves London Euston. *Below right* Union Pacific Co-co and helper unit push freight over hump in Los Angeles.

Harnessing the power of steam

Locomotive development 1800–1834

1800 It is no exaggeration to assert that the invention of the steam locomotive changed the face of the world. By paving the way toward unprecedented speed in transport it put the finishing touch upon the developments of the Industrial Revolution. It was the indirect, and highly competitive, association of two men, both ingenious mechanics, that first blazed the trail. In 1765 James Watt, mathematical instrument maker at Glasgow University, had to repair an instructional model of a Newcomen Cornish beam engine, and hit upon the idea of using a separate condenser as means for effecting a very great economy in the use of steam. His innovation created such interest that eventually he went into partnership with Matthew Boulton, an industrialist in the West Midlands. The firm of Boulton and Watt prospered exceedingly, in the building of stationary steam engines, but it was when they began to receive orders for pumping engines in the Cornish tin mines that the practice developed by Watt had its first and only influence on the future of rail transport. One of the young men who saw the Watt engines installed in Cornwall was Richard Trevithick, and while Watt was timorous and self-effacing, albeit a superb mechanic, Trevithick was bold and confident to the point of rashness.

1814 Although Trevithick himself took very little part in the development of his locomotive after this first experiment, those who followed profited by its failures. It frequently broke down, and its relatively great weight compared with horsedrawn wagons broke many rails. Matthew Murray, of Leeds, for example, suggested having two cylinders working cranks at right angles to each other. This eliminated the "dead center" position and dispensed with the huge fly-wheel. This suggestion was incorporated in Blenkinsop's locomotives put to work on the Middleton Colliery railway near Leeds, in 1812. It had been thought that the contact between a smooth rail and a smooth wheel tire would not provide a good enough grip to enable a locomotive to haul a heavy load, and Blenkinsop had, in 1811, taken out a patent for a toothed rail laid to one side of the running rail, in which a gear mounted on the axle of the locomotive worked as a pinion in a rack. Locomotives of this type, hauling trains of coal cars, achieved a certain degree of reliability, though progress was slow and the geared arrangement expensive. One of the Blenkinsop engines was purchased by Blackett, for trial at Wylam Colliery, Northumberland, and the outcome was that the toothed rail arrangement was considered unnecessary. By the time this engine was at work George Stephenson was beginning to come into the picture. With financial backing from Lord Ravensworth he built his first locomotive for the Killingworth Colliery in 1814. It had many shortcomings, and the second Killingworth locomotive, in which Isaac Dodds was the joint patentee with Stephenson, was a vast improvement. The noise of exhaust, about which many complaints were made was practically silenced by turning the exhaust steam into the chimney, where it performed a second function, that of sharpening the draft of the fire and increasing the rate of steam production. Then the complicated gear drive was superseded by connecting the crosshead directly to the driving wheels through the connecting rod. In this locomotive, Stephenson and Dodds together had reached nearly all the fundamental points of the orthodox, classic, steam locomotive, in 1815: two cylinders, simple direct drive, exhaust turned from cylinders into chimney to increase draft on the fire. The partners had, in the second Killingworth locomotive, incorporated a synthesis of all the best features of the pioneer work of Trevithick, Blenkinsop, Matthew Murray, and Blackett, and the way was clear to introduce steam locomotive power on the projected Stockton and Darlington Railway.

The world's first ever railway locomotive was built by Richard Trevithick and tried out on the Pen-y-Darren tramway, in South Wales, on February 21, 1804.

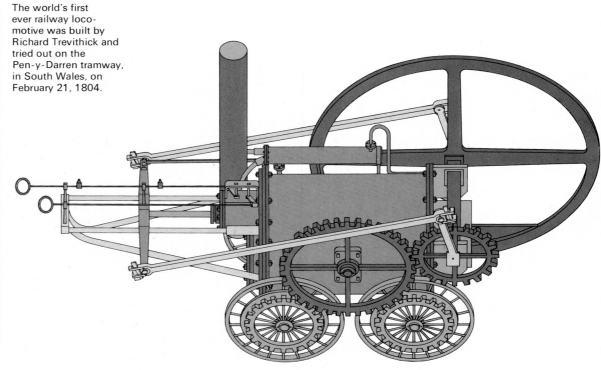

An early atmospheric stationary engine.

Watt used steam at comparatively low pressure; Trevithick at once began to build engines using much higher pressure, and instead of condensing the steam after use he exhausted it into the atmosphere: his first engine was nicknamed "Capt. Dick's Puffer."

From stationary engines used in the Cornish tin mines, Trevithick turned to rail traction, but not before he had made experiments with a locomotive on the roads in Cornwall, to the alarm of the populace. In 1803 a demonstration in London led to the "road carriage" getting out of control and tearing down the railings outside a private house. He became associated with industrial activities in South Wales and then there came the famous wager that led to the building of the first steam railway locomotive. The bet, between two prominent ironmasters, challenged Trevithick's "tram wagon" as it was called, to haul a load of 10 tons over the 15.6 km (9.75 miles) from Pen-y-Darren to Abercynon Basin on the Glamorganshire Canal. That Trevithick won the bet for his sponsor is a matter of history, and now interest centers around the design of the locomotive. It had but one cylinder, and to carry the drive over dead center there was an enormous fly-wheel. The piston, through the conventional crank-connecting rod mechanism, rotated a small pinion wheel which drove a large gear wheel. This engaged with gears mounted on the same axles as the road wheels of the locomotive. It was a triumph but had shortcomings.

William Hedley was the first to build a locomotive running on smooth edge-rail, in 1813: the *Wylam Dilly*. Here, *left*, it is seen much later, after rebuilding into the form of the *Puffing Billy*, 1815.

1827

The celebrated *Locomotion*, engine No. 1 of the first public railway in the world, incorporated all the best features of the Killingworth colliery locomotives, but the working conditions on what was virtually a main line, by comparison, were much more severe. The *Locomotion* was found incapable of steaming continuously for any length of time, and stops had to be made to raise steam. In the meantime, George Stephenson was away and engaged with the surveys and estimates for the Liverpool and Manchester Railway. He had left his faithful assistant Timothy Hackworth in charge on the Stockton and Darlington, and to that painstaking and very able man fell the task of making the pioneer locomotives reliable work units. In 1827 he built the *Royal George* locomotive at Shildon Works. It was much larger than any of the previous engines built by Stephenson, and had six coupled wheels. In it Hackworth increased the steaming capacity by arranging the flue from the firebox to the chimney in the form of a U, instead of a single large pipe, and so presented an increased area of flue tube in contact with the water. Hackworth was also the inventor of the blast pipe, a narrowing cone through the nozzle of which the exhaust steam passes at high velocity and creates an intense draft on the fire. The *Royal George* steamed very freely, but it was a curious thing to look at. Because of that return flue the firedoor was at the chimney end of the boiler, and the fireman rode on a separate tender propelled in front of the engine, while the engineer was at the rear end, where there was a second tender carrying the water supply tank. The greatly improved performance of the *Royal George* was in many ways a turning point in railway history, because until then in the later 1820s there were many who felt that locomotives could not be made sufficiently reliable, and that cable traction would be the only preferable alternative.

On the Liverpool and Manchester Railway, construction of which was nearing completion, the directors decided to stage a competition, the Rainhill trials, for the best type of locomotive to work the line. Although Hackworth had done so much to pull the Stockton and Darlington Railway around from failure, George Stephenson and his son, Robert, felt that his *Royal George* type of locomotive was rather clumsy and slow, and in entering a locomotive for the competition they introduced some further novel features, particularly in the boiler. To promote rapid evaporation by increasing the hot surfaces in contact with the water, the flue from the firebox to the chimney was split up, so that the hot gases of combustion instead of passing through one large tube passed through a nest of much smaller ones. This feature was suggested and incorporated not by a fellow engineer but by the secretary of the company, Henry Booth. As the first of its kind it gave much trouble in the constructional stage, because great difficulty was experienced in fitting the tubes to the boiler ends without leakage occurring. But Robert Stephenson persevered and eventually turned out a first-class job. The engine was the ever-famous *Rocket*, which steamed very freely.

Hackworth also entered the competition, and at his own expense built a four-wheeled engine, the *Sans Pareil*, having the return flue type of boiler. But the conditions of the competition staged at Rainhill did not require such a massive engine as the *Royal George*, and the *Sans Pareil* had only one tender, propelled in front. The engineer stood on a small platform jutting out at the rear. Hackworth's engine was sound enough in conception but he was rather let down by some of the suppliers of parts. One of the cylinders was badly cast and burst at one point, and then the feed pump supplying water to the boiler failed, and that of course put an end to the engine's participation. The third competitor, the *Novelty* of Braithwaite and Ericsson, made some spectacular runs, but broke down frequently, and eventually the *Rocket* of George and Robert Stephenson was the only one of the three to stay the course. Not only did it win the competition, and ensure that the *Rocket* type became the first standard engine type of the Liverpool and Manchester Railway, but it became a world prototype, incorporating all those basic features of design that were perpetuated for more than a hundred years in locomotives of increasing size all over the world, culminating in the gigantic "Big Boys" of the Union Pacific Railroad, which were built in 1941.

1830

When it came to day-to-day working on the Liverpool and Manchester Railway the *Rocket* type did not prove entirely satisfactory, and Robert Stephenson obviated the trouble from jerky and rough riding by introducing the *Planet* type in 1830, which had the cylinders between the frames, situated beneath the smokebox. All the machinery became largely concealed; but while this produced a much smoother riding engine, a problem of another type was introduced, that of a driving axle that had to incorporate two cranked features between the frames. The problems were, however, of manufacture rather than of principle, and locomotives with inside cylinders became very popular in Britain. The *Planet* type followed the *Rocket* type in having only a single pair of driving wheels, though situated at the rear instead of at the leading end of the locomotive. A single pair of driving wheels was favored for passenger trains, because it afforded a greater freedom in running; but the four wheels coupled type, as in the *Locomotion* and the *Sans Pareil*, was more suitable for freight trains, as providing greater adhesion in hauling a heavy load, and locomotives of this latter type were among the first exported from Great Britain to North America. They were, however, not to have any lasting influence on this continent.

In the USA the first ever railway, the Baltimore and Ohio, had from its inception in 1827 relied upon horse power; but in 1830 a New York industrialist and inventor,

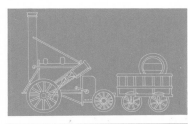

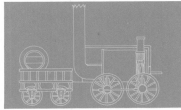

Top The successful entrant at the 1829 Rainhill trials was the Stephenson's locomotive *Rocket*. *Center* The exacting nature of the Rainhill trials defeated the *Novelty*. *Bottom* The *Sans Pareil* was the only serious rival to the *Rocket*, but it was crippled when a cylinder failed.

Peter Cooper, had made a large investment in Baltimore and Ohio land, and in his determination to see the railway succeed he set to work to produce a steam locomotive. Working in the Mount Clare shops at Baltimore, with scrap iron and borrowed wheels, and using gun barrels for boiler tubes, he built America's first home-made railroad steam locomotive, the *Tom Thumb*. It had a vertical boiler with the stack extending directly from the boiler end, and although having many defects arising from the primitive methods used in its construction, it paved the way to

The first train to run in New York State was hauled by the locomotive *De Witt Clinton*, in August 1831. It reached 24 km/h (15 mph).

success and was followed by locomotives of the same general type, built by the firm of Davis and Gartner. The *Atlantic*, built by the same partners in 1832, was the first of the so-called "grasshopper" type, again with vertical boiler, and the cylinders acting through large rocking shafts on the top of the boiler.

In the pioneer days of American railroading some strikingly original forms of steam locomotive were tried, none of any lasting success, but of great interest historically. The first locomotive ever to run in America, as distinct from the indigenous *Tom Thumb*, was imported from England by the Delaware and Hudson Canal Company in 1829. It was a typical English four-wheeler of pre-*Rocket* days and named the *Stourbridge Lion*. While Peter Cooper's *Tom Thumb* was going through its teething troubles on the Baltimore and Ohio Railroad, a much larger engine of the vertical boiler type was put to work in December 1830 on the South Carolina Canal and Rail Road Company. This was named the *Best Friend of Charleston* and goes down in history as the first locomotive to operate a regularly scheduled passenger run in the USA. Another notable American locomotive of early days, more in the contemporary British style, was the *De Witt Clinton* of 1831 which began work between Albany and Schenectady. This was an 0-4-0 with a horizontal boiler and a stack at the leading end after the style of the *Locomotion* on the Stockton and Darlington Railway. While American manufacturers were making their first attempts at locomotive building, the Stephenson inside cylinder 0-4-0 type, developed on the Liverpool and Manchester, had a limited phase of popularity, and in 1831 the firm of Robert Stephenson and Company of Newcastle supplied some locomotives of characteristic appearance, including the *John Bull*, to the Camden and Amboy Railroad.

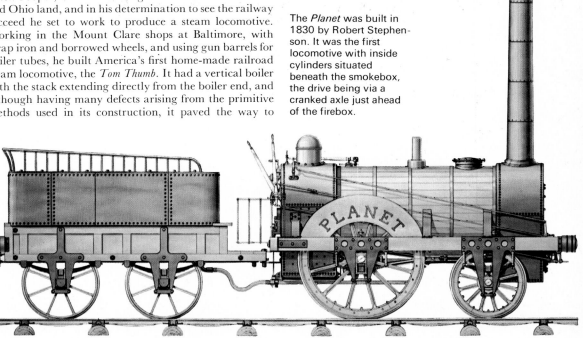

The *Planet* was built in 1830 by Robert Stephenson. It was the first locomotive with inside cylinders situated beneath the smokebox, the drive being via a cranked axle just ahead of the firebox.

Improving engine performance
Locomotive development 1835–1874

1835 By 1835 the steam locomotive had passed beyond the stage of a questionable gimmick.

The Liverpool and Manchester Railway was proving a very profitable investment, worked entirely by steam, and men like Robert Stephenson, having settled the fundamentals of operation, were becoming involved in finer points of performance. Speeds were increasing rapidly, more rapidly than development of the track, and the safe riding of locomotives became a point of much importance. The jerky action and rough riding of locomotives of the *Rocket* type, with outside cylinders, led to the production of Stephenson's famous *Patentee*, with inside cylinders, and this formed the prototype of many British locomotives exported to pioneer railway enterprises in Belgium, France, Germany and Russia. It came to be popular on the earlier British railways, and was exported to Canada and the USA. In North America, however, it was not successful. There was a great difference between the lavishly engineered, solid tracks of England, and the pioneer lines in America where, with little supporting capital, tracks were laid on meandering courses in river valleys and up steep hillsides, all with an absolute minimum of construction cost. The short, rigid wheelbased locomotives of conventional European type took unkindly to these sinuous, lightly laid tracks of America and derailments were frequent. A new concept of locomotive chassis design was therefore evolved on the simple principle of a three-legged stool or three-point suspension, which will stand on any rough ground. Thus came the American or 4-4-0 locomotive, in which the three points of suspension were the midpoints between the driving wheels on either side, with compensating levers to the axle boxes, and the pivot point of the leading four-wheeled truck. It was so successful that the American became the standard type of locomotive for any kind of duty all over North America, lasting in popularity for upward of 50 years.

Meanwhile a distinguished English engineer, Thomas Russell Crampton, who at one time worked on the Great Western Railway at Swindon, Wiltshire, was applying his own inventive mind to the problem of providing a smooth and safe-riding high-speed locomotive. He conceived the idea that if the large diameter driving wheels were placed at the extreme rear end, the center line of the boiler could be made low, thus securing greater steadiness of riding. A few of these picturesque stern-wheelers were put into service in England and Scotland, but it was in France particularly that the type found great favor, and so many of these engines were built that "prendre le Crampton" became a common phrase for "going by train." But even in the 1840s thoughts of some inventors were turning to alternatives to steam as the motive power, to avoid the use of coal and coke, emission of smoke and sparks, and the puffing noise. Thus came the ill-starred experiment with the so-called "atmospheric system" of traction, in which a large pipe was laid in the middle of the track; the power unit had a piston which fitted into the pipe, and the air in front of the piston was exhausted, thus drawing the unit along. The trouble was that the connection between the unit and the piston had to pass through a longitudinal joint in the pipe, normally sealed by a leather flap, but pushed aside by the movement of the piston connection and resealing afterward. Because the flap was made of leather, quick deterioration destroyed its sealing value. A vacuum could not be created ahead of the piston, and the system became useless.

It was natural that the early primitive steam locomotives working on the colliery lines in northeastern England should burn coal; but when plans were laid for more and more public railways, running through the green fields of the Midlands, those who opposed the building of railways managed to get restrictive clauses inserted into the Acts of Parliament authorizing them to prohibit the use of locomotives that did not consume their own smoke. At that early stage in the development that meant using coke instead of coal, and incurring the additional cost. This, however, could be regarded as no more than a temporary measure, and much experimenting was undertaken with coal-fired locomotives to reduce the emission of smoke to an acceptable level. In North America no such restrictions applied, but in areas distant from the coalfields wood-burning locomotives were built. This in turn brought problems with the throwing out of sparks. Many of the early American railways ran through densely forested country and sparks, whether from wood or coal, could cause serious forest fires. Sparks also occasionally set fire to the great timber trestle viaducts. While a major conflagration could lead to the complete loss of a viaduct, a smouldering insidious fire could lead to weakening of bridge members and result in a collapse while a train was crossing. Various spark-arresting devices of strange and picturesque appearance were fitted to the tall stacks of early American locomotives, giving them such names as "diamond stacks" and "balloon stacks" according to their shape. The first spark arresters were developed in the early 1830s and pioneered by such engineers as Matthew Baird. In all, over 60 types were tried on American wood-burning locomotives and became standard throughout the continent by the 1860s.

WTC No 5 Shannon locomotive, an early 0-4-0.

Left The atmospheric railway system of Jacob and Joseph Samuda. The cylindrical tube had a flanged slot at the top which was closed by a continuous flap of leather sandwiched between thin iron plates. The flap was hinged to the flange on one side and was free on the other, so that it could lift to allow the passage of the arm connecting the piston and the carriage. Air was expelled from the tube in front of the train thus creating movement by air pressure on the rear of the piston.

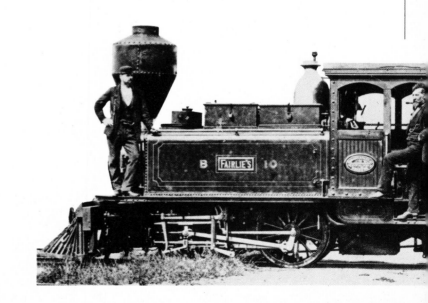

1859 In Great Britain while experiments were in progress to eliminate the use of coke there were interesting developments in the boiler itself. Robert Stephenson himself introduced what was known as the "longboiler" type, in conjunction with a relatively small firebox. The object was twofold: by having a long barrel, and making the products of combustion pass a considerable way before being exhausted, the fuel would be more completely burned; the long boiler would act as a large reservoir for steam, ready for use, while the small grate would need less coal to keep the fire bars covered while the locomotive was standing. It seemed an ideal type of boiler for freight trains, which spent a good deal of their time standing or switching, and using relatively little steam. The solution to the coal burning problem came ultimately in a very simple form – namely the firebrick arch, built transversely across the firebox. The flames and gases from the forward part of the grate were drawn back and around the rearward edge of the arch by the draft from the smokebox and, except at the times when the locomotive was being fired, gave a clear exhaust from the stack. This arrangement was first used on the Midland Railway in England in 1859, and thereafter the firebrick arch became a universal feature.

Locomotives of the 2-2-2 type, with outside, and sometimes with double frames were at one time popular for passenger work in Great Britain, and both varieties were exported to Europe. An important English variation must be noted, namely the "Jenny Lind" type which had outside framing for the leading and trailing wheels and inside frames for the single pair of driving wheels. On the London and North Western Railway, Southern Division, J. E. McConnell used inside frames only for a notable series of 2-2-2 express locomotives, nicknamed "bloomers." Before the end of the period, however, locomotives of the 2-4-0 type were coming into general use for passenger work, with notable examples in France, Belgium, Holland and Germany, in addition to those of Great Britain. In France, so long using the Crampton stern-wheeler type, the change to four coupled wheels was accompanied on the Paris, Lyon and Mediterranean by use of the "long-boiler"; but as the locomotives in question tended to pitch when running at speed, the 2-4-0 wheel arrangement was changed to the 2-4-2, a type which at a later date in the USA became known as the Columbia. While the 4-4-0 or American type with outside cylinders, leading truck and three-point suspension remained the standard design for general service all over the USA, larger locomotives were being introduced for heavier freight duties, and the Mogul (2-6-0) and the Consolidation (2-8-0) were coming increasingly into service. Speeds were not high, and competition in speed for such important traffic as that between New York and Chicago had scarcely begun to play a major role.

The Englishman Robert Fairlie patented an early design of articulated locomotive, and a few were built in the 1860s and 1870s. The 28-ton *Snake* was imported into New Zealand about 1873.

2-2-2
1-1-1

4-4-0
2-2-0

0-6-0
0-3-0

0-6-2
0-3-0

4-6-0
2-3-0

4-6-2
2-3-1

2-8-4
1-4-2

2-10-0
1-5-0

● Power transmission
Continental European notation in italics

Above Steam locomotive wheel notation, though perhaps a mystery to the uninitiated, is in fact a remarkably simple system. A distinction is made between driving and trailing wheels.

Right The moving principles of Walschaert's valve gear. Such mechanisms, though apparently complicated, operate purely to ensure that steam is let into and out of the cylinder to provide motion to the piston. Orange: high pressure (live) steam; yellow: medium pressure steam; blue: low pressure steam; green: steam under compression.

1863 The opening of the Metropolitan Railway in 1863, the first purely underground line in the world, involved the design of locomotives that literally consumed their own exhaust steam. No exhaust, however clear, could be permitted in the tunnels, and to meet this requirement a remarkably successful range of tank engines of the 4-4-0 type was introduced. The exhaust steam was diverted from the blast pipe into a large pipe on either side entering the top of the side tanks and was discharged upon the surface of the water. At one time no fewer than 120 of these locomotives were in service in the London area.

An interesting phase in the development of the steam locomotive came to center around lines of substandard gauge, principally in the USA, but a focus point of world attention came to be the 600 mm (1 ft 11½ in) gauge Festiniog Railway, in North Wales. Eminent engineers of the day stated that it would be impossible to design steam locomotives to operate satisfactorily on so narrow a gauge. After building some small locomotives of the 0-4-0 type that were limited in their capacity, C. E. Spooner, engineer of the Festiniog Railway, decided to try one of Robert Fairlie's patent double engines, which were in effect two tank engines arranged back to back on a single frame. Each engine unit, with its cylinders and running gear, was carried on a swiveling truck having ball and socket joint connections for the steam pipes below the smokebox at each end. These locomotives had two inside fireboxes, with doors alongside, stoked by the fireman who rode on one side of the central platform, the engineer riding on the other. The first of these engines, named *Little Wonder*, was put into service in 1869 and was an outstanding success. Several engines of the same type were added subsequently, and one is still working on the Festiniog Railway today. Locomotives of the same general type, but much larger and for the 1,435 mm (4 ft 8½ in) gauge, were built in England for service on railways in Mexico, Russia, South America and Sweden.

By 1874 the speed of passenger trains was becoming an important consideration in Great Britain. The British Post Office, for example, had definitely specified an average speed of 68 km/h (42 mph) overall between London and Holyhead for the Irish Mail; maintaining such an average, inclusive of the lengthy stops needed for postal traffic at such stations as Rugby, Stafford, Crewe and Chester, involved running at over 96 km/h (60 mph) on the open stretches of line. By the 1870s, indeed, speeds up to about 113 km/h (70 mph) were being reached on favorable stretches, not only with the Irish Mail, but on the Great Northern line from London (King's Cross) and on the steep though well-aligned descents of the west coast main line north of Lancaster. At that time, both in scheduled speed and in maximum speeds attained, the leading railways of Great Britain stood alone in the excellence of their performance, though this supremacy was not to last for many more years. While every credit must be given to the locomotives and their designers, this standard of running could not have been sustained without a track that was solidly built to the highest standards and thereafter scrupulously maintained.

Compound locomotives and superheating

Locomotive development 1875–1905

1875 By 1875 the steam locomotive had passed well beyond various experimental stages and was the predominant asset in the worldwide development of land transport; but its overall efficiency, in terms of work done in hauling a train in relation to the latent energy in the coal or other fuel consumed, was very low, something less than 8 percent. The attention of engineers in Great Britain, France, Germany, Austria and the USA became directed toward the improvement of this low return for the fuel consumed. Theoretical studies were made of the stages in which steam was produced and used, and by common consent the use of two-stage or compound expansion of the steam appeared to show the best prospects for improvement. It was an attractive theoretical concept, first put into practice by Anatole Mallet, who in 1875 built a small tank engine for the Bayonne and Biarritz Railway. Instead of being admitted simultaneously to two cylinders, steam was admitted only to the one high-pressure cylinder, and after expanding in that, it passed into the one low-pressure cylinder to complete its expansion before exhausting to the atmosphere. By this means Mallet was able to secure a greater pressure range over the whole expansion of the steam than if it had been passed through only one cylinder. Because the steam was at a much lower pressure on entering the low-pressure cylinder, it had to be made of much larger diameter, to ensure that each cylinder had a roughly equal thrust on the piston. Had this not been so the motion imparted to the locomotive as a whole would have been irregular and therefore conducive of rough, dangerous riding.

Mallet's ideas were quickly taken up by other engineers, first by A. von Borries of the Prussian State Railways, who in 1880 built two locomotives of his own design. One of the problems immediately confronting designers of compound locomotives was that of starting. In a conventional two-cylinder locomotive using single expansion and cranks at 90 degrees to each other, if one cylinder happened to have its crank and connecting rod on dead center, the second

flow of steam. But a further factor that handicapped these three-cylinder locomotives was that the two pairs of driving wheels were not coupled. This did not help with starting, when one pair might slip independently of the other and thus cause a lack of synchronization in the flow of steam. The Webb three-cylinder high-speed compounds of which there were 100, in five separate classes, did a great deal of hard work, but it might have been done much more easily had the two pairs of driving wheels been coupled. Webb's whole achievement as an engineer was unfortunately criticized because of the failure of his compound engines.

A very important trend that came to affect all aspects of locomotive design, maintenance and their work out on the line was the general introduction of steel instead of wrought iron as the basic material of construction, and also of rails. With harder rails and harder tires on the wheels both locomotives and rolling stock could run more freely. In Great Britain it was so remarkable to find

locomotives of good reputation, which in the 1870s were rarely exceeding 113 km/h (70 mph), speeding up to well over 130 km/h (80 mph) in the 1890s. Although claims of very high speed had been made for the Empire State Express in the USA, these have never been fully authenticated, and the climax in speed achievement took place in Britain in the Race to the North in 1895, when competition between the east and west coast routes from London to Scotland led ultimately to an all-out race between the sleeping car expresses leaving Euston and King's Cross at 8:00 p.m. for Aberdeen. The west coast record of 512 min for a run of 870 km (540 miles) with three intermediate stops, each to change locomotives, remained unsurpassed on the world's railways for many years to follow. It is perhaps significant that all the fastest start-to-stop runs on both coasts were made not by compounds but by single-expansion engines, 2-4-0 type on the London and North Western, and 4-4-0 on both the Caledonian and the North Eastern railways.

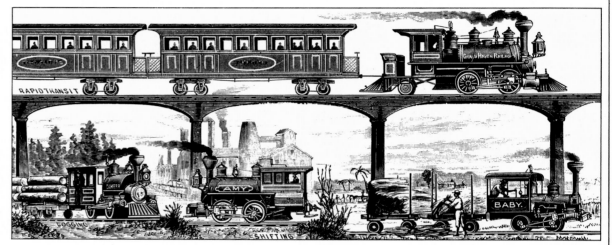

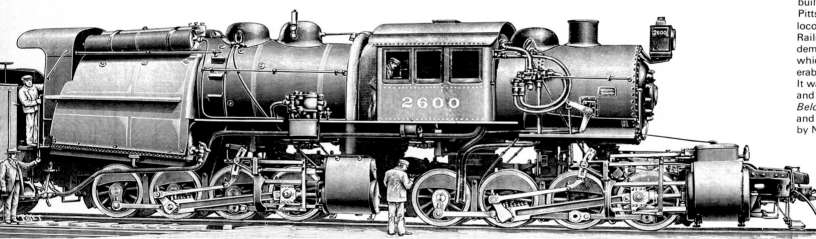

Above Light locomotives built by H. K. Porter, Pittsburgh Pa. *Left* A locomotive of the Erie Railroad Company in 1908 demonstrating a design which was to be considerably developed. It was truly gigantic and weighed 155 tons. *Below Rob Roy*, Midland and GWR, built in 1873 by Nelson & Co.

crank would turn the wheel and start the motion. But in a two-cylinder compound engine, if the high-pressure cylinder was on dead center the engine would not start. Von Borries designed a special starting valve that allowed a small amount of steam to pass directly into the low-pressure cylinder on starting and allowed the engine to get away in all circumstances. Many locomotives of this type were built for service in Germany, while an adaptation of it was successfully used on the North Eastern Railway in England. One of the best known, yet unfortunately the least successful, of the compound systems used in England was that of Francis William Webb on the London and North Eastern Railway. Webb was chief mechanical engineer on the London and North Eastern for a period of 32 years and helped to organize locomotive building to a very high standard of workmanship. But for some reason, never fully explained, Webb chose to employ three cylinders – two very small high-pressure ones outside, exhausting into one huge low-pressure cylinder between the frames. It was a curious arrangement, not helped by the low-pressure cylinder which despite its size was too small to take the exhaust without somewhat restricting the

1885

Although larger locomotives were being introduced as prototypes to the very end of the nineteenth century the 4-4-0 type remained a world favorite for passenger work. In America outside cylinders were universal, and the traditional American of earlier days was the same, though greatly enlarged, as the pioneers designed in the first place to run on lightly laid track. The celebrated *999* of the Empire State Express, for which a maximum speed of 179 km/h (112 mph) was claimed, was of this type. In France, Germany and Austria, the various types of compound had outside cylinders, but in Great Britain, followed by Holland and Belgium, inside cylinders were generally preferred. Much emphasis was set upon a neat and compact outward appearance, and these traditions were reflected in British locomotives exported to India, Australia and South America. Locomotive development on the Caledonian Railway must be specially mentioned because there particular attention was paid, by Dugald Drummond, to the design of the steam passages leading to and from the cylinders to ensure a free flow of steam. Drummond's locomotives were notably fast runners, and produced a high output of power.

Compound locomotive development in Austria and France took different ways. In Austria Karl Gölsdorf had to provide for severe hill climbing on main lines through the Alps, and used a two-cylinder system at first. With the outside cylinders of different sizes, these locomotives looked curious when seen from the front; but the 2-8-0 type designed specially for the Arlberg Tunnel route in the Tyrol acquired a very high reputation, and some were still in service 70 years after their first introduction, though transferred to other areas after the electrification of the Arlberg line. In France the major development was due to one of the pioneers of steam locomotive compounding – Alfred de Glehn – who was technical head of the Société Alsacienne, Belfort. He used four cylinders, two high-pressure outside and two low-pressure inside. The system was applied first on 4-4-0 locomotives of the Northern Railway of France, and though his experimental prototype had the two pairs of driving wheels uncoupled as in F. W. Webb's system, this engine, built in 1885, remained the only one of its kind. All subsequent de Glehn compounds

had the two pairs of driving wheels coupled. The de Glehn compounds were complicated engines to operate, and their outstanding success was due to the French custom of allocating each locomotive to one engineer only, who not only had exclusive charge of it in service, but who went into the repair shops and worked as a fitter on the engine when the time came for overhaul.

1904

The de Glehn system of compounding, as applied to the Atlantic express locomotives of the Northern Railway of France, came prominently to the notice of British travelers on the boat trains between Paris, Boulogne and Calais, and the purchase by the Great Western Railway of three for comparative trials in England led, under G. J. Churchward, to a successful development, not with compound, but with four-cylinder single-expansion locomotives. This range of 4-6-0 locomotives, that in 1923–7 led to the famous Castle and King classes, included a number of de Glehn design features. At the same time, however, Great Western boiler design was being derived largely from American practice with tapered barrel and a high raised Belpaire (or flat-topped) firebox. In 1904, older Great Western locomotives were prominent in making new speed records, including the first authenticated instance of a speed of 160 km/h (100 mph) by the engine *City of Truro*, and the running of a stretch of 113 km (70 miles) at an average of 130 km/h (80 mph) by the 4-2-2 engine *Duke of Connaught*. These two locomotives were responsible, in succession, for running an Ocean Mail special from Millbay Docks, Plymouth, to London (Paddington) – a distance of 394 km (246.5 miles) in 225 min, inclusive of a 2 min stop at Bristol to change engines. This run, with its overall average of nearly 106 km/h (66 mph), was the fastest ever up to that time.

An important development was then in progress in Germany. Up to then locomotives had used the steam just as it was boiled – saturated steam as it is termed. Dr Wilhelm Schmidt was applying the principle of superheating to certain locomotives of the Prussian State Railways. After formation the steam was heated further before use. This had the advantage of considerably increasing its volume and thereby its capacity to exert power in the cylinders. Of course in getting more steam, additional heat

Adams Radial locomotive, preserved today in immaculate working condition on the Bluebell Railway, England.

and therefore more coal had to be used. But the advantages far outweighed the cost, and although by the turn of the century the practice was only in its infancy, superheaters were to become a universal item of equipment on nearly all new locomotives from about 1912 onward.

With the twentieth century came the era of extremely large locomotives. In Great Britain the 4-4-2 and the 4-6-0 types began to supersede the 4-4-0 for passenger work, while in America the transition from the traditional outside cylinder 4-4-0 was very rapid. The intervening stages of the 4-4-2 and 4-6-0, known in America as the Atlantic and the Ten-Wheeler respectively, quickly gave place to the Pacific or 4-6-2. In the USA compounds were built on the Vauclain and the tandem system, both being generally favored to the systems then popular in Europe because they allowed the cylinders to be mounted outside the frames. Both employed four cylinders. In the Vauclain the high- and low-pressure cylinders were mounted in two pairs, one on each side of the engine. The high-pressure cylinder was immediately above the low-pressure cylinder, and their pistons were connected to a common crosshead. In the tandem system one high- and one low-pressure cylinder were mounted on a common horizontal axis, and the pistons for each cylinder were mounted on one continuous piston rod. Many locomotives of both types were built in the USA. The Vauclain system derived its name from Samuel Matthews Vauclain, who became superintendent of the Baldwin Locomotive Works in 1890 and eventually became chairman of Baldwin in 1929. He also designed engines for railway systems in many other parts of the world, including heavy freight engines for Brazil and engines for Japan.

The era of technological innovation

Locomotive development 1906–1926

1907 By the end of the nineteenth century it seemed that railway administrations in all parts of the world aimed to have the smallest locomotives that would work the traffic, while within a matter of ten years the pendulum had swung strongly the opposite way. Heavier and much more luxurious rolling stock was being built; dining and sleeping cars were being added to many of the principal trains, and while the urge to accelerate services had lessened, there was no deceleration. In all countries very much larger locomotives were built, and for the first time – in Great Britain at any rate – size and weight began to approach the maximum that the lines would take. Civil engineers placed limits upon the maximum axle loads that they were prepared to accept; but in Great Britain the crisis in this respect was postponed by the introduction of superheating. Smaller locomotives thus equipped could do greatly superior work to their predecessors of equivalent size and overall weight. Certain locomotives of a size unusual by previous standards and of the 4-6-0 type were built by the Caledonian and by the London and South Western Railways, but for sheer size in Great Britain Churchward's Pacific *The Great Bear*, on the Great Western Railway, surpassed all. This was only the second locomotive of the type to be built in Europe, the first being on the Paris-Orléans Railway in 1907. *The Great Bear*, completed at Swindon in 1908, was virtually an experiment in boiler design in readiness for future requirements, which in fact did not materialize.

The problem of maximum axle loading in locomotives was becoming much more acute on the continent of Europe. The massively built and well maintained British main lines were mostly capable of taking axle loads up to 18 or 19 tons, but this was not so in Holland, for example. In the early 1900s, traffic across that country, particularly in conveying the Anglo-German mails, was becoming increasingly heavy, and the elegant British-built 4-4-0s of the State Railway could not cope with the trains single-handed. Larger locomotives were needed, and that in the ordinary way would have meant heavier axle loads, which the civil engineers could not permit, because of the nature of much of the foundations on which the lines were laid. The matter of engine balancing became critical. In any locomotive the revolving cranks and reciprocating rods and pistons set up a degree of imbalance, which, if not compensated for, can give rise to unsteady and unsafe riding. So, a degree of balance was provided by putting compensating weights in the wheels. These, while resulting in a smooth riding engine, impart a "hammer blow" effect on the track that increases in seriousness as the speed rises. On some British 4-4-0 locomotives the hammer blow at 113 or 120 km/h (70 or 75 mph) was equal to 50 percent of the static axle load, giving a total load on the track of 28 or 29 tons. If, however, four cylinders are used instead of two,

and all four drive on to the same axle, the movements of the pistons, cranks and rods exactly compensate each other and there is no hammer blow at all. On the Netherlands State Railways the civil engineers were prepared to accept heavier axle loads on larger locomotives providing they were built with four cylinders. A very fine range of powerful 4-6-0 locomotives were built.

In the USA the equipping of all freight trains with the continuous automatic air brake enabled very long and heavier trains to be safely controlled when descending steep grades, and the size and power of the locomotives needed to haul such trains on level track and adverse grades had to be increased accordingly. For this the Mallet articulated compound type proved suitable, and it was enlarged to unprecedented length and tractive power. Some of the largest built in the period 1906–15 were 2-6-6-2s for the Chesapeake and Ohio, weighing 270 tons, and 2-8-8-2s for the Southern Pacific, weighing 265 tons. With such large boilers and fireboxes the rate of coal consumption was far greater than could be sustained by a single fireman, and mechanical stokers were introduced whereby coal from the huge tenders could be fed directly on to the firegrate and distributed evenly over its wide area. The stokers were so designed that the rate of feed could be regulated by the fireman according to the needs of the journey. These giant locomotives were four-cylinder

compounds, and the low-pressure cylinders carried on the forward articulated engine unit were often as large as 101 cm (40 in) diameter. The working of American freight trains did not require any fast running, and that these compound Mallets became rather unstable at any speed over about 48 km/h (30 mph) was then of no consequence: no higher speeds were needed. This instability was later shown to be due to an uneven distribution of the weight between the front and rear engine units, correction of which enabled more recent articulated locomotives to be run safely up to 113 km/h (70 mph) with the express freight trains of the 1930s.

This electric locomotive was introduced on Switzerland's Emmenthal-Burgdorf-Thun Railway as early as 1910.

Left The Great Eastern 0-10-0 No 20 *Decapod* was built by James Holden to achieve high acceleration. It failed because it was too heavy for existing track.

1912

One of the most important advances in this period was in the technique of locomotive testing. From an early date in the history of railways, dynamometer cars had been used by which the pull exerted by a locomotive could be measured – a sophisticated version of the simple spring balance. But such measurements taken while a locomotive was working a service train were necessarily subject to all the incidentals of daily railway operation, checks because of adverse signals, and so on; and in the USA plant was set up at Purdue University and at the St. Louis Exhibition of 1904, on which locomotives could be tested under laboratory conditions. The wheels were supported on rollers, and the driving wheels could be made to rotate the test plant rollers against an applied load. This could be varied according to requirements, and the task of hauling a train of any load and at any speed could be simulated. The behavior of the locomotive, steam production, coal consumption and all other workings could be observed in the carefully regulated atmosphere of a laboratory, instead of in the rough and tumble conditions of daily service on an ordinary railway route.

At the conclusion of the St. Louis Exhibition in 1904, the test plant on which the working of a number of dissimilar American locomotives had been demonstrated was removed and set up on a permanent basis at the principal locomotive works of the Pennsylvania Railroad at Altoona. In Great Britain modern dynamometer cars were built by the Great Western, North Eastern, London and North Western and Lancashire and Yorkshire Railways, but it was only the Great Western that followed the American example and built a stationary testing plant. In the beginning this plant was not used to a great extent, reliance being placed upon tests with the dynamometer car on service trains. On the London and North Western Railway in November 1913, during tests with one of the four cylinder 4-6-0 locomotives of the Claughton class, the highest output of power registered with a British locomotive was attained, namely 1,669 hp at a speed of 113 km/h (70 mph). This was not surpassed until considerably larger locomotives were in service after the First World War.

By the year 1912 the era of the "mixed traffic" locomotive was beginning. With the acceleration of freight services the need was felt for units that could haul a fast freight train but could also be used in medium-speed passenger services. Valve gears were being improved, and locomotives with coupled wheels of no more than 1,676 mm (5 ft 6 in) diameter were able to make speeds up to 113 km/h (70 mph) economical. This trend, and the locomotives that were coming into service in Great Britain as a result of it, was particularly advantageous when motive power had to be supplied for serving the battle-fronts in the First World War. Dual purpose locomotives

Interior of the cab *Caerphilly Castle*, 1923.

were ideal for both troop and munition trains. But the bringing of railways under government control both in Great Britain and France, due to the war emergency, led those with overall responsibility to look toward a far greater degree of standardization of locomotive design than had been thought desirable previously. Committees were set up and new standard designs drafted. In France events moved somewhat faster than in Great Britain, because one sector of the French railway network was actually owned by the state; and the government took the standard Pacific engine design of that railway, and a 4-6-0 dual purpose type, and placed large orders. Some were placed in Britain, because certain normal manufacturing facilities in France were in enemy hands. Arrangements were made for these new locomotives to be allocated also to the privately owned railways of France in the hope that they would subsequently be adopted as a standard. In Britain at the end of the war, the Minister of Munitions, then Winston Churchill, was anxious to place large orders for new locomotives, to avoid the large-scale unemployment that it was feared would result from the sudden end to the demand for munitions. This project never materialized, partly because the then separate independent British railways could not agree among themselves as to the individual locomotive designs and specifications that should be ordered.

1923

Just as the increasing size and weight of locomotives had brought continental engineers together in the earlier 1900s, so also in Great Britain, after the end of the war, locomotive and civil engineers were associated with scientific and university interests in the researches of the Bridge Stress Committee. The responsibility of this committee was to examine the effects that different types of locomotives had upon a variety of underline bridges. The outcome was to emphasize the beneficial effects of locomotives having three or four cylinders, and equally to underline the damaging effect of certain designs having only two cylinders inside. This confirmed the correctness of the policy of all four of the large groups set up by the Railways Act of 1921, the provisions of which took effect from January 1, 1923. Notable multicylindered high-speed passenger locomotives of the 1920s were the Gresley three-cylinder Pacifics of the LNER, the four-cylinder 4-6-0 Lord Nelson class of the Southern, and the three-cylinder 4-6-0 Royal Scot of the LMSR. Meanwhile the Great Western policy of building four-cylinder 4-6-0s for the heaviest passenger traffic continued with enlargements from the Churchward Star class of 1907 to the King of 1927 with the high nominal tractive effort of 18,280 kg (40,300 lb). The continued use of loose-coupled, unbraked cars on the majority of British freight trains meant that loads could not be greatly increased, and no significant increase in the size or power of freight locomotives took place in Great Britain throughout this period.

In France the allocation of government-ordered locomotives to some of the private railways did not have the desired effect. The Northern, and the Paris, Lyon and Mediterranean had always followed a strongly individual practice, and the new locomotives of the State Railway type were regarded as no more than temporary assistance and were transferred elsewhere after a short time. The Northern brought out a splendid new design of Pacific which did magnificent work on the very long English boat trains, while the PLM brought out a huge 4-8-2 for working over the steeply graded central section of the main line from Paris to Marseille, between Laroche and Dijon, where the line passes through the Côte-d'Or mountains. In the meantime the American Mallets were getting larger than ever, and in 1923 the Denver and Rio Grande Western took delivery of some compound freight engines of the 2-8-8-2 type that had grates of 9 m² (96.5 ft²) and a tractive effort of 48,353 kg (106,600 lb). The diameter of the low-pressure cylinders was no less than 1 m (39 in), and the total weight of the engine and tender was a staggering 332 tons.

This graceful 4-4-0 was built in 1913 by the North British Locomotive Co. in Glasgow, Scotland, to the order of the South India Railway. The tender cab is somewhat unusual, indicating that the engine was expected to run backward frequently.

The high point of steam

Locomotive development 1927–1934

1927 The years from 1927 until the outbreak of the Second World War were among the most momentous and productive in the entire history of the steam locomotive. In the mid-1920s it had reached practically to the limit of physical size in Great Britain, France and North America, and the multifaced challenge of increased tonnage requirements, the competition looming up from newer forms of motive power, and the economic conditions of the times presented engine designers with the urgent need to effect the basic improvements in the day-to-day performance of the machine itself, taking the term "performance" in its very broadest sense. The situation attained by 1927 was graphically portrayed at the time of the centennial celebrations of the Baltimore and Ohio Railroad, when a great pageant of locomotives was staged. At that time the Pacific type (4-6-2) was giving place to the 4-6-4, or Hudson, for the heaviest express passenger traffic, because a four-wheeled truck at the rear was advantageous in supporting the ever-larger fireboxes that were becoming necessary. Even so, the 4-6-4 was not considered large enough on some North American railways, and the 4-8-4 was being introduced. In the year of the Baltimore and Ohio celebration the Northern

Pacific took delivery from Alco of some huge 4-8-4s, while across the border the Canadian National was also using the type, in its celebrated Confederation class. At one time it was thought that eight coupled wheels would be restrictive upon the maximum speed a locomotive could attain; but 4-8-4s have been run regularly at 130 km/h (80 mph) and at even higher speeds.

Another important feature of then current American practice was the almost universal abandonment of multicylinder layouts. One of the last designs to have anything but the simplest two-cylinder arrangement of the machinery was a series of very large freight locomotives built by Alco for the Union Pacific in 1926. These were of the 4-12-2 wheel arrangement, with three cylinders, and a valve gear of the conjugated type introduced by Sir Nigel Gresley, on the Great Northern Railway of England, and standardized on all his principal designs for the London and North Eastern Railway. But by 1930 two cylinders only were used in North America, and on freight locomotives having tractive efforts approaching 45,359 kg (100,000 lb) the cylinders were necessarily very large. On a class of 2-10-2 built by Baldwin for the Reading Railroad in 1931 the cylinders were 77 cm (30½ in) diameter by

78 cm (32 in) stroke. Another important American development of the period was to design the main frames and their cross-stretchers as a single one-piece steel casting, instead of building them up from flat members. The cylinders were also included as part of this all-embracing "bed." One of the first instances of this development was in a class of 4-8-4 passenger locomotives for the Southern Pacific built in 1930. These large units had a booster engine on the four-wheeled trailing truck beneath the firebox which increased the tractive effort from 27,200 to 32,660 kg (60,000 to 72,000 lb) when it was put into operation.

Left The Royal Scot, c. 1927, preserved today. From the class of the same name, these three-cylinder 4-6-0s were designed to run on the LMS London to Carlisle route nonstop, a distance of 478 km (299 miles).

Left King George VI, built by GWR, pictured in the late 1950s at Bath spa, England. *Above* Nord Pacific-Bréville series, experimentally rebuilt with Cossart valve gear. *Right* 60 class Garratt 4-8-2 + 2-8-4 outside Nairobi shed.

1930

It was remarkable that, while American practice had swung so pronouncedly to the simplest of all machinery layouts, with two cylinders only and all the running gear outside, and the four "grouped" railways of Great Britain were using three-cylinder or four-cylinder single-expansion types for their principal express services, all of the French railways retained an unshakable preference for the four-cylinder compound, mostly continuing to use the de Glehn arrangement of cylinders. This was a complicated arrangement, both in the proliferation of the machinery and in the skill needed to drive it efficiently. But French railway traditions were more than equal to the need, and some outstanding work was performed around 1930. French expertise in all matters connected with four-cylinder compound locomotives was epitomized on the Paris-Orléans Railway, after the electrification of the sections leading out of Paris. Steam locomotive men feared that, with acceleration of service and increased tonnage capacity of the electric locomotives, unfavorable comparison would be made upon the standards of running south of Orléans. A very careful and scientific study was made of one of the existing Pacific engines, and certain weaknesses in the design of 20 years earlier were laid bare. The young engineer charged with this investigation, André Chapelon, recommended a redesign of the cylinders, improvement in the internal steam passages, and enlargement of the superheater. One engine was altered in accordance with his findings, and on test it was found that the capacity was increased by no less than 50 percent, while at the same time permitting the locomotive to run more freely. The features embodied in what became known in France as the "P. O. Transformations" became a yardstick for locomotive improvement throughout the continent of Europe.

In England Sir Nigel Gresley embodied Chapelon principles in a large new 2-8-2 design for use in heavy passenger service on the east coast main line between Edinburgh and Aberdeen, where increase of train loads had made double-heading a regular necessity while older types of locomotive had to be used. But one of the most important developments in Britain in the early 1930s was the mandate given to the new chief mechanical engineer on the London Midland and Scottish Railway to "scrap and build": to replace the somewhat heterogeneous stock of locomotives inherited from the constituent companies of the merger in 1923, with standard new designs of as few different classes as possible. Associated with this program was the aim to obtain greater monthly mileage from each locomotive. In total contrast to the continuing French practice of allocating one driver, and one driver only to each locomotive, the LMSR aim to secure maximum utilization involved the use of individual locomotives by several different crews in the course of a single journey.

There was one instance of six different crews manning a locomotive on successive stages of a 467 km (290 mile) journey. To meet such service requirements a locomotive of extreme simplicity for handling and outstanding reliability was needed, and W. A. Stanier, the chief mechanical engineer of the LMSR, provided such a locomotive in the mixed traffic 4-6-0 officially classed 5P5F, but known colloquially, as the "Black Five."

1934

Thus in the early 1930s major developments in locomotive design had taken place in Great Britain, France and the USA, while elsewhere the process of evolution was a reflection of the practice of one or another of the leaders, adapted to suit local conditions. From that time, however, a very distinctive development in two directions became evident on the sub-standard gauge railways of the world, and particularly in southern Africa. Hitherto the 1,067 mm (3 ft 6 in) gauge had been considered to impose a limitation upon size and the intrinsic merits of design; but on the South African Railways new locomotives of the 4-8-2 type were introduced which for characteristics of height, size, width and performance surpassed many of the medium-speed units operating in Europe on the 1,435 mm (4 ft 8 in) gauge. But the most remarkable development in Africa was in respect of the Beyer-Garratt articulated type. This type, on a substandard gauge line with extreme curves and a serious limitation on maximum axle loads, was shown in 1921 to have a considerable advantage over the Mallet articulated type in a series of comparative tests on the Natal main line of the South African Railways. The Garratt, with two separate but identical engine units and one huge boiler carried on a cradle slung between the two, proved an ideal locomotive for a sharply curved sub-standard gauge line. The boiler could be built to ideal proportions for free steaming – short barrel and large diameter – which was clearly impossible on the Mallet. The latter was very successful on the relatively straight standard gauge lines of the USA.

In India, another area of intensive utilization of steam locomotives, much was done by the Indian Railway Conference Association (IRCA) to standardize on locomotive design for the several once-independent railways that one by one, as their original concessions expired, were coming under national ownership and control. The IRCA produced three classes of Pacific, XA, XB and XC, for various conditions of passenger service on the broad gauge 1,676 mm (5 ft 6 in) lines, and two classes of 2-8-2 freight engine. At the same time those railways that in the early 1930s still remained independent, notably the Bengal Nagpur, pursued an individual line, and the BNR favored the de Glehn four-cylinder compound system in some large Pacific engines. Very powerful articulated locomotives of the Beyer-Garratt type were introduced for coal train use in Bengal.

In express passenger service the introduction of high-speed diesel powered trains in both Germany and the USA spurred steam locomotive designers to apply a degree of external streamlining to locomotives allocated to prestige high-speed trains. This was done to remarkable effect on the London and North Eastern Railway in 1935, when a new high-speed service was to be introduced to mark the Silver Jubilee of King George V. With a knowledge of what Chapelon had achieved in France, with internal streamlining of all the ports, passages and valves to facilitate the freest possible flow of steam, plus experience from his large 2-8-2 engines on the Edinburgh-Aberdeen route, Sir Nigel Gresley modified considerably the design of his standard Pacific engines, one of which had already attained a maximum speed of 173 km/h (108 mph). But with an eye to its publicity value and to the saving of a little coal by reducing air resistance, the new Pacific engines designed for the Silver Jubilee service were streamlined externally. It was not true streamlining but a form of aerodynamic screening copied from the external shape of some high-speed Bugatti railcars then operated on certain routes in France. This external streamlining, coupled with a silver-like finish that complied with the name of the new train, was most sensationally successful in its appeal to the public, and when the Silver Jubilee train attained a speed of 180 km/h (112.5 mph) on a preliminary demonstration run, its success as a commercial proposition was assured, in giving a service in four hours over the 429 km (268 miles) between London (King's Cross) and Newcastle. However, this train was as yet a once-off, traveling up from Newcastle to London in the morning and returning at 5:30 p.m.

Moving toward diesel power

Locomotive development 1935–1944

1935 Technical opinion in the advanced countries of the world was much divided in the late 1930s upon the relative merits of steam and diesel power. In the USA in particular, while railways operating prestige transcontinental services – such as the Burlington, the Rock Island, and the Union Pacific – were moving toward diesel power, some of the greatest of all American railways of that era – such as the New York Central, the Norfolk and Western, and perhaps the greatest of them all, the Pennsylvania – remained solidly with steam. The policy was to run long trains at speeds of 120–130 km/h (75–80 mph) on level track, rather than attempt to emulate the spectacular very high speeds of the diesel-hauled streamliners. An exception was that of the Milwaukee Road, which between Chicago, Milwaukee and St Paul was in competition with the streamlined diesel trains of the Burlington. The Milwaukee reply was to introduce the super-high-speed steam-hauled Hiawatha expresses, for which special streamlined locomotives were designed.

For working the high-speed Silver Jubilee express of the London and North Eastern Railway, introduced in September 1935, Sir Nigel Gresley built a new range of Pacific locomotives – class A4 – with important modifications from his previous standard A3 series. Apart from the striking form of external streamlining, and the silver-gray colors that attracted so much attention from the public, the internal steam passages and the valve ports were fully streamlined. This afforded the freest possible flow of steam, while the use of a higher boiler pressure – 17.58 kg/cm² (250 lb/in²) against 15.47 kg/cm² (219 lb/in²) – smaller cylinders and larger valves all contributed to a very free-running engine. Whereas the A3 class had to be pressed beyond their natural limit to attain speeds of more than 160 km/h (100 mph), the A4s ran up to 177 km/h (110 mph) and more with ease.

The form of streamlining on the LNER A4 Pacifics was very effective in deflecting the exhaust steam clear of the cab. This was at a time when the increased girth of locomotive boilers was causing difficulties on some types, with steam beating down and obscuring the view ahead from the cab. On the huge articulated freight locomotives of the Southern Pacific Railroad that worked over a route including lengthy tunnels on single-line sections, the locomotive was turned "back to front" as it were, the cab placed at the leading end to provide a clear view. The locomotives in question were oil burners, and the fuel supply was piped from the large tender attached to the smokebox end of the engine. A notable range of locomotives of this general type operated on the heavily graded coastal route north and south of Oakland, California, as well as on other, similar, routes in the United States.

In the USA the fastest regular running in the steam era was made by Hiawatha trains on the Milwaukee Road, which attained speeds of more than 160 km/h (100 mph) between Chicago, Milwaukee and St Paul. When these trains were first introduced in 1935, and the train consist was relatively light, special streamlined locomotives of the Atlantic type were used, built by the American Locomotive Company. But the service grew so much in popularity that much larger locomotives became necessary to haul the heaviest trains, and a class of 4-6-4s of similar appearance, styling and coloring was introduced in 1938. They had a tractive effort of 22,815 kg (50,300 lb) compared to the 18,144 kg (40,000 lb) of the Duchess class on the English LMS.

In 1941, Alco built a class of 4-8-8-4 Mallet-type articulated locomotives for the Union Pacific Railroad. They were the largest and heaviest steam engines ever built: together, engine and tender weighed 534 tons. Although designed primarily to work the heavily graded section through the Rocky Mountains, they were also capable of speeds of up to 130 km/h (80 mph).

Above The London Midland & Scottish *Coronation Scot* streamliner was introduced in 1937. It is seen here leaving Euston for Crewe on a test run on June 29.

Below This line-up of former LNER locomotives, at King's Cross shed in 1949, emphasizes the unusual shape of the streamlined A4 class Pacific 60033 *Seagull*.

1937 What was probably the zenith of British express passenger locomotive development was reached in 1937 with the introduction by Sir William Stanier of the LMS Princess-Coronation class of Pacific, originally streamlined for the Coronation Scot train, but later developed into a standard type for heavy express working on the Anglo-Scottish west coast route. In their nonstreamlined final form they were known as the Duchess class. Very powerful and free-running locomotives, they hold the British record for the maximum recorded performance in continuous "all-out" steaming, at a rate of 18,144 kg (40,000 lb) per hour from the boiler. They have also been timed at speeds up to 185.5 km/h (114 mph), although the record for British locomotives, and the maximum attained anywhere in the world with steam, was by the LNER A4 Pacific *Mallard* in 1938. When pressed to the limit, it reached 203 km/h (126 mph) on a special test run. These locomotives were capable of pulling up to 20 passenger coaches.

One of the most significant developments in the history of railway traction came in the later 1930s from the Electro-Motive Corporation of General Motors. Under the direction of Richard Dilworth the highly successful 567 diesel engine, designed and perfected by Charles F. Kettering and his son Eugene, was built into a standard main line diesel-electric locomotive. Using all standard components, they could be managed by a single crew without the expense of multiple manning that was necessary when heavy trains were double or triple headed by steam locomotives. While some of the American railways

Left Period Penn Central locomotives pictured on yard duty. The bullnosed locomotive comes from a class of 4,800 hp units which once pulled the eastern section of the Broadway Limited.

The high-speed service offered by the Hiawathas became so popular that extra trains often had to be run. The Atlantic locomotives built to inaugurate the service in 1935, and shown here, were thus replaced within 4 years by 4-6-4 locomotives able to haul twice the load.

such as the Burlington and the Rock Island introduced special streamlined diesel unit trains, Dilworth decided that the most profitable field for diesel traction was in direct replacement of steam, and his handsomely styled and brightly painted "first generation" locomotives began to do that most successfully.

Following the spectacular – but transient – success of the diesel-powered Zephyr trains in the Middle West of the USA, the development of the General Motors locomotives began the movement that was soon to sweep across the railways of North America like a prairie fire. This consisted of 1,800 hp units that could be made up into multiples of as many as four, to provide a locomotive of 7,200 hp with the completely standard 567 engine. The first passenger locomotive for long-haul duty was introduced in 1937, and the freight variation followed in 1939. The outstanding value of the diesel freight locomotive, in heavy-grade service lay in the high power output at low speed, roughly double that of a steam locomotive of equal nominal tractive effort.

1938 In France a remarkable development of the 4-6-4 type was interrupted by the outbreak of hostilities in 1939. After the general amalgamation to form the French National Railways in 1938, a central office for studies and design had been set up, and M. de Caso produced a plan for a super-high-speed 4-6-4 that would haul trains of 200 tons at a speed of 169 km/h (105 mph) on level track. Eight were eventually built, remarkably so during the German occupation. Three were three-cylinder single expansion machines, and the other five were four-cylinder compounds in the characteristic French style. They were never used for high speed, but in heavy-load use they did excellent work, until the lines they worked were electrified.

In 1938 the German State Railways had introduced a powerful 2-10-0 for general freight service, known as class 50. A large number were put into service. But with the onset of war, and the need to economize in use of all metals, an "austerity" version was produced. Known as class 52, or in Germany the *Kriegslok*, every part that could be dispensed with was discarded. Sections that could be made lighter or more economical were redesigned. None but the basest of materials were permitted. As a result, whereas the class 50 with its tender weighed 146 tons, the 52 *Kriegslok* weighed only 120 tons. During the war, in Germany itself and in the countries then under German occupation and control, no fewer than 10,000 of these "austerity" locomotives were built.

1941 It was in this same period that the articulated locomotive began to reach its ultimate size and tractive power. In the USA this took the form of an extension to the Mallet principle of having two "engines" carried beneath one huge boiler. The rearward "engine" was carried on the main frame, while the forward one was articulated and gave a degree of flexibility to the locomotive as a whole. While the general trend was away from the original Mallet concept which was that of a compound locomotive, in a few notable instances – particularly on locomotives designed for relatively slow and heavy freight work – the compound principle was retained.

The ultimate in steam locomotive construction for heavy fast freight service came in 1941, with the building by Alco of the celebrated 4000 class, 4-8-8-4 type, for the Union Pacific Railroad. They were the largest and heaviest steam locomotives ever built. The engine alone weighed 350 tons and the huge tender another 197 tons. This vast assemblage of 547 tons may be compared to the 162 tons of an LMS Duchess 4-6-2. The Union Pacific 4000 class locomotives were nicknamed the "Big Boys," but their tractive effort of 61,400 kg (135,400 lb) was not the highest achieved in the USA. They were essentially fast running locomotives, used mainly between Ogden, Utah, and Green River, Wyoming. Detailed to heavy priority freights, they performed invaluable service during the Second World War.

At this time the British firm of Beyer, Peacock, of Manchester, was continuing to develop the Beyer-Garratt type of articulated locomotive for use in difficult terrain and substandard gauge lines in the countries of the British Commonwealth. The development of this type of locomotive was by no means complete by the end of the particular period covered here, although one of the most successful designs ever produced by Beyer, Peacock, the 4-6-4 + 4-6-4 of the 15th class for the Rhodesia Railways, was first introduced in 1939. These were dual use units, used alike on heavy freights and on mail trains. Although coupled wheels are no more than 144.78 cm (4 ft 9 in) diameter, these locomotives run very smoothly at high speed on the 1,067 mm (3 ft 6 in) gauge, and their excellent tracking qualities enable them to take the curves without any appreciable reduction from the maximum allowed speed of 88 km/h (55 mph). These engines have a total weight of 179 tons, and a tractive effort of 21,544 kg (47,496 lb). Another remarkable Beyer-Garratt design was that of the EC3 class on the Kenya and Uganda Railway, on which the maximum axle load was then limited to 11.75 tons, on the meter gauge, against 23 tons on the main lines of Great Britain. The EC3 had the wheel arrangement 4-8-4 + 4-8-4, and the designers packed such power into the limitations imposed by gauge and track that these engines had a tractive effort of no less than 20,910 kg (46,100 lb). They were used essentially as heavy freight haulers.

Chapelon compound and Kriegslok locomotives preserved.

Locomotive power now

Locomotive development 1945 and after

1948 An outstanding event influencing the design of steam locomotives was the nationalization of the British Railways as from 1948, and the decision of the newly formed Railway Executive Committee that, for economic reasons, reliance must continue to be placed on steam power for some years to come. In 1948, after a series of interchange trials between express passenger, dual purpose and heavy freight locomotives of the four previously privately-owned companies, had shown no designs markedly superior to any other, the Railway Executive Committee decided to produce a series of new standard designs for future quantity production that would embody the best of the regional types. The first of these was the class 7P7F dual purpose Pacific, of which the first was No. 70000 named *Britannia*, and completed at Crewe in 1951. The Pacific, followed by 4-6-0s in various power classes, and new standard tank engines for short-distance traffic, achieved a considerable degree of success in the short time before the launching of the British Railways Modernization Plan of 1955, a major point of which was the elimination of steam power throughout Britain. The new standard locomotives of 1951 and subsequently, of which 999 were built, were therefore not fully developed, and included traits in their performance

greatly reduced turnaround time necessary with diesel-electric locomotives, as compared with steam. While on certain specially regulated runs, like those of the Santa Fe between La Junta and Los Angeles, a very high percentage utilization could be obtained from steam locomotives, such results were not generally practical. The swift replacement of steam locomotives by diesels in the USA had repercussions all over the world and led commercial rather than technical interests to press for similar "revolutions" elsewhere, nowhere more strongly than in Britain. This eventually led to the launching of the British Railways Modernization Plan of 1955 and the elimination of all steam power on that system by 1968.

Cutaway of the steam locomotive *Britannia*, British Railways No 70,000. While no one locomotive can be said to be typical, as so many variations were produced, this model exemplifies the strong traditional lines reflected in post-1945 production. This series of locomotives represented, along with the 9F 2-10-0's, the last steam traction built in the UK – and some of the noblest. Their passing remains a sadness to all enthusiasts.

Above Southern Pacific locomotive, about 1951. The four-unit diesel engine had a total rating of 6,000 hp.

that were not eliminated before it was decided that all future development was to be concentrated on non-steam forms of power. Most successful of all the new standard designs was that of the 9F 2-10-0, designed primarily as a freight engine but so versatile in ordinary service as to be used in high-speed passenger service, attaining speeds up to a maximum of 145 km/h (90 mph).

In the USA the elimination of steam power was more rapid even than in Britain. The diesel-electric locomotive has traction characteristics definitely superior to those of steam, on units of nominally equal tractive effort, when working hard up a severe grade at speeds of 32 km/h (20 mph) or less, and its introduction came in areas where bad grades existed. On some of the eastern lines in the USA where grades are less exacting, extensive trials were conducted between diesel-electric locomotives and the latest steam designs, notably on the New York Central, but elsewhere steam was swept away, involving in many areas the replacement of relatively new locomotives that had run no more than a small part of their economic life. Two factors tended to hasten the end of steam power in the USA. The first was the uncertainty of fuel supply in the eastern United States because of severe and recurring labor troubles in the coal industry, and the second was the

The first main line diesel-electric train in Britain leaves Euston in 1948.

Above left Steam express in India today. *Left* Regional Transportation Authority locomotive arrives at La Salle Street Station, Chicago.

Above After withdrawal, the world's steam speed record holder *Mallard* was restored for display in Britain's National Railway Museum.

Below British Rail's High Speed Train (HST) power unit, containing a 2,250 hp diesel engine. Each trainset has one at each end.

1955

In France, and to a lesser extent in other countries on the continent of Europe, the drive toward modernization was no less strong, but to electric rather than diesel power. The mountainous regions of the Alps were favorable to the generation of hydroelectric power, while equally in these countries the large-scale importing of fuel oil was undesirable. Consequently much of the funds made available for reconstruction after the war were directed toward electrification. Leaving out of account certain obsolete systems, three forms of electric traction current supplies were in use in 1950: 1,500 volts dc in France and the Netherlands; 3,000 volts dc in Belgium and Italy; and 15,000 volts ac at $16\frac{2}{3}$ cycles in Germany, Austria and Switzerland. These systems were continued in the first reconstructions made after the war, notably on the Paris-Lyon-Marseille line of the French National Railways. One of the most notable developments, derived from the practice of the Bern-Lötschberg-Simplon Railway in Switzerland, was the adoption in France and elsewhere of electric locomotives in which all axles were powered. Earlier conceptions that some nonpowered guiding wheels were needed fore and aft on locomotives used in high-speed service were dispelled, first by Swiss experience and then by the remarkable performances of the new French locomotives, two of which attained a maximum speed of 330km/h (206mph) on tests.

In the USA, while certain routes over which very heavy ore traffic was conveyed had been electrified for upward of 30 years, all postwar development was in diesels; but while it was the so-called "first-generation" cab type that had been first in sweeping steam aside, as the diesel conquest continued to its conclusion the "second-generation" type predominated. This was a less elegant but more serviceable design with the walkways giving access to the engines out in the open, and affording much easier maintenance. Locomotives of this type, from both General Motors and the American Locomotive Company (Alco), virtually took over the entire freight working in the USA, operating trains of unprecedented length. On heavy grades, such as the Sierra Nevada, additional units were cut in at the midpoint of lengthy trains, radio controlled by the engineer on the head-end unit. In Britain the introduction of diesel power was not so clearcut. The policy of British Railways had been to give trial to a variety of makes and transmissions, and on the Western Region,

for example, all the new power first introduced had hydraulic rather than electric transmission, the former being generally favored in West Germany for use on nonelectrified lines.

The culmination of steam power on the railways of the world came to be seen in India and southern Africa. Economic conditions in India, since the attainment of independence, compelled the restriction of imported fuel to a minimum, and with ample supplies of coal available development of the steam locomotive continued. New standard designs for both the broad and the meter gauge, derived from experience with those used in imperial days, continued to be built in large numbers, until it was possible to extend electrification and import sufficient oil to make diesel power an acceptable alternative. Today the indigenous manufacture of both electric and diesel-electric locomotives is proceeding satisfactorily. In southern Africa the development of the Beyer-Garratt articulated locomotive continued to reach colossal proportions. On the Kenya and Uganda Railway, improved standards of track and road bed permitted of the use on certain routes of locomotives with a 21-ton axle load, and advantage was taken of this to introduce the exceptionally powerful 59 class, having the 4-8-2 + 2-8-4 wheel arrangement, a total weight of 252 tons and the very high tractive effort of 37,807 kg (83,350 lb). They are the most powerful locomotives ever to be built for meter gauge track, and they haul freight trains of more than 1,000 tons on 2 percent grades between Mombasa and Nairobi.

Electric power in France, and Britain, and subsequently in many other countries, took a new turn after experiments in France showed that by using 25,000 volts ac at the commercial frequency of 50 cycles per second, considerable savings could be made in the cost of installation. In the electrification schemes embodied in the British Railways modernization plan this form of power supply has been standardized, except on the Southern Region, where large areas were already equipped with the "third rail system" of pick-up instead of an overhead line. The locomotives used on the London Midland Region, operating the most intense main line express passenger service in the world, are carried on two four-wheeled trucks and develop 5,000 hp. They are capable of hauling a 12-car train of 420 tons up a 1 percent grade at 145 km/h (90 mph).

1978

Today the newest forms of rail traction are moving away from the locomotive-hauled train, for high-speed passenger service. In 1964 the New Tokaido Line of the Japanese National Railways was opened, with the so-called "bullet trains" running at speeds of 210 km/h (130 mph) on a specially designed track. The service has proved so popular that today there is one of these trains every 15 minutes from Tokyo to Osaka from 6:00 a.m. to 9:00 p.m. The same general principle is used in the British high-speed train (HST) sets now operating on the Western Region, except that these latter have a 2,200 hp diesel power unit at each end, whereas the Japanese trains are electric. The Western Region HST sets, running at a maximum speed of 200 km/h (125 mph), provide the fastest and most intense diesel operated service in the world, between London and Bristol and between London and South Wales. In France construction is now going ahead with an entirely new high-speed line between Paris and Lyon, on which electric trains of the unit type, like the Japanese "bullets" and the British HSTs, will run at speeds of up to 300 km/h (185 mph). In France the latest electric locomotives are of 8,000 hp, and can run at 200 km/h (125 mph).

Cattle cars to family lounges

Rolling stock 1800–1875

1800 The earliest form of vehicle for conveyance on rails was the colliery tram, or cauldron car, designed for carrying coal. It was a four-wheeler, of such a size that it could be pulled by a horse on one of the rough cart tracks of the day. When such cars were fitted with flanged wheels and ran on the early form of edge-rails, it was found that a single horse could pull three or four of these cars, and the type was in general use when the first locomotives were tried out in northeastern England. In early trials men climbed aboard these cars for the ride, and when the Stockton and Darlington Railway was opened in 1825 many of those participating, men and women alike, rode in the traditional cauldron cars. The earliest passenger cars varied according to the class of traveler. First-class cars were built to look like the familiar stagecoach, while for third-class passengers nothing more than an open car was provided. Between these two extremes was the second-class – an open car with seats and a canopy over the top to give some protection against the weather. Recalling how passengers traveled on the outside seats of the old stagecoaches, it was not surprising that thoughts turned to double-deck railway cars, and some quaint examples were built in France and the USA. But in Great Britain the reduced headroom necessitated by passing under bridges and through tunnels precluded the use of double-deckers in the early stages. Indeed, double-decker coaches in Britain have never raised any great degree of popular interest.

Although conditions of rail travel in the pioneer days were not greatly different from those on a stagecoach, at any rate for the outside passenger, the addition of smoke, steam and red-hot cinders from the locomotive stacks introduced new hardships, particularly as many more people than ever before were traveling. A general outcry against rail travel conditions in Great Britain led to the passing of Gladstone's famous Regulations of Railways Act of 1844. This Act laid down as a legal necessity that on every line of railways there should be at least one train every day on which properly covered-over third-class accommodation was provided, at a fare of one penny per mile and serving every station on the line. The so-called "Parliamentary trains," despite the covered cars, were not the height of luxury. On the first-class cars luggage was usually stacked on the roof and was sometimes set on fire by sparks from the engine. On the freight trains cattle

Top The *Experiment*, the first passenger coach, horse-drawn, Stockton & Darlington Railway, 1825. *Above* Bodmin and Wadebridge car, c. 1845, in National Railway Museum, York. *Right* Captain Powell's transferable car, from an old print. A typical eccentric scheme dreamed up for the existing world of railways.

1850 At an early stage of development larger cars were introduced on to the American railways for much the same reason as the traditional 4-4-0 locomotive was adopted. The short wheelbase freight cars and passenger cars did not ride well on the sharply curved and lightly laid tracks, and vehicles for both passengers and freight, carried on two four-wheeled trucks, were much preferred. Thus originated the American passenger car. There were entrances only at the ends; the inside was completely open, without any of the divisions that made a British, or a European, car a series of compartments. Usually they had a high clerestory roof. Whereas an English passenger train might consist of 12 or 15 four-wheeled coaches, an American train would have no more than three or four of these large cars. For third-class passengers there would be little difference in comfort – or lack of it: bare boards was the rule for all. Third-class cars were often in the form of a primitive, unlit, open saloon car with wooden benches across the center, ventilation being provided by a few doors and windows. The British four-wheeler of the mid-nineteenth century was a basic feature of operation, and so far as size was concerned the same applied to passengers, parcels, mails, or even horses. They were light and could be pushed easily by human effort. At the larger stations locomotives were not used for switching. On each of the tracks there were small turntables, large enough to take one four-wheeler. If it were necessary to transfer a vehicle from one line to a parallel track, it was pushed to a turntable; then the table was rotated 90 degrees, and the vehicle was pushed across the connecting rails on to the turntable for the next track and then turned until it was in line. These turntables were a built-in feature of most early British rail stations, and their existence explains to a considerable extent the reluctance of many railway managements to introduce large coaches.

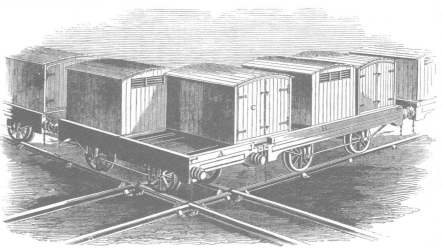

were carried in open cage-like vehicles, and the drovers traveled with the animals. While movement of coal had been the basic traffic of the earliest railways in the northeast of England, when railways were opened in the rural counties farther south it was considered *infra dig* to carry coal. When such business was offered to one railway manager he is said to have exclaimed with much indignation, "What, coal by railway – they'll be asking us to carry dung next!"

Above Early car from Stockton and Darlington Railway. Such designs were an inevitable result of the transfer from road to rail.

Right Cars on the Liverpool and Manchester Railway. One example of innumerable contemporary engravings of the period.

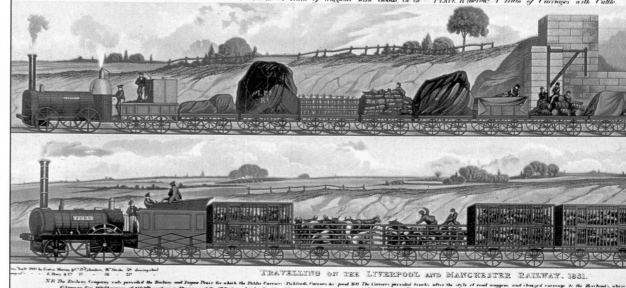

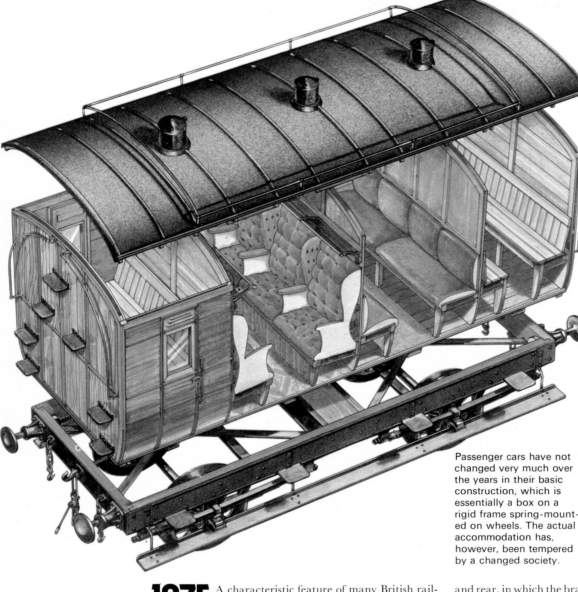

Passenger cars have not changed very much over the years in their basic construction, which is essentially a box on a rigid frame spring-mounted on wheels. The actual accommodation has, however, been tempered by a changed society.

1875 A characteristic feature of many British railways in this period was the family "saloon" or parlor car. This was usually a four-wheeler that could be chartered on payment of so many first-class fares and would on request be transported from anywhere to anywhere. It would be attached to advertised train services, though there could be a lengthy wait for the next connection at a junction. The accommodation comprised a drawing room with an adjoining compartment for family servants traveling in attendance. Sometimes in the case of wealthy patrons there would be horseboxes in addition, and these included accommodation for the grooms. During the shooting season in Scotland trains from England often included ten or more of these family saloons, many with horseboxes attached. The epitome of comfort and convenience was to be seen in the royal saloons built especially for Queen Victoria and her traveling court.

At this early stage in railway development the arrangements for braking were primitive. The British passenger train of the 1860s and 1870s had brake vans at the front and rear, in which the brakes were applied by the trainmen by hand. There was a whistle code, whereby the driver whistled for the brakes to be applied. It is remarkable to recall that by that time passenger trains were regularly running at 96 km/h (60 mph) or more. In America trains had a front and rear brakeman, and on freight trains, which were usually made up of a series of closed box cars, the brakeman would often be seen running along the top of the cars while the train was at speed, applying or releasing the brakes as required. On British freight trains, when a severe descending grade was being approached, it was necessary to stop for the hand brakes to be applied on a specified number of vehicles before the descent was begun. British freight trains were manned by a single trainman, in addition to the locomotive crew, and there was no facility for the work of a traveling brakeman to be done. Because of the carrying of most freight in box cars, the American freight train presented a more uniform appearance than its British, or Continental, counterpart in the latter part of the nineteenth century.

Top A lounge car of the London, Brighton and South Coast Railway, 1873
Above An artist's impression of the new Pullman car introduced on the Great Northern Railway in 1879.
Below Plan views of first-class car on the Moscow and Koorsk Railway around 1880.

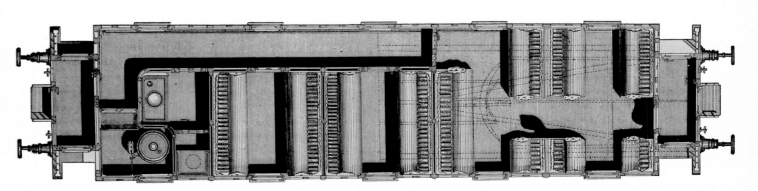

Traffic becomes specialized

Rolling stock 1876–1924

1874 In the last years of the nineteenth century there was a marked transformation in the size and comfort of passenger rolling stock in Great Britain, continental Europe and in colonial territories. The influence came from the introduction to certain English railways of the American Pullman car. It was a movement that found little favor at first. British railway managements were rather horrified at the size and length of these cars and feared that their inclusion in trains of conventional cars would cause havoc in the case of a derailment or a collision. But the move to provide better accommodation for the lower social classes, pioneered on the Midland Railway, gradually gathered impetus. Although the Pullman car as such was adopted on no more than a few railways, longer coaches, carried on two four-wheeled trucks began to come into more general use in the 1880s and 1890s in Britain. At the same time the four-wheelers, designed to suit the old station turntables, had given place to six-wheelers on most of the main lines, and these cars were built to quite remarkable lengths, particularly in certain postal cars in service on the east coast route from London (King's Cross) to the North. Even so, at the time of the exciting race to Aberdeen in August 1895, the 8:00 p.m. sleeping car express from King's Cross was composed entirely of six-wheeled cars, including sleeping cars of that size.

On the continent of Europe a great variety of passenger cars were in use, ranging from the very luxurious sleeping cars of the Wagons-Lit company to cramped ill-lit compartment vehicles that were not inaptly nicknamed "dog-boxes." All the older vehicles were built entirely of wood, and the inclusion of more modern steel-framed coaches in the same trains was at times disastrous. This situation prevailed throughout the period up to 1924, and traveling even on "rapides" running to sharp time schedules was apt to be hazardous. In the USA, with railways still providing the premier means of land transport, the large double truck cars were advanced to provide increased luxury for those who could pay substantial supplements over the ordinary fares and, in addition to including dining and sleeping cars on the night trains, lavishly appointed club cars, lounges and facilities for businessmen were added. For railway officials traveling on official business and entertaining guests, the so-called "business cars" were introduced. These were very large cars, including four or more sleeping compartments, a business lounge, private dining room with a first-class chef in constant attendance, and usually a near end observation platform. In Great Britain the corridor car came into general use on the principal express trains and, as on the continent of Europe, but unlike North America, the corridor was at one side of the car, from which entry was made into individual compartments. In America the cars remained open, with access to seats from a central aisle.

The developing traffic in all parts of the world led to the construction of many special vehicles for freight. The advantages of bulk transport were recognized, but with coal, for example, huge cars carrying 30 tons, or more, however excellent on the run, were not entirely convenient because of the difficulty of getting them to the mines for loading. They were used mostly by the railways themselves for locomotive coal. A problem so far as vehicles for special traffics were concerned was that they were loaded in one direction only, and had to be returned empty. In Britain a great number of collieries and individual coal dealers had their own private cars, and the liability of the railways to haul these put further restriction upon movement and the most economical use. Apart from coal, there were a great number of miscellaneous private cars in circulation. Some of the most interesting and specialized of freight cars were those specially designed for perishable goods, such as refrigerated cars for meat in transit across continents or taken from ships bringing imports from far overseas. Some British companies made a specialty of running express fish trains from northern ports direct to the larger cities. The cars used, although four-wheeled, were designed for running up to 96 km/h (60 mph) and were fitted with the continuous automatic brake, as on passenger trains. Cars were also fitted for carrying fruit, fresh vegetables, and spring flowers in bulk. Because of the relatively short journeys involved in transporting these perishable goods from one part of Britain to another, it was not thought necessary to install special refrigeration equipment in the majority of these vehicles.

Below left WCJS postal car built in 1883 and restored to its original livery for the PO Centennial in 1938. *Below* Iron covered freight car. *Lower* First-class coach for South India Railways.

Left Victorian mail sorting car – a railway post office.

Below Third class coach for Metropolitan Railway.

1900 Postal business required the provision of special cars. Traveling post offices were attached to many express passenger trains, and both Britain and the USA introduced several exclusively mail trains. In Britain, at a great number of points mail was collected and set down, without the train stopping, by means of the mechanical pickup apparatus. Mail was thus delivered to many relatively small communities lying on or near the mail train routes. The special mail cars included letter boxes at which members of the public could mail letters, for which convenience a small extra charge was made. Although these cars had aisle connections, these were not for the purpose of connecting up to the corridor of the passenger section of the train. The aisles were set to one side, instead of positioned centrally. This was done so that the entrances at each end of a mail car would be clear of the tables running from end to end, used for sorting mail.

Another specialized traffic on the British railways was that of milk. The large six-wheeled cars with slatted sides have been called "prisons on wheels," and into these were loaded in large numbers the once-familiar milk cans. From the rural districts of the West of England, and from west Wales, special trains at almost passenger train speed were run to London and other large city centers. More recently, however, the milk had been conveyed in glass-lined tank cars. Another familiar feature of British railways was the so-called tarpaulin-bar car. This was an open four-wheeler, which had a central horizontal bar. It would be used for any consignment that needed covering in transit; a tarpaulin was passed over the central bar and fastened at the two sides, giving the assembly the look of the gable of a house. Flat cars were also used on to which special consignments were loaded and secured. These included small private conveyances and containers, brought to the railway freight yards on road vehicles and there transferred to the railway car. This practice, which began in the early years of the twentieth century, was the beginning of what developed into the modern technique of the container train.

Left A third class car in Brittany, France, at the beginning of the 20th century. *Below left* The dining car of a French luxury train at the turn of the century. *Top right* Interior of GER first-class car around the turn of the century. *Center right* The overhead monorail system between Barmen and Elberfeld-Vohwinkel. This section of the line passes along the river Wupper.

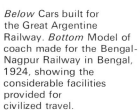

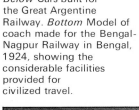

Below Cars built for the Great Argentine Railway. *Bottom* Model of coach made for the Bengal-Nagpur Railway in Bengal, 1924, showing the considerable facilities provided for civilized travel.

Freight improvements: commuter comfort

Rolling stock 1925 and after

1925 From 1925 onward there came a greater specialization in freight rolling stock to provide more efficient service and less damage in transit. In North America the universal employment of center couplers involved buffing and absorbing shocks when trains were starting, or being braked. The standard box car was gradually developed to enormous size, up to 27 m (85 ft) long and 5.5 m (18 ft) high, and the improvement in braking techniques enabled long trains of them to be controlled safely. In the USA refrigerator cars, nicknamed "reefers," are used for the transport of great quantities of citrus fruits from California eastward, and at specific points on the long journey the examination of brakes, running gear, and the servicing of locomotives is supplemented by examination of the cars' icing equipment. The trains are put on to what are termed icehouse tracks. Oil is another traffic that requires special cars, while the massive transport of coal, in enormous hopper cars from which the entire load can be dumped on to a conveyor belt in a few seconds, forms the lifeblood of railways like the Norfolk and Western and the Chesapeake and Ohio. In Britain transport of coal used to be a very profitable but exceedingly slow business, in lengthy trains of four-wheeled unbraked cars rarely traveling at more than 40 km/h (25 mph) and involving much tedious switching and reswitching and the subsequent return of empty cars to specific mines or other owners. Today the "merry-go-round" principle is used for conveyance of coal to regular standing orders, from colliery to electricity generating stations. The trains are made up of large hopper cars equipped with continuous air-brakes, and the diesel-electric locomotives remain coupled during the loading process and then transport the trains to the power station, running intermediately up to 80 km/h (50 mph) or more. The locomotive remains on the train during the unloading.

On the continent of Europe freight vehicles have been developed as long wheelbase four-wheelers, which have excellent riding qualities and which can be run at speeds up to 80 km/h (50 mph). Through the activities of the International Union of Railways (UIC), a great deal of standardization of size, couplings and brake equipment has been achieved, making convenient the interchange of

vehicles over the railways of Europe. A number have been built to run on the more restricted British loading gauge, thus facilitating the working of through loads to and from the Continent, by one or other of the ferry boat services. Road congestion in all the advanced countries of the world has led to arrangements for delivery of new automobiles by train. In the USA advantage has been taken of the height available for loading to build three-deck automobile carriers, and one "tri-level," as they are known, is loaded with 15 automobiles. In Britain and on the Continent two decks is the maximum that can be accommodated. The integration of transport services by road and rail has taken two forms. In Britain long flat cars are loaded at freight terminals with three containers, which are lifted from the road vehicles by special overhead cranes. In the USA with the advantage of extra height, the entire road vehicle, including its wheels, is loaded on to the railway flat car in what is termed a "piggyback" operation. Although primitive forms of such a system had been in use in the USA for many years, it was only in the 1950s that it became economically attractive and developed into the sophisticated operation seen today.

Left A simplified automatic air brake showing the principle of two compressed air tanks working in opposition to each other, to operate the brake cylinder. With the brake on the air is discharged out of the main system, isolating the main compressed air tank, thereby bringing the auxiliary compressed air tank into play to apply the brake. With the brake off the main tank is again fed into the system, supplying the auxiliary cylinder and discharging the air from the brake cylinder, releasing the brake shoe.

Brake on

Brake valve — Pressure regulating valve — Main compressed air tank

Brake pipe

Air discharged

3-way valve
piston moved to left by compressed air from auxiliary air tank

Auxiliary compressed air tank

Brake cylinder

Brake off

Compressed air — Atmospheric pressure

piston moved to right by compressed air from main air tank

Air discharged

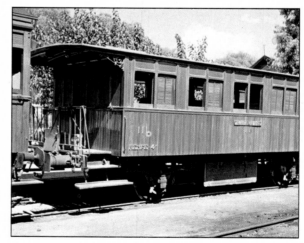

Top London-Paris night ferry of Cie Internationale des Wagons Lit, at Gare du Nord, Paris.

Above Breakdown train near Waverley, Edinburgh.

Left Third class, 4-wheeled wooden RENFE coach at Lorca, Spain.

Below Restored Field & Mackay post office car at Bridgnorth, England.

Above Stainless steel Railiner at Kingston Station, Jamaica.

Above right Modern double-decker commuter stock on SNCF, France.

Below Restaurant car of Iran National Railways in Tehrān station.

Lower Peruvian diesel railcar – for rail or road transportation?

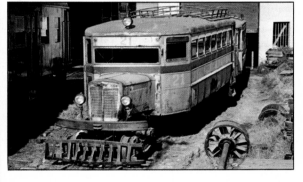

1964 So far as main line passenger service is concerned, one of the most important developments is the addition of air conditioning. The discomfort of long-distance intercity or transcontinental travel, in the USA in particular, with the accompaniment of drafts from open windows, dust, and smoke from heavily fired steam locomotives, is now receding into memory; and it is only when the air conditioning plant on a modern car fails temporarily that discomfort returns, in the form of stifling heat, because the windows cannot be opened. The general tendency in most parts of the world today is to make passenger accommodation on long-distance trains more like that of an airliner. This is partly because of the shortening of journey times, and the growing practice of offering "snacks" rather than the elaborate meals of a full dining car service. On an increasing number of modern trains arrangements are being made to serve "packaged" meals to every passenger at his seat, again in airline style. The coaching stock now being designed for the new super-high-speed service in France, from Paris to Lyon, and beyond, will have passenger seating with no greater space between seats than in a modern airliner. Prior to this present trend vehicles of great luxury were introduced on some routes in Europe, notably the "Grand Confort" coaches on some French trains, such as the all-first-class Mistral, Capitole and Aquitaine. In the USA advantage was taken of the height available to build coaches having seating on an upper deck, with baggage space, washrooms, and so on, below. The same principle has been used in the "dome" observation cars run on many American long-distance trains. In Japan, where there is more passenger travel per capita than anywhere else in the world, the practice of seat reservation by computer has been carried to an all-embracing extent, on the super-high-speed *Shinkansen* bullet trains, in that the act of booking a ticket also confers a reserved seat on a particular train. There are so many of these that if the next train, at the time of booking, is full, one can be fairly sure of getting on to the next following, 15 minutes later. Knowing the number of his coach by the seat reservation, the passenger can wait on the platform in exactly the right position for him to enter the train when the doors open.

The problem of the commuters is acute in all large cities, and in the USA and Canada many double-deck cars of breathtaking size have been built for service around Montreal, Chicago and elsewhere. In North America, however, the intensity of service required is not to be compared with that of London. The need for station stops of no more than 30 seconds would completely preclude the use of double-deck cars such as those used around Chicago, on which all passengers entrain or alight through one door on each side of one of these huge vehicles. Noncorridor compartment cars, with individual doors to every compartment, seems the only solution to a traffic situation such as that existing on the Southern Region of British Rail. On the so-called "rapid transit" lines now operating around cities in many parts of the world, the multiple-unit electric cars, with wide opening sliding doors, are designed to take a high proportion of standing passengers. It has been found that even with only two wide openings on each side of a car, the interior, designed to facilitate easy movement of passengers, and the limited length of individual cars, make it possible to stop briefly at stations even in the rush hours, and to close the doors despite crowding inside. It is only in certain Indian cities that commuters cluster so thickly round doors that they cannot be closed!

Below British Rail EMU of late 1950s, refurbished 1977, on Western Region.

Right Modern stock of Trans-Europe Express.

Building on the grand scale
Railway architecture

The arrival of the railways demanded innovative and inventive construction in the fields of mechanical and civil engineering. But the one structure that was totally new, and symbolized to the general public the power and prestige of the railways, was the station. In its early days the station was a relatively crude affair, matching the locomotives and cars that arrived and departed, but very soon, with the rapid expansion of services, stations were being constructed on a grand scale.

At important terminals, the demand for a roof span to encompass a great number of tracks and platforms led to the increasing use of cast iron – one of the most striking innovations of nineteenth-century architecture. Throughout Victorian Britain, and also in many other parts of the world, stations of impressive and enduring grandeur were built, combining imposing facades with miracles of train shed construction.

Britain

Before the 1830s the finest existing predecessor of the railway station was the Palm House at Kew, London, built between 1844–48. This collaboration of architect and engineer, Decimus Burton and Richard Turner, proved to be typical of many such projects and underlines the contrast between the Victorians' confidence in their technological skills and their conservatism regarding architectural style. This led to an alternation of Classical or Gothic facades that rarely related to the amazing great shed behind them. It is strange that the Crystal Palace, built at the same time as Kings Cross station, London, did not inspire complete stations in iron and glass. It did, however, provide an object lesson in prefabrication and the two great arched sheds at King's Cross resembled

Left Booking office, Worth Valley Railway, Yorkshire, England. *Above* St Enoch's Underground Station, Glasgow. *Below* Antwerp Station. *Right* Gare de Lyon, Paris.

Above Aerial view of
Bern station. *Below*
Modern Dutch station.

technically at least the transept of the original Crystal
Palace, although they were made of laminated wood (later
replaced by steel).

Lewis Cubitt planned King's Cross station, the year
before the Great Exhibition of 1851 was to give the greatest
boost to passenger travel that Britain has ever known.
Hundreds of thousands of travelers left their homes for the
first time and flocked to London by train. The general
confidence in rail travel gained by this enterprise led to the
building of many new imposing stations.

The exterior of Paddington station, London (1852–54),
is hidden by Philip Hardwick's Great Western Hotel, and
it is the spatial grandeur of the interior and the attempt by
its builders, Wyatt and Brunel, to relate the platform
buildings and shed to an unusual design of ornamental
metalwork that make it one of the finest early stations.

The most astonishing Gothic facade still remains at St
Pancras, London (1868–74), designed by Giles Gilbert
Scott. He collaborated with W.H. Barlow who constructed
the shed which spans 73.2 m (240 ft) and is 30 m (100 ft)
high (see pages 16–17).

Outside Britain

The rest of the world took Britain's lead for some years and
nearly all stations continued to show two methods of
construction, one for facades and the other for sheds. In
Stuttgart (1911–14), for instance, Paul Bonate and F.E.
Scholer produced one of the finest station exteriors of its
time. Unbroken masonry wall surfaces and plain rounded
arches provided a traditional approach to design that was
very different from Hamburg station (1903–06), in which
an attempt had been made by the builders, influenced by
the Paris Exhibition of 1889, to construct a station in a
more genuinely modern manner. In an attempt to improve
design, competitions were held in Germany in 1903 for
Basel station and in 1907 for Darmstadt. This practise was
followed in other countries and the most notable
competition winner was Eliel Saarinen who in 1904 won
the competition for Helsinki station which he built
between 1910–14. This complex and highly original
structure is his principal early work. In size and

Above Interior of Grand
Central Station, New York.
Below right Tunnel
keeper's house, Clayton
Tunnel, Sussex, England.

monumentality it rivals Stuttgart and is the most
outstanding railway station of the pre-1914 period. In New
York traditionalism still ruled and the Pennsylvania
Railway Station, built in 1906–10 and now demolished,
was a vast building obviously modeled on the Tepidarium
of the Baths of Caracalla in ancient Rome.

Eventually a nostalgia for styles of the past was replaced
by an enthusiasm for new forms of expression, offered by
new materials such as concrete, and a sense of
identification with the twentieth century. Florence station
(1934–36) was built in the "International Style" which
was prevalent in Europe between the wars and is identified
by its asymmetrical composition of cubic and rectangular
shapes devoid of moldings, smoothly rendered, and
relieved by large windows arranged in horizontal bands. It
was the most advanced station in the world before the
Second World War. It remains to be seen whether any
station built in the remainder of this century will surpass
Rome's outstanding Termini station, built in 1951.

Wherever in the railway world the traveler may find
himself, he is sure to discover many interesting stations,
from the grandiose city terminal to the often highly
individualistic, but no less architecturally interesting,
country stations. On these pages we have attempted to
illustrate some of this diversity.

The paraphernalia of railways

Apart from an architectural form, railways have helped to create a whole world of paraphernalia and related ephemera. Each railway company has moved through a series of images, each expressing its individuality through uniforms, badges, tickets, and a host of other detail. Indeed each railway engine, especially in the days of steam, had its own trappings, which when the day of doom struck made many a collector happy and many a dealer rich. The nameplate of a famous locomotive may well fetch over $2,000 today. While much of the past has been lost, the public in many countries has been left with a fine representative sample in a multitude of museums and railways preserved by enthusiasts. Meanwhile the paraphernalia continues to be generated.

Apart from the paraphernalia of the railways themselves, there are also its first cousins the postage stamp, the cigarette card, and especially the model locomotives built to a variety of scales. To these, too, the enthusiast rushes. Many a country has taken its railway system as a source of national pride and has issued a variety of postage stamps. But probably the most meaningful remembrance of the glories of the railway era is symbolized by the model train. While model racing cars now compete for interest, the sheer glamor of the locomotive and its rolling stock shines through and the child's love of his clockwork engine can turn into the grown-up's desire for the most finely detailed model locomotive – often at considerable expense.

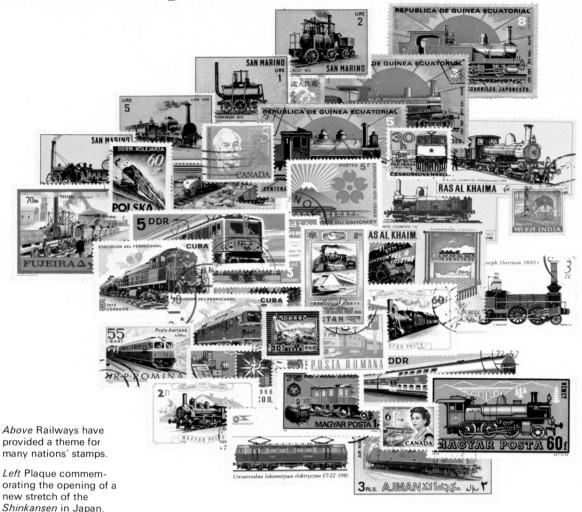

Above Railways have provided a theme for many nations' stamps.

Left Plaque commemorating the opening of a new stretch of the *Shinkansen* in Japan.

Above Brass locomotive model made in Japan.

Below Variety of US model stock.

Left Manufacturer's plate from German locomotive.

Below Tōkyō Express on the Imperial Railway, Japan. One of a set of cigarette cards published by the Imperial Tobacco Co Ltd, circa 1896.

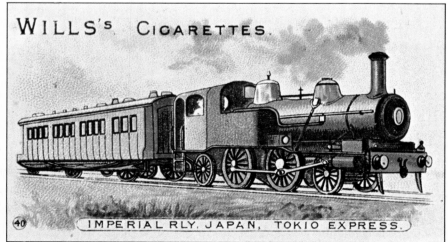

How Railways
Work Now

The eclipse of steam

The steam locomotive was unquestionably the simplest, cheapest and most reliable form of motive power ever devised for railways; but its cheapness related mainly to first cost. After the Second World War, when the immediate rehabilitation of British Railways was in hand and economic considerations were uppermost, R. A. Riddles, the member of the Railway Executive responsible for mechanical and electrical engineering, said that investment would first be made in the form of traction that gave the most tractive effort per pound sterling. At that time a diesel locomotive cost two and a half times that of a steam locomotive of equal tractive power. On a longer term view, however, steam locomotives had many disadvantages in the new era then opening out. Fuel was a major problem. Although railways in many parts of the world were using alternatives, coal was still the most generally used, and its cost was rapidly increasing. Furthermore, with the introduction of coal-cutting machinery in the mines, the form in which it was received on the railways was not ideal for locomotive firing, and troubles were frequently experienced with inadequate steam production. There was also the question of labor availability, because even the smallest steam locomotive needed two men in constant attention, and changing attitudes toward working conditions after the Second World War were tending to make work on a steam locomotive unattractive.

Quite apart from the actual manning and running of steam locomotives, their percentage availability was relatively low. While much had been done in the 1930s to reduce the work content of daily servicing, by the introduction of such devices as self-cleaning smokeboxes, hopper ashpans and streamlined processes of attention at running sheds, the fact remained that one could rarely schedule duties taking up more than about ten hours out of 24, and then only with the closest attention to all matters of servicing. The average utilization was much less. With steam locomotives spending a considerable time out of service space and housing were becoming uneconomical.

By contrast, the diesel locomotive started with several evident advantages, once the initial cost had been covered.

It needed very little in the way of daily servicing, and its first cost could be balanced by its much higher availability – roughly double that of steam. This meant that many fewer locomotives would be needed to work the traffic. With much less time spent out of service a great economy in space could be made – in fact locomotive roundhouses began to take the form of roadside filling stations, so little was the time that individual units were out of traffic. The most difficult problem to be faced was in covering the time of transition from one form of motive power to the other, because in one respect diesels, if not properly cared for, could become a far greater liability than steam locomotives. It was vitally necessary to keep steam and diesel servicing facilities separate. Diesels should not be housed, or serviced, amid the inevitable dirt of a steam shed.

The power to weight ratio of nonsteam locomotives is

often quoted to their advantage. In North America particularly the performance characteristics of a diesel-electric showed up to remarkable advantage over steam on severe grades. At speeds below 32 km/h (20 mph) the power to pull is roughly double that of a steam locomotive of nominally equal tractive power, whereas at 80 km/h (50 mph) and over the advantage, if any, would lie with steam. On the Euston-Glasgow route, electric locomotives of 80 tons total weight develop 5,000 hp, whereas the largest and most modern steam Pacifics, with an all-up weight of 160 tons, developed around 2,000 hp.

Steam today: *Above left* Barry scrapyard. *Above right* Taj Express, Delhi. *Below* Nairobi station, locomotive No 2423 simmers in the sun.

Diesel motive power

The diesel heavy-oil engine starts with a big theoretic advantage over steam in its much higher thermal efficiency, and in its use of a lower grade of fuel than is necessary for the ordinary motor car. Although not to the same extent as the gasoline engine, the diesel is a quick-running engine compared with the reciprocating steam locomotive, which drives direct on its "road" wheels. A steam express passenger locomotive with driving wheels of 2 m (6.5 ft) diameter will be making about 300 rpm when running at 113 km/h (70 mph), whereas the normal engine speed of diesels extends from about 750 rpm upward. But again, while the steam locomotive has a variable-speed engine, with a working range from 0 up to 300 rpm or more, the engine itself in a diesel locomotive needs to be kept running at approximately constant speed, and there must be interposed between the engine and the road wheels some form of transmission gear, as with a gasoline engine. Before describing the various types of diesel engine that have been used in rail operations, the two principal types of diesel engine in general use should be mentioned. The great majority are the relatively slow-running marine type, exemplified by the Sulzer, General Motors, and General Electric designs, which have an engine speed of about 800 rpm. But the other type, the Napier quick-running aero type "Deltic" engine, has had an outstandingly successful record in a small specialist application on the railways of Great Britain.

Among transmissions, the simplest is mechanical, though the power to be transmitted precludes the use of a purely manual gearbox, as on a motor car. One of the most successful early applications in Britain was on the former Great Western Railway, which in collaboration with the AEC of Southall, builders of London's buses, introduced diesel powered railcars in the 1930s, with a precisely similar type of engine and transmission to that then in use on the buses. This included the well-tried Wilson gearbox, which is the best-known application of epicyclic change-speed gearing to locomotives and railcars. This utilizes the so-called "sun and planet" type of mechanism, and can be built with either a four- or five-speed arrangement. The

Above 35 class diesel hydraulic, Nairobi.

Below British Rail diesel mechanical switcher. *Below right* West German diesel locomotive.

Right Wheel notation used for UK diesel and electric stock, with all their variations, appears more mysterious than that used for steam locomotives. Numbers are given for carrying axles, letters are used for driving axles: A=1, B=2, C=3. Axles which are individually driven are suffixed 'O'. This system is also used on the continent of Europe for steam locomotives.

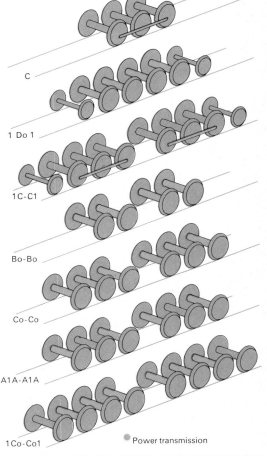

C

1 Do 1

1C-C1

Bo-Bo

Co-Co

A1A-A1A

1Co-Co1   ● Power transmission

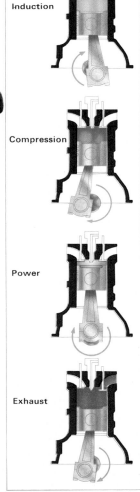

Induction

Compression

Power

Exhaust

gear changing was effected by compressed air cylinders, although in retrospect the traditional locomotive engine men, used to steam, were puzzled at first over the matter of changing gear. These railcars were introduced at a time when private cars were the exception rather than the rule among employees of British Railways. There is a story told of the driver who felt ashamed to go home and tell his wife that he had "been trying to drive a blue pencil motor bus." However, all the drivers became expert enough in a very short time.

Mechanical transmissions, however, could be used only for relatively small power units, and it was electric transmission that became the most usual in the very rapid changeover from steam to diesel power in the USA, in the years just after the Second World War. Before proceeding to a description of electrical transmission, it must be explained that a so-called diesel-electric locomotive is really an electric locomotive in all its traction characteristics, but one that carries its own powerhouse. A diesel-electric locomotive is entirely self-contained, as with steam, needing only supplies of fuel and water, to be taken at intervals according to the built-in capacity of its fuel and water tanks.

The diesel engine cycle might be mistaken for that of the gasoline engine, but the spark of the latter is missing. The power stroke depends on the compression taking place which provides the condition for ignition. Fuel is injected into the cylinder in an atomised state. Multicylinder diesel engines provide the power plant for mechanical and hydraulic transmissions to the wheel, and for conversion into electric power in diesel-electric systems. The main disadvantage of diesel systems is the high weight involved.

Electric and hydraulic transmissions

In a diesel-electric locomotive there is no physical connection between the engine and the road wheels. It should more correctly be called an electric locomotive that carries its own power generating station. In most designs the generator, and the diesel engine that drives it, are mounted on a common foundation, built as a single entity, while the electric traction motors are quite separate and carried directly on the driving axles of the locomotive. On the Peak class C + C of British Rail, for example, there are six traction motors, three on each truck. These locomotives have the Sulzer double-bank type of diesel engine, whereas the English Electric type is of the V-form, as is also the celebrated 567 engine of General Motors in the USA. The earlier British diesel-electric locomotives had the added complication of having to carry steam generators. They were introduced at a time when all main line passenger rolling stock in Britain was steam heated, and the auxiliary electrical generator, coupled to the main generator and part of the engine unit, had to have additional capacity to feed the steam generator when it was required. While the output of the main generator could be varied according to the immediate demands for power from the traction motors, the output from the auxiliary generator, providing power for lighting and so on, had to be constant.

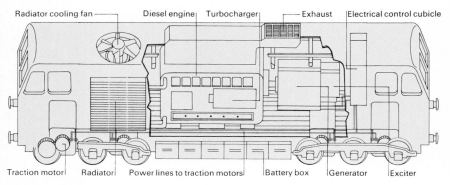

Radiator cooling fan — Diesel engine — Turbocharger — Exhaust — Electrical control cubicle

Traction motor — Radiator — Power lines to traction motors — Battery box — Generator — Exciter

The transmission of power between the main generator and the traction motors is controlled by the engineer, by a handle operating the power controller. This operates the traction motor contactors, regulates the diesel engine speed, and varies the excitation current of the main generator according to requirements. All these controls are interconnected and electrically interlocked one with another, actuated by the movement of the one throttle handle.

In West Germany the hydraulic system of transmission is favored, and for a time this system was standard on the Western Region of British Rail. German manufacturers have also exported locomotives of this type to many parts of the world. The transmission is different from that of diesel-electric locomotives in that there is direct mechanical connection between the engine and the road wheels. The diesel engine crankshaft is connected to the fluid transmission unit through a device called a Cardan shaft, which consists of a telescopic shaft with a universal joint at each end. There is a separate diesel engine for each truck of the locomotive, and the transmission unit is mounted so that its drive wheel is on the center line of the truck, in the case of a locomotive with two four-wheeled trucks. From this drive shaft Cardan shafts extend fore and aft to the final drive on the axle of the road wheels. The hydraulic form of transmission has the advantage that there is less weight actually carried on the truck, but the usage of diesel-hydraulic locomotives on British Rail is now virtually at an end, those on the Western Region being phased out.

When diesel-electric locomotives were first installed it was thought that the effect on the track would be less severe than with steam; that the smooth action, in contrast to the fluctuation of load due to the rotation of heavy parts, would be beneficial. In fact there was no advantage, because of the heavy weight of traction motors carried low down on the actual truck axles, which caused a pounding action not previously experienced. In the very successful "all-adhesion" electric locomotives introduced in Switzerland at the end of the Second World War, the traction motors are not mounted on the trucks. These types of locomotive have been used in other railway systems, the Swiss having always been leaders in this field.

Top SD 40 units 5581 and 5745 stand with a freight train in Vancouver yard.
Above left Basic layout in a diesel-electric locomotive, with the power flow from power unit to traction motor.
Right British Rail class 56 in erecting shop; the ventilator grill is being lowered into position, with one of the trucks in the foreground.

Right Lowering the diesel engine into a British Rail High Speed Train power car.

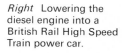

Electric power

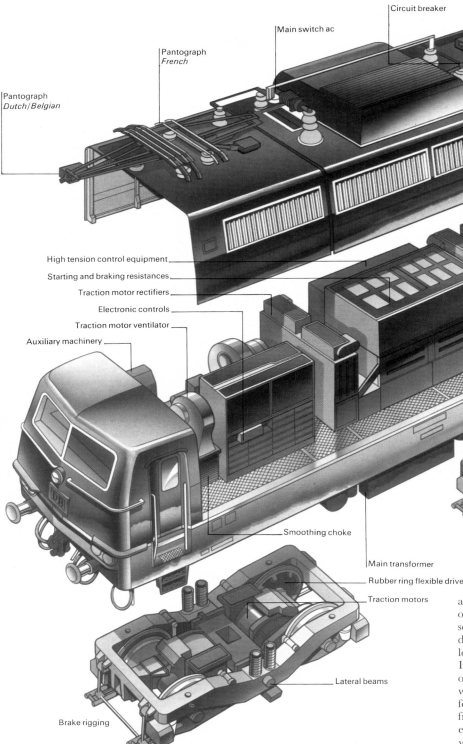

Series E 410 electric locomotive built for German Federal Railways. This is a multicurrent locomotive designed to run under all four of the main European current systems. This Bo-Bo locomotive has a 4,300 hp one-hour rating and a starting output of 6,800 hp, which for a mere 84 tons weight is a considerable achievement. Multi-current equipment carried is increased by the need to cope with the different systems, though this has been tempered with the introduction of thyristor controls. Nevertheless the mechanical parts had to be designed to be as light as possible to accommodate the considerable weight of electrical equipment. Other particulars include a total length of 16,950 mm, wheel diameter of 1,250 mm, an hourly output of around 3,200 kW (more on later models), a continuous power output at between 89 and 145 km/h of 3,000 kW, a maximum tractive effort of 28,000 kg and a maximum speed of 150 km/h (93 mph).

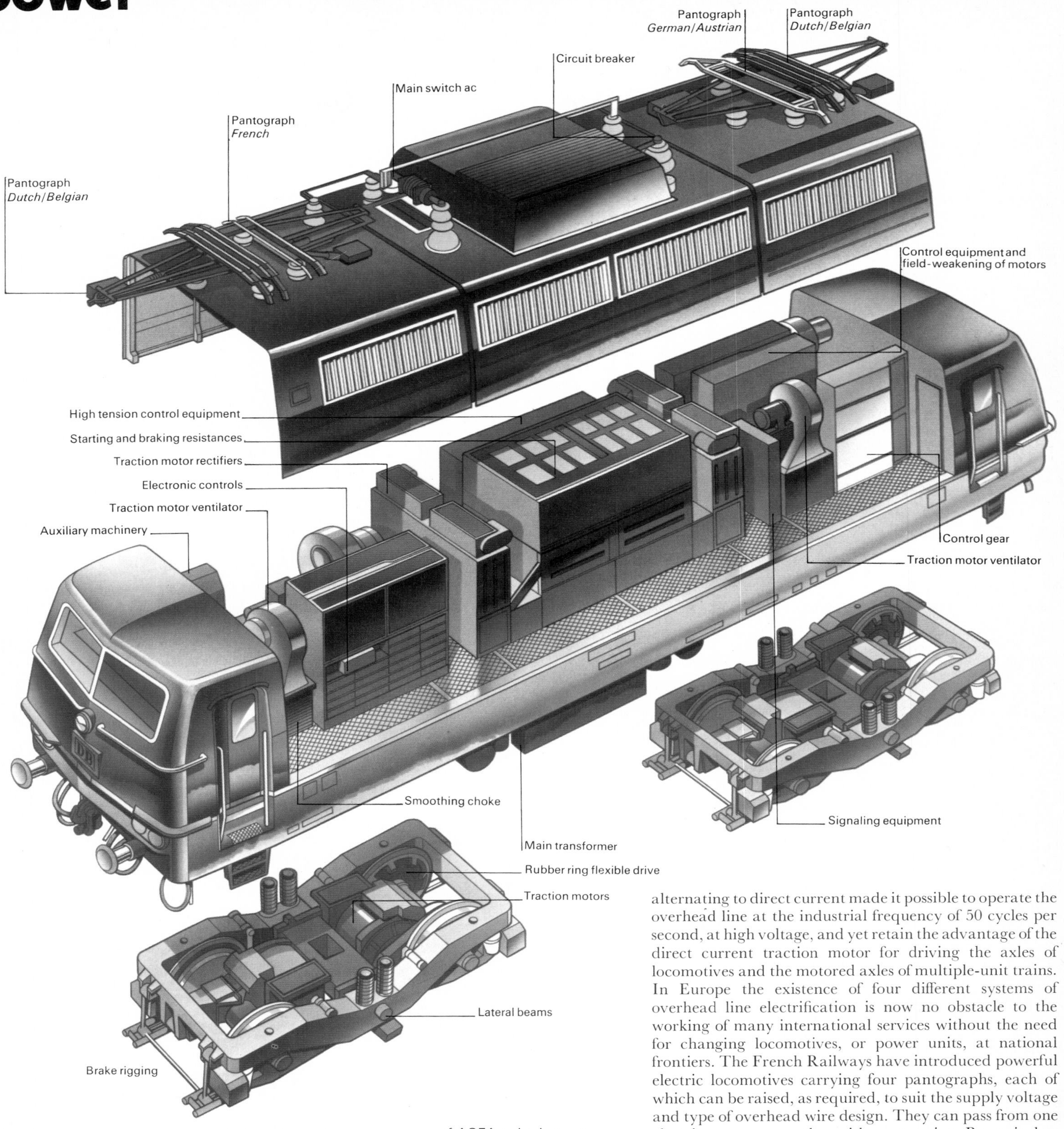

There is a considerable diversity of electric traction systems on the railways of the world, largely because of the different eras in which the various countries made major investment and consequent standardization. The four systems now in widespread use in Europe are: (1) 1,500 volt dc in the Netherlands and earlier French lines. (2) 3,000 volt dc in Belgium, Poland, Italy and Czechoslovakia, also extensively in Brazil, Chile and South Africa. (3) 15,000 volt ac at $16\frac{2}{3}$ cycles, in West Germany, Norway, Sweden, Austria and Switzerland. (4) 25,000 volt ac at 50 cycles, standard in Britain for all except the third rail dc system of Southern Region; it is standard for new works in France, and is being generally adopted in all countries installing main line electric traction today, notably in Hungary and India.

The 25,000 ac system has the advantage of being considerably cheaper to install, requiring lighter overhead conductor wires and lighter supporting structures. It was first adopted on a large scale in France, in preference to the previous standard 1,500 volt dc system, after extensive trials and close comparison of costs with a line largely used by heavy freight between Valenciennes and Thionville. The particular attraction of the system was not only the reduced initial cost of the trackside equipment, but that the development of static devices for converting

Below shows the construction of an electric locomotive at the Swedish firm of ASEA, who have contributed much to the development of modern electric motive power.

alternating to direct current made it possible to operate the overhead line at the industrial frequency of 50 cycles per second, at high voltage, and yet retain the advantage of the direct current traction motor for driving the axles of locomotives and the motored axles of multiple-unit trains. In Europe the existence of four different systems of overhead line electrification is now no obstacle to the working of many international services without the need for changing locomotives, or power units, at national frontiers. The French Railways have introduced powerful electric locomotives carrying four pantographs, each of which can be raised, as required, to suit the supply voltage and type of overhead wire design. They can pass from one electric system to another without stopping. Power is shut off on the approach to a frontier point, and the train allowed to coast until under the wires of the new network. Then the appropriate pantograph is raised.

The latest French electric locomotives working on the Eastern Region main line from Paris to Nancy and Strasbourg include a feature of control that enables the engineer to preset and automatically maintain the speed he requires. The route includes numerous changes in grade, while the maximum speed permitted is constant over long sections. The presetting device can be set, for example, to correspond with a line maximum speed of, say, 145 km/h (90 mph). Once this is done the locomotive will maintain that speed whatever the grade. The fastest French locomotive running today, however, performs over lines equipped with the 1,500 volt dc system, from Paris to Bordeaux and Paris to Toulouse. The locomotives working the 200 km/h (125 mph) trains on these routes are of approximately 8,000 hp. In Britain on the Euston-Glasgow route, with the aim of simplifying the drive between motors and axles, one series of 100 locomotives was built with the motors axle-slung, as on diesel-electric types. But lengthy experience, and a tendency to poor riding, led in later designs to a return to the previous use of frame mounted motors with a flexible drive.

Labels on cutaway diagram:

Pantograph *German/Austrian*
Pantograph *Dutch/Belgian*
Circuit breaker
Main switch ac
Pantograph *French*
Pantograph *Dutch/Belgian*
Control equipment and field-weakening of motors
High tension control equipment
Starting and braking resistances
Traction motor rectifiers
Electronic controls
Traction motor ventilator
Auxiliary machinery
Control gear
Traction motor ventilator
Signaling equipment
Smoothing choke
Main transformer
Rubber ring flexible drive
Traction motors
Lateral beams
Brake rigging

High-speed trains

In the railway context, "high speed" must necessarily be a relative term and describes something that travels a great deal faster than anything else on the particular line; but here we are referring to trains that run at more than 160 km/h (100 mph). There are still not many places in the world where the speed is achieved, having regard to the total of railway length. However, speeds are increasing and the marked trend is to further increase both maximum and overall speed. This urge to accelerate is affecting all the advanced countries of the world with new style trains being introduced in Italy, Canada and the Soviet Union, in addition to those of France and Britain. It is therefore extremely important to have a full appreciation of the manifold factors that are involved, quite apart from the vital primary need to provide constant tractive power in a form that will make higher speeds attainable and capable of being sustained – all with an economic use of fuel. Engineers of today are widely aware of all the different technological disciplines that must be satisfied, including the need for an economic use of fuel, before a super-high-speed service can be offered to the traveling public, and they are unlikely to fall into the traps that ensnared their predecessors of more than 100 years ago, who developed the steam locomotive to feats of speed before the track was ready to take it safely, and before the means of stopping it were adequate.

Two quite distinct ways of introducing high-speed trains are in progress today, the first by building special-purpose new railways, such as the Japanese *Shinkansen* and the French TGV, and the second by upgrading existing lines. From the engineering rather than the financial viewpoint the second method is by far the more difficult, especially on such old-established railways as those of Britain. The cost of realigning curves and remaking difficult junctions to

Above RTV 31 Hovertrain on test at Earith, England, in 1971. The project was unsuccessful as the manufacturers, Tracked Hovercraft Ltd, failed to receive enough government backing. *Right and above right* The French monorail prototype, which was also an ill-fated experiment.

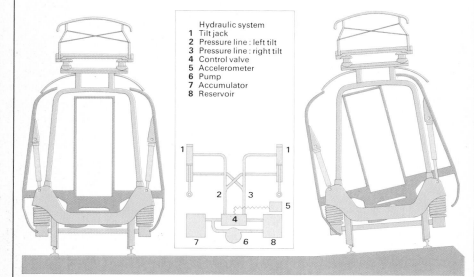

Hydraulic system
1 Tilt jack
2 Pressure line : left tilt
3 Pressure line : right tilt
4 Control valve
5 Accelerometer
6 Pump
7 Accumulator
8 Reservoir

permit uninterrupted high speed can be prohibitive, while in mountainous country the physical circumstances could well make the project impossible. It is to meet these conditions that the principle of the so-called "tilting" train has been developed. The first production units of the British Advanced Passenger Train are expected in service in 1978, and by utilizing a mechanism that causes the train to adjust itself to the curves by a tilting action of the body in relation to the trucks, it can safely negotiate existing curves at far higher speeds than are permissible with conventional rolling stock. Maximum speeds of up to 250 km/h (155 mph) are planned.

The braking on all high-speed trains, and the difficulties that arise on a "mixed" railway like those of Britain, are highlighted when a direct comparison is made of the signaling arrangements on the Euston to Crewe section of the West Coast Main Line and what is proposed for the Paris-Lyon TGV line in France. On the Euston-Crewe line the four-aspect color light signals are spaced, on an average, about 1,100 m (1,200 yd) apart. The leadup to a red signal is first a double yellow, and then a single yellow, so that the distance from the first warning to the red, where the train must stop, is 2,200 m (2,400 yd). This provides a safe margin for trains traveling at a maximum of 160 km/h (100 mph), consisting of ordinary passenger cars hauled

The tilting mechanism associated with all ultra high-speed trains today is shown *above* in the Italian Fiat model. The hydraulic system, which effects a maximum tilt of 9°, is that developed for the British Rail APT. Other systems exist in operation or development in North America, France and the USSR, but there is no doubt that a considerable spread will occur, though operation of such trains while utilizing existing track nevertheless demands the highest standards, which will be attainable only with complete reconstruction.

Above Part of the new Rome-Florence high-speed line, the Italian answer to modern regional intercity transit. *Left* Fiat tilting cars designed for the new high-speed services.

Left and right The French TGV prototype on test, destined for the new Paris-Lyon high-speed line. The basic prototype was powered by a gas turbine, as was the British APT, but likewise in the production overhead electric power will be used, for economic reasons. The mockup on the left is being pressure-tested by the passing of an in-service train.

by electric locomotives. The diesel powered HSTs are equipped with special braking equipment, which enables them to stop from 200 km/h (125 mph) in the same distance taken by ordinary trains from 160 km/h (100 mph). On the French TGV line, by contrast, the distance between signals is to be exactly double that between Euston and Crewe, and the normal stopping distance allowed is to be four sections, or 8,780 m (9,600 yd). Nevertheless, the trains will be equipped with brakes to permit an emergency stop in 3,750 m (4,100 yd), from a speed of 274 km/h (170 mph). The line can be signaled in this way because it will be used exclusively by the TGV trains.

Another important point to be considered in the running of very high-speed trains is that of passenger comfort. Again it is not the comfort "in flight," as it were, although the passenger has yet to experience the sensation on a considerable curve when the tilting feature of the Advanced Passenger Train, or its overseas counterparts, comes into play. In the ordinary way the passenger is not aware of curves when the speed is precisely that for which the cant of the track has been designed. It will be the sensation in the train when the brakes are applied because of an adverse signal. Up to now the effect on a diesel-powered HST when braked hard from 200 km/h (125 mph) is not noticeably different from that in an ordinary train in similar circumstances from 153 or 160 km/h (95 or 100 mph), though the initial rate of deceleration is necessarily higher. From 250 km/h (155 mph) it may be noticeable. A further consideration is that of seeing signals at such speeds, with color light signals already coming up, on the Euston-Crewe line, every 25 seconds at 160 km/h (100 mph), and with audible signals in the cab to mark each location. This can be compared with the more secluded atmosphere in the cab of a Japanese *Shinkansen* train, with no visible or audible signals and only the speed direction to observe. Also the *Shinkansen* line does not have to provide for other classes of traffic in addition to the 160 km/h (100 mph) "flyers." On the French TGV line, at 290 km/h (180 mph) the signal locations will be passed at intervals of about 28 seconds, which will compare closely with British Rail's Euston-Crewe system.

Left The British Rail APT-P power car fitted for overhead electrical pickup. The livery is still provisional. The power car will be in the center of the trainset providing limited access between the two sections. This is to prevent extensive buckling. *Below left* The APT-E prototype set. Here the power unit is at the end as in this early prototype gas turbine motive power was used.

It is interesting to compare the locomotive power on the high-speed lines. As mentioned previously, the latest electric units on the Euston-Glasgow route are of 5,000 hp and they haul trains of up to 12 coaches on the fastest schedules. The Western Region HST trains of seven passenger coaches are powered by two 2,200 hp diesel units, for running at 200 km/h (125 mph) on level track. On the Japanese *Shinkansen* trains, which consist of 16 cars, every axle in the train is powered, making up a total of 16,000 hp. The designed speed on the later sections is 257 km/h (160 mph), but the distribution of power throughout the train gives a very smooth ride, and almost imperceptible braking. On the French TGV trains, which will have eight cars and six trucks out of 13 powered, the combined horsepower of the two power units is 8,500. It is considered that this is not excessive considering the speeds to be run; but the designers hope that a certain amount of power will be saved at the very high speeds by the elaborate streamlining of the nose and tail of these trains. The weight of the eight passenger cars of these trains is 405 tons, compared to the maximum of 610 tons hauled by the CC6500 class 8,000 hp electric locomotives at 200 km/h (125 mph) on the Paris-Bordeaux route.

A model of the Japanese linear motor train. This plan, like others in the UK and Germany, has failed to continue development with any reasonable momentum, but many think it is the motive power (if that is the correct description) of the future. Operation depends on electrification by magnetic repulsion or in some cases hovering devices, motion then taking place by linear means.

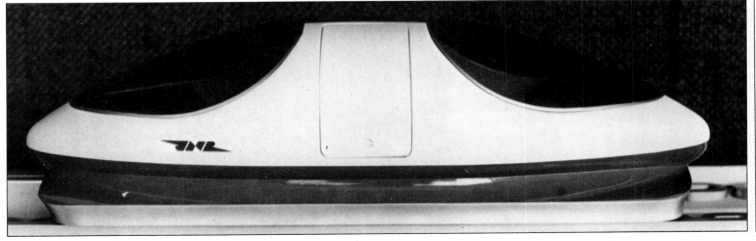

Permanent way: laying the track

New railways for heavy modern traffic are being built in Iran, France and Japan, and have recently been completed in Australia. Also on certain British main routes what is virtually a new railway has been built over the tracks of one more than 100 years old. The very heavy utilization of refurbished British and French routes, and their success in carrying fast and frequent traffic at unprecedented speeds, has provided an invaluable fund of experience for the building of new railways. The problems in laying out and building new railways in countries like Iran and in the remoter parts of Australia differ considerably, because even with today's modern equipment there are difficulties of terrain, of procuring indigenous labor, and of climate, that can well dictate much of the form a new railway will take. The traffic forecast can also play a major part. For example, a new line in the style of the Japanese *Shinkansen* would not be engineered if the principal traffic was likely to be in heavy minerals.

A major consideration is the economic factors involved in alternative methods of construction. While it is clearly desirable to avoid heavy grades as far as possible, because this will lessen operating costs on a completed line, with modern motive power this is not so important as in the days of steam power. The spectacular civil engineering of some of the early British lines, through relatively easy country, was due to the limited tractive power of early locomotives and their inability to climb a grade at good speed with a paying load. It is interesting to compare the approximate relative costs of laying a new railway by hand, as might be

Ditch to intercept run off from above
Side ditch
Side drain
Track
Ballast
Lower drain
Lower intercepting ditch

Below The point of contact and ultimate limiting factor of railways: the flanged wheel meets the rail. This type of rail chair is now disappearing.

Pipe drain to catch water permeating ballast

Although it is possible to run trains over a lightly engineered track formation, any line over which it is hoped to run trains at speed, and/or locomotives and cars with a heavy axle loading, has to be properly built.
Standards recommended for main lines by the American Railway Engineering Association are shown, *left*.

Two types of clips are shown *below*, both used extensively today, and both of which can be used in conjunction with concrete or wooden ties, and different types of tie plates. The accent is on strength and flexibility, but ease of installation is also a major factor.

Below Track is maintained to high standards in certain countries, but in many parts of the USA this is not the case and derailments are frequent.

considered in a country having an abundance of local labor, and by mechanized methods. In the simple preparation of the roadbed, removing topsoil, trimming sides and cutting drainage slopes, the difference for an 18 m (60 ft) length of single track would be between 150 man hours by hand, and four man hours by machine. It can be imagined what the difference would be if deep cuttings or high embankments had to be formed. On new lines the ballasting is often done in two stages, one-third of the total volume being put down in advance of track laying and two-thirds afterward. In the actual laying of the track itself, the difference in cost can be relatively small where labor is cheap, but mechanical laying is four to five times as fast and would therefore cause less interference to the laying of the bottom ballast. On double or multiple-track routes where a close parallel track is available for railborne supplies, replacement of old track can be expeditiously effected by laying completely prefabricated track direct from transporter vehicles alongside.

The most remarkable example of new railway construction in recent times is that of the new French line from Paris to the southeast, which is being planned for continuous running at 300 km/h (185 mph). All the preliminary work was preceded by comprehensive aerial surveys, and with particular regard to the environment, great care has been taken to avoid towns and villages. Because there will be an abundance of power built into the

new electric trainsets, grades as steep as 3.4 percent are included. Although the line has been engineered to provide a notably straight course, and consequent freedom from speed restrictions on account of curves, the inclusion of such steep grades has meant that in hilly country tunnels are avoided, although there are several lengthy viaducts. By use of modern earthmoving equipment, construction has proceeded rapidly, and with the surveys providing for convenient "cut and fill" techniques, the spoil excavated from relatively shallow cuttings has been readily moved to form the contiguous shallow embankments in the undulating countryside.

The underlying reason for the construction of the new French line, an addition to the network of the national railways, was that the existing main line of the former Paris, Lyon and Mediterranean Railway was at times approaching traffic saturation point. The new line, with its anticipated acceleration of service, is expected to attract much extra traffic. The Japanese *Shinkansen* lines were built for similar reasons. In contrast, however, some of the most interesting lines built recently in Australia have been entirely private commercial enterprises, connected with long-range projects for the export of coal and iron ore. The cost of a first-class main line railway, through harsh and barren country, has been no more than one part of the capital investment in mining plant, mechanized handling equipment at the mines and port of shipment, and

provision of houses, shops and recreational facilities to attract workers to an otherwise unattractive part of the country.

The evolution of track itself has passed through several stages to arrive at its present standard of excellence and general reliability. The one-time highly favored British "chaired" track is now obsolete, though considerable lengths of it will no doubt remain in service for many years, on secondary, and slower running lines. It arose from the concept of the great pioneer engineer Joseph Locke, who propounded the idea of a rail that was shaped like a dumbbell, having the same sized heads which could be turned over when the upper edge was worn, thus doubling its life. It was not successful, because the undersurface resting in the cast iron supporting chair became damaged with the constant pressure of traffic. But although the equal-headed rail was abandoned the bullhead type survived and until the end of the Second World War remained the British standard. Nearly everywhere else in the world the Vignoles, or flat-bottomed rail was standard; but a British investigation toward a future standard favored the flat-bottomed rail, because it had a greater lateral stiffness for the same weight per length and was thus likely to need less work in maintaining a good line. This was an important feature at a time when labor was scarce and the cost of it steadily rising.

On most overseas railways up to the end of the Second World War, flat-bottomed rails had been spiked directly to the cross-ties, or sleepers as they are known in Britain; but a feature of British track had always been a slight inward inclination of the rails toward each other to give a centering effect and to counteract quickly any tendency of locomotives or rolling stock to yaw from side to side. To achieve the same effect with flat-bottomed rails involved the insertion of slightly tapered tieplates between the tie and the foot of the rail. At the same time the need was felt for a more positive form of anchor than the simple dog spike used in America. Great ingenuity was shown among British manufacturers in the design of spikes, or clips which had a spring feature, and these have been used in great quantities on the modernized high-speed routes in Britain and are now becoming favored on some of the most heavily used railways in the British Commonwealth. Tie design has also become a specialized job. A rectangular section of timber is of course the simplest, but is still almost universal in North America, where ample supplies of suitable wood are available. In Europe, and particularly in Britain, reinforced concrete is generally superseding wood, which previously was of Baltic pine. Concrete ties can be designed in a shape to provide strength in conformity to the distribution of stress due to passing traffic, and it has been used with conspicuous success on the high-speed electrified line from London (Euston) to the north. The French railways are also adopting concrete ties, but in a different form. Whereas the British design consists of a continuous concrete member, the French has two concrete blocks, one beneath each rail, connected by a steel tie-bar. This design is also giving excellent service on high-speed routes.

An essential of all track – and particularly where continuous welded rails are used, as on most high-speed routes in Britain – is a solid and well maintained bed of ballast. This is usually provided by granite rock chips of regular size solidly packed beneath and around the ties and having an outer frame of considerable width beyond the ties. With such adequate and well maintained ballast no trouble is experienced with continuous welded rails, which do not have the freedom to expand longitudinally with changes in temperature: the stresses due to temperature change are taken up internally. Another essential of good track is a carefully designed system of drainage, with close attention to areas where the subsoil is clay. There is a tendency for clay to work up and impregnate the ballast, but this is counteracted by the insertion of a thick "blanket" of finely powdered granite between the clay and the bottom of the ballast. Experiments have been made in France and Britain with the so-called "slab-track" used on parts of the Japanese *Shinkansen* lines. Instead of the ballast there is first a base slab of concrete extending to the full width of the ordinary ties, and on top of this is a paved slab. This latter takes the place of the ties, and in it are set the fastenings for the rails and their tieplates. One of the great advantages of this design is in tunnels, in the reduction in depth it makes possible. It was installed to useful effect in certain tunnels in the approach to Glasgow from the south, when the line was electrified and the rails needed to be lowered to give space above for the overhead electric wires.

The need to reduce the cost of track maintenance and at the same time provide a road of consistently high quality

The most advanced method of track laying, utilizing a continuous concrete bed, is still under development in the UK. PACT (Paved Concrete Track), *below*, has already been used to overcome the problems of underbridge electrification where ballast bedding provides insufficient clearance. 40 m (130 ft) of PACT can be laid by a "paving train" in one hour.

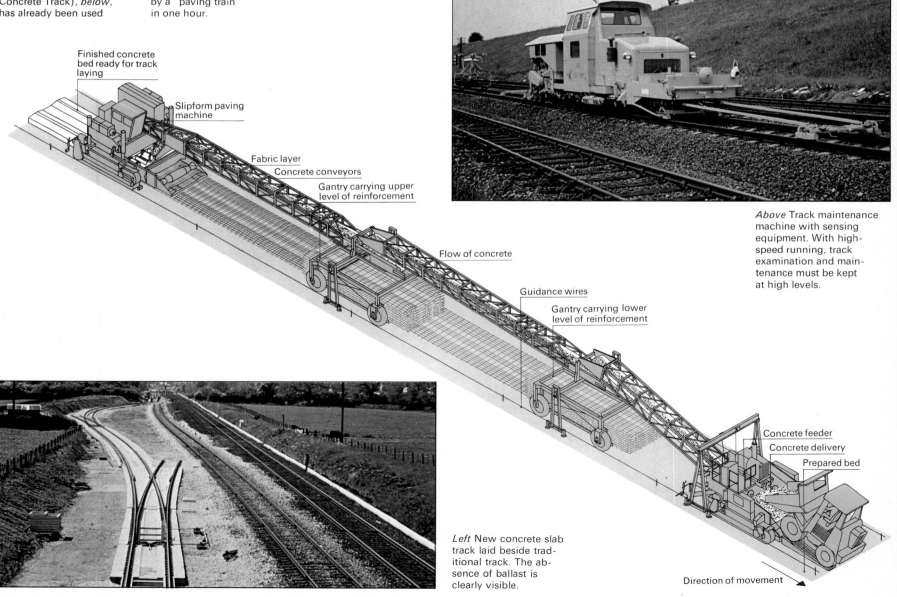

Finished concrete bed ready for track laying

Slipform paving machine

Fabric layer

Concrete conveyors

Gantry carrying upper level of reinforcement

Flow of concrete

Guidance wires

Gantry carrying lower level of reinforcement

Concrete feeder

Concrete delivery

Prepared bed

Direction of movement

Above Track maintenance machine with sensing equipment. With high-speed running, track examination and maintenance must be kept at high levels.

Left New concrete slab track laid beside traditional track. The absence of ballast is clearly visible.

Permanent way: smooth running

Left An empty oil train pulled by class 47 locomotive leans on the main line curve while leaving Hunslet oil terminal, Yorkshire, England. Right Welded rail joint showing original joint bar holes.

on which speeds of 160–200 km/h (100–125 mph) can be run with complete safety has led to the design of many ingenious machines for such tasks as ballast cleaning, checking alignment, and, when repairs are needed, for changing ties without disturbing unduly the adjoining ties and ballast. In former days the alignment was checked by the gauger getting down on to his knees and simply looking along the rails. These men, with a lifetime of experience, were consummate experts at the job, and with two or three plate-layers on hand with their crowbars, any slight irregularities in line were quickly corrected. Today there is neither the time nor the labor for this skilled task. Nowadays one of the greatest boons to track maintenance is the automatic self-leveling and tamping machine, the word "tamping" meaning the packing of the ballast around the ties. Many variations of this machine are used throughout the world, one of which has an alignment feature combined.

In keeping with the great advances in the basic design of track on what is termed "plain line" – that is where there are no switches, crossings or other intersections – have been the developments in switches and the method of their operation. As in so many aspects of modern railway equipment and working, it is often a question of line capacity. For example, at the branching of two first-class main lines, one route will probably be straight and the other involve a curve. Even with the most advanced type of junction switch in use until recently, a speed restriction to about 72 km/h (45 mph) would have been called for on the diverging route. But today what are called "high-speed turnouts" are installed, enabling the divergent line to be taken at 113 km/h (70 mph). These are also used on certain quadruple track sections to enable a train to change tracks at 113 km/h (70 mph).

Right The frog or nose point of a crossover.

Below left A very worn point on a switch in a US yard. Below right Series of crossovers on the entrance to a German station.

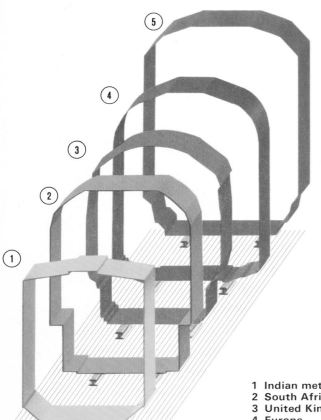

These examples reflect the wide variety of existing loading gauges. Interesting differences to note are the large dimensions permitted on South African Railways, where the rolling stock is taller than in the UK although the gauge is narrower; and the great size of North American stock. Those shown are no more than a representative selection of the world's loading gauges. Perhaps the two most notable ones not illustrated are that of the Indian broad gauge which permits a maximum width of 3.6 m (12 ft), and the Russian loading gauge. Russian engines can be the largest and most impressive in the world, permitted as they are to be more than 5.2 m (17 ft) above rail level.

Right South African Railways 4-8-4 at Kimberley shed showing huge size of loading gauge as compared with rail gauge.

	rail gauge		maximum height		maximum width	
1 Indian meter gauge	1,000 mm	*3'3⅜"*	3.429 m	*11'3"*	2.591 m	*8'6"*
2 South Africa	1,067 mm	*3'6"*	4.140 m	*13'7"*	3.048 m	*10'0"*
3 United Kingdom	1,435 mm	*4'8½"*	3.861 m	*12'8"*	2.819 m	*9'3"*
4 Europe (Bern Conference)	1,435 mm	*4'8½"*	4.280 m	*14'0½"*	3.150 m	*10'4"*
5 North America	1,435 mm	*4'8½"*	4.724 m	*15'6"*	3.277 m	*10'9"*

In heavily worked areas, particularly within city boundaries where there is an intense commuter traffic and much complicated track work, the wear on the rails is often severe on the switch points in a switch layout. It is also a characteristic of the power units of multiple-unit suburban trains, with the electric motors carried on the trucks, to be very hard on the track. In consequence it has become the practice for the most vulnerable parts of switch layouts, switch points in particular, to be made of high wear-resisting cast manganese steel, instead of from ordinary rail steel. Over many years it has been found that for standard rails a medium manganese steel, gives the best service in heavy high-speed traffic. The operation of switches and crossing is actually the job of the railway's signal and telecommunications engineer, in that he provides the apparatus to move the switches; and where this is electric, as in all modern installations, he designs the electric circuits for the control, with appropriate interlocking with the signal control circuits. The principles of interlocking are referred to in more detail on pages 70–71. A modern electric switching machine has three functions. Before the points can be thrown the facing switch lock must be withdrawn. The provision of a facing switch lock is a legal requirement at all switches over which passenger trains run in the facing direction. Then when the lock is withdrawn the switches are moved over, and the lock reinserted, securing the switches in their new position. The last function is the setting up of electric detection to prove that the switch point has gone fully home, and is fitting snugly against the stock rail. Only when this is proved is it possible to clear signals for a train to pass over the switches. The electric switching machine completes all these functions in about three seconds.

Right Locomotive washing facility, UK. The thoroughness of such behind-the-scenes operations is not fully appreciated by the commuter.

Top Vehicle used for lifting derailed trucks back on the rails in a US yard.
Above Vehicle above in operation. Such derailments are common in the US where high capital costs have led to a lack of maintenance, even on main lines. On some railway systems speed limits are kept low to avoid accidents. This is the major problem in providing faster services.

Bridge and tunnel construction

Bridges

The provision of relatively straight track to serve the needs of modern high-speed railways, has meant the construction of long bridges and tunnels over and through geographical obstructions. On these new railways the appearance of the bridges is notably different from the masonry arched viaducts of the pioneer lines, or the timber trestles of North America. On the Japanese *Shinkansen* line between Tōkyō and Osaka, for example, there are eight bridges more than 457 m (500 yd) long, the longest being the Fujigawa, no less than 1,508 m (1,650 yd), within sight of Mount Fuji. The foundations of these bridges are mostly in the form of pneumatic caissons 15.5–18 m (17–20 yd) in depth, on which piers of reinforced concrete are built. The superstructure varies, but where steel trusses are used they are made continuous, from one end of the bridge to the other. Erection takes place by the cantilever method, extending stage by stage outward from the completed part of the steelwork which is anchored to the piers. On the *Shinkansen* lines the standard length of span, from one pier to the next, is 59 m (65 yd).

In certain locations prestressed concrete girders are used. These are of remarkable design and provide complete support for a double track high-speed railway, with its ballast and roadbed with a total width of top platform of about 11 m (36 ft). The girder portion, providing the strength to carry the weight of the trains, consists of four deep beams approximately beneath the running rails. The total length of this cast, prestressed concrete unit is 23 m (25 yd). These bridges, with their

Above Construction of the Overvaal Tunnel in South Africa, well illustrates the scale of works necessary in tunneling. While techniques have improved enormously over the years, working conditions can often be harsh. *Right* A level crossing in the United States, one example of many different approaches to the problem when road meets rail. Nevertheless, one of the major sources of railway accident statistics is found at the crossing gate, or lack of it.

sleek, modern appearance, are wholly in keeping with the external decor of the *Shinkansen* lines. While new railways are being built covering new locations, ingenious work is often involved where old bridges have to be strengthened or renewed to meet the needs of present-day traffic. Where complete renewal is necessary and a new location is available, straightforward modern techniques can be used, a remarkable example of this being provided by the Rajahmundry bridge on the Howrah-Madras line of the Indian Railways, 900 m (1,000 yd) downstream of the original bridge, with the piers in water about 12 m (40 ft) deep. Here the foundations are on massive concrete wells sunk to a depth of 30 m (100 ft) below low water mark to ensure sufficient grip in the river bed, even in conditions of maximum erosion during high floods – always a hazard on Indian railways. This great new bridge, which has a total length of 2.8 km (1.75 miles), carries a roadway built to Indian national highway standards on the upper level, with the double line railway inside the 12 m (40 ft) high K-type trusses, which form the superstructure of the bridge. These girders were erected by the cantilever method.

Tunnels

Tunneling, despite all modern aids to excavation and subterranean survey, still involves very much of a plunge into the unknown, and methods have to be varied according to the nature of the soil and rock encountered, sometimes after excavation has proceeded some way. In good ground, a favored way of cutting through mountains and hillsides is known as the "bottom heading and half section" method. A pilot heading is driven along the bottom line of what will be the finished tunnel, as a means of access and a way for the removal of spoil. When this has

been driven an adequate distance, excavation to the full size begins in the upper half section. Then arch shuttering is put in to support the concreting of the top arch, until this is set. With the upper half section complete and the top arch in place, side cutting on either side of the bottom heading is carried out, working outward to the full width of the tunnel, until the side walls are ready to be concreted. In bad ground twin headings at the bottom inside of a single heading on the center line of the tunnel are cut. When this is done, a heading is driven along the line of each side wall, so that massive side walls at the lowest level can be got into place at an early stage, providing protection against ingress of water or shale and support for the shuttering when the time comes to install the top arch. In some of the long tunnels on the *Shinkansen* line the side heading method had to be used for part of the bores where the ground was considered too treacherous for any other method to be used.

Another method used where there is a prospect of good ground throughout is known as the "top heading and bench cut." Excavation begins with a heading in the upper half of the tunnel, which is enlarged out to the full profile and the top arch fully concreted. Then, using bulldozers, the lower half is excavated out to the full width and the side walls put in. In recent years, however, when the task of carrying railways beneath waterways has arisen, excavation beneath the river or canal bed has been avoided altogether by use of the "submerged tube" method. In Rotterdam when the Métro was projected, it was at once known that excavation for the underground sections in the

style of London or Paris would be quite impracticable: the excavations would immediately fill with water. Therefore a channel was dug on the line of the proposed Métro, allowed to fill with water, and then the prefabricated tunnel sections were lowered into it. The tubes were constructed with sealed ends, and when lowered into the water and butted accurately together, connection between adjoining tubes was made. The same "submerged tube" form of construction was used for the Bay Area Rapid Transit line, at San Francisco in passing beneath the bay to Oakland. The tube is 6.4 km (4 miles) long and it is possible for trains to travel between the two centers in as little as 8 min.

Top Stone viaduct in India. *Above* Bridge on the Kuranda-Cairns line in Queensland, Australia.

Above left Forth railway bridge, Scotland.

Right Modern viaduct in Spain built to massive proportions.

Passenger cars : early days

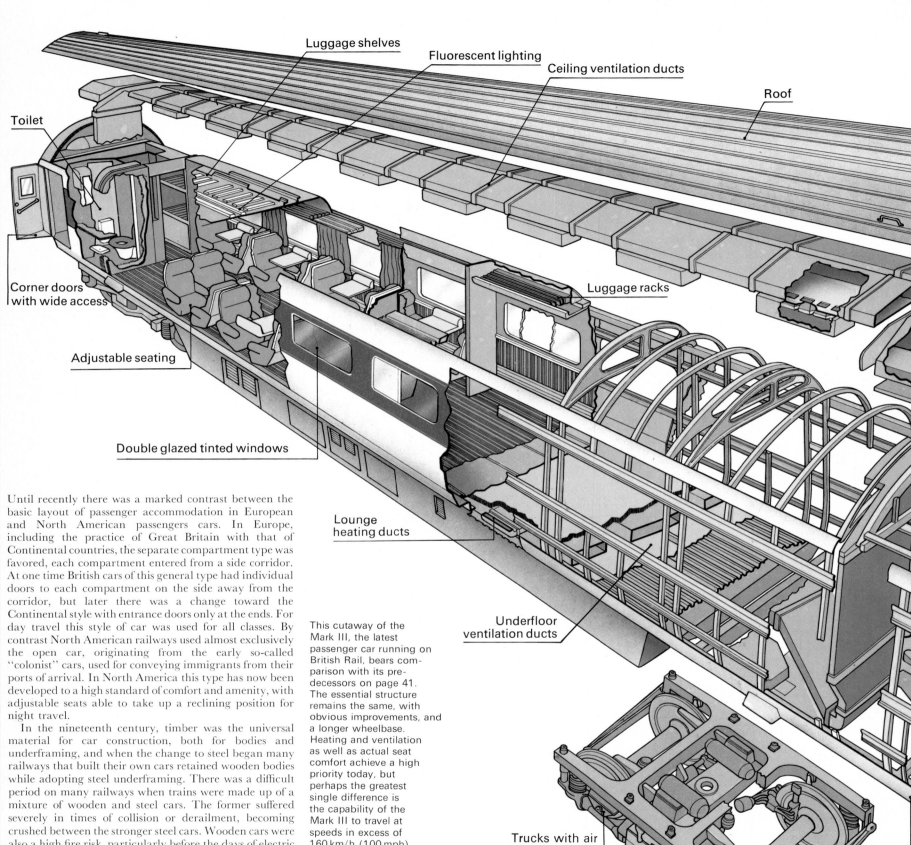

Toilet

Luggage shelves

Fluorescent lighting

Ceiling ventilation ducts

Roof

Corner doors with wide access

Luggage racks

Adjustable seating

Double glazed tinted windows

Lounge heating ducts

Underfloor ventilation ducts

Trucks with air springing and disk brakes

Steel shell construction

Until recently there was a marked contrast between the basic layout of passenger accommodation in European and North American passengers cars. In Europe, including the practice of Great Britain with that of Continental countries, the separate compartment type was favored, each compartment entered from a side corridor. At one time British cars of this general type had individual doors to each compartment on the side away from the corridor, but later there was a change toward the Continental style with entrance doors only at the ends. For day travel this style of car was used for all classes. By contrast North American railways used almost exclusively the open car, originating from the early so-called "colonist" cars, used for conveying immigrants from their ports of arrival. In North America this type has now been developed to a high standard of comfort and amenity, with adjustable seats able to take up a reclining position for night travel.

In the nineteenth century, timber was the universal material for car construction, both for bodies and underframing, and when the change to steel began many railways that built their own cars retained wooden bodies while adopting steel underframing. There was a difficult period on many railways when trains were made up of a mixture of wooden and steel cars. The former suffered severely in times of collision or derailment, becoming crushed between the stronger steel cars. Wooden cars were also a high fire risk, particularly before the days of electric lighting.

Today, the open type of passenger car is becoming quite widely adopted on the continent of Europe and is universal in new construction on British Rail. While some passengers

This cutaway of the Mark III, the latest passenger car running on British Rail, bears comparison with its predecessors on page 41. The essential structure remains the same, with obvious improvements, and a longer wheelbase. Heating and ventilation as well as actual seat comfort achieve a high priority today, but perhaps the greatest single difference is the capability of the Mark III to travel at speeds in excess of 160 km/h (100 mph).

Below High Speed Train with Mark III coaches.

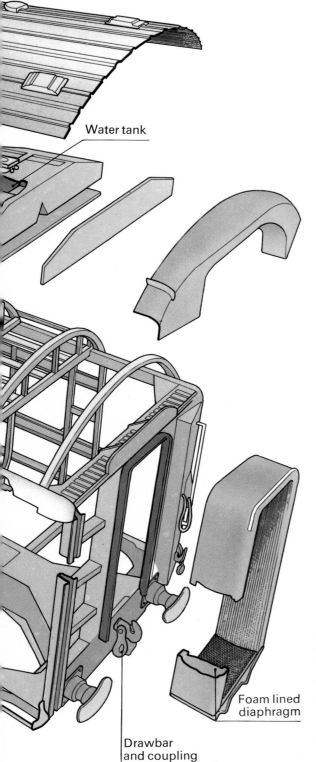

Water tank

Foam lined
diaphragm

Drawbar
and coupling

prefer the seclusion of separate compartments, the open car offers so many advantages in modern travel, in which the journey times are being progressively reduced. To the businessman the tables are a convenience, on which papers, books, or documents may be studied en route, or impromptu discussions or conferences held with colleagues; while on many trains a cart service of drinks and snacks is provided for those who do not wish to walk several coaches to a buffet car. On the fast intercity trains of British Rail there is often insufficient time to take a full dining car meal. For others, traveling with families, the four seats with table between is ideal for picnic meals, and other incidentals of an excursion outing. On the continent of Europe on some of the TEE services providing luxury as well as high-speed, the traveler can choose between compartment or open cars at the time of seat reservation. On the frequent intercity services of British Rail, seat reservation is usually unnecessary, but it is essential on most Continental express trains and obligatory on some.

The provision of dining cars on long-distance trains became an attractive accompaniment to travel around 1900, and the serving of breakfast, lunch, or dinner became something of a ritual with stewards specially selected for the task and taking as much pride in their service as the head waiters in fashionable restaurants. Echoes of this age in railway travel are to be seen on some prestige trains on the continent of Europe, but for the most part railway meals are nowadays simpler and taken in greater haste, often from the bar counter of a buffet car. Nevertheless, the counter service steak and french fries breakfast on Australian interstate express trains, taken in 20 to 25 minutes, is not so far removed from the slick movement required in the dining car of the prewar Cornish Riviera Express, when in the height of the holiday season the steward served three sittings of lunch during a journey of

four hours! In the modern trains of open type cars, certain parts of the train are set aside for the service of meals and are available only to those passengers requiring them. At one time a walk from one's seat to the dining car provided a welcome diversion during a long journey, but an advertised amenity of many prestige trains today is that meals are served at every seat, if required.

The evolution of the sleeping car has followed different paths in many parts of the world. In Europe little was done in early days to provide any additional comfort for night travel, whereas the much longer continuous journeys made across the American continent led to forms of seclusion in the early "colonist" or open cars, including blinds that could be lowered on either side of the central gangway, behind which passengers could to some extent undress. In Britain, when sleeping cars were introduced, for first-class passengers only, they provided completely private compartments for one, whereas on the continent of Europe even the first-class sleepers on the prestige international trains included two berths, one above the other in a compartment. This form of accommodation is still in use today. In Britain "third-class" (now second-class) sleepers were introduced in 1928, and these have two-tier bunks in a compartment. The accommodation consisted of no more than a bed with pillow and blankets, at each level.

Much has been done in recent years to improve the smoothness of the ride. In earlier days certain British railways famed for the smoothness of travel achieved their high standards by close and meticulous maintenance of the trucks. More recently, faced with the need to minimize the extent of railway work, new and advanced designs of truck have been introduced that give an excellent ride over long periods, at much higher speeds than previously, with a minimum of attention. The methods of suspension have been the subject of constant research.

Right and below left Construction of the Mark III in British Rail engineering works. *Below right* interior of the Mark III coach.

Passenger cars : modern improvements

Above New stock on the Wuppertal Monorail, Ruhr, West Germany.

Left Older type of Dutch DMU at Utrecht station.

Below Modern stainless steel EMU – northeast United States.

The great distances traversed by transcontinental trains in North America, and also in Australia, led to a demand by wealthy patrons for a luxury of accommodation beyond that of the ordinary first-class car and its associated dining and sleeping cars. Cars including private suites were introduced, while more generally available bar-lounges, club cars and observation lounges were run on certain trains. In Britain, both from Manchester and Bradford, from which at one time there was a high-class daily commuter traffic for businessmen living at seaside resorts and traveling daily, there were club cars, entry to which was open only to members of a traveling club. Cars of this kind were attached to certain express trains between Manchester and Blackpool, Manchester and Southport, and Bradford and Morecambe. They each had their own regular stewards and all the facilities of a first-class city club.

Modern tendencies in the highest class main line service are all toward airline style in passenger accommodation. The technical features that have developed to provide a comfortable ride in conditions of very fast running are to a large extent epitomized in the new cars now being built for

the Paris-Lyon TGV (*très grande vitesse*) line in France. On this line it has been decided to adopt powered trainsets, in preference to locomotive-hauled cars, with no more than moderate axle loading, considered essential for stability at 300 km/h (185 mph). The coaches are articulated, with trucks between the car bodies, which make possible a reduced height and therefore lower resistance to their passage through the atmosphere. To provide for rapid acceleration, six trucks out of the 13 in each trainset are powered. The trains themselves consist of eight passenger cars with a power unit at each end and will provide seating for 375 passengers.

An important accompaniment of the introduction of very fast new trains is a more complete understanding of the relationship between wheel and rail. For some time a roller test plant has been in operation at Pueblo, Colorado, USA, on which track conditions can be simulated and the reaction of vehicles passing over it observed under very precise laboratory conditions. This test plant, and one also recently brought into operation near Munich, West Germany, provides a parallel activity to that of stationary locomotive test plants, in that the unit to be examined can be run at maximum road speed, without moving from the test bed. In the case of the Pueblo and Munich plants, the

Above left New London Transport electric train entering Paddington.

Above Modern suburban EMU on Moorgate-Hatfield line, north London.

plants, the effects of such track features as curves and transitions, together with defects such as kinks and hollows, can be studied. It is not necessary to have a complete vehicle for satisfactory tests to be made. A bogie can be loaded to correspond with the loaded or unloaded weight of a coach. Furthermore, when new designs are proposed incorporating novel features, prototypes can be built and tested thoroughly before mass production is started.

The introduction of new rapid-transit commuter services in many cities of the world has been accompanied by some notable advances in the technology of rolling stock design. Some years ago, in an attempt to minimize noise when passing through tunnels, rubber tyred vehicles were introduced on a new underground line of the Paris Métro. Like other urban rapid-transit projects, the trains themselves were of the multiple-unit "set" type, but unlike other applications of pneumatic tyres such trainsets could not be steered, and means for guidance had to be provided in the form of additional wheels, on vertical axes, in contact with the vertical side of the concrete trough in which the main wheels ran. Also, further additional wheels were needed, to be brought into operation when these unusual trainsets had to be switched on to other routes, when entering a maintenance depot or stabling yard. They had, therefore, three times as many wheels as on a normal trainset. This type has been used on only one of the Paris Métro lines, but it was adopted for the Montreal subway, and has been installed on the Marseille rapid-transit line.

Some of the latest techniques in car production for

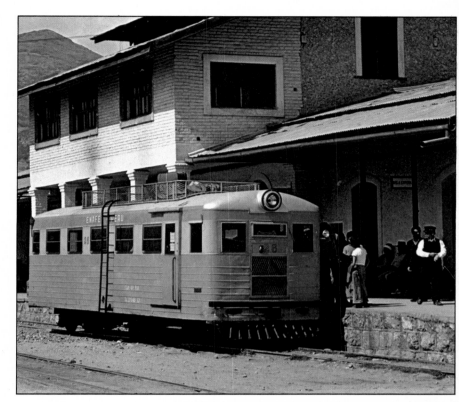

Right Tiny diesel railcar of ENAFER, Peru.

Below Air-conditioned double-deck stainless steel EMU for long haul work, comprising 2 × 2 car and 1 × 4 car units; Central Station, Sydney.

rapid-transit lines are embodied in new stock for the Paris Métro. Until recently, aluminium as a material for car bodies, while attractive from the viewpoint of weight reduction, has been impracticable because of its higher cost over steel; but now, with major progress in aluminium assembly techniques, French manufacturers have for the first time been able to achieve lower constructional costs for aluminium, and large orders have been placed, not only for Paris, but for several other cities. The older lines of the Paris Métro impose restrictive space conditions, which are non-existent on the notable "express" underground routes of the RER (regional express métro), which allow locomotives and trains of main line dimensions to run through the new tunnels. However, the body design of the new cars for the older Métro lines incorporates much structural ingenuity to provide additional space for passengers. An outstanding feature is the use of three pairs of sliding doors on each side of the car, which when fully opened provide space for entering equal to one-third of the total length of the car. As in all rapid-transit cars there is a large amount of space for standing passengers.

For the commuter services on certain of the main lines around Paris, some very handsome new double-deck passenger cars are now in use, hauled by electric locomotives. The set of cars and the locomotive make up a two-directional trainset, in the same way that steam locomotives were used on earlier commuter trains. The locomotive is not uncoupled, and while hauling the cars in one direction it propels them in the reverse. The car furthest from the locomotive has a driving cab, from which the locomotive is remotely controlled. This was also practised with steam, but the fireman had to remain on the locomotive at all times, and when propelling he and the driver were at opposite ends of the train.

Below Local passenger train passing through Ellis Park station, South Africa. Hillbrow in background.

Right Interior of dining car, Benguela Railways, Angola: note the wood panelling and luxurious Pullman style.

Freight cars : specialization

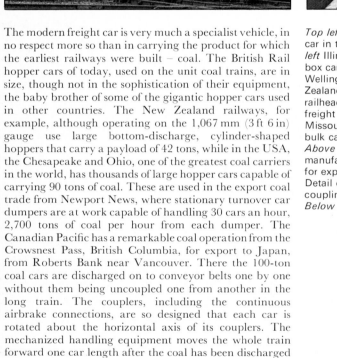

The modern freight car is very much a specialist vehicle, in no respect more so than in carrying the product for which the earliest railways were built – coal. The British Rail hopper cars of today, used on the unit coal trains, are in size, though not in the sophistication of their equipment, the baby brother of some of the gigantic hopper cars used in other countries. The New Zealand railways, for example, although operating on the 1,067 mm (3 ft 6 in) gauge use large bottom-discharge, cylinder-shaped hoppers that carry a payload of 42 tons, while in the USA, the Chesapeake and Ohio, one of the greatest coal carriers in the world, has thousands of large hopper cars capable of carrying 90 tons of coal. These are used in the export coal trade from Newport News, where stationary turnover car dumpers are at work capable of handling 30 cars an hour, 2,700 tons of coal per hour from each dumper. The Canadian Pacific has a remarkable coal operation from the Crowsnest Pass, British Columbia, for export to Japan, from Roberts Bank near Vancouver. There the 100-ton coal cars are discharged on to conveyor belts one by one without them being uncoupled one from another in the long train. The couplers, including the continuous airbrake connections, are so designed that each car is rotated about the horizontal axis of its couplers. The mechanized handling equipment moves the whole train forward one car length after the coal has been discharged and the car has subsequently been rotated back to its normal position.

Discharge through bottom hoppers, or by the rotating process, is not always possible, especially in the conveyance of waste products in industrial plants, such as blast furnaces and steel works. In the USA, and more recently in South Africa, side-dumping cars are used. The bodies resemble an extramassive version of an ordinary gondola but are supported on four huge compressed air cylinders. If it should be required to dump to the right-hand side of the line, air is applied to the two cylinders on the left-hand side and the extending of their pistons tilts the body to the right – pivoting about the center line of the vehicle. For dumping to the left, the tilting is provided by the cylinders on the right-hand side.

The "covered wagon" or box car has now been built to great size. It may be nothing more than a "box," designed to carry general merchandise, but many designs include highly specialized equipment for carrying sperishable goods or even newsprint, which needs particularly careful carrying when in large quantities.

The transport of automobiles and road trucks has become another specialized part of rail freight business. In Britain and on the continent of Europe, the cars are loaded on two levels, while the extra height of the North American

Top left German terry car in the UK. *Above left* Illinois Central box car, USA. *Above* Wellington Harbor, New Zealand, an important railhead in modern-day freight terms. *Top right* Missouri Pacific Railroad bulk carrier, Los Angeles. *Above right* Dump car manufactured in the UK for export. *Right* Detail of back-eye car couplings in US yard. *Below* Santa Fe boxcar.

loading gauge enables three levels to be used. On the latest American car transporters, 15 cars are carried, five on each deck. In Britain, however, whatever limitations in height are imposed by the loading gauge are made up for in length. The articulated principle has been applied to produce four-unit articulated trucks, each unit of which carries seven cars. With intermediate articulation only five trucks are needed to support the four units, and fully loaded with 28 automobiles the entire assembly weighs as much as 93 tons. These remarkable vehicles are designed to be run at 120 km/h (75 mph) if necessary. In the USA, because of vandalism, side protection of multi-level auto carriers has been found necessary, and in the latest designs the whole surface, except the ends, is completely covered in. At inland stations where automobiles are delivered, both to private purchasers and distributing agencies, special ramps are installed to permit easy unloading of the upper decks. The export of automobiles from Japan sometimes leads to unusual railway sights in North America: the passage of a heavily loaded westbound train of American automobiles, heading for San Francisco, is met by an equally long eastbound train loaded with their Japanese counterparts.

The introduction of special-purpose vehicles has grown to a remarkable extent in the USA where strenuous efforts are being made to win back traffic that had been lost to truckers. In no respect has this trend been more noticeable than in the cooperation between the railways and individual manufacturers for delivery of their products. In a joint conception of the Southern Pacific Railroad and

General Motors, the ingenious vert-a-pac car carrier was evolved, specially to convey new automobiles from plant to distribution centers. The vert-a-pac, as its name suggests, carries cars in a vertical position. On each side of these enormous box cars there are 15 doors, which are hinged at the bottom; when opened they form an inclined ramp on to which an automobile is driven. It is then secured for transit on to this ramp, and when the door is shut the automobile

Below Loading piggyback trailers on to a Union Pacific train in Argos Yards, Seattle, USA, using a mobile crane. Piggyback transport is of growing importance in North America where ocean shipment is not included and simple container flexibility is required.

is in a vertical position inside the vehicle. Loading takes place on both sides, and with a full complement 30 automobiles can be loaded into this one vehicle and ensconced in a totally enclosed box car. Another special vehicle is that known as the "stack back" flat car, used widely in the US for transporting heavy trucks, which are delivered from the manufacturers with nothing more than the chassis and the driver's cab. It was on the Louisville and Nashville that the ingenious idea of stacking them in an inclined position originated. The first in the line is positioned with its front wheels about 60 cm (2 ft) above the level of the platform with the flat deck in the rear of the driver's cab inclined downward. The second truck then has its front wheels on the back of the first truck and its hood almost touching the cab of the first.

Below "Piggy Packer" vehicle, which can lift 40-ton trailers, working on Chicago & North Western railway.

Above Piggyback car – not as neat as a container car, but just as effective.

Below British Rail Motorail train running by south Devon coast near Dawlish, England.

Right Canadian National car transporter with a particularly graphic device. Over long distances auto transportation achieves greater importance, though even in the United Kingdom Motorail has created a growing market.

Freight cars: automation

A major difficulty that at one time confronted Australian railways when it came to interchange of traffic between the different states was that at every state boundary except one, between Victoria and South Australia, there was a change of rail gauge. In one or two major cases this has been partly resolved by the building of new standard gauge lines, but this does not apply everywhere and on certain through runs, in particular those concerning the State of Victoria, special vehicles are used on which the cars are changed at the point where there is a change of gauge. The vehicles are lifted bodily from one set of trucks and lowered on to a second set for the altered gauge. At the frontier between New South Wales and Victoria it is not unusual for 20,000 vehicles to be truck-changed annually.

These difficulties led to the modern concept of the container train, which is being developed extensively in Europe. The idea of a sealed container that can be transferred from rail to ship, and then back to rail again, is not a new one, because it was practiced for very many years in the days of steam operations on the Continental boat-train services from London, across the English Channel to France. The modern rail concept is to have a fixed-consist set of flat cars for each scheduled service and not to alter that consist even though a full complement of containers is not available on the particular day. For example a nightly service from Garston Docks, Liverpool, to Glasgow would contain a set of 20 flat cars, each capable of carrying three containers – 60 to a train. If, however, by loading time the traffic of the day has produced only 47 containers, the train would be dispatched with some of the flat cars not fully loaded. The transit of these trains is given top priority in the night. During these hours express passenger trains are run at considerably lower speeds than in the daytime; and the container trains, or "freightliners" as they are called, running continuously at 120 km/h (75 mph), are equally fast. A fully loaded 20-flat container train would represent more than 1,000 tons, or roughly double that of a heavy night passenger train, and on the heavy grades in the north of England and Scotland two

Above left Loading containers after manufacture. *Above right* Harwich at night, loading containers. *Right* Oil train from Milford Haven to London moving through Sonning Cutting. *Below left* Container train, administered by Intercontainer, an international coordinating body. *Below right* US oil tanker.

5,000 hp electric locomotives are needed to maintain the fast scheduled speeds.

The transport of livestock needs specially equipped freight trains. In Britain in former days sheep and cattle were transported in single-deck four-wheeled cars, with open caged sides; but this traffic has largely ceased. In other countries, however, it is still a major item, and the modern general concept of the high-capacity car has been applied to this traffic. Large double-decked sheep vans are run on the Iraqi State Railways, and even larger ones in the USA. The Atchison Topeka and Santa Fe railway has also introduced double-decked stock cars that were adjustable.

Specialized cars are used for the bulk transport of materials in powder and pellet form. On British Rail, while the private owners' cars of former days are no longer to be seen as individual loads in freight trains, contracts have been arranged with large industrial concerns for the running to regular schedules of daily unit freight trains carrying a single product. The Rugby Portland Cement Company has a fleet of large four-wheeled cylindrically shaped cars, which have a gross laden weight of 50 tons and

are run at speeds up to 96 km/h (60 mph). Considerably larger are the 100-ton cars operated for the Blue Circle Cement group. These carry a maximum payload of 78 tons, and are also run at speeds of 96 km/h (60 mph). Their appearance is striking, with the cylindrical bodies inclined in sections to facilitate the easy flow of the material when loading. All these large vehicles impose an axle load of about 25 tons on to the track. This can be accepted only on main trunk lines because it is of the same order as that of locomotives. Another special vehicle on British Rail is a 100-ton bulk powder tank cars used for conveyance of raw material needed for detergent manufacture. In tune with the actual containers themselves, whether it be consignments loaded into containers or minerals and materials conveyed in bulk, is the design of the trucks to permit safe and steady running up to 96 km/h (60 mph). Every effort is made to reduce unsprung weight, to incorporate load-sensitive dampers and to equip them with disk or clasp brakes. All British fast freight trains are fitted with the Westinghouse automatic air brakes permitting the safe and smooth control of the heaviest trains in the most adverse circumstances.

In North America, although there have recently been a number of mergers reducing the number of companies and setting up large combines such as Conrail, the Burlington Northern, and others, there are still a vast number of different owners and an equally great variety of cars. With computerization of operational controls in great classification yards, some mechanized process was necessary to eliminate the human recording of car types, ownership and destination of individual loads as freight trains came into the receiving tracks so that they could be correctly routed. This too is now done by computer, but the computer has to know such information as destinations and weights. To do this the system of Auto-

matic Car Identification has been tried out. A color-coded panel is fixed to every freight car in major railway service. It is a rectangle 60 cm (24 in) high and 25 cm (10 in) wide and includes 14 horizontal strips of color in combinations of red, blue, black and white. By varying the relation of adjacent colors, a very large combination of codes can be obtained, which when decoded identify the type of vehicle and the owning railway. As a train enters the receiving tracks at a classification yard, it passes a photoelectric scanner, which automatically reads the code on the side of the vehicle and immediately transmits the information to the computer in the control tower, from where the switching for train classification is set up.

Above Zilletalbahn, Austria, showing how the standard gauge cars are transported.

Below Truck of US tank car showing springing and braking arrangements. Such tankers may carry up to 70 tons of oil products apiece, which requires considerable stability.

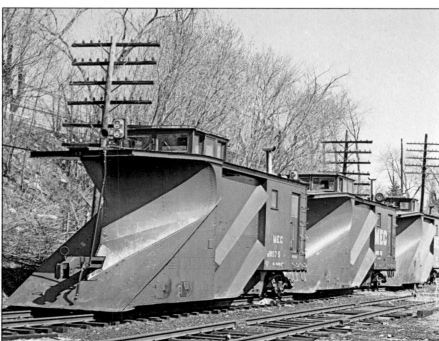

Left Snowplows, Maine Central, Bangor.
Right The Automatic Train Control plate from a truck, which details for an electronic eye to read, full information regarding destination etc. This system is not entirely successful as the plates become dirty, thus confusing the automatic reading. Many classification yards have installed hybrid computer equipment to deal with some sorting work.
Below right Canadian Pacific caboose at the end of a coal train.

Modern signaling

The function of modern signaling is primarily to ensure the safe movement of trains, but equally, by giving clear and unmistakable indications, to give engineers confidence to run at the maximum speeds permitted by the physical characteristics of each section of line. While originally semaphore signals were devised and installed to tell drivers when to stop, today modern signaling is the one feature of railway technology without which it would be impossible to run high-speed services, or intense commuter programs. The modern signal is the day color light type, which, unlike the old semaphore signals, gives essentially the same indication to the driver by day and by night. The code of indications varies in different countries, but the underlying philosophy is generally the same. The code used on British Rail for what is termed "multi-aspect signaling" is the oldest, first introduced in 1925 and by far the simplest, and is second to none in its record of safe operation. At junctions it tells the driver what route he is to take, whereas the standard code in North America instructs the driver at what speed he should travel. This latter method involves a considerable proliferation of signal lights, but is very effective in operation. On the continent of Europe, systems of color light signaling are of more recent origin and vary from country to country, some involving a blend of the British "geographical" and the North American "speed" aspects.

The fundamental safety feature underlying all modern signaling is the track circuit. Each line of railway is divided into a number of sections, insulated from each other, into which an electrical feed is made at one end. Connected across the rails at the other end is a relay, which acts as a multipurpose switching device. If there is no train or other

Approach to Rotterdam station.

vehicle, in the particular section, the relay is energized and certain contacts are made. If the electrical feed along the rails to the relay is in any way interrupted, by the presence of a train or the misfortune of a broken rail, the relay is deenergized. The contacts of the track relay control the signal indication at the entering point to the track circuit, and by other contacts enable the whereabouts of all trains to be shown on the illuminated diagrams in the dispatchers office. The track relay, which is a highly sophisticated instrument with upwards of 80 years' research and development behind it, is at the heart of the interlocking that performs a number of vital functions. It prevents conflicting signals from being displayed; keeps following trains on the same line at a safe distance apart while the interlocking of units in electrical circuits prevents the clearing of signals until the line ahead is correctly set through switches and crossings; and prevents the establishment of a line-up of switches that would intersect the line-up of another and so give rise to what would become a "collision course."

The safeguards against the chance of a signalman's error are now so complete as to make modern systems virtually accident-proof as far as track relay systems are concerned. With the modern push-button control consoles, there is nothing physically to prevent a signalman pushing a wrong button; but the interlocking in the system is such that if he did so the function concerned would not respond. There would be no answering indication light to show that all had correctly worked, and he would realize that he had nearly set up a potentially dangerous situation. At the present time, however, there is no corresponding safeguard

for the engineer, although a great deal is done to help him. It is considered that the control of the running of the train should not be taken out of his hands except if he is ignoring the warnings given by a signal or the warning apparatus in his cab. The question as to how and when warnings should be given and direct control applied have been the subject of much debate, with differences of viewpoint in various parts of the world. On British Rail it is now standard practice on main lines to give an audible warning in the cab at every signal on color light multiple-aspect routes and at the "distant" or warning signal where semaphore signals remain. In multiple-aspect territory on the approach to a green (clear) signal, a bell is rung briefly in the locomotive cab, while on approach to a first warning double yellow, or a final warning single yellow, a horn is sounded. In the case of the clear indication, no action is required from the engineer, but at the warning the horn continues sounding until an acknowledging lever is operated. If the engineer acknowledges promptly it is taken as an assurance that he is alert, and full control of the train remains in his hands. Should he fail to acknowledge after a brief time, the brakes are automatically applied and the train stopped. Varying degrees of cab warning and control are used in other countries.

Left Modern four aspect and junction signals, British Rail.

Above Manual signal box preserved on the Bluebell Line, UK.

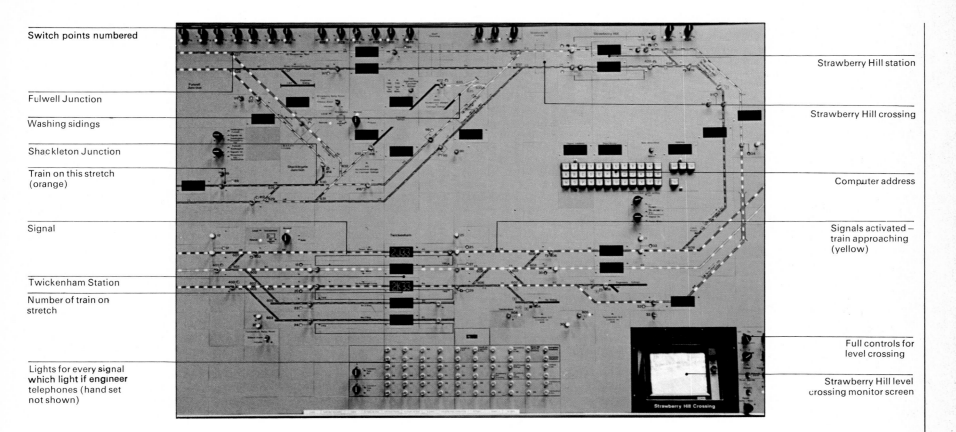

Switch points numbered

Fulwell Junction

Washing sidings

Shackleton Junction

Train on this stretch (orange)

Signal

Twickenham Station

Number of train on stretch

Lights for every signal which light if engineer telephones (hand set not shown)

Strawberry Hill station

Strawberry Hill crossing

Computer address

Signals activated – train approaching (yellow)

Full controls for level crossing

Strawberry Hill level crossing monitor screen

Above A general view of the interior of Feltham signal box in southwest London. The main display is on the left, angled in five panels. The main panel featured on this page (above) is the second from the left. The small television screens which monitor all level crossings on this section are visible at the base of the panels. The main control desks are to the right, and hidden behind them are computer printout machines giving information regarding traffic flow, schedule changes and cancellations.

Above The public address control at Feltham. From this panel a controller can give messages over the public address systems of all the stations on the section. Not only can recorded messages be played announcing trains, but also the whole system can be overridden and direct address effected using the microphone which is visible. This is necessary when train delays occur.

The regulation of traffic on important routes has been greatly improved by the concentration of control at a few large centers, instead of having a chain of small signal boxes along the line. The modern panel British Rail signal box controls anything up to 160 km (100 miles) of high-speed main line in addition to all the local working around a large station or junction. The whereabouts of all trains are indicated by lights on the illuminated track diagram, while a system known as "train description" pinpoints the position of individual trains by displaying their numbers in illuminated characters on dark rectangles at key positions on the diagram. These numbers progress from one rectangle to the next as the train proceeds on its journey. At junctions or among the diversity of routes around a large station, the routes are set by the signalmen. Unlike the earlier days of mechanical signaling or the first installations of electric operation, there is now no need to operate each individual function separately. A complete route is set up by the pressing of two buttons. The system is known as "entrance-exit." The signal immediately before a junction may lead to a number of different routes and first the entrance button is pressed; then the signalman selects the button at the exit of the route he requires. If the interlocking is free, because no conflicting movement is signaled, the pressing of the exit button sets up the whole route. When all the switches in the route are correctly lined up and have been detected, the signal at the entrance to the route clears automatically and the traffic is able to proceed.

On the busiest routes of the London Underground, the practice of route setting has been carried a remarkable stage further. Dealing with nothing other than multiple-unit passenger trains working to an intense schedule, the operation for a whole day's running is controlled by an instrument called a "program machine." In simple terms, all the signal and switch operation required for the service set out in the schedule is, as it were, put on to tape, and as the trains pass through the various junctions, such as Camden Town or Earls Court, the tape is advanced one step and automatically sets the route for the following train. In the traffic control centers the dispatchers watch the progress of the trains but have no need to intervene except in cases of late running or emergency. It is a remarkable example of automated traffic control. On the Victoria Line of the London Underground the trains themselves are automatically operated, except that the engineer presses two buttons simultaneously to close the doors and start the train, once the "right away" is given from the platform.

Above The supervisor's desk at Feltham. Clearly visible are the key switches for entry into the computers used to control operations and the keyboard for addressing the computer. Of interest are the "signal address" and "description" panels which give details of any train present at any signal point. The code given in the description panel is that carried on the locomotive. The first digit gives the class of train, the letter indicates the destination, and the final digits constitute a train number.

Traffic and scheduling : main line

Planning a passenger schedule on a line carrying a variety of traffic usually involves striking a balance between the immediate demands of the business offered, the economic use of rolling stock and motive power, and what is practical in the way of speed. Clearly, the rolling stock should be worked to the best advantage, securing maximum utilization, but an ideal backward and forward movement of a consist of cars might not fit in with the traffic flows, and some runs might be no more than lightly loaded. On the other hand it has been demonstrated many times that the introduction of regular interval services between important centers throughout the day attracts traffic. Undoubtedly trains running in the off-peak periods will sometimes be sparsely loaded, and in early days it was often the practice to work these periods with fewer cars. But the fixed formation trainset presents no problems with switching and the time and labor saved thereby amply compensates for the underutilization of the seating accommodation in off-peak hours. On the busiest intercity services on British Rail, trainsets shuttling between major cities on single journeys of 160–240 km (100–150 miles) do not leave the terminal stations at either end. There is no question of their being worked as empty cars to some storage yard. In many cases these intercity trains are at the terminal platforms for little more than half an hour, before leaving again often fully loaded for the return trip.

The intensity of car utilization today creates its own problems. The attractions of a fast, frequent service will be dimmed somewhat if there are times when the equipment of the cars is faulty, quite apart from major considerations such as the quality of the ride. But in addition to engineering maintenance, which on trains providing an intense daytime intercity service has to be carried out at night, there are points that are small so far as the overall planning is concerned, but are important from the viewpoint of public relations. Nothing can be more irritating or repellent to passengers entering a car at the start of their journey than to find old newspapers and other debris left by the occupants on the incoming journey, and however briefly a trainset may rest in a terminal station platform between incoming and outgoing trips, time must be allowed for maintenance personnel to clean the train's interior.

Provision for maintenance of the track also governs the scheduling of intense high-speed passenger services. On the electrified line of British Rail northward from London (Euston), the traffic today is enough to justify an hourly service throughout the day from London to Liverpool and to Manchester, and a half-hourly service to Birmingham.

Crowded passenger train in India: the answer to high passenger densities.

Perhaps the reason for its sudden haste between stations C and D is that a faster train is following it, not stopping at all stations, which therefore has to overtake it. As seen *below*, the slower mixed train is scheduled to wait half an hour at station D, perhaps to switch, while the fast passenger train will wait only 2 min at the station, overtaking the slower mixed train at the same time.

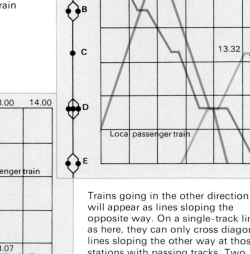

Loca passenger train

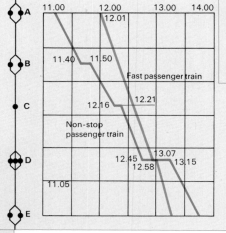

Trains going in the other direction will appear as lines sloping the opposite way. On a single-track line, as here, they can only cross diagonal lines sloping the other way at those stations with passing tracks. Two trains moving the other way are shown *above*: one nonstop from E to A crosses the mixed at B, without stopping, and a slower, all stations, train. Note that just before 1:00 p.m. there are 3 trains in station D.

This series of diagrams explains the workings of a *scheduling graph*, of which the section *below* is seen as representing a small part. One of the axes of such a graph ought to have 24 hours marked out along it, not 3 as here. Such a graph would also, normally, cover a greater route length than the 120 km (75 miles) here. The line is single track, with passing places at all stations except C.

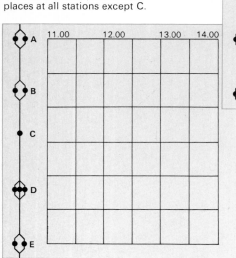

As the time scale moves from left to right, horizontally, the train, *above*, is traveling from A to E. The steeper the diagonal line between stops, the faster it is traveling. The longer the horizontal line at a station, the longer it stops. This, therefore, is a slow train, perhaps mixed, averaging less than 60 km/h (37 mph) between stops, except between stations C and D where it manages 100 km/h (62 mph).

Traveling through the Rockies in leisurely style.

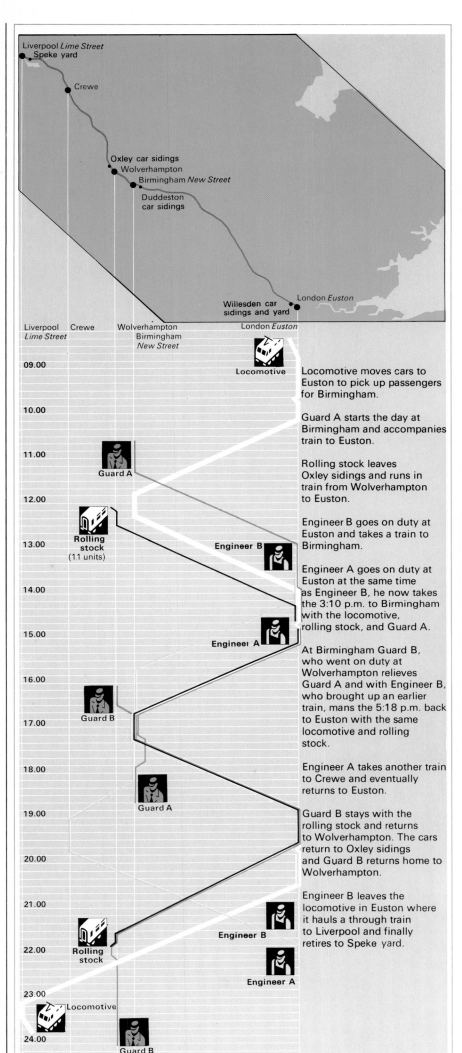

Liverpool *Lime Street*
Speke yard
Crewe
Oxley car sidings
Wolverhampton
Birmingham *New Street*
Duddeston
car sidings
Willesden car
sidings and yard
London *Euston*

Liverpool *Lime Street*	Crewe	Wolverhampton Birmingham *New Street*	London *Euston*

09.00 — Locomotive — Locomotive moves cars to Euston to pick up passengers for Birmingham.

10.00

11.00 — Guard A — Guard A starts the day at Birmingham and accompanies train to Euston.

Rolling stock leaves Oxley sidings and runs in train from Wolverhampton to Euston.

12.00 — Rolling stock (11 units)

Engineer B goes on duty at Euston and takes a train to Birmingham.

13.00 — Engineer B

Engineer A goes on duty at Euston at the same time as Engineer B, he now takes the 3:10 p.m. to Birmingham with the locomotive, rolling stock, and Guard A.

14.00

15.00 — Engineer A

At Birmingham Guard B, who went on duty at Wolverhampton relieves Guard A and with Engineer B, who brought up an earlier train, mans the 5:18 p.m. back to Euston with the same locomotive and rolling stock.

16.00

17.00 — Guard B

Engineer A takes another train to Crewe and eventually returns to Euston.

18.00 — Guard A

19.00 — Guard B stays with the rolling stock and returns to Wolverhampton. The cars return to Oxley sidings and Guard B returns home to Wolverhampton.

20.00

Engineer B leaves the locomotive in Euston where it hauls a through train to Liverpool and finally retires to Speke yard.

21.00 — Engineer B

22.00 — Rolling stock — Engineer A

23.00

24.00 — Locomotive — Guard B

The diagram, *left*, follows the movements, throughout their working day, of the staff and equipment used for a single return operation of a locomotive-hauled passenger train between London (Euston) and Birmingham. Although the trains are the 3.10 p.m. Euston–Birmingham and the 5.18 p.m. Birmingham–Euston, the diagram shows, for the rest of their day, the different paths of the men and equipment who come together briefly to work these trains.

Every hour also there are fast trains serving other northern destinations, in addition to which there are, at slightly longer intervals, trains to Scotland. To provide an adequate time interval for small items of track maintenance and the operation of trains which intersect the high-speed main lines, the regular interval trains are grouped in "flights," leaving London at 5-minute intervals beginning at 40 minutes past each hour until 10 minutes past the next hour, thus leaving a full half hour free for local movements and other essential maintenance work to be carried out on the line.

The intensity of regular passenger train operation in Britain has no counterpart elsewhere, because even the *Shinkansen* lines in Japan are dealing with a fixed-interval service of one particular class of train. In France today, the very fast intercity services are planned to enable a traveler from the provinces to make a visit to Paris, have a full afternoon for business, and return by a train reaching his home destination before midnight. French passenger train travel at its greatest intensity is seen at seasonal holiday periods, when a vast number of extra trains are run from Paris to resorts in Switzerland, on the Côte d'Azur, and in Spain. In the days just before Christmas, for example, it is not unusual in the six hours before midnight for about 60 long-distance trains to be dispatched from the Gare de Lyon alone. Only six or seven would be regularly scheduled services; the rest are extras. But such is the reserve organization available that this intense provision

A London-Birmingham train leaving Euston.

can be worked punctually, with most trains covering between 120 and 130 km (75 and 80 miles) in the first hour out of Paris, and serving such diverse destinations as Athens, Rome, Nice, Grenoble, Milan, Interlaken and Genoa.

In France the prestige passenger train services entering and leaving Paris have to be interwoven with the commuter traffic, which is intense in the peak hours, though on all the principal routes approaching the city there are four tracks from distances of about 32 km (20 miles) inward. On the main route from Paris to the southeast, particularly over the 316 km (195 miles) southward to Dijon, the line, although quadruple-tracked for most of the way, is at times being worked to full capacity; because of this the new TGV line is being built to cope with this intensity.

Traffic and scheduling : commuter

The operation of an intense commuter service presents a totally different set of problems from those posed by main line operations. Paramount is the inescapable fact that a very large amount of rolling stock has to be available to cater for the morning and evening peak periods, but which is necessarily idle or much underutilized during the rest of the day. There is also the problem of storage, because the great volume of cars needed for the morning peak cannot be accommodated in the immediate area of the city terminal stations; it has to be worked outward to suburban centers before standing by during the off-peak hours. Because of the underutilization of much of the stock on the basis of a 24-hour assessment, the working of commuter services tends to be uneconomic, despite progressive increases in fares. The nature of the cars essential for such a service – whether it be the non-corridor compartment type of the Southern Region of British Rail, the subway type with as many as three pairs of sliding doors a side, or the huge double-decker cars of Chicago – makes it quite unsuitable for any other kind of duty in the off-peak hours. Today, however, while the situation in the immediate environs of great cities is acute and likely to remain so, the acceleration of main line services with the latest forms of motive power has resulted in many more city workers commuting from further afield. In earlier days many businessmen traveled to London daily from Brighton, Eastbourne or Worthing, and today travelers commute daily from as far afield as Peterborough (122 km; 76 miles) and Bath (171 km; 107 miles).

A criticism directed at many commuter services is that while trains may run at frequent intervals, the overall time from outer residential stations to the city center is relatively slow, because of the frequent stops. This is a criticism that could well be leveled at the latest extension of the London Underground to Heathrow international airport, from

The train routes of the Waterloo to Windsor line from 6:00 p.m. to 12:30 a.m. are shown in chronological order of departure.

The intensity of train utilization on a fast commuter service is geared to passenger demand and does not simply involve the continuous running of trains from a city terminal to the suburban centers and then back again. The diagrams along the bottom of these two pages represent trains running on British Rail's Waterloo–Windsor line for the 6½-hour period from 6 p.m. to 12:30 a.m. on a weekday. Each train is represented by a ball colored according to the train's time of departure and is coded according to its place of destination, eg C – Windsor (see first panel), and its order of running eg C2 – second train to Windsor. Trains which at some point split, usually an eight-car set splitting in two with each half going to a different destination, are indicated – C2a, C2b, etc.

The block of small panels (above right) indicate the individual routes of each train set in chronological order of departure from Waterloo. A double line indicates a return journey, while further lines show additional journeys by the same set in the time period covered. As mentioned above, where sets split, this is also shown. Thus if we start with the small panels at A1 and refer to the first of the larger panels

we find that in the half hour 6 to 6:30 p.m., A1 has reached Staines, B1 is nearly in Brentford, C1 and D1 are between Richmond and Twickenham, and B2, A2 and E1 are on their way to Richmond, the latter having just left Waterloo. This progression can be followed through with other sets appearing on the scene.

The operation shown here represents movements on one section of track out of Waterloo during the evening peak and later evening, and well illustrates the complexity of traffic movements which must be planned.

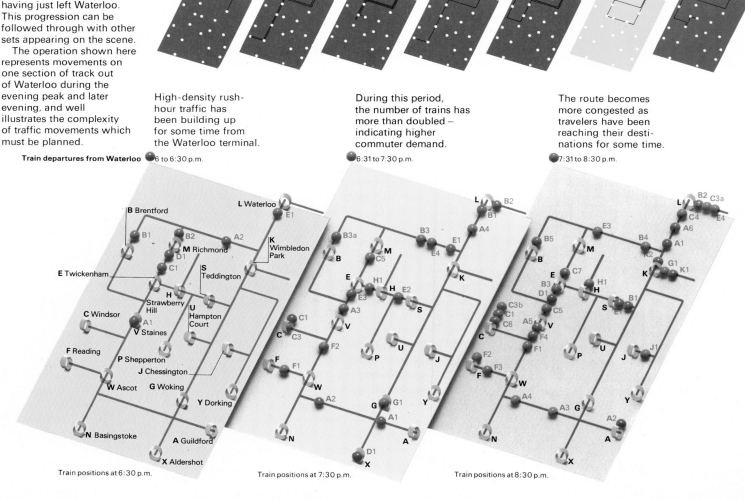

High-density rush-hour traffic has been building up for some time from the Waterloo terminal.

During this period, the number of trains has more than doubled – indicating higher commuter demand.

The route becomes more congested as travelers have been reaching their destinations for some time.

Train departures from Waterloo ● 6 to 6:30 p.m.

● 6:31 to 7:30 p.m.

● 7:31 to 8:30 p.m.

Train positions at 6:30 p.m.

Train positions at 7:30 p.m.

Train positions at 8:30 p.m.

which the trains entering the central area must necessarily take their turn among the swarm of other subway trains. A striking attempt has been made to overcome this problem in Paris by the construction of new deep-level express lines. By the use of these lines a great deal of the congestion at main line terminals has been relieved by diversion of commuter trains to the new deep-level underground lines. The new network is known as the Regional Express Métro, and its outstanding feature is the provision of no more than a few stations in the central area, in contrast to the closely spaced stations of the original Paris Métro, and on the London Underground. For example, the distance between the stations Auber and Defense is 7.2 km (4.5 miles), and the time allowed only 6.5 minutes inclusive of a 20 second intermediate stop at Étoile. The track and rolling stock are fully up to main line standards, though even on the Regional Express Métro provision is made for a large number of standing passengers at the peak periods. The total seating accommodation of a three-car train is 40 first-class, 160 second-class, seated, and 658 second-class passengers standing.

One of the most remarkable modern examples of complete railway schedule integration is that now in operation on the Netherlands State Railways. Connecting all the major cities, such as The Hague, Rotterdam, Amsterdam, Utrecht, Zwolle, Eindhoven and Maastricht, there is a half-hour service of fast electric trains, so that a traveler can arrive at a city station and be sure that within half an hour at the most there will be a fast train. The service may require a change of trains en route, but the connecting service will arrive within a matter of minutes, and therefore the continuation of the journey will be equally fast. To the outermost centers, such as Leeuwarden, Groningen, and Vlissingen (Flushing), there is a one-hour service of fast electric trains. In the operation of such a network everything depends upon strict punctuality, and all trains entering the Netherlands from surrounding countries, and all freight trains, are subjugated to this basic national electric train network. So regular, standardized and punctual is the operation that it is regulated by computer program to suit the planned schedule. At the large centers the traffic supervisors keep no more than a watching brief, and manual intervention takes place only when some unusual circumstance arises, or when some train from outside the country approaches one of the frontier stations at a time outside its scheduled time. The electric trains operating the half-hourly and hourly services in the Netherlands are all of the multiple-unit type. The only passenger trains that are locomotive hauled are the international through services.

Left Double-deck commuter coach, Burlington Northern, waiting in Chicago Union Station.

Below When railways were first built, their terminals were on city edges, but as cities have grown the stations have become relatively more convenient. This diagram shows how important the main lines have become for short-distance commuting, even in Paris with its Métro.

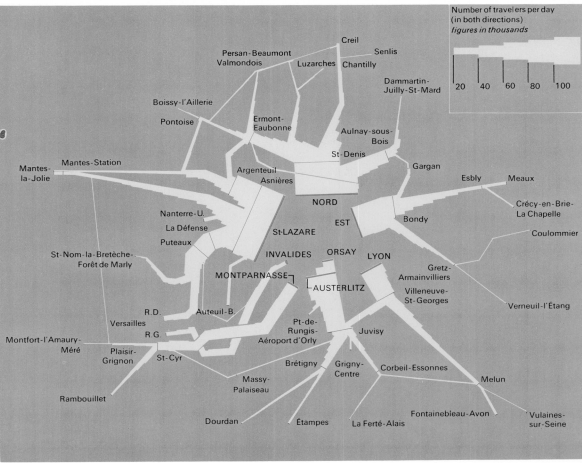

Number of travelers per day (in both directions) *figures in thousands*

20 40 60 80 100

By this time the number of rush hour trains has begun to diminish as the pressure is taken off Waterloo.

8:31 to 9:30 p.m.

From 9:30 p.m. onward there is a gradual buildup of trains returning from the suburbs to Waterloo.

9:31 to 10:30 p.m.

A limited number of trains are leaving Waterloo on their final journeys and many more are in the sidings.

10:31 to 11:30 p.m.

The last train has departed from Waterloo and the whole route has become virtually deserted.

11:31 p.m. to 12:30 a.m.

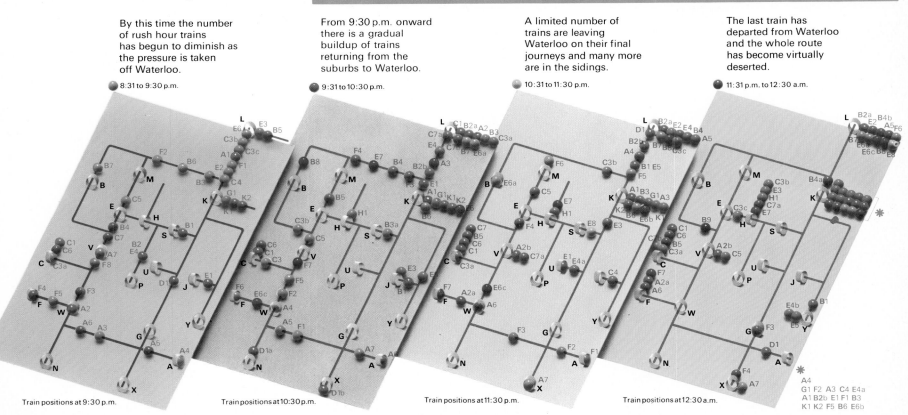

Train positions at 9:30 p.m.   Train positions at 10:30 p.m.   Train positions at 11:30 p.m.   Train positions at 12:30 a.m.

A4
G1 F2 A3 C4 E4a
A1 B2b E1 F1 B3
K1 K2 F5 B6 E6b

The science of freight handling

Freight car being slowed in classification yard by retarders.

The principle of classification yard operation is illustrated *below*. The central problem is usually how to split a train of cars for mixed destinations and reassemble it into an order in which efficient delivery can be effected. Here there are 16 cars bound for 12 different destinations. The cars are sorted by two "moves" into the correct order for delivery. It is the job of the "yard master" to see that the moves are carefully worked out to economize on the operation. This task is usually aided today by computer operation.

The great variety of consignments handled by the freight department of a modern railway makes essential a scientific study of traffic flows and the demands of commerce. In all parts of the world the problem of using tracks to the best advantage is severe and continuing, and whether the railway is an intensively used "mixed" line, like most of the trunk routes of British Rail or the principal main routes in France and West Germany, or consists of lengthy stretches of single line as on some of the great transcontinental routes in North America, the ultimate aim is similar, though on a different scale: to run the longest freight trains it is practical to operate to secure minimum line occupation. This involves the making-up, or classification, of these lengthy formations, and inevitably the individual freight cars are coupled up one behind the other as they arrive from their various originating stations. Switching, and the subsequent classification after a long run to some distant distributional center, is an expensive business, to be avoided wherever possible. While in Britain, particularly today, and to a lesser extent in other countries there is a general trend toward the running of block loads of a single commodity that need no switching at the start or classification afterward, this method cannot be adopted in the majority of instances.

While switching is a relatively simple mechanical operation, consisting of adding vehicles in ones and twos to the rear end of a train, its classification at the end of a long through run can depend upon geographical circumstances, particularly when freight is arriving for shipment from a large port. Some of the largest and most elaborately equipped classification yards are located a few miles inshore from extensive dock areas. There, arriving trains from many different inland centers, bringing a great variety of freight loads, have to be sorted out and classified into trains to go to individual loading points at the docks. Notable examples of this kind of operation were established at Hull and Middlesbrough, in northeastern England, and at Melbourne, Australia. There is also the matter of city distribution of incoming freight at a time when traffic congestion on the highways is becoming critical. From the railway point of view there is a great attraction in concentrating the dispatch and receipt of goods at a few large stations which will be well equipped with mechanized loading and unloading facilities. But highway transport is involved between the actual senders and the consignees, and this inevitably slows down the overall operation. The time cycle has, however, to be considered in relation to the length of run by rail, and in this the shorter runs within the confines of a small country such as Britain cannot be compared even to western Europe, still less to North America.

The lengthy train of mixed traffic, which modern conditions require to be run at speeds at least up to 96 km/h (60 mph), continues to present a field for constant study and evolution in the practice of train handling. In North America formations of 150 cars are common, and these are more than 2.5 km (1.5 miles) long and weigh anything up to 10,000 tons. Pulling power, with modern diesel-electric locomotives, is perhaps the least of the problems facing operators, because two, three or four locomotives may be coupled together electrically as well as mechanically so that they can be controlled by a single man, who may have 12,000–15,000 hp at his disposal. The science of controlling such a train at speed, and especially on long descending grades, has now become one of the most sophisticated in the entire extent of train operation. The trains are air braked throughout, but the art of braking has advanced immeasurably from the basic principles patented by George Westinghouse 100 years ago. Numerous refinements have been added to ensure smooth

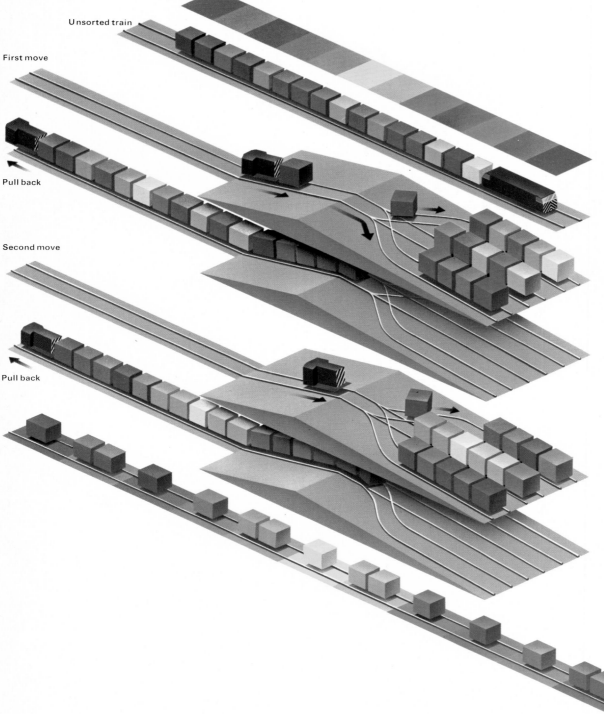

Destinations

Unsorted train

First move

Pull back

Second move

Pull back

application throughout an enormously long train. The principle of dynamic braking is used to minimize wearing of brake shoes and heating during long periods of downhill running. This reverses the action of the engines on the locomotive units and causes them to be put "on compression" as it were. Finally, the engineer is in radio communication with the conductor and brakeman riding in the caboose at the rear end of the train, and also with the dispatcher at the control center of the area in which he is running. As it frequently happens that the head end and rear end of an American freight train are completely out of sight of each other for long periods of the journey, radio communication is essential.

Such a freight train may have its consist unchanged for a distance of 1,600 km (1,000 miles) or more, except that "helper" locomotives may have to be used on certain steeply graded sections. When this happens with very long and heavy trains that may require three or four diesel-electric units of 3,000 hp continuously at the head end, the helper units are cut in intermediately, at about the half-way point of the total train. In certain cases the "helper" consists of another three or four locomotives, and is under radio control from the driver of the lead units. However, if the section of severe grade is relatively short, the "helper" may be manned by local enginemen. The cutting in of the "helper" involves stopping, dividing the train, and recoupling.

Above Chicago yards showing a wide variety of box cars in the foreground, with piggyback trailers ready for loading in the middle distance, and beyond such trailers loaded up. At the top of the picture cars are seen loaded on to multiple-storey car transporters. This scene gives a good impression of the complexity and scale involved in modern classification operations.
Left Garratt pulling freight train in East Africa.

The great classification yards

The location of some of the great classification yards of North America shows the philosophy of modern freight train operation on the grand scale. On Canadian Pacific Rail there is Alyth, for example, just to the east of Calgary, which lies at the intersection of two major routes with the transcontinental main line to Vancouver. The line from the south into Calgary serves a large group of prairie stations and brings in a vast amount of wheat traffic, while that to the north goes to Edmonton and the mineral-bearing regions of north Alberta. There is Conrail's great Conway Yard west of Pittsburgh serving an enormous concentration area of heavy industrial traffic (see page 80). Out in the west, in addition to Barstow, the Southern Pacific has a very finely equipped modern yard at Colton, near Los Angeles, a concentration and classification point for north, south and east directions, as well as for terminal traffic in Los Angeles itself.

The basic activity in a modern mechanized classification yard is simple. A train from some distant starting point is brought into one of the receiving tracks, and then its individual cars have to be sorted and routed into one of about 30 classification sidings, each of which collects traffic for one destination. The sorting is often done in one continuous propelling movement over an intervening "hump." It is a continuous flow operation, in which many divergent factors have to be taken into account in order to maintain smooth operation.

The makeup of a train arriving in a big yard is checked by a photoelectric scanner as it comes in, and this information is transmitted automatically to a main computer, which stores all the information concerning type of car, destination and ownership. This is because in North America there is a great number of individual, privately owned railways whose cars are pooled for certain traffics, and which can claim distance rates for use by other companies. The mechanization in a modern classification yard applies to the degree of braking applied to the cars as they roll down from the hump. The cars for different destinations have to be uncoupled by men called "pin-pullers" as they pass toward the crest of the hump, and then rolling down the steep grade beyond they separate sufficiently for the switches to be thrown between successive cars, or groups of cars coupled together, known as cuts.

Once the propelling movement starts from one of the receiving tracks, with a locomotive pushing from the rear end, the computer in the main control tower takes charge. It sets the switches according to the route required for each cut, and applies braking to the cars according to a bank of information it has collected. The extent to which a cut

Barstow yard looking over control tower, showing the desert conditions in which the yard was constructed. An extensive tree-planting program will change the landscape completely in a few years' time.

Trains approach Barstow from three different directions. Those from northern and southern California enter straight into the receiving yard, while those from the east are directed via the hump area and enter at the opposite end.

BARSTOW YARD

to San Francisco · Mojave

Mojave Desert

San Fernando

to N. East and S. East

Los Angeles · San Bernardino

Pacific Ocean

Receiving yard
The capacity of the receiving yard allows trains to arrive from all directions without disrupting operations in the yard. All trains enter this yard on arrival from where incoming locomotives move to the diesel service area for necessary attention. The receiving yard contains ten tracks.

Departure yard
Following the sorting of vehicles in the classification yard, cuts of cars are moved to the departure yard to be assembled into trains. The capacity here of nine tracks, which can accommodate about 1,370 cars, allows the formation of three trains, one each to northern and southern California and one eastbound. The neighboring through train inspection yard is for the examination of trains not requiring processing at Barstow.

1 Locomotive washing plant
2 Administrative office building
3 Diesel service building
4 Supervisor's tower
5 Car repair
6 Hump master's tower
7 Mechanical temperature control building
8 Hump conductor's building
9 Caboose service building
10 Mini-hump control building
11 Bowl master's office

View of Barstow yard as seen from hill in picture, top left.

○ Receiving yard
○ Classification yard
○ Local yard
○ Departure yard
○ Diesel service area
○ Caboose service area
○ Freight car repair
○ Through train inspection yard
○ Mini-hump
• Retarders

Classification yard
After trains in the receiving yard have been inspected and routes checked with the control office, they are shoved over the crest of the hump for entry to the classification yard. At the hump a total of three on-line computers have already stored information about all cars, and following individual uncoupling, vehicles are guided into any one of 44 tracks by a system of computer controlled switches and braking devices. Four tracks are provided for any resorting of stock. The classification yard has the capacity for over 2,000 vehicles.

Left Barstow yard with hump in the foreground. Sets of retarders can be clearly seen.

requires braking will depend upon how much space is available in the classification siding to which it is routed; this the computer "knows" from information constantly collected from the track itself. Then the nature of the route leading into that siding has to be considered: some have more curves on the way than others. The direction and strength of the wind must also be taken into account, because a strong adverse wind can seriously retard the running of a large box car. Lastly there is what is termed the "rollability" of the car – whether it is a good or a bad runner. This cannot be determined before it actually begins to run by gravity down the hump. But a mechanism in the track is available to measure this characteristic, calculations being made instantly and fed into the main computer in time for account of the rollability to be taken in applying brake pressure. The brakes, although electronically or hydraulically controlled, apply purely mechanical pressure by gripping the wheels of a car as it makes its way through the yard.

While the great classification yards are focal points of concentrated activity in freight train handling, no less vital are the centers of overall scrutiny and direction. At the headquarters of the Southern Railway System in Atlanta, Georgia, can be seen, on remotely controlled illuminated track diagrams, the whereabouts of every train on this far-flung railway network, extending on its long western and

northgoing main lines from New Orleans, Memphis and Cincinnati, around its central complex in Alabama and Georgia to its east coast extensions into Florida, the Carolinas and northward to Washington, DC – an extraordinary panorama of a railway on the move. Each dispatcher in charge of a particular part of this wide-ranging area is able to tell at once the contents and ultimate destination of every freight train under his control. There is, however, one important outcome of this remote supervision. There are few men along the actual lines to scrutinize the passage of trains, and with the freight trains so long it is impossible for either the engineer or the caboose crew to see what is happening all along the train. There is the possibility of journal boxes overheating, which if unattended could deteriorate to the point of collapse and lead to derailment of the car. Accordingly a compre-hensive program of installing "hot-box detectors" has been carried out on American railways. On the extensive Southern Pacific, for example, whose lines extend westward from New Orleans just north of the Mexican border and up the Pacific coast to Portland, Oregon, and includes such busy centers as Los Angeles and San Francisco, there are no fewer than 448 locations fitted with hot-box detectors, which give warning to train crews and dispatching offices of journal boxes running hotter than at normal conditions.

The Conrail experiment

The Consolidated Rail Corporation (Conrail) is a private, profit-making corporation established in the USA by the Regional Rail Reorganization Act of 1973, chartered in the Commonwealth of Pennsylvania, and is composed of portions of six bankrupt railways, namely the Penn Central, the Central of New Jersey, the Lehigh Valley, the Lehigh and Hudson River, the Erie Lackawanna, and the Reading. It began operations as Conrail on April 1, 1976. Of the constituents, Penn Central was by far the largest and was itself the product of a huge merger in 1968 between the Pennsylvania and the New York Central railways. The New York, New Haven and Hartford was subsequently included in Penn Central. The reasons for the decline and eventual bankruptcy of all these companies was ascribed to the introduction of competitive modes of transport, supported in part by large government financial resources. This led to a heavy fall in railway business, and a decline in railway capital resources.

Now, with access to government investment funds of up to $2,000 million to launch operations and achieve the goal of long-term viability, Conrail is rebuilding on a massive scale. It operates some 27,200 km (17,000 miles) of route, of which Penn Central contributed more than 20,800 km (13,000 miles). A great program of track improvement is in progress to enable speed of trains to be restored to the high standards achieved in the heyday of all the constituent companies, which include some of the most famous names in American railway history. The system network covers all the states in the northeast corridor, from Washington to Boston, and intensively those of Pennsylvania, Ohio and Indiana, with westward penetrations into Illinois and northward into Michigan. It operates 4,500 diesel locomotives, and 148 electrics, and runs an average of 1,500 freight trains daily, using more than 151,000 freight cars. There are now eight operating regions, with headquarters situated in New Haven, New York, Philadelphia, Pittsburgh, Newark, Detroit, Chicago and Indianapolis.

Above Lackawanna locomotive, a one-time constituent company of Conrail.

The USA's Consolidated Rail Corporation, or Conrail, began operation on 1 April 1976, with the emblem, *left*, on its rolling stock.

Conrail train.

Conrail locomotive.

Great Routes

Through the Alpine fortress 1

The first proposals for a great railway under the Alps were made in 1848, for a connection between the Italian province of Piedmont and the French one of Savoy. But the times were not propitious, with war between Austria and Italy impending. It was not until 13 years later, under the joint efforts of Count Camillo Cavour, of Garibaldi, and of King Victor Emmanuel of Sardinia, that the project of a tunnel from Modane to Bardonecchia under the Mont Cenis pass, was revived. At first the idea was made light of, but when it was appreciated that the promoters were in earnest, much was written of the dangers to be incurred – of the folly of tampering with nature to the extent of driving a tunnel through "the bosom of the mighty fortress," as one English newspaper expressed it. But the Italian engineers persevered and succeeded. It was a task without precedent. In the ordinary way, with tunnel construction as pioneered by George Stephenson and others, it was the practice to sink a number of intermediate shafts to provide both additional access and a surface check on the alignment; but nothing of the kind was possible at the Mont Cenis, where the line passed beneath a mountain 3,500 m (11,500 ft) high.

To secure bearings for the direction of the bores that were to begin at Modane on the French side, and at Bardonecchia on the Italian, it was necessary to use the process known in surveying as indirect triangulation. A geometrical linkup had to be obtained between the lines of entry at the two portals, and this was obtained by taking a succession of bearings up the valley of the Maurienne, high above Modane, over the Mont Cenis pass, and then along the southern side of the pass to Bardonecchia. The survey was conducted with marvelous accuracy, despite the fact that the geometrical link between the two ends was some 64 km (40 miles) long through Alpine mountain country. The Mont Cenis route was constructed as a first-class main line, with double track throughout, and the main tunnel is

The Alpine tunnels are all close together: only the Mont Cenis is not contained on the main map, *right*. It lies between Lyon and Turin (*below*); its northern portal is at Mondane.

terrain over 1,000 m (3,280 ft) shown in brown

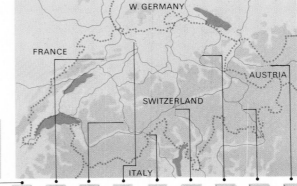

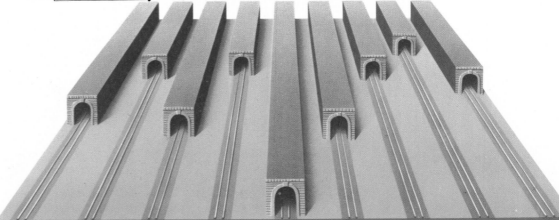

The Alpine tunnels are the world's most impressive group. However, tunneling now in progress in Japan will dislodge the Simplon from its position as the world's longest: that between the islands of Honshu and Hokkaido will be one of 54 km (33.5 miles) long. The diagram, *below*, shows the first Simplon Tunnel opened: a second driven parallel to it and opened in 1922 is slightly longer.

Mont Cenis	Grenchenberg	Lötschberg	Hauenstein	Simplon I	Gotthard	Ricken	Albula	Arlberg
13.590 km	8.578 km	14.415 km	8.134 km	19.803 km	14.998 km	8.603 km	5.865 km	10.250 km
8.445 mls	*5.330 mls*	*8.957 mls*	*5.054 mls*	*12.306 mls*	*9.320 mls*	*5.346 mls*	*3.645 mls*	*6.369 mls*
open 1871	open 1915	open 1913	open 1916	open 1906	open 1882	open 1910	open 1906	open 1884

An early boring machine used in Alpine tunneling.

13.6 km (8.5 miles) long. The changeover from French to Italian operation of the trains takes place at Modane, so that operation through the tunnel is entirely Italian. The tunnel is probably unique among the world's great pioneer engineering projects in that the time of construction was very much overestimated. When the work was started in 1857, such was the original nature of the undertaking, and the unknown conditions in those mountains into which the engineers were boring, that it was expected the 13.6 km length would not be completed in less than 25 years. Actually it would seem that the engineers were a little fortunate in not meeting any undue hazards. The final breakthrough, when the parties working from Modane and Bardonecchia met on Christmas Day 1870, received less notice than it might otherwise have had, because the newspapers at that time were full of dramatic stories of the Prussian siege of Paris that had followed the catastrophic military defeats suffered by France in the early stages of the Franco-Prussian War of 1870–71. The completion of the Mont Cenis Tunnel, in 1871, provided a through route from Paris to Turin, and thence to Genoa, and it is the route followed by the Rome Express of today. The experience gained by the Italian engineers in carrying out the work on the tunnel was of immense importance when the time came for even longer tunneling projects.

The second great Alpine tunnel was the Gotthard, of which the spiral alignments leading to it are described on

Above Summit of the Gotthard line. *Below left and right* Early prints of the Gotthard railway: left, the Rohrbach viaduct; right, the bridge and tunnel at Wassen.

page 19. The Gotthard Tunnel opened an important new international main line from Germany through Switzerland into Italy, leading direct to Milan. It was possible by using the Eastern Railway of France, to Belfort and Basel, to travel from Paris to Milan via the Gotthard Tunnel. But it was a rather roundabout route, and after the war of 1870–71 one could well imagine that French travelers would wish to avoid passing through German territory if possible, and so the great project of the Simplon Tunnel was launched. This was a route of great historic interest. In 1805 Napoleon had ordered the construction of a "diligence" road over the Simplon Pass into Italy, and a great triumphal arch was erected in Milan to celebrate the completion of the work. The tunnel, which was projected in the 1890s, was to be a continuation of the Jura-Simplon Railway, which ran along the north shore of Lake Geneva, from Lausanne and then up the Rhône valley to Brig. It would provide a remarkable short route from the Paris, Lyon and Mediterranean line to northern Italy.

Work began simultaneously at the two ends, near Brig in the Rhône valley, and at Iselle. Unlike the Gotthard the Simplon Tunnel marked the crossing of the international frontier. The grade was rising on a moderate inclination from each end to a summit point near the middle of the tunnel, and almost exactly below the frontier, which is at the head of the Simplon Pass. It was originally intended that the line would be worked with steam locomotives, and because of the single-line bore of the main tunnel this bore was made very large: 5.9 m (19 ft 6 in) high and of a maximum width of 4.9 m (16 ft 5 in). Every precaution was taken in design to try to ensure there should be no trouble from a concentration of exhaust fumes in a very small space. At first all went well – so well that there were high hopes of the tunnel being completed in far less than the estimated time. Then troubles began to grow. In the workings from the Swiss side the temperature rose to almost unbearable heights, and at a point about 8 km (5 miles) in, it rose to 53°C (127°F). It was found that the only way to keep conditions fit for men to work in was to bring in ice-cold water and spray it on to the rocks. Once these natural hazards were mastered the contractors introduced round-the-clock working in three shifts to speed up the operation, and eventually in February 1905, more than a year later than the time originally anticipated, the breakthrough between the Swiss and Italian teams was effected. But more than a year was to pass before the tunnel was completed and train services began. The actual date of opening to traffic was May 30, 1906, but on one track only. So advantageous was the shortened route from France to Italy that very soon the single-line section was proving a bottleneck, and plans were prepared for enlarging the pilot tunnel to full size. The second tunnel was opened for traffic in December 1921.

The fourth of the great main line Alpine tunnels was the Lötschberg. In view of the forthcoming opening of the first bore of the Simplon the need was expressed for a main north-south line from central Switzerland to link up with the Jura-Simplon line and provide yet another direct connection into Italy. So the Bern-Lötschberg-Simplon Railway was projected, and to reach Brig from Bern and the beautiful shores of the Lake of Thun the line would have to be carried through the heart of the Bernese Oberland. The great tunnel at the summit, just over 14 km (9 miles) long, was to be carried beneath the lofty peaks of the Balmhorn and the Altels, but one of the great initial difficulties was that, unlike the Mont Cenis, the Gotthard and the Simplon, the routes to the tunnel entrances did not lie on any existing highways. The Lonza gorge, leading to the south portal at Goppenstein, is as desolate a ravine as could be imagined, and subject to avalanches. Due to a

The northern portal of the Simplon tunnel.

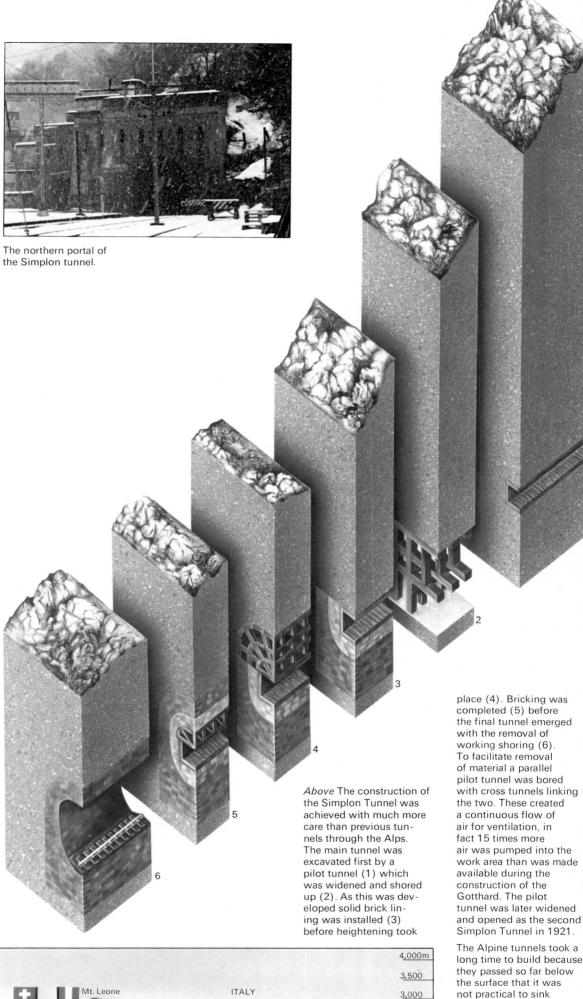

Above The construction of the Simplon Tunnel was achieved with much more care than previous tunnels through the Alps. The main tunnel was excavated first by a pilot tunnel (1) which was widened and shored up (2). As this was developed solid brick lining was installed (3) before heightening took place (4). Bricking was completed (5) before the final tunnel emerged with the removal of working shoring (6). To facilitate removal of material a parallel pilot tunnel was bored with cross tunnels linking the two. These created a continuous flow of air for ventilation, in fact 15 times more air was pumped into the work area than was made available during the construction of the Gotthard. The pilot tunnel was later widened and opened as the second Simplon Tunnel in 1921.

The Alpine tunnels took a long time to build because they passed so far below the surface that it was not practical to sink shafts into the line of the tunnel to provide extra working faces. The Simplon is 2,100 m (6,890 ft) below the surface at one point. It was initiated in 1898, and completed only in 1906.

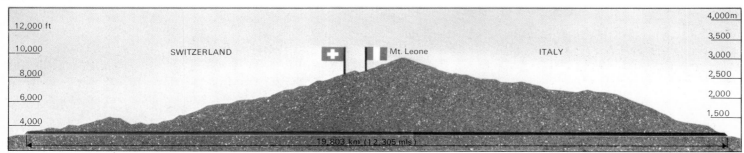

SWITZERLAND   Mt. Leone   ITALY

12,000 ft   4,000m
10,000   3,500
8,000   3,000
6,000   2,500
4,000   2,000
  1,500

19.803 km (12.305 mls)

Through the Alpine fortress 11

series of disasters, involving much loss of life (see page 19), the route from the Kandersteg end had to be diverted. In July 1913 the Lötschberg line was completed and opened.

The meter gauge Rhaetian Railway includes some extraordinary spiral and tunneling locations as it climbs up the Albula valley, making its way on a continuous ascent of 3.4 percent to its summit point in the Albula Tunnel. From there it descends into the Upper Engadine to serve the famous Alpine resorts of St Moritz and Pontresina. Looking down on the railway from the heights above Bergün one sees an extraordinary location that looks more like the efforts of some skillful model railway enthusiast, with little space at his disposal but anxious to include as many spirals, viaducts and tunnels as he could into the minimum space. Traveling in the smart electric trains of the Rhaetian Railway one loses all sense of direction when negotiating such a stretch, while from the privileged viewpoint of the locomotive cab the succession of curves, high viaducts and tunnels, negotiated at a surprisingly high speed, is simply breathtaking. The stone viaducts are works of art, and adorn rather than disfigure the magnificent scenery; some idea of the skill in engineering this particular location can be gathered from the gain in vertical height of 416 m (1,365 ft) in a direct distance of 6 km (4 miles). This distance, if climbed directly, would mean a grade of 6.6 percent, but by means of the spirals and reversals of direction the actual grade is 3.4 percent. The speed is maintained at around 48–56 km/h (30–35 mph). The civil engineering and the maintenance of the track in these spectacular locations is of the highest order and the riding of the coaches so smooth that, even when rounding curves on the edge of near-vertical precipices, there is no sensation of danger – only of wonder.

Below Two modern electric Swiss trains in a mountain station.

Above Spiral tunnels on the Gotthard line, one of the lines on which these tunnels were pioneered.

Most of the Alpine lines were originally worked by steam, including the Rhaetian Railway, owners of the Albula line and one-time owners of the 1902 0-4-4-0 Mallet type tank engine, *below left*. In only 6 km (4 miles) as the crow flies, the Albula line of the

Rhaetian Railway climbs 416 m (1,365 ft). The grade has been kept to a manageable 3.4 percent by a series of spiral tunnels. In the diagram, *right*, the mountainside has been cut away to show how the line loops back on itself when climbing to the summit tunnel from the south.

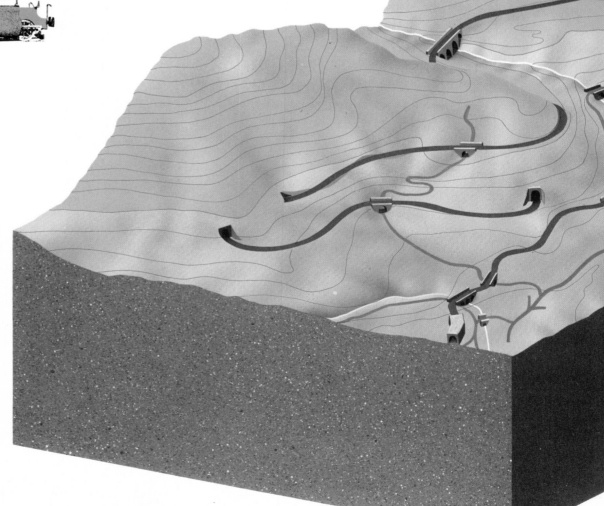

meters	feet
2300	7546
2100	6890
1900	6233
1700	5577
1500	4921

Furka Oberlap train, on Grengiols viaduct.

The ARB rack railway, Switzerland.

Trans-Europe Expresses

It was in 1957 that the idea was conceived among the original six countries of the European Economic Community, and Switzerland, of a network of fast intercity trains providing comfortable accommodation for businessmen and other regular travelers. The idea was to combat the loss of railway travel to air services and to provide out-and-home journeys on the same day, with time for business at the further destination. It has since been extended considerably to include trains of the same standard running into Austria, Denmark and Spain. On some routes, as between Paris and Brussels, Amsterdam and Munich, Paris and Hamburg, there is more than one train in each direction, though in the case of the longer journeys such as Hanover-Vienna by the Prinz Eugen or Paris-Venice by Le Cisalpin, it is not possible to apply the original out-and-home concept. All the Trans-Europe Expresses (TEE) are so named, and some trains that were already well established on their own account have been designated TEE by the standard of their accommodation, speed and service. Such trains are the French Mistral (Paris-Nice); the Rheingold (Netherlands-Germany-Switzerland); and the Étoile du Nord (Amsterdam-Paris). All TEE trains are first-class only and require a special supplement, according to the distance traveled. On some trains it is necessary to specify at the time of booking the type of meal required, because this determines the section of the train where the passenger's reserved seat would be allocated.

Six types of TEE train

The first are operated jointly by the French and Belgian railways, and consists of six- to twelve-car trains, according to traffic requirements, hauled by electric locomotives. The passenger accommodation is in compartments and open lounges, and meals are served at the passengers' own seats. When booking seats it is necessary to state whether meals are required. The Étoile du Nord is made up of Pullman-type stock. The load is usually considerably increased by extra coaches at Brussels, for the nonstop run to Paris. The second type of TEE train is that of the German Federal Railways and is known as the Rheingold type. The accommodation varies according to route, with three to nine cars in compartments and open saloons, and meals are served in a separate 42-seat dining car. Some trains in this category are locomotive hauled, as with the Rheingold itself, while others, like the Parsifal, between Paris and Hamburg, via Cologne, are unit trains with power units at each end. The third category of TEE train includes, among others, the French 200 km/h (125 mph) flyers Aquitaine, L'Étendard and Le Capitole. The accommodation ranges from seven to nine cars, with separate 42-seat dining cars. The Cisalpin, running through to Venice, includes some Swiss coaches in its formation. The trains in the third group are electrically hauled except for L'Arbalete, from Paris to Zürich, which takes the eastern region line through France, via Troyes, and is diesel hauled as far as Basel.

The fourth group of TEE trains includes only the "heavyweights" of the PLM route in France, the Mistral and the Rhodanien. Both are specified as providing 470 seats in 14 cars; meals are served in the open saloon-type cars, or in a separate restaurant. Furthermore, the Paris-Nice section of the Mistral includes a bookstall, bar and hairdressing salon. The Mistral, with a nine-hour run between Paris and Nice, is an afternoon train in each direction, but the Rhodanien, leaving Marseille at 7:10 a.m., provides nearly four hours in Paris (1:44 to 5:37 p.m.), with the return train arriving in Marseille just after midnight. These trains with their great weight provide some of the most interesting and severe locomotive duties to be found anywhere in the world at the present time. The Rhodanien runs the 507 km (317 miles) between Paris and Lyon nonstop, in each direction, in 223 min southbound, and 226 min northbound, at respective average speeds of 136.5 and 134.7 km/h (85.3 and 84.2 mph). The Mistral calls additionally at Dijon and does the 312 km (195 miles) from Paris (Lyon) in 139 min southbound, and 140 min northbound. The former entails an average speed of 134 km/h (84 mph). Taking into account the slow running in the suburbs of Paris, both the Mistral and the Rhodanien must run at 160 km/h (100 mph) for most of the way, and on the long southward

Left Göschenen station, north entrance to the Gotthard Tunnel.

Above TEE express leaving Bozen-Brenner tunnel in Italy.

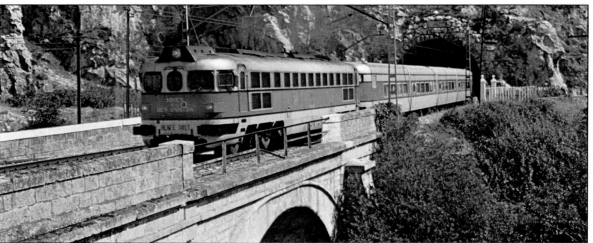

Above Talgo train, Pancarbo, Spain.

Below TEE express at San Remo, Italy.

climb into the Côte d'Or mountains to the summit at Blaisy-Bas tunnel, south of Dijon, the speed is not usually much below 152 km/h (95 mph).

The fifth group of TEE trains includes those operated by the Swiss Federal Railways, which are five-car unit train sets, electrically worked, and have seating for 168 passengers, in open lounges, with a separate dining car. One of these is the Gottardo, between Basel and Genoa, running nonstop over the highly picturesque Gotthard line between Zürich and Lugano. This train arrives in Genoa with just enough turnaround time for the same trainset to make the return journey. But a businessman can leave Zürich at 8:47 a.m., reach Milan at 1:35 p.m., and have more than four hours in this latter city before returning at 6:00 p.m., to reach Zürich at 8:57 p.m. The other TEE trains in the fifth group run between Brussels and Zürich via Luxembourg, Strasbourg and Basel. During the winter months the Iris leaves Brussels at 7:01 a.m. and reaches Zürich at 1:59 p.m. The return time is 3:42 p.m. and arrival at 10:39 p.m. The complementary service is that of the Edelweiss, leaving Zürich at 6:59 a.m., and departing from Brussels on the return run at 4:11 p.m.

The sixth group is that operated by the Italian State Railways, and includes some very interesting trains, like the Settebello, described on pages 118–119. These are electrically operated and have accommodation varying between four and eight cars, according to service. There are two other trains on the Milan-Rome line in addition to the Settebello: the Ambrosiano and the Vesuvio, which runs through to Naples. Then there is the Lemano, working between Milan and Geneva, which is named for its long run beside Lac Leman (Lake Geneva) and the Ligurian Sea. This train runs between Milan and Avignon, via Genoa, the Ligurian Riviera, the Côte d'Azur and Marseille. It is a long run, of more than 7 hr, but it is interesting as providing connection at Avignon with another TEE, the Catalan-Talgo, which runs between Geneva and Barcelona. This one is unique among the TEE trains because it is made up of the special Talgo type of coach, each of which seats only 17 passengers in an open lounge. There are nine of these cars, and meals are served in a separate 48-seat dining car. On this service the coach wheel sets are adjusted at Cerbère from the French gauge to the Spanish, in each direction. The full journey is a long one, taking 9½ hr, traveling via Lyon, Avignon and Narbonne, and, after crossing the frontier between Cerbère and Port Bou, via Gerona in Spain.

TEE ferry

One other TEE requires particular mention, namely the Merkur, between Copenhagen and Stuttgart. This is the only train, so far, in which transport by ferry is involved at one stage. The train leaves Copenhagen at 9:45 a.m., but does not reach Hamburg until 2:27 p.m. Afterward the train calls at many well-known German industrial centers, including Bremen, Dortmund, Essen, Düsseldorf, Cologne, Koblenz, Mainz, and Mannheim finally reaching Stuttgart at 10:58 p.m. The cars on this service are of the German Federal Railways type.

TEE between Weinberger and Rhine, Germany.

1	Étoile du Nord	**23**	Van Beethoven
2	Ile de France	**24**	Rheingold
3	Rubens	**25**	Erasmus
4	Oiseau Bleu	**26**	Adriatico
5	Brabant	**27**	Molière
6	Memling	**28**	Rembrandt
7	Aquitaine	**29**	Helvetia
8	L'Étendard	**30**	Roland
9	Le Capitole	**31**	Prinz Eugen
10	Le Mistral	**32**	Gottardo
11	Le Rhodanien	**33**	Mediolanum
12	Le Cisalpin	**34**	Blauer Enzian
13	L'Arbalète	**35**	Settebello
14	Stanislas	**36**	Ambrosiano
15	Kléber	**37**	Vesuvio
16	Parsifal	**38**	Merkur
17	Catalan-Talgo	**39**	Cycnus
18	Ligure		
19	Saphir		
20	Edelweiss		
21	Iris		
22	Lemano		

The network of TEE trains consists of 39 differently named expresses, working over 31 different routes. The routes with more than one train are: Brussels–Paris, with 4; Brussels–Strasbourg–Zürich, with 2; and Milan–Rome, also with 2.

The great British route: London to Glasgow

Known as the West Coast main line, the 642.4 km (401.5 mile) section from London (Euston) to Glasgow is one of the most historic in Great Britain. It includes major lengths of two great pioneer railways, the London and Birmingham, built by Robert Stephenson, and the Grand Junction, built by Joseph Locke. North of Lancaster it includes two of the earliest fast running main lines built through mountain country, the Lancaster and Carlisle, passing through the eastern flanks of the English Lakeland mountains, and then the Caledonian, continuing the line to Glasgow. Both these great routes were engineered by Joseph Locke. An important cutoff link in England was the Trent Valley line, from Rugby to Stafford, on which through trains to the north bypassed the complicated area around Birmingham. Always a very busy main line, it was until January 1923 worked by two great railways in partnership, the London and North Western, in England, and the Caledonian north of Carlisle. From 1923 they were amalgamated into the London Midland and Scottish Railway, and then became separated again at the time of nationalization of the British Railways in 1948 into the London Midland and the Scottish Regions of the new organization.

The heritage was a diverse one. When the London and Birmingham Railway was built the capacity of steam locomotives was very limited. Robert Stephenson, as a designer and manufacturer, was well aware of this and in

planning the line he decided that the steepest grade should be 0.3 percent. Although the country in the south of England did not involve crossing any mountain ranges, there were chalk escarpments on the north side of the Chiltern Hills, a northeastern extension of the Cotswold limestone at Blisworth and the Kilsby Ridge. To avoid steep grades, Stephenson had to excavate, by hand, some tremendous cuttings and the tunnel under the Kilsby Ridge was one of the most troublesome works on the line. But the result was a magnificent route over which heavy loads could be operated with relatively small locomotives. Indeed, the rapid increase in the volume of traffic became an embarrassment, and before the nineteenth century was out two additional 96 km (60 mile) running tracks had to be laid. Most of this Trent Valley line is quadruple tracked, as is the line north of Stafford as far as Weaver Junction, 280 km (175 miles) north of London.

The London and North Western, and the Caledonian Railways were regarded as the premier lines of England and Scotland, respectively. They had the largest annual revenues, and their preeminence was shown indirectly on their coats of arms. The LNWR adopted "Britannia" herself, while the Caledonian took the Royal Arms of Scotland. The West Coast main line was also the principal artery of mail traffic between London and the North, as well as to Ireland via Holyhead, and it was known as the Royal Mail Route. Trains carrying traveling post offices from many parts of Great Britain fed into the postal trains of the West Coast main line at Tamworth, Crewe, Preston and Carlisle. Both companies prided themselves on their punctuality of running. The nineteenth-century chairman of the LNWR, Sir Richard Moon, always said that the publication of a schedule was the promise of an English gentleman and should be honored as such. The prosperity

of the NNWR was continually enhanced and the company set toward insuring the future by allocating large proportions of the profits toward improvements on the line, such as new signaling, classification yards and improved junction layouts.

It has never been a purely Anglo-Scottish route. In fact, the very intensity of the present-day traffic and the justification for the great modernization works carried out on it in recent years lie in the number of important centers that are served from its main line. Over the most southerly 131 km (82 miles), between London and Rugby, there are separate services to Birmingham and Wolverhampton, to Liverpool, to Manchester, to North Wales, and over the Irish Mail route to Holyhead, to Blackpool and the Fylde coast, and to west Cumbria – all these in addition to the Anglo-Scottish services, which again are quite separate. The section between Euston and Rugby, where Birmingham trains diverge, is without question the most intensively used section of railway in the world. When the great modernization plan for British Railways was launched in 1955, it was not surprising that this line was chosen for conversion to electric power, together with the northward continuation to Liverpool and Manchester and the main line network through Birmingham and Wolverhampton. Experience elsewhere in the world had shown that electrification of railways always seemed to attract new business, what is sometimes called "the sparks effect," and the modernization plan as it was developed provided for considerably more elaborate service than previously, and a great increase in scheduled speed. Whereas in steam and diesel days the hallmark of a fast express was a start-to-stop average speed of 96–105 km/h (60–65 mph), the new services were planned to raise that speed to 130 km/h (80 mph).

With many more trains, and higher speeds, the track and all the equipment obviously had to be strongly upgraded. The line itself was virtually rebuilt, putting in new rails, continuously welded, with the latest type of

reinforced concrete cross-ties, and extra deep granite ballast. The system of electrification chosen was 25,000 volts, alternating current, at the commercial frequency of 50 cycles per second, with overhead line current pickup. The standard of speed on the open line for express passenger was set at 160 km/h (100 mph), although when the line was first brought into service in 1966 there were many places, junctions, curves and such like, where reductions were necessary. Some of these restrictions have now been removed by the completion of realignment schemes. Color light multiple-aspect signaling was installed throughout.

The task of carrying out the work of modernization was immense, because it all had to be done while operating what was even then one of the busiest railways in the world. Numerous temporary speed restrictions had to be enforced while track was renewed. The actual work of relaying was done mostly at weekends, but during the preparation for such work, and during the consolidation afterward, long stretches of line at a time had to be covered at 50 km/h (30 mph) or less. Late running was frequent, and at a time when train times were at their best scarcely competitive with a fast car, let alone with internal airlines, there was an acute danger that traffic might be lost, and once lost difficult to regain. To travelers by train there was ample evidence that a great amount of work was in progress, with installation of poles for carrying overhead

Far left Night electric Scot, British Rail.
Above Intercity express departs from London, Euston.

The electrification of the London (Euston) line through to Glasgow, largely carried out in the 1960s, marked a considerable step forward in the history of Britain's railways. Stages in electrification meant a progressive reduction of time to make the route competitive with the air shuttle between the two cities. Further improvement will come with the introduction of the Advanced Passenger Train.

The process of electrification used on the London to Glasgow route.

Left to right:
Raising bridges to make room for overhead wires.

Digging a new track base.

Digging holes for the erection of metal poles to hold the catenary system.

Pouring cement into the holes from a special cement train, equipped with a number of mixers.

Raising catenary poles for bolting on to the concrete base.

Erecting new four-aspect colored light signals.

Erecting the overhead wiring, slung from the catenary poles. Performed from the flat roofs of special cars.

Running the test train to check proper circuitry.

The opening of the line for high-speed running using electric motive power. When the line first opened between Crewe and London there was an immediate saving of 30% on the original journey time.

wires and the rebuilding of stations. Then section by section the electrification was completed: Manchester to Crewe first, then southward to Nuneaton; a phenomenal change came over the train running in the almost uncanny acceleration from a stop, and in the smoothness of travel at high speed. The management of the London Midland Region was, however, anxious that the improved service on the electrified line should be reflected in the important connecting services that must remain for some time diesel operated, and an intricate pattern of cross-country connections was devised, centered upon Birmingham, whereby trains from the southwest of England and South Wales connected by cross-platform interchange with trains to the northwest and Scotland. No longer were long waits for connections to be tolerated, or missed connections through late running. New Street station, Birmingham, was to be the focal point of the entire service, with the direct Liverpool, Manchester and Scottish trains using the Trent Valley line, and bypassing Birmingham was so timed that on the critical London–Rugby section their running fitted in with London–Birmingham trains involved in the New Street connectional pattern.

The continuation of the electrified system northward to

Carlisle and Glasgow was a much discussed, and somewhat delayed, project. Although the through train services from London to the Scottish cities were joined north of Preston by those from Liverpool and Manchester, there was not the same density of passenger traffic as on the line south of Crewe, and there was at first some difficulty in establishing financial justification for the capital outlay. But with electric operation there was the possibility of spectacular acceleration of service on the mountain grades of the north country. Between Carnforth, on Morecambe Bay, and Shap Summit, for example, the line rises 270 m (885 ft) in 50 km (31.5 miles), and with heavy trains in preelectrification days one could not expect to cover that distance in much less than 35 min. But the powerful electric locomotives were able to climb a 1.3 percent grade at 145 km/h (90 mph) with a 12-car train, and it has been possible to schedule a point-to-point time of 22 min up that long climb, an average speed of 137 km/h (85 mph). The curves in places preclude maximum speeds, but today the 145 km (90 miles) between Preston and Carlisle are regularly run in less than 65 min, start to stop.

The acceleration is the same in Scotland where the formidable Beattock Bank has to be climbed – 16 km

(10 miles) at an inclination of 1.3 percent. As a result of electrification, passenger train speeds north of Preston are 160 km/h (100 mph) wherever the track permits, except on the steepest grades. But no less important is the manner in which the very heavy night freight trains are operated. The basic speed for these is 120 km/h (75 mph), and with the maximum tonnage freightliners, carrying 60 containers on 20 flat cars (three on each), a pair of electric locomotives are used in order to maintain the high speed required uphill, which is little below 120 km/h (75 mph), on a 1 percent grade.

With electric locomotives of 5,000 hp and trains of 12 modern air-conditioned cars, the time over the 642 km (401.5 miles) between London and Glasgow is 5 hr, an average of 130 km/h (80 mph) including one stop, or a few minutes longer on trains that make more than one intermediate stop. It is planned to introduce the Advanced Passenger Train on to this route, which through its tilting feature will allow the curves as at present engineered to be taken at considerably higher speed. With the APT sets in operation it is expected that the overall time between London (Euston) and Glasgow will be reduced to 4 hr, an average from start to stop of 160 km/h (100 mph).

Rail versus air: a real contest

In the early 1960s there was much talk in the advanced countries of the world that railways had become obsolete, except for crowded and unattractive commuter areas, where they would continue to compete with the increasingly congested road approaches to large cities. The experience of the great long-distance railways in the USA in losing practically all their high-class passenger business to airlines seemed a pointer to what could happen elsewhere. In Europe railways had taken a terrible beating in the Second World War and recovery at first was not rapid; and when the modernization plan for British Railways was first launched, there were some influential people who did not believe that any appreciable acceleration of service was either necessary or desirable: all that was needed was to get rid of steam power. Fortunately, wiser counsels prevailed, and as in France, and to a slightly lesser degree in West Germany and Italy, the cue has been taken from the astonishing success of the *Shinkansen* lines in Japan. In Britain, as in France, the target for intercity overall speed is being pressed to well above 130 km/h (80 mph). In both countries there are intermediate stages of lengthy intercity journeys from one intermediate station to another, booked at start-to-stop average speeds of more than 160 km/h (100 mph), with overall averages, including intermediate stops, of around 145 km/h (90 mph).

This tremendous upsurge in passenger train speed, coupled with on time performance, smoothness of running, and reliability in all but the most extreme of winter weather conditions, is definitely reversing the trend of travel habits in countries having the journey times at present prevailing in Europe. It is, however, not likely that any appreciable change will be seen in countries such as the USA, in which the distances are so great that air travel holds an advantage that not even the most dramatic of railway accelerations can surpass. But in Britain, with the regular journey time between London and Liverpool, and between London and Manchester, down to no more than $2\frac{1}{2}$ hr, that between London and Birmingham at $1\frac{1}{2}$ hr, and between London and Bristol less than $1\frac{1}{2}$ hr, the advantage is passing to the railways. The service is from city center to city center, avoiding all the delay and frustration of travel to the airports, inevitable delays at crowded air terminals and, with the dependence of air travel upon good weather conditions, the risk of cancellation or prolonged delay.

Fog and other conditions of bad visibility – hazards to air traffic – are no longer hindrances to the running of high-speed railway services. Color light signals themselves

By air
By rail

New York – Chicago
4 hrs 10 mins *air*
18 hrs *rail*

New York – Washington
2 hrs 40 mins *air*
4 hrs 6 mins *rail*

Paris – Lyon
3 hrs 30 mins *air*
3 hrs 45 mins *rail*
1 hr 45 mins in 1982

Center-to-center journey times are increased by air travel because of the time spent traveling to the airport; this can make rail travel very competitive though there is a limit as to how far such speed-ups will be possible.

Tokyo – Osaka
2 hrs *air*
3 hrs 10 mins *rail*

Hamburg – Zurich
3 hrs 20 mins *air*
9 hrs 24 mins *rail*

Hamburg – Munich
3 hrs 6 mins *air*
7 hrs 35 mins *rail*

London – Glasgow
3 hrs 10 mins *air*
5 hrs *rail*

Left Modern electric intercity train on Euston-Glasgow line.

have a far greater range than the oil lamps of the previously-used semaphores, but today most high-speed main lines in Europe have some form of cab signaling to supplement the trackside signals, and on lines such as that from London to Bristol, or the electrified line from Euston to the North, the continued incidence of audible signals in the cab as every color light signal is passed gives the necessary confidence to run at full speed. On the Japanese *Shinkansen* lines there are no trackside signals at all, and the visual indications in the cab, derived from an inductive linkup with electric currents flowing in the track circuits, display to the driver the speed at which he must run. If conditions on the line ahead require a reduction of speed, this is immediately shown on the display panel in front of the driver, and if within a short time he has not taken appropriate action the train brakes are applied. Such equipment serves to show that, even while the speed of passenger trains has increased to such an extent as to give

Above Munich station, a modern intercity train – clean, sleek, fast and exciting.

them a distinct advantage when competing with air travel over relatively short distances, increase in speed has not been achieved at the expense of the safety that is such a cherished attribute of rail travel the world over. Neither does the present level of passenger train speed represent the foreseeable limit. The Advanced Passenger Train will set newer limits, and the French are now building the new TGV line between Paris and Lyon, which will be the fastest railway in the world. It would appear therefore that in the battle for supremacy as a means of efficient transport, the railway networks of the world – with their intrinsic advantages – are still very much a force to be reckoned with.

Paris-Lyon: tomorrow's way

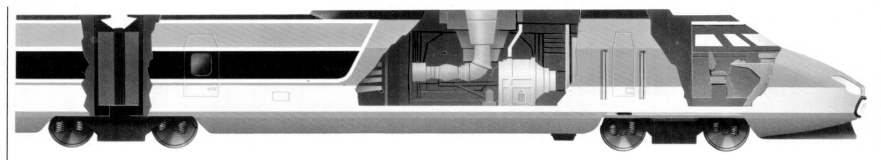

High tension power lines and Substation

Paris

Melun

Sens

St. Florentin

Montbard

Dijon

Chalon-sur-Saône

Macon

Lyon

The French National Railways have pressed the aim of high-speed services with a great deal of success on lines to the southwest, over the routes of the former Paris–Orléans–Midi Railway, now covering the 580km (360 miles) between Paris and Bordeaux nonstop in 3 hr 50 min, an average speed of 151 km/h (94 mph). The "rapides" on this route run at 200 km/h (125 mph) on favorable stretches of line, but it was not on this route that the most urgent need for development presented itself. It was the southeastern route from Paris to Dijon and Lyon that was becoming saturated, and by its nature it could not accommodate speeds of more than 160 km/h (100 mph). The decision was taken to build an entirely new line on which speeds of 300 km/h (185 mph) could be run. Like the British HST sets, and the Japanese *Shinkansen* trains, the new French *très grande vitesse* (TGV) sets will be entirely self-contained electric consists, and it is the intention that all day services leaving Paris from the Gare de Lyon will eventually be of this type. Although traveling to a diversity of destinations beyond the new line itself, the TGV trains will run at the new level of high speed while on the new line, and beyond it they will run at the maximum now permitted on the existing routes.

This arrangement will make possible some striking accelerations that will make it difficult for the airlines to compete. For example, the fastest train time from Paris to Lyon, 507 km (317 miles) is 3 hr 44 min, an average of 137 km/h (85 mph). By the TGV route the time will be 2 hours. Continuing beyond Lyon along the route to the south, the present and future times to Avignon are 5 hr 37 min and 3 hr 49 min, and to Marseille 6 hr 33 min and 4 hr 43 min. Over a distance of 856 km (535 miles) from Paris this represents an average speed of 180 km/h (113 mph), even though 349 km (218 miles) are over an ordinary not a TGV line. The new line now being built runs through very hilly country to the west of Dijon, but in order that TGV trains can reach Dijon and continue from there to the Swiss frontier at Vallorbe, and on to Lausanne, connection with the existing main line is made at Saint-Florentin. Similarly, connection is with the existing line at Mâcon for passage on to the line to Geneva and Turin via the Mont Cenis Tunnel. Again the service accelerations forecast are impressive, reducing the time from Paris to Lausanne from 4 hr 37 min to 3 hr 29 min, and to Geneva

The new Paris-Lyon line, which will open in 1982, is being built to cater for a high passenger traffic demand. It will link urban areas which contain 40% of the French population, and also provide a high-speed connection for international travelers. The new line conforms to very high standards consistent with speeds of 300 km/h (186 mph) by the new TGV series of motive power. This will reduce journey time over the route from the present 3 hr 44 min to just 2 hr.

from 5 hr 30 min to 3 hr 19 min. This latter saving of more than two hours on a journey of international importance will be of great advantage to a large number of rail users.

The new line does not actually enter Paris, but begins at a junction with the existing line at Courbs la Ville. South of that station progress will then be so swift that passengers will see little of the intervening country, and its place among the great railway routes of the world will be based solely on statistical performance, rather than on any accompanying appreciation of the passing scene. This latter is of course very much the case with air travel, and it is with the air that the TGV trains will compete. Like the *Shinkansen* lines in Japan, this new French line will carry only passenger trains; but their removal from the existing line will leave that splendidly equipped railway relatively free to carry the ever-increasing freight traffic. This is due to development of the port of Fos between Marseille and the Rhône delta.

One important feature of the TGV sets now under construction is that their electrical equipment will need to accommodate different systems of electric power supply. The existing PLM line into Paris, and south of Lyon, is operated on 1,500 volts dc, but the new line will have the present French standard system of 25,000 volts ac, at 50 cycles. Furthermore, on the TGV sets that work to Lausanne, provision will be made to operate on the Swiss system at 16,000 volts ac at $16\frac{2}{3}$ cycles per second. The equipment is so designed to facilitate changing from one to another at the changeover points without stopping. Although from a sightseeing point of view there will be complete uniformity in the appearance and speed of all trains using the new lines, it will nevertheless be regarded as an epoch-marking step forward in the history of rail transport in the twentieth century.

Right Construction in progress on the new Paris-Lyon route cutting through open country with the minimum of disturbance.

Across Asia: the eastern goal

It has been said that the Trans-Siberian Railway is the backbone of the USSR. It is the longest continuous railway in the world, for the distance from Moscow to Vladivostok is nearly 10,000 km (6,000 miles). The Russians began their eastern progress in the sixteenth century, and the first Russian troops to reach the Pacific were a regiment of Cossacks in 1639. The absorption of Siberia into the Russian Empire continued during the following 200 years and it was in 1858, during the worldwide railway mania, that the first proposals were made for a Trans-Siberian Railway to the Pacific. The Russian government turned a deaf ear to these proposals, for the Crimean War had drained the Russian treasury and it was not until 1875 that the Ministry of Communications dared to put forward an official plan, and even then it was not approved. But the seed had been sown, and a succession of official and semi-official plans were put forward during the following years. In the late 1880s a survey and estimates were made, and in 1891 the government gave its official approval and, later in the same year, Crown Prince Nicholas broke the first ground at Vladivostok during his Far Eastern tour.

By that time the Russian railways had reached across the Siberian border to Čel'abinsk and construction began at both ends. But the Russian Finance Minister was still daunted by the estimated cost of the line at a period when a succession of bad harvests had caused financial stringency, and it was not until Sergius Witte, a professional railwayman, became Finance Minister that progress on a large scale began, partly with loans from French and other sources. A Trans-Siberian Committee was formed, with Prince Nicholas in the chair and a membership that included almost every important figure in government circles, and the whole vast undertaking was put on a business footing.

The projected line passed through Omsk, Novosibirsk and Krasnojarsk, to Irkutsk, near Lake Baykal. Thus far the project was fairly straightforward, as the line would be comparatively level, passing through the fertile strip

bounded on the north by tundra and on the south by arid country. From Irkutsk, however, engineering difficulties began, for the country was mountainous from Lake Baykal eastward. After consideration the Committee decided that it would save time and money to cross the lake by train-ferry rather than to circumvent it by rail. From the eastern shore of Lake Baykal the line would pass through Ulan-Ude and Čita.

The engineers had put in a pessimistic report about the section of the railway circumventing the Chinese province of Manchuria. The country north of the Amur river (the frontier) was very rough and much earthwork would be

Top An early view of Obi, one of the stations on the Trans-Siberian Railway, showing a wood-burning locomotive fitted with a spark-arresting stack.

Right The dramatic sight of huge Russian stock hauling a train across the frozen wastes traversed by the Trans-Siberian Railway.

needed, which would consume time and money. The committee decided that it would be much better if some arrangement could be made with the Imperial Chinese government which would allow the railway to be built through the comparatively flat land of Manchuria, as this would be both shorter and cheaper. The coronation of Tsar Nicholas II in 1895 gave the Russians an opportunity of meeting high Chinese officials, and invitations were sent. They were pleased when the Imperial Chinese government selected Marquis Li Hung-chang as their envoy, for not only was he the most capable man of his time, but he was a believer in railway construction. Furthermore, he was known to be apprehensive of a war with Japan and thus inclined to seek other friends. An agreement resulted to create the Chinese Eastern Railway, a joint Sino-Russian company stretching across Manchuria and thus permitting the completion of the Trans-Siberian Railway. The agreement went further and permitted the Russians, jointly with the Chinese, to construct a branch of the Trans-Siberian line southward about 800 km (500 miles) to Talien (Lüda) and Port Arthur at the southernmost tip of Manchuria. These were both ice-free ports and thus preferable to Vladivostok.

The Russians lost no time in forming the company and in pushing ahead with construction. They had, however, difficulties with the Hung Hudze, wild and aggressive

tribes that looted construction camps and stole wire from the railway. The railway police, almost wholly Russian in personnel, were reinforced to keep order, and the Russians became dominant in northern Manchuria. The lack of hard roads was another difficulty faced by the engineers, who finally decided to build a supply rail line of low quality along the selected route, with the permanent line alongside it. This saved time and money.

In 1903 the Chinese Eastern Railway was complete, not only the west to east line, but also the branch to Port Arthur. As the connecting lines on both frontiers had already been built, through running from St Petersburg (Leningrad) to Vladivostok was possible, except for the line around Baykal, completed in 1904.

The quality of the line was low, however, due to the original orders of the committee. The line had been laid with light rails which allowed an axle load of only 13 tons, and the ties were untreated, while ballast was very thin due to shortage of stone on several sections of the route. The Chinese Eastern line also gave much trouble. Nevertheless the line was completed and traffic began to flow, hindered only by numerous derailments. A big program of improvements, the cost of which would be met partly out of revenue, was instituted and lasted for many years, although the advent of the Russo-Japanese War held up development. The railway was in no fit state to cope with

large-scale military traffic, and its limitations were an important, if not the prime, cause of the Russian defeat. The peace treaty included the concession to the Japanese of two-thirds of the southward Trans-Siberian line and the loss of Talien and Port Arthur.

The committee had already decided that it was necessary to circumvent Manchuria and the Chinese Eastern Railway, and construction began. It was difficult and was not completed until 1916 when it was at once used to its full capacity in carrying war material from Japan and the United States to help Russia's war effort in the First World War. By that time, however, the quality of the whole Trans-Siberian Railway had been much improved and it withstood the traffic satisfactorily.

The line was vital in the civil war that followed the Russian Revolution, but after a pause the program of improvements continued and has, in fact, never ceased. The Russians sold their share of the Chinese Eastern Railway to the Japanese in 1935, but have pushed on with railway construction in their own territories. The line from Moscow to Irkutsk has now been double tracked and electrified, while the remainder is now worked almost wholly by diesel power. The quality of the passenger accommodation is now on a par with the Wagons-Lit Company trains of the 1900s, which were regarded as equal to anything in the world at that time.

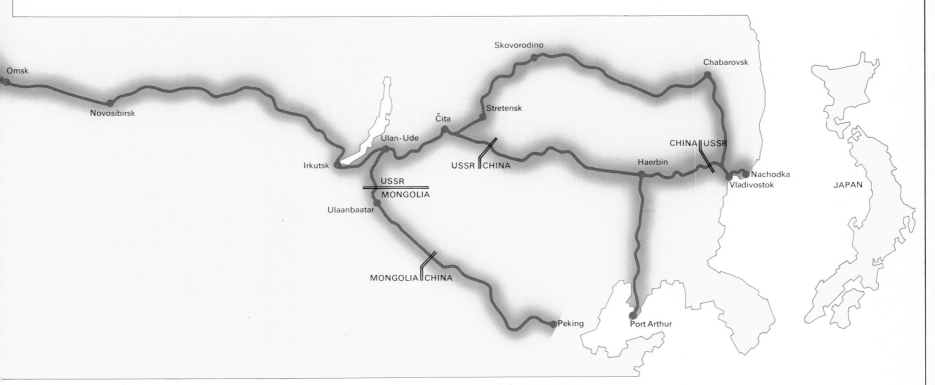

The Trans-Siberian Railway from Moscow to Vladivostok was built at a cost of $250,702,000. The construction of a more northerly line, from Lake Baykal to the River Amur, has recently been announced with completion due in the 1980s. Basically seen as a strategic plan, the new 2,880 km (1,800 mile) route will have the added advantage of opening up eastern Siberia for settlement and trade.

View from Trans-Siberian Railway.

Across Asia: the great dream

The Trans-Asian Railway

It was not until recently that the name "Trans-Asian Railway" came into prominence, the reason being that although the railways in Turkey, Iran, Pakistan, India, Bangladesh, Burma and Thailand were all developing and extending over the years, it was a comparatively short time ago that governments and railway authorities gave attention to the possible advantages of linking them up. In recent years the United Nations Committee for Asia and the Pacific (ESCAP) became interested, and now holds biennial meetings to review progress. ESCAP's researches indicate that although it is unlikely that long-distance through traffic will be large, short-distance traffic on sections of the Trans-Asian Railway will often be considerable, and they cite the example of Turkey and Iran where there has been a big increase of international traffic since the railways were linked up in 1971. ESCAP also estimates that the costs of freight traffic overland will be competitive with those of seaborne traffic.

The Trans-Asian Railway starts at Haydarpasa, Istanbul's eastern terminus across the Bosporus. The railway from Europe to Istanbul was completed in the 1880s and train ferries now take railway rolling stock across the Bosporus, until such time as the planned railway tunnel under the straits is built. From Haydarpasa the line climbs to Eskişehir and then runs eastward across rolling country to Ankara, the capital. From there it runs through Kayseri and Malatya to Tatvan on the shore of Lake Van. Train ferries carry trains across the lake, and so to the Iranian frontier at Qaṭūr. In Iran the line skirts Lake Urmia to Tabrīz and continues on to Tehrān, through hilly and windswept country. From Tehrān the line runs south to Qom Junction and from there southeastward for some 800 km (500 miles) to Kermān, the present railhead. From Kermān the line has been surveyed to a junction with the isolated section of the Iranian State Railway running from Zāhedān to Mīrjaveh on the Pakistan border, a distance of less than 500 km (300 miles). At Mīrjaveh the gauge of the railway will change from standard gauge to the Pakistan and India gauge of 1,676 mm (5 ft 6 in). This means that all passengers and freight must be transhipped; though later it is intended to reduce the amount of transhipment by changing the gauge of through cars, as is done between France and Spain. The branch line of the Pakistan Railway which runs to Mīrjaveh will be rebuilt to main line standards to take the anticipated through traffic. Trans-Asian trains will use this line, crossing the Indus at Rohri and from there they will continue at speed on the electrified main line to Lahore.

From Lahore the line runs to the Indian border and from there to Delhi, and so down the Ganges valley to the neighborhood of Calcutta.

Once the gap between Kermān and Zāhedān is filled, there will be a through rail route from Europe to Calcutta, and the economic forecasts are favorable. The remainder of the Trans-Asian route, however, is not as yet finally settled. It will diverge from the line to Calcutta some

Train crossing Turkey on an early part of the route.

300 km (186 miles) north of the city. All railways in Burma, Malaysia, Thailand, Cambodia (Khmer) and Vietnam are built to meter gauge and there must, therefore, be a transfer point from 1,676 mm (5 ft 6 in) gauge to meter gauge for all traffic somewhere in eastern India or in Bangladesh. Where this transfer point is situated will depend on where the Brahmaputra River is bridged. If this is done at Bāhāburābād, as seems most probable, the change of gauge is likely to be made at Katihār, where a transfer point already exists.

The Trans-Asian Railway will then cross into Bangladesh and run through the lush delta country to Chittagong. Its projected route is not yet settled. The government of Burma has already given its approval in principle to the plan of a railway across Burma but has not yet indicated what route it prefers the railway to follow. One alternative would be for the line to run south from Chittagong through Cox's Bāzār and on toward Sittwe before turning east, penetrating the Arakan mountains and crossing the Irrawaddy to Myingyan. From there it could run on existing lines to Thazi Junction and on to Taunggyi before turning south on new construction to cross the Salween River to Thailand. Once across the frontier, in very mountainous country, it could join the Thailand State Railway at Chiang Mai. This is one alternative, but there are several others, all equally difficult from the engineering viewpoint, and depending also on political decisions. The only point that seems to have been decided is that the line built in 1943–44 will not be followed.

Once on the Thailand State Railways, the Trans-Asian Railway will descend to the plains and pass through Bangkok. From there it will run in an easterly direction to the frontier of Cambodia at Aran Pradet (Paôy Pêt), and from there to Phnum Pénh, the capital. This is the present railhead, but a line has been surveyed from Phnum Pénh to Ho Chi Minh City (Sai-gon). The Vietnam Railways system runs from Ho Chi Minh City to Hanoi along the coast, and then turns inland to Pingxiang which is the frontier town of China. At Pingxiang there already exists a transhipment point where all traffic must transfer from meter gauge to Chinese standard gauge.

Chinese railways

The Chinese railways have, in recent years, come to appear more obviously Chinese. This might seem surprising, because until less than 50 years ago there were no Chinese standards and specifications, and each railway adopted the methods and designs of the country that financed the railway's construction. As a consequence, British, French, American, Japanese, Russian, and even Dutch and Belgian, designs could be seen at work, which lent the railways a colorful variety unmatched elsewhere. While Chinese standards and specifications are now used, they are still influenced by the good railway ideas of other nations. The net result, however, is without any doubt Chinese.

There are just eight rail entrances to China. As China is an enormous country, covering one-eighth of the habitable area of the world, this may seem very few, but China has

Development of the Trans-Asian Railway, Istanbul to Peking, is now controlled by a United Nations committee. As shown, the majority of the route is already in existence, although with a variety of gauges, and only a few stretches remain to be built, of which Zāhedān-Kermān is scheduled for completion by 1980. Burmese plans have yet to be announced, however, and the project is hindered by war in Indo-China. It is likely to be many years before operation of such a route will be effected.

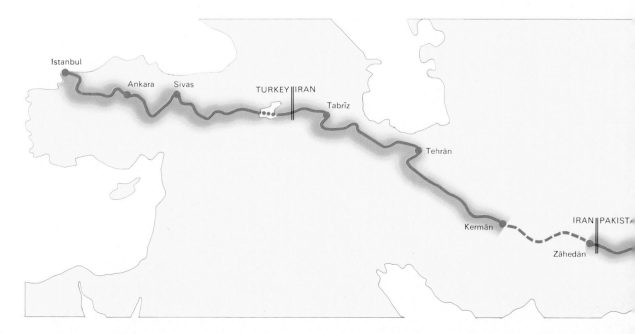

never encouraged intercourse with other nations. Of the eight existing entrances, only two are in common use, these being the railway between Hong Kong and Canton, and the entrance from eastern Europe, which is a line leaving the Trans-Siberian Railway at Ulan-Ude, crossing the Gobi Desert, and reaching Jining in China where the trucks of Russian 1,524 mm (5 ft) gauge are changed for others of the Chinese standard gauge. Of the remaining entrances, two are from North Korea, two from Vietnam, and two others from the Trans-Siberian Railway in Manchuria, the last four all requiring a change of gauge.

The Chinese railways are well maintained, well run, and profitable. The standard gauge track is solid and well ballasted. Bridges are being strengthened and loading gauges give ample room. A relic of British influence is that on many railways high platforms are in use, though passenger cars always have end aisles and steps, with a deck that is used at high platforms. Passenger cars have an eastern European general appearance, and the freight cars, though based on British and Japanese designs, have a generally American appearance. Motive power is at present mainly steam, though electric power is used on lines with heavy traffic and heavy grades. In districts where water is short and fuel has to be transported long distances, diesel locomotives are being built to handle passenger traffic.

The principal lines run a distance of 2,260 km (1,400 miles), from Canton in the south to Peking in the north, via Wuhan, where the Yangtse is crossed on a magnificent road and rail bridge. The route is mainly through hilly and attractive farmland, though after crossing the Yellow River on another remarkable bridge, the hills disappear, and the line crosses the great North China Plain to Peking.

A second main route is that from Peking, through Tientsin and Tsinan in Shantung, to Nanking on the Yangtse, crossing even a finer and larger bridge en route.

From Nanking the line runs southeast through rice fields to the outlying factories of Shanghai, one of the largest cities in the world. From Shanghai it runs south to Hangchow, onward in a southwesterly direction through lush farmland becoming slowly more hilly, until it joins the Canton-Wuhan line at Chuchou.

Perhaps the most remarkable of the Chinese railways is that which runs east and west across China, with interconnections with the two main routes already described, this enters loess country where the scenery becomes spectacular, especially as seen from a shelf above the Yellow River. The line continues through Sian, an ancient capital of China, Lanchow, a rapidly developing city, and then runs over 1,000 km (620 miles) westward to Tumen, with its oil wells, on to Urumchi, and finally to Kelamayi, another oil city.

Two separate lines now unite China proper with Manchuria, both reaching Shenyang (Mukden). This is at the center of a highly industrialized district with the great Fushun open-cast coal mine and the great Anyang steelworks a short distance to the south. From Shenyang railways run south to Lüda (Talien), southeast to Korea, northeast to Hailung, and north to Changchun and Haerbin, an industrial city on the former Chinese Eastern Railway which has junctions with the Trans-Siberian Railway to east and west.

There are many other lines in China, but those already mentioned are the most important. The most spectacular one of all, however, is the line running northwest from Peking through the Nankow Pass, under the Great Wall, to Kalgan and from there westward to Baotou and Lanchow. As can be seen from the foregoing account, China's railways are on a par with any others in Asia and are expanding faster than any in the world.

First train across the Yangtse bridge, China.

Steam train in front of Agra fort, India.

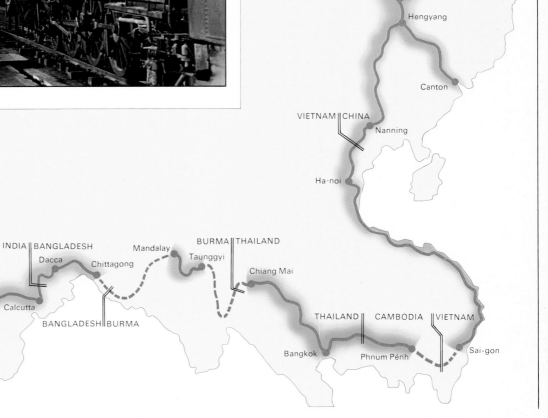

Australia: crossing the arid continent

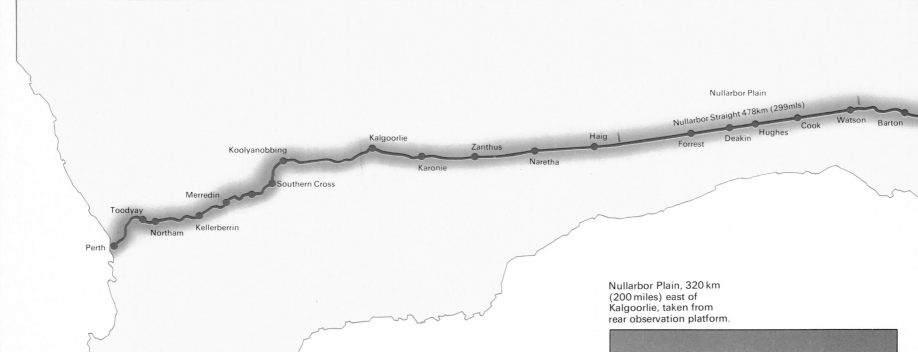

Nullarbor Plain, 320 km (200 miles) east of Kalgoorlie, taken from rear observation platform.

When the proposal was first put forward to integrate the individual Australian colonies into a unified federation, Western Australia stood apart. She was alone, separated from the rest by the virtually unknown desert lands of the Nullarbor Plain and saw no advantage in being united with the rest. Yet it was felt that without her, federation could not be a success, and as an inducement for her to join the federal government, it was offered that a railway would be constructed eastward from Kalgoorlie to join the nearest point of the South Australian system, which was then at Port Augusta. On the strength of this, and of other inducements, Western Australia agreed to join, and the Commonwealth of Australia was inaugurated on New Year's Day 1901. Between Kalgoorlie and Port Augusta, however, lay more than 1,600 km (1,000 miles) of virtually unexplored territory, and with no more than a few handfuls of Aboriginal tribes scattered over the land, it is not surprising that it took some time to launch the actual constructional work on the railway.

Lines across the desert

The prospectors went out on camels. The expeditions took some preliminary organizing, because there would be no chance of living off the land. It was so absolutely devoid of physical features and human habitation that any survey party would have to go out furnished for a stay in a waterless desert. One thing the early surveyors did find, however, was that the line could be made literally straight, and practically level for hundreds of miles. Many years passed before estimates could be placed before the federal government to get the expenditure approved, and it was not until September 14, 1912 that the first earth was turned, with great ceremony, by the Governor-General of Australia. The building of the line was like nothing that had gone before: no great mountain ranges to cross, no primeval jungles to cut through, no hostile natives, no attacks by wild animals. The working parties had to be completely self-contained. In the 1,682 km (1,051 miles) between Kalgoorlie and Port Augusta there was not a single running stream, and the provision of water supplies for the constructional gangs was the greatest problem of all. Water had to be divined, wells sunk, and reservoirs constructed, and out in the open, with not a tree for hundreds of miles, the midday heat was intense. Track laying began in 1913, and four years later the first through train steamed out of Kalgoorlie.

It was not a through train in the ordinary sense because

the "Trans," as it is still called today, was laid to the 1,435 mm (4 ft 8½ in) standard gauge, and at both ends the gauge was 1,067 mm (3 ft 6 in). Why the difference? At the time the "Trans" was authorized, the problem of different gauges in Australia was highly controversial. Only New South Wales had the standard gauge. But the federal government had set its sights on ultimate standardization, and the standard gauge seemed the logical one to use, rather than the 1,600 mm (5 ft 3 in) of South Australia and Victoria, or the restrictive 1,067 mm (3 ft 6 in) of Western Australia and parts of South Australia. The decision was a far-sighted one, because in recent years commercial interests justified the construction of a standard gauge line from Kalgoorlie through Western Australia to the Indian Ocean, and the final linkup with the standard gauge of New South Wales came in 1970.

When the Trans-Australian section of the Commonwealth Railways was built, in 1913–17, a vital consideration was the means of servicing steam locomotives. The line had to be entirely self-contained. At each end it was flanked by narrow gauge lines over which its locomotives could not run. Along its vast length of 1,682 km (1,051 miles) the stations were spaced not because of any need to serve local communities, because these did not exist, but to suit the operating requirements of the line. They were sited to suit the coaling and watering requirements of locomotives and for their changing and remanning on the way. Three major intermediate depots were set up, so as to equalize roughly the run from Port Augusta to Kalgoorlie; these depots were at Tarcoola, Cook, and Rawlinna, and gave successive distances of 412, 409, 485 and 376 km (257, 256, 303 and 235 miles). At each depot engines were changed, but the crews changed more frequently. All along the line little townships were built to house and provide for the needs of men working on the line. When first opened the journey time for the whole distance was 37½ hr, giving an average speed of 45 km/h (28 mph). There were three passenger trains a week in each direction, and long before the introduction of regular air mail services an excellent connection was provided from the fortnightly mail steamer from England. Landing at Fremantle and traveling over the 1,067 mm (3 ft 6 in) gauge line to Kalgoorlie, passengers could then change to the "Trans" and eventually reach the eastern cities of Australia. This service allowed the passenger to save 48 hours on the journey from London to Melbourne, and 3 days if proceeding to Sydney.

Nowadays, with powerful modern diesel-electric locomotives, there is no need for any changing of engines between Port Augusta and Kalgoorlie, but the crews change at Tarcoola, Cook, and Rawlinna. They work successive stages on a four-day roster from their home station. Thus a Kalgoorlie crew would work to Rawlinna the first day, lodge and then go on to Cook the next day. On the third day they work back to Rawlinna, lodge again, and make the final run home on the fourth day. Similar schedules are organized from Port Augusta. It is an extraordinary experience to ride in the engine cab over the 475 km (297 mile) straight section of the "Trans." When the line was first built the ties were laid on the surface of the ground with very little ballast; but now the line is heavily ballasted, and speeds up to 113 km/h (70 mph) are permitted on some sections. It is the feeling of absolute nothingness that holds one enthralled: there are some areas of low bluish scrub, but nothing else on the horizon all around. The effect is extraordinary again when approaching one of the passing stations. First there are a few specks on the far horizon, which are gradually revealed as low buildings, and then the realization that they are being sighted over the curve of the earth, as in the first sight of islands or approaching ships at sea.

The Indian-Pacific

In 1970 the through train service across Australia was inaugurated – the "Indian-Pacific," named from the

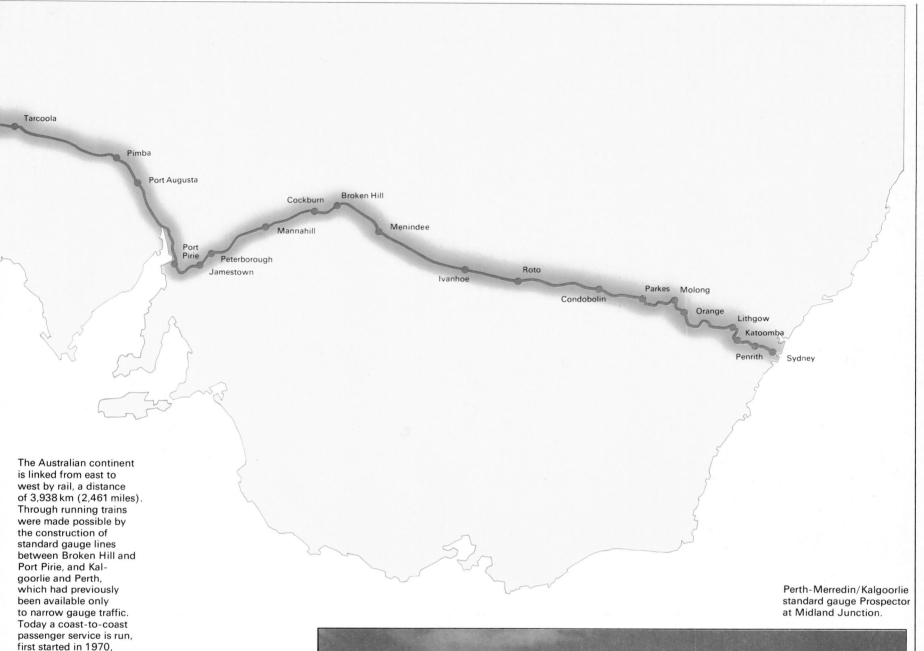

Tarcoola
Pimba
Port Augusta
Cockburn
Broken Hill
Mannahill
Menindee
Port Pirie
Peterborough
Jamestown
Ivanhoe
Roto
Condobolin
Parkes
Molong
Orange
Lithgow
Katoomba
Penrith
Sydney

The Australian continent is linked from east to west by rail, a distance of 3,938 km (2,461 miles). Through running trains were made possible by the construction of standard gauge lines between Broken Hill and Port Pirie, and Kalgoorlie and Perth, which had previously been available only to narrow gauge traffic. Today a coast-to-coast passenger service is run, first started in 1970, providing four trains in each direction each week.

Perth-Merredin/Kalgoorlie standard gauge Prospector at Midland Junction.

oceans at each end of the 3,938 km (2,461 mile) journey. It travels over 1,166 km (729 miles) of New South Wales tracks and 347 km (217 miles) on the South Australian before reaching the "Trans" at Port Pirie. The section of 91 km (57 miles) from this latter important junction to Port Augusta was changed to standard gauge many years ago. The Indian-Pacific now runs four days a week, leaving Sydney on Mondays, Wednesdays, Thursdays and Saturdays at 3:15 p.m. The arrival in Perth is at 7:00 a.m. on the fourth day, after two changes in time. The run over the "Trans" section takes from 4:45 p.m. on one evening at Port Pirie to 8:30 p.m. on the next day at Kalgoorlie. However, because of the change from Central to Western time at Cook, the actual journey time is $28\frac{3}{4}$ hr, at an average speed of 63 km/h (38.5 mph). The intermediate stops are Port Augusta, Pimba (serving Woomera), Tarcoola, Cook, and Rawlinna. The fastest intermediate running is across the Nullarbor "straight," which begins 117 km (73 miles) east of Cook. From the latter station the 485 km (303 miles) to Rawlinna, 358 (224) of them on the long straight, are covered in 7 hr, at an average speed of 70 km/h (44 mph). This, of course, includes stops as required at some intermediate passing stations. Passenger rolling stock on the Indian-Pacific is of the highest standard in Australia – and compares favorably with TEE and other prestige passenger stock. The stainless steel cars are completely air conditioned and there are many on-board amenities.

New Zealand: southernmost route

Between 1863 and 1870 a number of short lines were built, mostly projected by the various provincial governments. These had several different gauges, but in 1870 the central government passed an Act that required all future railways in the colony to be built to the 1,067 mm (3 ft 6 in) gauge. Today the principal main line in the North Island runs from Wellington to Auckland, and there are important branches terminating at New Plymouth on the west coast and Gisborne on the east. In the South Island the principal main line runs south from Christchurch to Dunedin, and Invercargill in the far south. There is an important northward connection from Christchurch to Picton, on the Cook Strait, while the east-west line, passing through the Southern Alps in the Otira Tunnel, connects to the industrial and mining centers of Greymouth and Westport. In a mountainous country the railways of New Zealand include many spectacular feats of engineering, dating from earlier years when the cost of deep tunneling could not be justified. The Otira Tunnel was not

Above left 2-6-2 at Ferrymead Museum.

Above 4-8-4 near Arthur's Pass on final run, now in Ferrymead Museum, Christchurch, New Zealand.

commenced until 1908, but partly because of delays through New Zealand's participation in the First World War, it was not completed until 1923. It has a total length of 8.4 km (5.3 miles).

An early highlight of New Zealand railways construction in the North Island was the Rimutaka Incline on which the line ascended 300 m (1,000 ft) in 23 km (14 miles), and then descended 265 m (869 ft) in less than 5 km (3 miles). A center rack rail was employed, with special brake cars with brakes gripping the center rail when descending, while tank locomotives with horizontal grip wheels were used to haul the trains up – often four locomotives to one train. Now the mountain range is pierced by the Rimutaki Tunnel, which is 8.75 km (5.47 miles) long, the longest in the British Commonwealth and opened in November 1955. Modern machinery and expertise enabled it to be built in a fraction of the time taken for the Otira. The secondary line to Napier and Gisborne, running for much of its northern part along the east coast of North Island, includes the highest viaduct in New Zealand, the Mohaka; at its maximum it is 97 m (318 ft) high, and consists of a series of latticed steel towers, tapering sharply in width toward their bases.

Since the early days, now that traffic has increased, and with it the weight of locomotives and cars, some considerable improvements have been made to the alignment in places to permit faster running; but one of the most spectacular locations on the North Island main line remains. Running south from Auckland and entering the central mountain massif, the line comes to Raurimu, and ahead is the task of climbing 213 m (700 ft) in the next 5.6 km (3.5 miles), in the direct line. Such a grade as 4 percent would have been quite impracticable for the moderate powered steam locomotives originally employed; but the track was laid out in the form of an ascending spiral. It includes a complete circle, two horseshoe curves, and two short tunnels, and so artificially increases the distance between Raurimu and National Park to 11 km (7 miles), with an average grade of 2 percent. Once up at Park the traveler can behold at relatively close range one of several active volcanoes.

The division of New Zealand into two halves by the Cook Strait has inevitably been a point of transport difficulty; and although there are of course air services that facilitate the rapid transit of such passengers who are in a hurry, there has always been the need to transfer railway freight cars and road vehicles. In 1962 there was introduced a 4,226 ton Rail-Road ferry between Wellington and Picton, working on the roll-on, roll-off principle, and this and two similar ships have certainly revolutionized interisland transport. Except in the approaches to the Otira Tunnel, the railways in the South Island do not include such spectacular engineering as in the North Island; but this is amply compensated for by the great historic interest of some parts of the system, and the survival of steam power. The very first railway in New Zealand was built between the port of Lyttleton and Christchurch, a distance of 6.8 km (4.25 miles). Lyttleton is backed by a range of hills, and the original proposal was to go directly through by a tunnel 2 km (1.25 miles) long; but this promised to be too expensive. Today part of the route of this pioneer line, at Ferrymead, is operated by a steam preservation group.

The journey south from Christchurch by a diesel train called the Southerner has the particular fascination of leading further south than anywhere else in the world by train. The journey of 589 km (368 miles) from Christchurch to Invercargill takes just 10 hr, and from the latter town the rails continue, but without any regular passenger service, to Bluff, the furthest south. The main line south, after keeping beside or near to the east coast for the first 448 km (280 miles), to Balclutha, then swings inland and westward before turning south again at Gore. This station is the junction for Lumsden, whence one can travel during the summer season by one of the most fascinating, but alas most remote, steam trains in the world. A branch line runs from Lumsden into the mountains to Kingston, lying at the foot of the most beautiful Lake Wakatipu, and here one meets the Kingston Flyer – a train with a pedigree extending back nearly 100 years.

In the 1880s the branch line service between Gore, Lumsden and Kingston was run by three gorgeous little 2-4-0 tender engines built by Rogers, in the USA. They were highly decorated with a wealth of polished brass and copperwork, and their engineers used to run the branch trains in such dashing style that they were nicknamed the "Kingston Flyers." In 1971 the idea was born of running New Zealand's only vintage steam trains over the same route, and two of the celebrated Ab class Pacific engines were saved from the scrap heap and restored to first-class working order to run the modern Kingston Flyer. One cannot expect speed as it is known today on all the railways of the world, because it now takes $1\frac{1}{2}$ hr to cover the 61 km (38 miles) between Lumsden and Kingston.

The total length of the New Zealand Railways covers

Two Ea locos about to be uncoupled at Arthur's Pass. Three together can haul a 500 ton train up a 3 percent grade in Otira Tunnel at 32 km/h (20 mph).

The Auckland-Wellington line and that from Christchurch to Invercargill, constitute the north and south trunk routes, respectively. In the daytime the Silver Fern, a luxury railcar, runs on the northern route, followed at night by the Northerner. In the South Island the route is served by the Southerner, with distinctive blue paintwork, which provides a daily service. The other named train in New Zealand is the Endeavour which runs in daytime between Wellington and Napier. All these lines are single track but are used an increasing amount by passenger traffic.

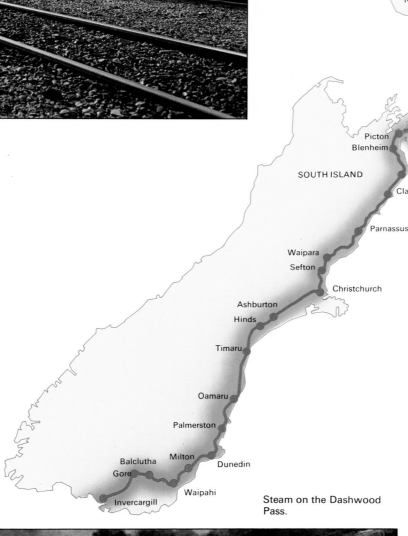

Auckland
Otorohanga
Mangapehi
Taumarunui
Spiral tunnels
Raurimu
NORTH ISLAND
Ohakune
Mangaweka
Marton
Palmerston North
Waikanae
Picton
Wellington
Blenheim
Ward
SOUTH ISLAND
Clarence
Parnassus
Waipara
Sefton
Christchurch
Ashburton
Hinds
Timaru
Oamaru
Palmerston
Milton
Balclutha
Dunedin
Gore
Waipahi
Invercargill

Steam on the Dashwood Pass.

about 4,800 km (3,000 miles), and about 75 percent of the revenue comes from freight traffic. Passenger business, though very efficiently operated, mostly in handsomely styled diesel railcars, is quite small, not amounting to more than about 5 percent of the total earnings. The remaining 20 percent of the revenue comes from various ancillary services, including the Wellington-Picton train ferry. Operationally the New Zealand Railways, so far as general equipment is concerned, are among the most complete and up-to-date in the world. They were one of the pioneers, outside the USA, of Centralized Traffic Control (CTC), which has now been applied to most of the main lines. Today further cutoff lines are in course of construction, involving long tunnels. The passenger services on most routes run during the daytime, but on the busiest route and the longest through run, that between Auckland and Wellington, there are both day and night services. The distance is 680 km (425 miles) and the daytime Silver Fern does the journey in about 13 hr, with five intermediate stops. This is a railcar type of train with buffet included. The real show train of the service is the Silver Star, leaving the two cities at 8:00 p.m., and including full dining and sleeping cars. The journey time is $12\frac{1}{2}$ hr in each direction.

99

Japan's Shinkansen 1

The first railway in Japan, built along the old Tokaido Trail in 1872, had no pretensions to being a speedway. On the recommendation of British engineers, it was built to the 1,067 mm (3 ft 6 in) gauge, as in South Africa, New Zealand and much of Australia; and to minimize the cost of construction it took a meandering course near to the east coast, skirting obstacles and including sections of steep grades. At first this did not matter. As a nation, the Japanese of the nineteenth century had a complete inability – indeed a reluctance – to hurry, and the trains were very slow. They became little faster as the line was extended southward to the furthest extent of the main island of Honshū. How, in a mere 50 years, the Japanese changed from this pastoral, easygoing existence, first to defeat Tsarist Russia in a major war and then to advance to become one of the leading industrial and military powers of the world, is one of the phenomena of history. In the process, the Tokaido line of the Imperial Japanese Railways, though enlarged to double track throughout and with the addition of several cutoff lines to ease grades and reduce overall distance, became completely saturated. In the late 1930s, although its 552 km (345 miles) of route between Tōkyō and Osaka represented only 3 percent of the total Japanese railways, it was carrying 25 percent of the total passenger and freight traffic. This was perhaps not surprising since 40 percent of the total population of the Japanese islands, and 70 percent of the industrial output, was concentrated in the narrow belt of land between the central mountain range and the sea and served by what can be called the Old Tokaido line.

A scheme was then worked out for an entirely new line, that would cut the time between Tōkyō and Osaka to $4\frac{1}{2}$ hr. This was a startling proposal because such a time would involve an average speed of 120 km/h (75 mph) – infinitely faster running than anything that had previously

Above Local railcar set.

Left C61 class 4-6-4 at Miyazaki on Kyūshū.

Below Shinkansen and highway: direct routes.

been made in Japan. But the country's precipitate entry into the Second World War, and the tremendous damage to her railways and industries that ensued before her surrender, necessarily caused suspension of the great plan. When it was revived after the war it took an even more ambitious form. With the speeds that were proposed it was considered that the 1,067 mm gauge would be inadequate, and this led to the conception of a new *Shinkansen* line on the standard gauge, quite separate from the existing 1,067 mm (3 ft 6 in) gauge network. Moreover, having taken this decision the Japanese National Railways determined to build a line of such straightness and massive construction that the standard passenger train speed on it would be 200 km/h (125 mph). By comparison with what has been achieved previously in Japan, this was a staggering proposition. In August 1957 the government decided to set up an investigation committee. A year later an aerial survey of the route was made, in March 1959 funds for construction of the line were included in the

Royal engine at
Miyazaki.

Existing
Under construction
Surveys authorized 1977

The first stretch of
the *Shinkansen* network
between Tōkyō and Osaka
was opened in 1966 and
was later extended to
Hakata. Extensions to
this basic network were
started, but financial
problems led to consid-
erable disruption of
work and surveys. Thus
the Seikan under-
water tunnel between
Hokkaidō and the main-
land was commenced
and work continued
while the lines leading
to it were actually
stopped. It was not
until 1977 that the
future of the tunnel
in the *Shinkansen* net-
work was ensured.

national budget, and in weeks these were approved.

The incredible speed with which the line was built was fully in keeping with the fast service that was promised. No more than one week after the project had been approved by Parliament, a ceremonial first ground breaking was performed, and in the astonishing time of five years and five months, full commercial service between Tōkyō and Osaka began. In view of the work involved this time does indeed take some believing. To permit uninterrupted high speed there was, outside the city area of Tōkyō, no curve with a radius of less than 2.4 km (1.5 miles). There were no road crossings, and in that densely populated strip of country the line was carried for the most part on viaducts high above the towns, and especially where there might have been intersections of any kind. Lengthy viaducts were built to take the line on the level across river valleys, and where there were mountains blocking the direct line of the railway, there was no thought but to tunnel straight through. In view of the high speeds to be attained and the intense utilization of the tracks forecast, very great care was taken in forming the embankments to secure an adequate degree of compactness in the piled-up earth. The tremendous amount of work put into this feature of the construction was vitally necessary seeing that a high-speed passenger service was to be inaugurated at once. On older railways in Great Britain and elsewhere it was usually the practice to run at moderate or even slow speeds at first, while all the earthworks were fully compacting; but the time schedule permitted no such settling in period on the New Tokaido line. In crossing urban areas the line is carried on elevated track structures with rail level about 6.4 m (21 ft) above ground, consisting of concrete rigid frames. These required a much narrower right-of-way at ground level than if conventional embankments had been built.

There were some very long bridges on the new line, mostly crossing the estuaries of rivers and the adjoining marshland. One of these gives a magnificent view of the sacred Mount Fuji and has from the outset been a favorite place for publicity photographs of the new trains at speed. Great care has been taken in the design of these bridges, many of which are in localities of natural beauty. The frequency of trains, both in these areas and where the line crosses urban complexes, has led to the need to minimize noise. High parapet walls have been built on many viaduct sections. There are no fewer than 66 tunnels between Tōkyō and Osaka, and by this more direct alignment the length of the line was reduced from the 552 km (345 miles) of the Old Tokaido line to 515 km (322 miles). Twelve of the new tunnels are more than 2 km (1.25 miles) long, and in all of them the aerodynamic effect of two trains passing at speed, which would be more than 400 km/h (250 mph), had to be taken into account. The standard distance between the nearest rails of opposing tracks in Great Britain is 1.8 m (6 ft), but in the tunnels of the New Tokaido line this distance has been made 2.7 m (9 ft). This is the standard "distance between" on the new line as far south as Osaka, but south of that city, and on subsequent extensions where speeds of 257 km/h (160 mph) are provided for, this width has been increased to 2.9 m (9 ft 6 in).

Traffic operation on the New Tokaido matches the basic conception and the magnificent civil engineering. From 6:00 a.m. to 9:00 p.m. one of the *Hikari*, or "Lightning," trains leaves Tōkyō approximately every 15 min for Osaka, covering the 515 km (322 miles) in 3 hr 10 min inclusive of brief stops at Nagoya and Kyōto. This is an average speed of 160 km/h (100 mph) and the volume of traffic can be imagined – each train consisting of 16 cars and providing seating for about 1,400 passengers. The

loading averages about 1,000 passengers per train, taking an average over the entire day, and over all 365 days in the year. At midday most of the trains are completely full. Taking the averages over the year one can indeed wonder why 55,000 people want to travel from Tōkyō to Osaka every day, while another 55,000 are traveling in the reverse direction. As a scenic ride the *Shinkansen* is a rather disappointing journey. The windows in the air-conditioned coaches are placed rather high up in comparison to those of modern British or continental European trains, and one gets the impression of a landscape sweeping past, and of built-up areas passing swiftly below. It is only when crossing the broad river valleys, and where there are glimpses of distant mountain ranges, that the lookout is appealing. Then again, so much of the line is in tunnel. This is not so marked on the original section as it is on the newest stretches south of Osaka. On the Sanyō *Shinkansen*, south of Okayama, through Hiroshima to the very south end of the island of Honshū, where the island itself is narrowing, nearly 55 percent of the line is in tunnel – nearly 225 km (140 miles) of it. It is hardly the kind of journey one would choose for sightseeing, though it is certainly excellent for getting quickly to one's destination. Today the 1,030 km (640 miles) from Tōkyō to Shimonoseki take 6¾ hr.

The new section south of Osaka, to Shimonoseki, is 509 km (318 miles) long, and the *Hikari* trains cover the distance in 3½ hr. But the fastest trains running south of Osaka do not stop at Shimonoseki, but continue by means of the tunnel under the Kanmon Strait to the island of Kyūshū. There the *Shinkansen* line terminates at Hakata, which is reached in 6 hr 56 min from Tōkyō. The Kanmon Strait is quite narrow, between relatively high ground on both sides, with the 1,067 mm (3 ft 6 in) gauge line tunneled beneath on a location that involved sharp curves

Japan's Shinkansen 11

at each end and steep grades. The *Shinkansen* line, on which high speeds are required throughout, needed a much longer and deeper tunnel, and the effect of this is seen in the schedules operated by the faster of the new trains, which do not stop at Shimonoseki, and which cover the 213 km (133 miles) from Hiroshima to Kokura in 74 min – an average of 172 km/h (108 mph) start-to-stop. The accompanying map shows the routes proposed for further extensions of the *Shinkansen* network, north of Tōkyō. None of these have yet progressed far, but a major project which will benefit the existing 1,067 mm (3 ft 6 in) system in the north of Honshū, as well as the projected *Shinkansen* extension, is the great undersea tunnel between Honshū and the northernmost island of Hokkaidō.

The Seikan Tunnel, as it is to be named, will be the longest undersea tunnel in the world, longer indeed than the tunnel under the English Channel was planned to be. Although the Seikan will have an overall length of 54 km (33.5 miles), only 23 km (14.5 miles) will be actually under the sea. It was originally planned for completion in 1979, but unexpected and serious difficulties have arisen in the construction, despite the most exhaustive preliminary surveys. There was every reason for embarking on this daring project. At present communication between the two islands is by train ferry, and the crossing from Aomori to Hakodate takes four hours. It can be a very stormy

passage and on one occasion a ferry sank, with heavy loss of life. The surveys revealed a vast fault on the sea bottom, near the middle of the strait, from which unlimited volumes of water at high pressure would flow. Because of this, it was thought essential to have the roof of the tunnel 100 m (110 yd) below the sea bed, and at a depth of 247 m (270 yd) below sea level. This great depth in the center has resulted in the tunnel being so much longer than the actual distance across the strait, despite the use of fairly steep grades on either side. As planned there will be a level stretch for about 4 km (2.5 miles) in the middle of the tunnel, and to reach this there will be a descent 22 km (13.5 miles) long on a grade of 1.2 percent from the Honshū side. To reach the higher ground on the Hokkaidō side, an ascent of no less than 28 km (17.5 miles), also at 1.2 percent, will be necessary. So far as power is concerned such grades will not trouble the *Shinkansen* trains, with every axle powered and 1,000 hp available for every car in the trains. But it is intended that the tunnel will be used also for 1,067 mm (3 ft 6 in) gauge trains, and the one main tunnel will carry tracks for both. This will enable the more

Right, the passage of *Shinkansen* trains in both directions as observed from a point approximately 150 km (95 miles) from Tōkyō, close to Mount Fuji, over an 18-hour period. Though all trains, which are 16 car sets, average almost 160 km/h (100 mph) the Hikari (Lightning) stop at less intermediate stations than the Kodama (Echo). The high traffic density handled on the network is one of the greatest of any system in the world, and calls for highly developed systems.

Shinkansen passing Mount Fuji in the position taken by the observer in the opposite diagram.

local trains from either side to benefit from the tunnel and make the use of the train ferry unnecessary.

The method of constructing the tunnel is interesting, in view of the exceptional depth below the sea. Along the line of the main tunnel what is termed the "bottom drift" method has been used. A pilot tunnel is driven first, to a distance of about 0.5 km (0.33 mile) ahead of the main working to investigate rock conditions. Then the main tunnel is excavated to its full size in two stages, first the upper half and then the lower. The concrete for the arch is put in, before the lower section, and then lastly the side walls are built in. In the course of the work many additional pilot tunnels have been driven to test rock conditions on either side. The completion of this great work will be awaited with the utmost interest, but at present authorization of *Shinkansen* extensions north of Tōkyō has not yet been forthcoming. It is likely, however, that these lines will differ from the Tokaido and Sanyō *Shinkansens* in that they will carry a mixed traffic instead of being exclusively passenger. It was the original intention that the Tokaido *Shinkansen* should be mixed, carrying freight traffic at night; but such was its success as a mass-carrier of passengers that a great number of additional trains had to be run beyond those originally planned, up to the present maximum of four *Hikari* per hour, and the night time was needed for track maintenance. There was no chance to do anything in the brief intervals between trains in the daytime.

Today 90 *Shinkansen* trains a day leave Tōkyō for the south. The pattern has changed a little from that in operation before the extension beyond Okayama was open. A typical set of departures is 12:00, 12:12, 12:16, 12:24, 12:36, 12:40, and 1:00 p.m. The 12:16 and 12:40 are "Kodama" and "all stations" to Osaka, which means only three more stops than the *Hikari* at the other departure times. Already, however, the line is becoming saturated, and the Japanese National Railways are considering the construction of yet another line to cater for the exceptional section Tōkyō-Nagoya-Kyōto-Osaka. Because of its construction features as the pioneer, the running speeds on the present line cannot be increased above the present 210 km/h (130 mph). The crunch is expected to come after 1980, and the concept at present is that another entirely new line might be constructed, but this time not using a conventional railway at all, but the principle of magnetic levitation. It is the basis of the experiment made both in Great Britain and France with the so-called "hover trains." In Japan experiments have been in hand for some time with a car propelled by a "linear motor," and

Above The Seikan Tunnel under construction on 1.2 percent grade. The tunnel, started in the late 1960s, was continued in the face of economic difficulties. For some time it was doubtful whether *Shin-kansen* trains would ever be able to use the tunnel, but the situation was resolved favorably. When it opens the Seikan Tunnel will be the longest in the world. *Right* Monorail, Tōkyō. *Below* Shinkansen train.

although there is still much to be done the prospects are enthralling. The Japanese set new standards with the building of the Tokaido *Shinkansen* line, when they reduced the Tōkyō-Osaka time from the 6 hr 40 min of the 1,067 mm (3 ft 6 in) gauge limited express trains to 3 hr 10 min; but with magnetic levitation, and cars propelled by linear motors, the target time is only one hour. It is thought that a new line operated in this manner would take the ultraprestige traffic, leaving the original Tokaido *Shinkansen* to cope with the many who would be content with a 3 hr 10 min run between the two cities.

Crossing North America 1

Routes in the USA

A the zenith of steam operation in the USA, busiest among the great trunk routes were the rivals operating between New York and Chicago. The New York Central, with its "water level" route, had the advantage of no grades, but the Pennsylvania had the shorter distance. The physical characteristics balanced each other, however, and both were maintaining a 16-hour service between the two cities, by the two world-famous trains, The Twentieth Century Limited by the NYC, and The Broadway Limited, with average speeds of 96 and 90 km/h (60 and 56.25 mph) over 1,536 and 1,440 km (960 and 900 miles), respectively. The Pennsylvania Railroad had much the harder route, because it cut through the very heart of the Allegheny mountains. From Harrisburg the quadruple tracked main line makes a picturesque course up the valley of the Juniata River to Altoona, where the great workshops of the Pennsylvania Railroad were situated, and then by means of the great Horseshoe Curve it climbs to its summit in the mountains in the Gallitzin Tunnel. Then comes an equally severe and picturesque descent to Pittsburgh. The New York Central, on the other hand, went due north at first,

beside the Hudson River, and then at Albany turned west to run through the Mohawk river valley and then near the south shore of Lake Erie – mostly level, but hard going with loads of more than 1,000 tons needing to be hauled continuously at around 130 km/h (80 mph).

Westward from Chicago, the Atchison Topeka and Santa Fe Railway provides a truly great route to the west coast. The main line of the Santa Fe from Chicago to Los Angeles is 3,577 km (2,223 miles) long. It runs through seven states and three time zones, crosses three great mountain ranges, and witnesses daily some of the fastest passenger and freight operation in the USA. At the peak of the steam era, during the Second World War, when an efficient service of very heavy trains to the west coast was a national necessity, only two locomotives were needed for the entire journey. A 4-6-4 was used over the relatively level eastern section of 1,595 km (990 miles) from Chicago to La Junta, Colorado, and there it was changed for a 4-8-4, which took the trains over the 1,982 km (1,232 miles) on to Los Angeles, through the mountain ranges of New Mexico, Arizona and California. The mountains are stark, rugged, and near-desert in places,

Below Once the mountains in the east had been crossed and the Mississippi reached, the railway builders in North America turned their minds to the great leap to the west coast. Vast sums of money were involved, even by 19th-century standards; thousands of men struggled in frightening conditions and thousands more argued about the relative desirability of such schemes. The transcontinental routes which emerged, forged two nations and certainly as far as the United States was concerned provided the impetus to further expansion and development.

Above US narrow gauge in Colorado. Silverton train, Rio Grande.

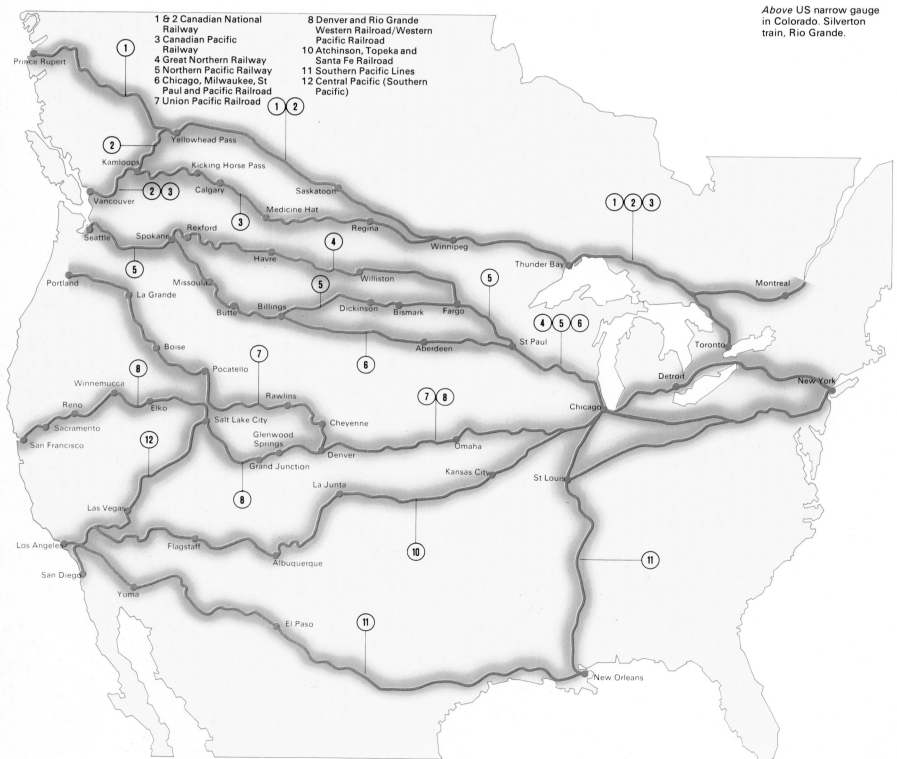

1 & 2 Canadian National Railway
3 Canadian Pacific Railway
4 Great Northern Railway
5 Northern Pacific Railway
6 Chicago, Milwaukee, St Paul and Pacific Railroad
7 Union Pacific Railroad
8 Denver and Rio Grande Western Railroad/Western Pacific Railroad
10 Atchinson, Topeka and Santa Fe Railroad
11 Southern Pacific Lines
12 Central Pacific (Southern Pacific)

and show magnificent coloring under the blistering heat of cloudless skies. The full journey takes more than two whole days, and there is much night traveling. The great train of steam days was the Chief, supplemented by the diesel-hauled Super Chief. Today's successor, under Amtrak, is the Southwest Limited.

For sheer spectacular country and superb train operation, however, the Denver and Rio Grande Western, between Denver and Salt Lake City, can scarcely be surpassed. The present main route, used by the thrice-weekly Rio Grande Zephyr, and daily by a dozen or more large freight trains in each direction, is a composite one. The original main line took a rather circuitous route, running due south at first from Denver to Pueblo, then turning west to cut through the Colorado Rockies in the breathtaking Royal Gorge, and from there over the Tennessee Pass, with its fearsome grades. The distance from Denver to Salt Lake City by this route was 1,192 km (745 miles). By 1934 the magnificent line of the Denver and Salt Lake Railroad had been connected to the original Rio Grande by the "Dotsero Cutoff" line, and the end-to-end distance was reduced to 912 km (570 miles). Although without the scenery of the Royal Gorge, the shorter route via the Moffat Tunnel is itself magnificent and also inspiring to the student of railway engineering. It climbs from the plains of Denver for 61 km (38 miles) on a continuous grade of 2 percent and passes through 30 tunnels hewn from solid rock in a distance of 23 km (14 miles), even before reaching the great Moffat Tunnel under the main range of the Rockies. Beyond this summit, in canyon and near desert country, the line crosses the states of Colorado and Utah eventually breasting Soldier Summit in the Wasatch mountains of Utah before descending to Salt Lake City.

The Southern Pacific, the manifold activities of which extend from New Orleans almost to Seattle, in the Pacific northwest, carries a great train called the Coast Starlight between Los Angeles and Seattle, passing through Oakland (San Francisco) intermediately. Like most of the American railways of today, the Southern Pacific is a mighty freight operator, with originating traffic in two distinct areas, namely in the cities of Texas and the Gulf of Mexico, and in California. These two areas are connected by the long main line running from Los Angeles near to the Mexican border; and then there are the two great prongs by which the Southern Pacific takes its traffic to hand over to the Union Pacific at Ogden, Utah, for its run to Chicago, and northward to link up with the Burlington at Portland, Oregon. In the steam era the Southern Pacific was distinguished by its cab-in-front articulated loco-motives of gigantic proportions, for the freight trains, and by its brightly painted 4-8-4s on the north-to-south passenger trains. The Coast Starlight of today is a night train only between Eugene and Oakland (San Francisco); for the rest of the long journey in both directions it runs in daylight, and even on the northbound run in high summer it is light enough, soon after daybreak, to see the scenic gem of the whole route, the exquisite Mount Shasta, shortly after passing Dunsmuir. The southern part of the same journey includes much fine coastal scenery, both north and

Logo of the Grand Trunk Western Company.

Preserved American steam. Note the powerful headlamp, the warning bell, and rather small cow-catcher.

south of Santa Barbara, and except where the curves demand caution the modern diesels wheel their heavy trains along at 113 km/h (70 mph).

The eastward line of the Southern Pacific today is the route of the one-time Central Pacific, climbing over the Sierra Nevada range, and heading for the historic end-to-end meeting point with the Union Pacific, at Promontory, Utah, where in 1869 the last spike of the first transcontinental railway across America was driven. Then the line was carried around to the north of the Great Lake on a considerable detour, but now, with the aid of a causeway, the line is carried across the lake, and the place where the "last spike" ceremony took place is now no more than a tourist attraction, with the two restored locomotives standing rather forlorn facing each other in the desert.

The Union Pacific, on to whose rails eastbound trains pass at Ogden, is another great railway. It cuts through rugged country in the mountains of Utah and Colorado and then makes fast time across the plains of Nebraska to reach the west bank of the Missouri River at Omaha to make connection with the third partner in the chain of communication between Chicago and San Francisco – the Chicago and North Western. Until the recession following the Second World War, the passenger trains to and from the west traveled on the direct line from North Platte to Cheyenne, but now the San Francisco Zephyr, the only through passenger train between Chicago and San Francisco, under the auspices of Amtrak, travels via Fort Morgan and Denver, going from there due north to regain the former route at Cheyenne. Ogden, Utah, is in many ways the grand junction of the Union Pacific. For while the running further west on the transcontinental line is taken up by the Southern Pacific, the UP had main lines running southwest to Los Angeles, north to Butte, Montana, and northwest to Portland, and today its distinctively colored diesel locomotives are a familiar sight.

Another great route to the west is that now followed by Amtrak's Empire Builder – running between Chicago and Seattle. This is a most interesting journey because it uses parts of three different railways. From the scenic point of view the eastbound run is the more rewarding, leaving Seattle just before noon. The name of the train, which Amtrak inherited from the Great Northern, is in memory of the great nineteenth-century tycoon, J. J. Hill, who was once a member of the famous syndicate of four who organized the formation of the Canadian Pacific Railway Company. But he disagreed with the others so violently over the route to be followed, which he wanted south of Lake Superior, and so through American territory, that he left the syndicate, and initiated his own all-American line to the west coast – the Great Northern. Through his vigorous and successful prospecting of railways in all directions Hill eventually became widely known as "the Empire Builder."

The train of today, however, takes the former Northern Pacific line out of Seattle (now part of the Burlington Northern system), and from East Auburn, where it turns

Crossing North America 11

away from tidewater, the long ascent through the Cascade Range begins. There follows over an hour of delightful traveling, through densely wooded mountain country as the train climbs to nearly 900 m (3,000 ft), and there are many glimpses of the great Mount Rainier. By nightfall it reaches Spokane, a general junction, and there the train passes on to the former Great Northern line. It is just daylight again when the train runs beside the Glacier National Park, and then comes the fast day-long run across the prairies of Montana and North Dakota. Yet another night passes in the train, with breakfast soon after leaving Minneapolis. The line is now that of the Chicago, Milwaukee, St. Paul and Pacific – the "Milwaukee Road" – over which the steam-hauled Hiawathas of prewar days used to speed at 160 km/h (100 mph). The line at first makes a delightful course beside the upper reaches of the Mississippi River, leaves the great river at La Crosse and passes eastward to reach the shores of Lake Michigan at Milwaukee. From there, almost within sight of the lake for the rest of the journey, it arrives at Chicago.

Routes across Canada

Canada has been wittily described as a country 5,000 km (3,000 miles) long and two railroads wide. It is nothing more than plain truth that the building of the Canadian Pacific Railway helped enormously in welding the far-scattered provinces of Canada into a single, strong and united nation; and the route by which it went through the great mountain ranges of British Columbia befits, in every respect, its role in what has been so aptly called the National Dream. It was the section between Calgary and the canyons of the Fraser River, by which van Horne defied earlier advice, which determined that the route must go farther north through the Yellowhead Pass. In the

City of Los Angeles in Echo Canyon, Utah.

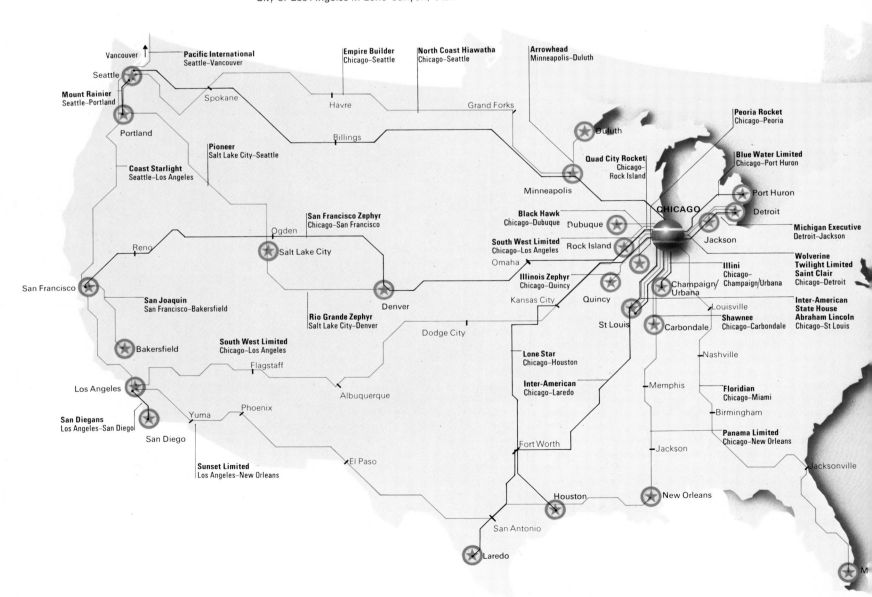

well-nigh incredible adventures that the pioneers had in finding any sort of a route at all through that maelstrom of mountain peaks, densely forested slopes, and swift flowing rivers, in the magnificent engineering embodied in building the line, and in the never-ceasing challenge its curves, grades and tunnels make to the locomotive men of today, it must remain a route without parallel on the world's railways. It is no mere mountain track built to open up a virgin land, but a major artery, nevertheless so terribly graded that on one stretch, the Beaver Hill, it needs 13 3,000 hp diesel locomotives to lift every one of the 10,000 ton coal trains – four every day – that run from the Crow's Nest Pass to Vancouver, for export to Japan. This great operation, which is only one of many services, takes place in the shadow of some of the grandest mountain scenery to be enjoyed from a train anywhere in the world.

Although the Canadian Pacific was first through to the west coast, the Yellowhead Pass did not have to wait so very long for its railway. Two rivals to the Canadian Pacific struck out west-northwest from Winnipeg, both heading for Edmonton, Alberta. The Canadian Northern and the Grand Trunk Pacific strove to open up different parts of the intervening country, but they were never very far apart, and when both were merged into the Canadian National system, the line through Saskatoon was chosen for the through transcontinental services. That great pioneer engineer Sandford Fleming had good reason to recommend this route on the score of gradients, because west of Edmonton the approach to the great range of the Rockies is relatively gentle. The scenery is beautiful as the line draws near to Jasper and passes through its nature park. There is, it is true, some stiff climbing in the final approach to the Yellowhead Pass; but on the westbound Super Continental train it is night, and the passenger is

Amtrak locomotive
in Union station,
Los Angeles.

conscious of difficult country only when riding high up in one of the dome cars, watching the way the locomotive headlight swings from one side to another when rounding the many curves. From Edmonton to the Yellowhead Pass the present main line is a synthesis of the best locations of the previous two rivals, sometimes Grand Trunk Pacific, sometimes Canadian Northern, making up a splendid fast-running main line.

Beyond the Yellowhead the routes diverge. The Super Continental train turns south and downhill into the valley of the Thompson River, coming in the early morning to Kamloops. Then follows an amazing run down the canyons where the Canadian Pacific is on one side and the Canadian National on the other, never out of sight of each other until reaching tidewater, and never more dramatically than when they execute a scissors movement – each crossing from one side to the other, as the viaduct of one strides over the viaduct of the other at Cisco.

The Fraser River, into which the Thompson River enters at Lytton, provides travelers on both the Canadian Pacific and the Canadian National routes to Vancouver with some grand spectacles, quite apart from the "scissors" location at Cisco. But even these are perhaps less astonishing than the first sight of the Fraser River from the Caribou Dayliner of the British Columbia Railway, when descending from Williams Lake to Lillooet, on the southbound run from Prince George to North Vancouver. This is a route of astonishing scenic variety, ranging from an almost pastoral Scottish quality between Prince George and Williams Lake and finishing alongside Howe Sound in fiord-like scenery, stretching from Squamish to Vancouver. This last section now has the compelling attraction of a vintage steam run, regularly scheduled, and worked by one of the magnificent Royal Hudson 4-6-4 locomotives.

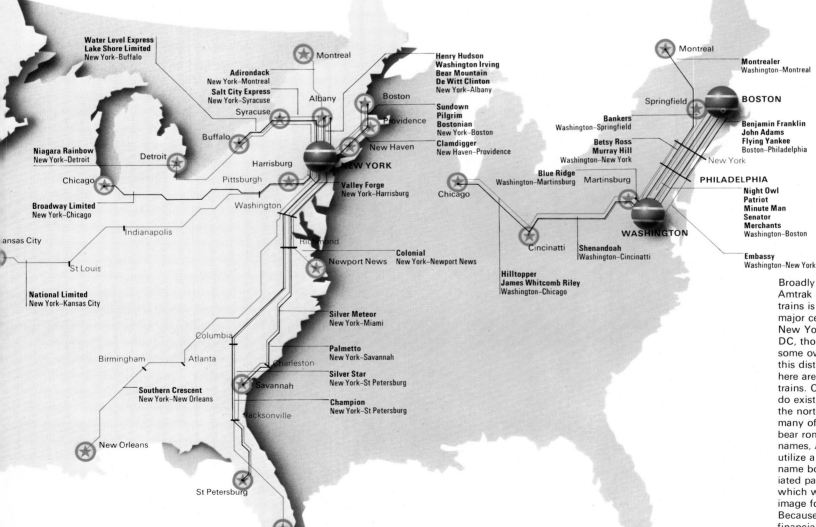

Broadly speaking the Amtrak network of named trains is based on three major centers, Chicago, New York and Washington, DC, though there is some overlap involved in this distinction. Shown here are only the named trains. Other services do exist, particularly in the northeast. Though many of these trains bear romantic and colorful names, Amtrak does not utilize a system of name boards and associated paraphernalia which would enhance their image for the enthusiast. Because of a worsening financial situation, Amtrak has been forced to reduce service availability.

The Andes: highest in the world 1

The trans-Andine railways include seven major routes. Two connect Chile and Argentina, three give the landlocked country of Bolivia access to the Pacific Ocean, one links Lima with the mountain valleys and mineral region of central Peru, and the most northerly connects Guayaquil and Quito in Ecuador. These railways were built, mainly between 1870 and 1914, to a variety of gauges: standard gauge in Peru, 762 mm (2 ft 6 in) and meter gauge in Chile and Bolivia, and 1,067 mm (3 ft 6 in) in Ecuador. At the time they were built they helped to bring some political unity to the scattered and diverse populations of the countries they served, but their main function was economic and their main interest freight traffic. They were, and still are, vitally important to the mining industries of Peru, Chile and Bolivia. Passenger traffic has never been more than a troublesome obligation.

Crossing the Andes meant building the highest railways in the world. The Peruvian Central Railway reaches 4,829 m (15,845 ft), the now-closed Collahuasi branch of the Antofagasta (Chili) and Bolivia Railway 4,826 m (15,835 ft), and the Río Mulatos-Potosí line in Bolivia 4,787 m (15,705 ft). The Andes rise steeply from the Pacific coast of South America. They consist of a number of mountain ranges and plateaus dissected by deep, narrow

Diesel locomotive of ENAFER, Peru.

Below The network of the Central Railway of Peru, the most important railway in South America for engineering scale. Much of it was built by Henry Meiggs, and it was his most staggering achievement.
The line from Huancayo to Huancavelica includes 103 tunnels and 76 bridges.

Above Cuzco-Machu Picchu line, Peru.

valleys. Railway construction presented civil engineers with serious problems, for they had, in a confined space and short distance, to build railways over passes which exceeded Mont Blanc in altitude. The solutions they adopted were tight curves, switchbacks, and, in two cases, rack sections. Operating the lines created further difficulties: steep grades, the lack of local sources of fuel, heavy wear and tear on motive power and rolling stock, and frequent landslides and washouts. Only the southernmost route, from Los Andes in Chile to Mendoza in Argentina, encountered the hazards of heavy snowfalls and avalanches. Despite road and air competition in the last 20 years, all the seven lines remain in operation, though with varying degrees of efficiency and reliability. They offer the traveler some of the most exciting railway scenery on any line in the world.

The Central Railway of Peru

The Peruvian Central is perhaps the most impressive of the seven routes. The engineering of the route involved immense problems. From Lima to Chosica grades are gentle and the route is straightforward. East of Chosica, though, the deep Rímac valley, the only feasible route to central Peru, narrows to a maximum width of perhaps 200 m (656 ft). Within its limits the engineers had to find a way of climbing from 854 m (2,802 ft) above sea level at Chosica to 4,783 m (15,693 ft) at Ticlio, a distance of no more than 76 km (47 miles) by the modern direct road which runs along the bottom of the valley. The twists and turns which the railway needs to gain height have made the rail distance far greater: 117 km (73 miles). To keep the

Goyllarisquizga

Cerro de Pasco

Mina Rangra

Carhuamayo

Huaythayo

PERU

La Oroya

Matucana

Cocachacra

Chaclay

Lima

grade down to 4.3 percent, the single-track railway has to use the whole width of the valley, crossing frequently from one side to the other, and even this would be impossible without the use of the famous switchbacks to gain height. Between Chosica and Ticlio there are six double and one single switchbacks, 66 tunnels and 59 bridges to cross the Rímac and the valleys which enter it.

Contrary to the general belief it was not the famous American entrepreneur Henry Meiggs who surveyed and laid out the route, but a former Peruvian government engineer, Ernesto Malinowski. Meiggs's task was to convince the skeptics of the practicability of the route and to contract and organize the necessary labor and materials. Construction of the line, which began in 1870, presented many problems. Thousands of workers died of a mysterious disease at Verrugas, and by 1877, when Meiggs died, Peru was bankrupt and the rails extended only as far as Chicla, 129 km (80 miles) from Lima and 3,723 m (12,215 ft) above sea level. Meiggs had, however, laid out the roadbed as far as the summit at Ticlio, 29 km (18 miles) farther on, and the Peruvian Corporation, which took the railways on lease from the Peruvian government in 1890, therefore had a comparatively straightforward task in completing the line to the proposed terminus at La Oroya,

209 km (130 miles) from Lima and 3,712 m (12,179 ft) above sea level. Later extensions took the tracks on to Cerro de Pasco (1904), Huancayo (1908), and a meter gauge line was constructed from the latter point to Huancavelica in 1926.

For many years the Central Railway's commercial returns were disappointing, and as late as the 1890s the management was still considering ways to drive off the competition of 800 miles which took advantage of the graded route the railway offered between La Oroya and Lima. Only in 1897, when a rise in prices made it economic to mine copper in Cerro de Pasco, Morococha and Casapalca, did the Central Railway begin to give an adequate return on the capital invested in it, and the large quantities of mineral traffic gave it about 30 years of commercial success, ended by the world depression of the 1930s. The problems faced by the Central Railway were common to most high-altitude railways. The costs of operating forced it to charge some of the highest freight tariffs in the world. The large number of bridges and tunnels made engineering maintenance expensive. Seasonal rains, between January and April, caused landslides which at best closed the railway for a few days each year, and at worst left behind a huge repair bill. Floods in 1925

caused $350,000 of damage and interrupted traffic for 82 days. Steam locomotives had to be strong enough to withstand the rough conditions and powerful enough to haul heavy freight trains up the continuous grades. British locomotives invariably proved too weak for these demands, but the management's record in adapting to the problems was extraordinarily good. They made several attempts to save on the heavy fuel bill. They prospected for coal in the region, in 1909 converted their locomotives to burn oil, and later considered plans to electrify part of the line. The mechanical department developed the powerful Andes class of 2-8-0 locomotives, which could negotiate the tight bends and steep grades with a payload of 180 tons of freight. They also constructed special cars which could be used to haul oil up the hill and minerals down, thus cutting down on expensive transport of empty rolling stock. After 1930 the railway's financial problems worsened. The Central Highway, which ran parallel to its tracks, was completed in 1935 and attracted much of the more valuable traffic. The government proved reluctant to allow the railway to raise tariffs or to protect it from this competition. In the 1960s, however, foreign loans financed a modernization plan. By 1967 Alco diesels had replaced steam locomotives. The expense, though, led the railway

After the first 40 km (25 miles) the line climbs steeply, reaching the Galera Tunnel at 4,832 m (15,848 ft). The highest summit is at La Cima, 4,818 m (15,806 ft). The line is notable for its switchbacks.

Above Cuzco-Santa Anna train, passing through mountain gorge, Peru.

Below Ecuador-Guayaquil and Quito line, switch-back at Devil's Nose.

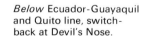

into even more financial difficulties, and the government nationalized the line in 1972.

The chief interest of the Central Railway has always been freight, and it remains essential to the mining industry. Fortunately, however, the ordinary traveler too can still depart from Desamparados station in Lima at 7:00 a.m. on any day of the week to enjoy the nine-hour journey to Huancayo. Except for those unfortunate travelers who suffer from altitude sickness and have to be given oxygen by the green-coated attendants, all will marvel at the ingenuity of the men who built this railway and at the ability of those who have operated it since, amidst some of the most rugged landscapes on earth.

Southern Peru and Bolivia

Three railways serve the *altiplano*, a grassy plain 3,900 m (12,800 ft) above sea level, which extends for about 300 km (200 miles) from north to south in southern Peru and Bolivia. The Southern Railway of Peru, a standard gauge line, was largely built by Meiggs between 1869 and 1875. It runs from Mollendo through Arequipa, the second city of Peru, to the town of Juliaca on the *altiplano*. There it divides. A short, level 46 km (29 mile) line runs around the shores of Lake Titicaca to the port of Puno. A 338 km (211 mile) line runs north to Cuzco, the ancient Inca capital, crossing a summit of 4,314 m (14,154 ft) at La Raya. A steamer service across Lake Titicaca gives the Southern Railway access to Bolivia, where in 1906 it completed a short meter gauge line from Guaqui, the Bolivian port, to the capital city of La Paz.

Although the Southern Railway climbs, at Crucero Alto, to 4,471 m (14,668 ft), it presented no serious engineering problems. The average construction cost of the 523 km (325 miles) between Mollendo and Puno was less than half that of the Central Railway's Callao-Chicla

The Andes: highest in the world 11

section. The line is single track throughout. Passenger trains have succumbed, on the Mollendo-Arequipa section, to road competition, but east of Arequipa, on the mountain section, passenger traffic has increased in the past few years and extra trains have been put on to cope with the demands of a growing tourist trade. Like all the Andean railways, passengers have never provided the Southern Railway with more than a small fraction of its revenue. The freight traffic for Bolivia has always been important, making the navigation of Lake Titicaca an integral part of the railway's operations. There were steamers here in the 1860s, before the railway. The *Yavarí* and *Yapurá*, which were carried up from the coast by mule and assembled on the lake, can still be seen at Puno. Later the Peruvian Corporation added three more steamers on the Puno-Guaqui run, and in 1971 introduced a train ferry service across the lake to the Matilde mine in Bolivia.

The 458 km (284 mile) railway between Arica and La Paz was completed in 1913. It was built by the Chilean government to fulfill the terms of the 1904 peace treaty between Chile and Bolivia. Construction was extremely lengthy and difficult, and until the firm of Sir John Jackson took over the contract it seemed unlikely that it would be completed. It includes a 42 km (26 mile) rack section of the Abt two-bar type between Central and Puquios. There were no commercial reasons for the construction of another route between Bolivia and the Pacific, and the railway made a loss until 1922. The problems were manifold. All ascending trains had to be broken into three parts to traverse the rack section, and government control of both the Chilean and Bolivian sections brought inefficient management. This dated back to the opening of the line when the official party, consisting of leading figures from both countries, arrived at La Paz to find that their baggage had been left behind at Arica. The port, moreover, was little more than an open roadstead, and gained an unhealthy but deserved reputation for thieving and delays. Except for the times when, for political reasons, the Bolivian government has encouraged traffic to use this route, the line has been an economic failure, although its strategic importance to both countries is considerable.

The Antofagasta (Chili) and Bolivia Railway, usually known as the FCAB, lies farther south and it is the longest of the lines serving Bolivia. The FCAB started life in the 1870s as a 762 mm (2 ft 6 in) gauge line running inland from Antofagasta to the nitrate *pampas*. After the Pacific War (1879–1883), Chilean capitalists extended it inland to the Bolivian town of Uyuni, which it reached in 1889. In the same year British interests bought out the Chileans, and built the railway on to the mining center of Oruro on the *altiplano*, 930 km (680 miles) from Antofagasta. The line has always been the most profitable of all the Andean railways. There were few engineering problems to raise costs and the management could rely on three major sources of traffic: nitrates and copper from the Chilean section and tin from Bolivia. In 1908 the FCAB took over the recently constructed meter gauge line between Oruro and Viacha, changed its own line to meter gauge as far south as Uyuni, and began the construction of branches to the important cities of Potosí and Cochabamba. Both railways involved a climb to over 4,100 m (13,450 ft) in the eastern chain of the Andes, and their construction posed far more serious problems than anything found on the main line.

The Southern Railway of Peru, the Antofagasta, and the Arica-La Paz lines cannot match the splendor of the Central Peru, yet their scale is still impressive. The Southern approaches Bolivia by way of ferry across Lake Titicaca; Arica requires rack working to reach the heights; and the Antofagasta has seen better days as the Bolivian political instability prevents through traffic. Yet it is said by travelers that the approach to La Paz must rate as one of the railway wonders of the world.

The Southern Railway of Peru does not require the switchbacks of the Central yet reaches 4,472 m (14,668 ft) 357 km (223 miles) from the coast. At Puno passengers must take to ship in order to cross Lake Titicaca; the railway company maintains five for this purpose and the voyage takes 12 hours.

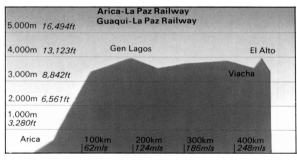

The Arica-La Paz line never achieved the importance of its neighbors even though at 471 km (293 miles) it is easily the shortest route between the capital and the coast. This was because the port facilities at Arica were poor, and also because 42 km (26 miles) of the climb are operated by rack on a 16.6 percent grade.

Below Although no longer properly operating through Bolivia, many parts of this system are utilized in Chile and Bolivia. The main summit reaches 4,084 m (13,396 ft) but an old branch to Punto Altobut reached 4,826 m (15,835 ft).

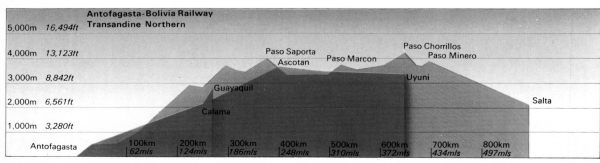

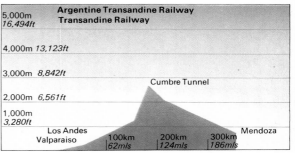

Freight train hauled
by steam locomotive
running through mining
countryside in Bolivia
near San Juan.

Top and above Part
of the trans-Andine
railway is the line
between Valparaíso in
Chile and Mendoza in
Argentina. It is not a
remarkable line though it
reaches its summit at
the Cumbre Tunnel 3,187 m
(10,452 ft). Rack working
is necessary on both sides
of the summit.

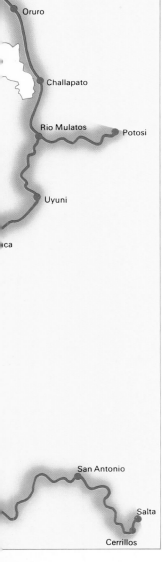

Each of the three routes serving Bolivia had disadvantages. On the Peruvian line freight had to be transhipped twice to cross the lake. On the Arica line the rack section caused delays and expense. And until 1928, when the FCAB in a carefully planned operation changed the gauge of its Chilean section, all freight on that route had to be transhipped at Uyuni. None of the ports, until the construction of Matarani in southern Peru in 1948, had adequate warehousing or harbor facilities. The major engineering problem, though, with the exception of the difficult section of the Arica route, was not the crossing of the Andes, but the descent into the city of La Paz, which lies in a ravine 700 m (2,300 ft) below the *altiplano*. The Peruvian Corporation's Guaqui-La Paz line, completed in 1906, had to use grades of 7.1 percent and electric power to descend into the city. The FCAB completed its own line in 1917 but frequent landslides and washouts caused it to relocate the line in 1924 with a ruling grade of 3 percent. The modernization of these routes since the 1950s has had varying degrees of success. The Southern Railway introduced Alco diesels and new rolling stock, including lightweight coaches, after 1958, and the line has been completely operated by diesels since the mid-1960s. Current financial problems, following nationalization in 1972, are impeding the purchase of spare parts, and services are frequently interrupted by breakdowns. The Bolivian railways faced similar problems after nationalization in 1964. Despite attempts to undertake the comprehensive dieselization of the railways in the late 1960s, frequent breakdowns and slow repairs meant that steam locomotives were still common in parts of Bolivia in the mid-1970s. The Chilean section of the FCAB escaped nationalization in the early 1970s, and is now the only railway in South America still under British control.

The Argentine-Chile links

Two routes, both of them uneconomic, connect the Chilean and Argentine railway systems. The younger, a

meter gauge line between Antofagasta and Salta, was not completed until 1948. The dream of connecting the Atlantic and Pacific by rail, though, had been held since the mid-nineteenth century, and the first rail connection was completed in 1910 after over 20 years of construction. This meter gauge line runs from Los Andes, between Valparaíso and Santiago, to Mendoza in western Argentina, a distance of 254 km (159 miles). It is not high in comparison with the other trans-Andine railways, rising only to 3,186 m (10,453 ft) in the Cumbre tunnel, but it includes six rack sections on the Chilean side and seven on the Argentine, using the Abt three-bar system. Moreover, it is far enough south to suffer quite severely from snow and avalanches, unlike the other trans-Andine routes. Landslides and washouts have always been common. One, in 1934, destroyed part of the Argentine section, interrupting through rail traffic for ten years. The railway has never justified the hopes of those who promoted it a century ago.

The Guayaquil and Quito Railway

The G & Q (misleadingly nicknamed the "Good and Quick") connects the two major towns of Ecuador: Guayaquil on the coast and Quito in the mountains. Work began in 1871, but it was not until 1908 that the contractors completed this rather rare 1,067 mm (3 ft 6 in) gauge railway. It extends for 463 km (288 miles) and climbs to 3,609 m (11,841 ft). Curves are tight, and the maximum grade of 5.5 percent is quite staggering for a steam-operated adhesion railway. Like the Central Railway of Peru, the Guayaquil and Quito uses switchbacks to gain height in a confined space. It has never been a commercial success, and the resulting lack of money for spare parts and replacements has given it a dreadful reputation for chaotic administration, breakdowns and derailments. Its locomotives and other equipment are often virtually antique. The fact that it continues to operate is perhaps more amazing than the fact that it was ever built.

Mountain climbing: rack and pinion

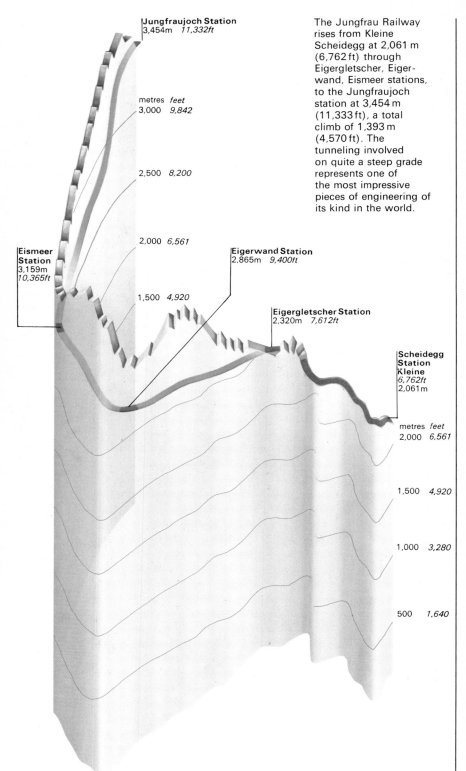

Jungfraujoch Station
3,454m *11,332ft*

metres *feet*
3,000 *9,842*

2,500 *8,200*

2,000 *6,561*

1,500 *4,920*

Eismeer
Station
3,159m
10,365ft

Eigerwand Station
2,865m *9,400ft*

Eigergletscher Station
2,320m *7,612ft*

Scheidegg
Station
Kleine
6,762ft
2,061m

metres *feet*
2,000 *6,561*

1,500 *4,920*

1,000 *3,280*

500 *1,640*

The Jungfrau Railway
rises from Kleine
Scheidegg at 2,061 m
(6,762 ft) through
Eigergletscher, Eiger-
wand, Eismeer stations,
to the Jungfraujoch
station at 3,454 m
(11,333 ft), a total
climb of 1,393 m
(4,570 ft). The
tunneling involved
on quite a steep grade
represents one of
the most impressive
pieces of engineering of
its kind in the world.

The breathtaking panorama to be enjoyed from the summit of a high mountain is normally not one to be attained without a great deal of physical effort of a skilled and specialized kind; but daring and highly ingenious railway engineering has enabled some of the most famous peaks in Europe to be ascended by train. The very first mountain railway in the world, however, was constructed in the USA in 1869 when Silvester Marsh, using a ladder type of rack between the rails, with circular rungs engaging with a vertical pinion under the locomotive, built a cogwheel railway to the summit of Mount Washington, the highest point in the White Mountains of New Hampshire, 1,918 m (6,293 ft) above sea level. This pioneer line is still worked entirely by steam. In 1871 the first mountain railway in Europe was opened, to the summit of the Rigi, overlooking the Lake of Lucerne. The engineer was Niklaus Riggenbach, and while using the same general principle as the rack pioneered by Marsh, he used a greatly improved form of rung in the ladder, which ensured a better locking effect on the locomotive pinion wheel. Nevertheless, the maximum inclination permitted was 20 percent. In the meantime another inventor, Edouard Locher, had designed a remarkable form of rack rail. It is provided with two parallel sets of horizontal teeth and each axle of the electric motor coaches has double horizontal pinion wheels. These engage and grip the central rack on both sides, and with this arrangement it was safe to have grades up to a maximum steepness of 50 percent.

In 1889, the sensational rack railway up Mount Pilatus was built, again overlooking the Lake of Lucerne. It climbs from a station on the lakeside to a height of 1,629 m (5,344 ft) in no more than 4 km (2.5 miles), making an average grade of 36 percent throughout. It was steam operated at first. The seating in the present electric powered cars is in step formation, so that the passengers are sitting roughly level on each step as the ascent is made. At

The north face of the Eiger, showing the position of the Eigerwand station windows, high up on the north wall.

times the outlook from the car is breathtaking, but nowhere more so than when the stark, precipitous face of the Eselwand is rounded, and the track is carried on a ledge blasted out of a solid, almost vertical, rock wall with a dizzy drop below on the left-hand side. Near the summit the line is taken through a tunnel hewn out of the rock, to emerge on a plateau between mountain tops at the summit and to find the hospitality of two hotels waiting at an altitude of 2,066 m (6,778 ft) above sea level.

In sheer altitude, however, the Pilatus railway is far surpassed by that of the Jungfrau, in the Bernese Oberland, which mounts to a ridge between the great mountains Jungfrau and Mönch at a height of no less than 3,454 m (11,333 ft) above sea level. At that great height a deficiency of oxygen in the air may cause faintness when a passenger steps out of the train at the summit. As a piece of mountain tunnel engineering, the Jungfrau Railway is magnificent, but because so much of it is in tunnel the ride

is not as interesting or as thrilling as that up the Pilatus. The approach ride, throughout from Interlaken, is one of great natural beauty, with superb mountain scenery; but the Jungfrau Railway proper begins at Kleine Scheidegg, and it is then 9.2 km (5.75 miles) to the summit station of Jungfraujoch. That run takes 65 min, and for no less than 50 min the train is continuously in tunnel. For mountain grandeur, however, apart from sheer sensation, the Gornegrat Railway, from Zermatt, easily takes first place, because the ascent is made in full view of that most majestic and striking of Alpine peaks, the Matterhorn. From the engineering viewpoint the Gornegrat Railway is notable as being the first in Switzerland to be operated by electricity from the outset. It was opened in 1898, 14 years before the completion of the Jungfrau line. The ruling grade is 20 percent, and the passenger is lifted 1,485 m (4,872 ft) in 9.2 km (5.75 miles). The ascent from Zermatt is made in 43 min, inclusive of stops.

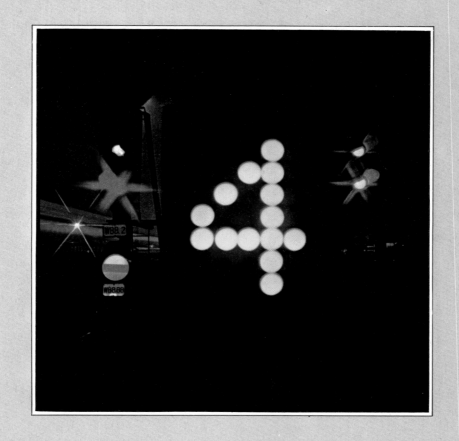

Great
Expresses

The Orient Express: the glory that faded

Few trains have been surrounded by a greater aura of mystery and romance than the Orient Express, yet few outside the most erudite of railway scholars knew its routes and their ramifications. Unlike many other great trains of the world, the Orient Express has varied and greatly diversified since it was first put on in 1883. Then its purpose was to provide a through service between Paris and Constantinople, but at that time it was not possible to travel the entire distance by train. The through coaches from Paris could go only as far as Giurgevo, a town on the Danube in Romania where that river formed the frontier with Bulgaria. Passengers crossed the Danube by ferry, and continued by train across Bulgaria to the Black Sea port of Varna, thence by steamer to Constantinople. From the winter of 1889 however the line through Turkey was completed, and the Orient Express, running once a week only beyond Vienna, took the main line of the Hungarian State Railway, southward from Budapest, and traveled via

The route of the Orient Express varied over the years and it used many types of train. The main routes shown on the map, *below*, are:
1 1900 Paris–Vienna.
2 1900 Paris–Constantinople. 3 1932 London–Bucharest. 4 1932 Simplon Orient Express. 5 1932 Arlberg Orient Express.

6 1932 Ostende–Vienna.
7 1932 London–Bucharest/Istanbul. 8 1977 Paris–Bucharest. The great romantic era of the Orient Express was in the interwar period, when it was possible to cross the Bosporus at Constantinople and travel on to Baghdād and Tehrān.

Zaribrod, and on to the Baron Hirsch Railway in Turkey. The distance by this route from Paris to Constantinople was 2,970 km (1,857 miles). Travelers left Paris by the Eastern Railway of France on Wednesday night at 7:30 p.m. and arrived in Constantinople at 5:35 p.m. on the Saturday evening, an overall average speed of 43 km/h (27 mph). No fewer than ten railway companies and six countries were involved.

There were at first many peculiarities in its operation. It was organized by the International Sleeping Car Company, and substantial supplements over the ordinary first class fare were charged. These varied over different parts of the route, and for this the car company was sometimes blamed. Actually the Sleeping Car Company received no more than a fraction of the supplement. The railway companies "cashed in" on the luxury traffic and charged what they liked, according to whether there were any competitive services.

After the introduction of the through service to Constantinople via Belgrade, a connecting train ran twice weekly from Vienna to Bucharest. It is this service that today still carries the famous name Orient Express. It leaves Paris nightly at 11:35 p.m. and arrives in Bucharest at 11:45 a.m. on the third morning. The journey time today is 36 hr 10 min, giving an overall average speed of 68 km/h (42.5 mph) over 2,448 km (1,530 miles). While there are through coaches between Paris and Bucharest the sleeping car service is not continuous.

The Direct Orient

When the Simplon Tunnel was opened in 1906 a rival to the original Orient Express was put on, using the Paris, Lyon and Mediterranean route in France and traveling through Switzerland, Italy, Austria and into Serbia. It was

named the Simplon-Orient Express, and more recently the Direct Orient, and it is this through service, between Paris and Constantinople (Istanbul) that was withdrawn in May 1977. It was a service that was twice interrupted, during the First and Second World Wars, and now it has disappeared again. The Simplon Express runs from Paris to Belgrade, and if a traveler wishes to continue to Istanbul it means an overnight stay in Belgrade and taking the Marmara Express next morning. Before the withdrawal of the Direct Orient Express in May 1977, departure from Paris (Gare de Lyon) was at 11:53 p.m. and arrival at Istanbul at 8:25 a.m. on the fourth morning, a total of $56\frac{1}{2}$ hr for the 3,024 km (1,890 miles), or 53.6 km/h (33.5 mph) overall. There was a time, after the end of the Second World War, when the service was yet again interrupted, during the civil war that broke out in Greece. Then it was necessary to detrain at the Bulgarian frontier station of Svilengrad, take a motor truck through the Grecian province of Thrace, and climb into another train at Uzunköprü. When the service was restored in 1949, and it was possible once more to travel in a through car from Paris to Istanbul, the journey through Thrace was considered somewhat hazardous. One intrepid traveler has described how five empty freight cars were propelled ahead of the locomotive, to explode any mines that might have been placed on the tracks. Immediately behind the locomotive came four Turkish RPO cars, followed by the dining car and two through cars. Following these came some very old coaches carrying soldiers "at the ready"; and finally a truck carrying an armored car armed with a field gun – also at the ready. Traveling in this way through Thrace, the maximum speed attained was no more than 32 km/h (20 mph).

At the present time, since normal operation has been

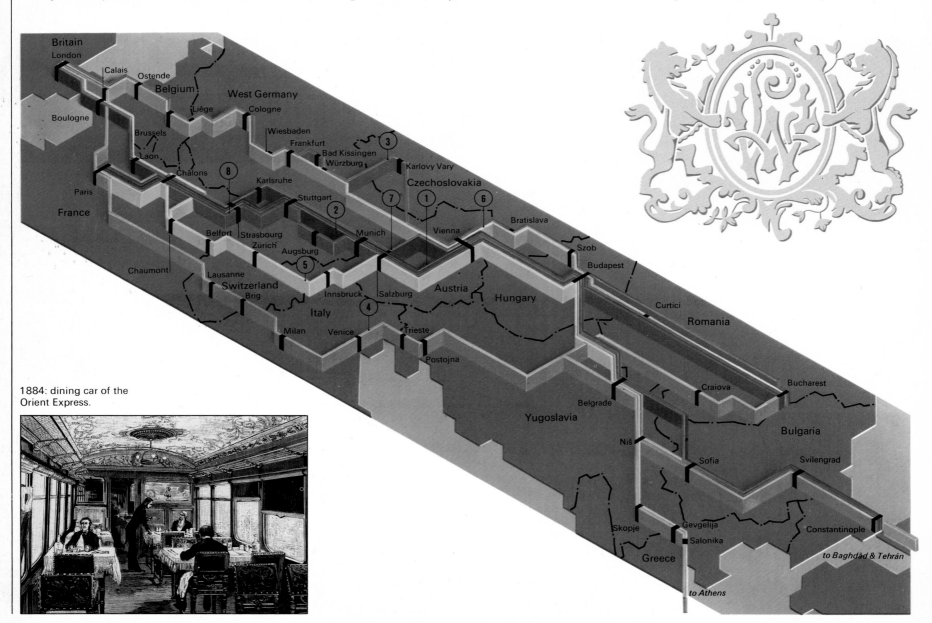

Britain
London
Calais
Ostende
Belgium
Boulogne
Liège
Brussels
Laon
Chálons
Paris
France
West Germany
Cologne
Wiesbaden
Frankfurt
Bad Kissingen
Würzburg
Karlsruhe
Karlovy Vary
Czechoslovakia
Stuttgart
Vienna
Bratislava
Belfort
Strasbourg
Zürich
Augsburg
Munich
Chaumont
Lausanne
Switzerland
Brig
Innsbruck
Salzburg
Austria
Hungary
Szob
Budapest
Italy
Milan
Venice
Trieste
Postojna
Curtici
Romania
Craiova
Bucharest
Belgrade
Yugoslavia
Niš
Sofia
Bulgaria
Svilengrad
Skopje
Gevgelija
Salonika
Constantinople
Greece
to Baghdād & Tehrān
to Athens

1884: dining car of the Orient Express.

Above Postcard showing French high-speed engine on the Orient Express, c.1900. *Right* The Direct Orient in Yugoslavia, pulled by two 05 4-6-2s. *Below* Scenes from the EMI motion picture *Murder on the Orient Express*, taken from the Agatha Christie novel.

Above North Iraq, the Istanbul-Baghdād train, linking direct with the Orient Express.

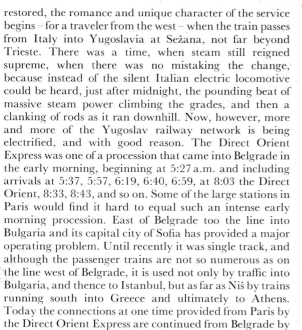

restored, the romance and unique character of the service begins – for a traveler from the west – when the train passes from Italy into Yugoslavia at Sežana, not far beyond Trieste. There was a time, when steam still reigned supreme, when there was no mistaking the change, because instead of the silent Italian electric locomotive could be heard, just after midnight, the pounding beat of massive steam power climbing the grades, and then a clanking of rods as it ran downhill. Now, however, more and more of the Yugoslav railway network is being electrified, and with good reason. The Direct Orient Express was one of a procession that came into Belgrade in the early morning, beginning at 5:27 a.m. and including arrivals at 5:37, 5:57, 6:19, 6:40, 6:59, at 8:03 the Direct Orient, 8:33, 8:43, and so on. Some of the large stations in Paris would find it hard to equal such an intense early morning procession. East of Belgrade too the line into Bulgaria and its capital city of Sofia has provided a major operating problem. Until recently it was single track, and although the passenger trains are not so numerous as on the line west of Belgrade, it is used not only by traffic into Bulgaria, and thence to Istanbul, but as far as Niš by trains running south into Greece and ultimately to Athens. Today the connections at one time provided from Paris by the Direct Orient Express are continued from Belgrade by the Athens Express.

East of Belgrade, the Direct Orient Express used to make slow progress. There were frequent stops to pass trains traveling westward, and many of these would be extremely long. At one time the Direct Orient Express carried its Athens and Istanbul sections – the present Athens and Marmara expresses – combined as far as Niš; but the loads became too great. The pastoral scene, as the train rolls placidly through the eastern part of Yugoslavia, is fascinating, but the traveler thinking of sustenance will be disappointed, because the dining car service, once such a special feature of the International Sleeping Car Company's train, is now largely nonexistent. The Direct Orient Express used to have a dining car on the Yugoslav part of the journey, but now the would-be diner has to wait until the length of Bulgaria has been traversed, entirely in darkness, and until 2:00 a.m. next morning when the Turkish dining car is put on at Kapikule. When operated by the Sleeping Car Company, it purchased its supplies from each of the countries passed through, since it was not permitted to convey food across international frontiers. The train does not exactly hurry across Bulgaria. It takes 2 hr 18 min to cover the 72 km (45 miles) from Dimitrovgrad to Sofia, and another 4¾ hr for the 312 km (195 miles) on to Svilengrad. But it is unimaginable that many business people, or men of affairs, have ever taken this train for its romantic associations.

Between the wars

The Orient Express proper, to Bucharest, and the Direct Orient, to Istanbul, were at their heights of prestige and popularity in the years between the two world wars. Stories of mystery and intrigue have been written around the journeys of the "King's Messengers" from the British Foreign Office who traveled alone in reserved compartments with their diplomatic bags. One of these distinguished servants of the country in his reminiscences has written, "Romantic writers tell us of beautiful spies and glamorous young secret agents who haunt the international trains for the purpose of extracting information from couriers, but the Greyhound knows his business far too well to mix dalliance with duty. A King's Messenger I knew – a noted Lothario – was scandalized at the suggestion that he might have commerce with the sirens of the Orient Express – 'besides,' he added naively, 'I have never seen them'."

The Direct Orient Express, or the Marmara Express of today, reaches the Turkish frontier in the early hours of the morning. It is however at Edirne that the traditional atmosphere of the Orient first strikes the traveler. On the station, in English, French, German and Italian, is a large board carrying the words "Welcome to Turkey," and if it is sufficiently light the first minarets may be glimpsed from the train. Locomotives and cars carry the crescent and star in large embossed characters on their sides. Then begins the final run toward Istanbul which takes only 6½ hr and brings the Marmara Express in at about 8:30 a.m. the next day. The terminus is at Sirkeci, on the banks of the Bosporus, beside the junction with the Golden Horn, and from this station ferries cross the waterway to the Haydarpasa station, where one takes the train for Ankara and the rest of Turkey.

The Irish Mail: over a century of service

Communication between London and Dublin was a vital feature of transportation within the British Isles long before the coming of railways, or indeed that of stage-coaches. When the British railway network began to develop rapidly in the 1840s there was controversy as to where the principal packet station for the Irish traffic should be located. Robert Stephenson was engineer for the projected Chester and Holyhead Railway, while his friend and rival, Isambard Kingdom Brunel, proposed a broad gauge line from Worcester through the heart of central Wales to Porth Dinllaen, on the Lleyd peninsula, near to the present village of Nevin, near Pwllheli. Stephenson's route was preferred, and the line was ready for the inauguration of the Irish Mail train service on August 1, 1848. It can be claimed as the first named train in the world, although it did not carry its title on the car roof boards until 1927. In 1848 one could not travel the entire way from London to Holyhead by train, because Stephenson's greatest work on the Chester and Holyhead – the great Britannia tubular bridge over the Menai Strait – was not finished. Passengers, luggage and mail had to be detrained at Bangor, travel by stagecoach across the strait over Telford's beautiful suspension bridge, and join another train at Llanfair, for the journey across Anglesey. The Britannia Bridge was completed in 1850, and from that time the Irish Mail was carried through from Euston to Holyhead by train. One picturesque tradition of earlier days remained and was continued for nearly 90 years. Each evening the "King's Time" was sent from London to Dublin by a watch sent from the General Post Office in St Martin's le Grand, conveyed by the Irish Mail train, thence by the packet steamer to Kingstown (now Dún Laoghaire) and finally by train to Dublin.

Until 1850 the sea portion of the journey had been carried out by Admiralty packets, but in that year the contract, lasting for ten years, was awarded to the City of Dublin Steam Packet Company. The magnificent inner harbor at Holyhead had not then been built, and ships sailed from the Admiralty pier. The City of Dublin company retained the contract for 70 years, and this brought a complication. The Admiralty pier would not take the weight of the express locomotives working the train from Chester, and engines had to be changed at the junction where the line to the pier left the main line into the inner harbor station. The principal service was at night, leaving Euston at 8:45 p.m., but there was also a day mail, leaving at 8:30 a.m. and carrying a traveling post office

and all the facilities of its senior partner that ran at night. In later years the day mail carried dining cars, while the night mail had sleeping cars. The times of both trains were arranged to suit the convenience of the Post Office, and the mail contracts stipulated the speeds that had to be run, both on land and sea. The contract of 1860 required an overall speed of 68 km/h (42 mph) between Euston and Holyhead, and the total journey time between London and Dublin took 11½ hr. This was a remarkable achievement for that period, because it included the necessary intermediate stops. These were certainly cut to the minimum, and it was, in fact, to permit of nonstop running over the 135 km (84 miles) between Chester and

Although the arrival time of the Irish Mail service in Dublin is a convenient 7:30 a.m., it must not be forgotten that passengers have to change from train to ship at Holyhead at 2:00 a.m., and have to be ready to leave the ship again at Dun Laoghaire at 6:45 a.m.

Top In London and North Western days: the down day mail (8:30 a.m. from Euston) leaving the Britannia tubular bridge, hauled by a Precursor 4-4-0.
Right Mail pick-up at speed using traditional system, now phased out.

Dublin
535km (332mls)
arr 07:30

Holyhead
424km (263mls)
arr 02:28
ferry dep 03:15

Dun Laoghaire
524km (326mls)
arr 06:45 dep 07:05

ferry crossing

Chester
318km (198mls)
dep 00:47

Crewe
254km (158mls)
dep 00:07

Rugby
133km (83mls)
dep 22:21

London (Euston)
dep 21:10

The route of the Irish Mail once followed the coach road built by Thomas Telford: communication between London and Dublin has long been of paramount importance, and at first the trains ran to a schedule set by the Post Office.

Left The day mail in the last years of steam leaving the Conway tubular bridge, hauled by a Britannia Pacific locomotive.

Above The Irish Mail
waiting to depart from
London, Euston.

In the days of steam power,
this headboard
adorned the front of the
Irish Mail's locomotive,
usually at the top
of the smokebox.

Holyhead that the first water troughs in the world were laid down near Aber, east of Bangor. As the train passed over them the fireman would lower a scoop, through which water was forced into the tender "on the fly."

To meet Post Office requirements the outward-bound night mail arrived at Holyhead around 2:00 a.m. – a grisly hour for passengers to change from train to the steamer, out on the end of the Admiralty pier! As traffic between England and Ireland increased, the London and North Western Railway, with its own steamers, put on two additional express trains between London and Dublin, the day express leaving Euston at 1:20 p.m. and the night at 9:50 p.m. These connected with steamers sailing from the inner harbor at Holyhead, and were much more convenient for passengers. After the First World War, when, because of political troubles, traffic to Ireland was much reduced, the ordinary day and night expresses were not revived, and the day and night mail trains provided the only service. At the same time the London and North Western Railway secured the mail contract for the sea passage, and the packets thereafter sailed from the inner harbor at Holyhead. When the London and North Western became part of the London Midland and Scottish Railway, in 1923, the coach and engine livery became crimson lake, and in 1927 the car roof boards were added. By the time the famous train celebrated its centennial, in 1948, it was being worked by the nationalized British Railways.

The Settebello: speed and luxury

A free translation of the Italian name for this fast luxury train of today is "the lucky seven," and travelers on it are indeed lucky in comparison with their forebears who had to travel on the so-called *Rapidos* of Italy, in pre-Fascist days. Certainly the passenger has to pay a substantial supplement over the regular first-class fare for the privilege of traveling on any train now designated as a Trans-Europe Express (TEE): but by and large it is worth it. In pre-Fascist days even the main line express trains and famous international services such as the Rome Express were haphazard, to put it mildly, in their operation. But Mussolini said, among a great many other rhetorical utterances, that Italian trains must run on time – period! And railway operation was certainly improved to an almost unbelievable extent. The Settebello provides a high speed luxury service between Milan and Rome, but in light of the previous reference to the Rome Express, it should be explained that the latter old-established and famous express does not use at any time the route of the Settebello. The Rome Express, leaving Paris just before midnight, comes into Italy through the Mont Cenis tunnel, stops at Turin, and then takes the historic line of I. K. Brunel down to the Mediterranean at Genoa. It then takes the coastal route to Rome, through Pisa, where someone on the platform will undoubtedly try to sell the unwary traveler a model of the leaning tower.

The Settebello, leaving Milan now at 7:50 a.m. does however follow the same route as that famous international express train, the Italia, which brings sleeping cars through from Calais, Hamburg and Brussels to Rome. This train does not go into the huge central station at Milan, which is a terminus. Coming in from the north, from the Gotthard line, it takes the avoiding line, and stops at the Lambrate station of Milan. But it joins the main line to the southeast close on the heels of the Settebello, only 7 min later; but being a much heavier train the time interval between gradually lengthens until it is nearly three quarters of an hour behind, on arrival in Rome. This does not mean, however, that the Italia is a laggard. The days are long past when Italian trains were composed of rather primitive wooden coaches with bare boards in third class and red plush on the seats in first.

Self-contained and high speed

The Settebello itself, introduced in 1953, was something of a pacesetter, not only in speed. The Italian Railways were one of the first to realize that if traffic was to be saved from passing to the airlines, and the private automobile driven in the Italian style – flat out, with horn blaring most of the time – the railways had to provide something more than comfortable compartment coaches and trains that ran at 120–130 km/h (75–80 mph) between stops. Something very much faster was needed to entice the busy executive, and the more opulent tourist. Great progress had been made after the end of the Second World War with electrifying the principal main lines in Italy, and improving the quality and maintenance standards on the track; the next step was the concept of a push-pull train with power units at both ends. This avoided the use of separate locomotives, and changing locomotives at a station like Florence, a terminal where through trains changed their direction of running. So the Settebello was designed as a self-contained seven car unit train.

The new train set a standard of speed and luxurious traveling accommodation previously unknown in Italy, rivaling anything else on European rails and, indeed, anything throughout the world, at that time. The high supplement charged for this service, as already mentioned, is virtually double the regular first-class fare, but the passenger is offered a service which is comparable to that of a five-star hotel. Each coach consists of five spacious compartments containing comfortable armchairs and couches. There are tables and lockers for hand luggage. The toilet facilities include showers and special ladies' rooms. All the coaches are completely soundproofed and there is an extremely efficient system of air conditioning. The three middle coaches of the train contain a restaurant, bar and kitchen; a baggage room where passengers' luggage is stored at the beginning of the journey; and also an office where a traveler can make a telephone call to anywhere in Italy. The interior decor is elegant and tasteful.

It is a style of high-speed express passenger train that has

07:50

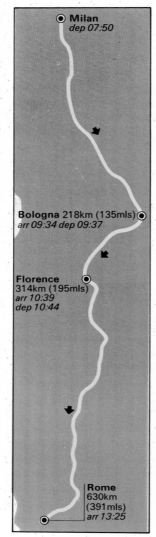

● **Milan**
dep 07:50

Bologna 218km (135mls)
arr 09:34 dep 09:37

Florence
314km (195mls)
arr 10:39
dep 10:44

Rome
630km
(391mls)
arr 13:25

13:25

Right The Settebello –
still sleek after twenty
years' service.

Above The forward observation car in the Settebello, engineer's compartment above.

IL SETTEBELLO

Settebello is an Italian game, "the lucky seven", where seven points gives victory and *the* card to hold is a seven. The Settebello is obviously *the* train to catch!

since been followed on railways in several parts of the world, including diesel-powered TEE trains running between French and German cities, the spectacular *Shinkansen* "bullet" trains in Japan, and quite recently the HST units providing such an intense service of high speed running on the Western Region of British Rail. In one fascinating respect the Italian ETR-300 trains operating the Settebello service differ from all their successors. In the rounded, streamlined ends of the seven car set there are observation lounges, supplementary to the ordinary registered seating accommodation, where passengers can ride at the very front and rear ends of the train, and enjoy a completely uninterrupted view of the line ahead. The engineman's controls are located in an upper "flight deck," above the lounge, exactly in the style of the first-class accommodation in the jumbo jet airliner, except that the arrangement was first used on the Settebello.

The Settebello now

When the Settebello gets going it leaves everything else well behind on the opening run from Milan over the straight level track to Bologna. In its earlier days the train left Milan at 5:50 p.m. and reached Rome at 11:40 p.m., so covering a large part of the journey in darkness, even in the height of the summer. Then there was only one train set shuttling back and forth, the northbound service leaving Rome at 10:50 a.m. Now there is a Settebello in each direction in the mornings, the northbound leaving Rome at 8:05 a.m. The overall time in each direction is 5 hr 35 min including stops at Bologna and Florence, 3 min and 5 min respectively, and the average running speed over the complete 630 km (390 miles) between Milan and Rome is 113.9 km/h (71.2 mph). This is a very similar average to that of the *Flying Scotsman*, over the 632.5 km (393 miles) between London and Edinburgh. With the rescheduling of the Settebello, and use of another fast TEE train, the Vesuvio, it is possible to leave Rome or Milan in the morning, have a full afternoon in either city, catch the

respective train and be back in one's home city before midnight. The Vesuvio is not quite as fast as the Settebello, taking 5 hr 50 min in each direction.

On its present schedule the Settebello normally runs at its fastest over the 218 km (135 miles) between Milan and Bologna, the time being 104 min southbound and 102 min northbound. The latter represents a start-to-stop average speed of 130 km/h (80 mph). The central section of 96 km (60 miles) between Bologna and Florence is the slowest, being allowed 62 min. This is due not so much to the severe grades over the ascent to the great Apennine Tunnel as the restriction on speed necessary over the many curves leading up to the piercing of the mountain range. This is indeed a thrilling stretch over which to ride in the forward observation lounge, with the track curving first to one side and then to the other, magnificent views over the countryside as the train gathers height, and the passage through the tunnel itself 18.4 km (11.5 miles) long. Until recently an observer riding at the head end of the train through the tunnel would have been surprised to see what looked like a station midway between the two ends. There was indeed a regularly manned tower box there that controlled the entrance and exit from two long sidings. These were made to provide refuges for slow-running freight trains, and the towerman down there, at Precedenze, as the tower was called, surely had one of the strangest jobs on the world's railways, hundreds of feet below the crest of the mountain, and about 8 km (5 miles) from daylight at the nearest end.

The southern end of the journey provides some further splendid sightseeing. The line from Florence to Rome makes a winding course through mountainous country; but there is more opportunity for fast running here, and the 326 km (203 miles) are covered in 161 min. This is nothing to what is intended when the new Direttissima is complete. The track distance between the two cities will be reduced to 251 km (157 miles), and the average speed is hoped to be about 160 km/h (100 mph).

The Aquitaine: pioneer of electric power

The main line between Paris and Bordeaux has from the middle of the nineteenth century been one of the most enterprising of French express routes. The Basque coast was already a favored vacation area, and at the same time the route formed an important link on the international line from Paris to Madrid and Lisbon, even though there was, as now, a change of rail gauge at the Spanish frontier. At that time the Paris-Orléans was the owning company as far south as Bordeaux, beyond which town the Midi Railway took over. The name "Aquitaine" for one of the fastest trains on this line, and indeed one of the fastest in all Europe, has been only recently bestowed; but the present magnificently appointed 200 km/h (125 mph) electric train is one of the manifestations of a great heritage of express passenger train operation. Although the route is now all electric, in the years until the advent of electric operation, the Paris-Orléans railway operated one of the greatest steam locomotives the world has ever seen.

The Orléans company

To take the story back nearly 100 years, the Orléans company had a deluxe train from Paris to Bordeaux that was the fastest long-distance express on the continent of Europe. But there was a big difference in the overall time. Leaving Paris at 6:58 p.m. it was not due in Bordeaux until 3:30 a.m. the following day, whereas the Aquitaine leaves at 5:53 p.m. and after a nonstop run arrives at 9:43 p.m. The respective average speeds are 68 and 150.9 km/h (42.5 and 94.3 mph) – a startling example of the advancement of railway service on this route in 90 years. The train of 1888 stopped at Les Aubrais (Orléans), St-Pierre-des-Corps (Tours), Poitiers, Angoulême, and Coutras. The stopping times were 4 min at each place except Coutras. At Bordeaux it was taken over by the Midi for the rest of the journey to Biarritz. On the Orléans it was hauled by the strikingly picturesque 2-4-2 locomotives designed by M. Forguenot.

Early in the twentieth century the Orléans company purchased some very fine compound Atlantic engines of Alfred de Glehn's design, and these locomotives provided the power for acceleration of service with heavier trains. In 1907 the company was the first in Europe to introduce locomotives of the Pacific type. At the same time most of the cars on the trains from Paris to the towns and cities of

Above The Aquitaine at speed, an SNCF publicity photograph.

The sleek and shiny headboard carried by today's Aquitaine symbolizes the SNCF's modern approach to rail transport.

Aquitaine were four-wheelers, though relatively large, with a long wheel base. The compartments inside were comfortable with tasteful decor, though with rather feeble oil lighting. Between stops the Atlantics and Pacifics used to wheel their long trains at speeds up to 113 km/h (70 mph) along the tracks. Then 120 km/h (74.5 mph) was the maximum speed permitted by law anywhere in France, and it was a limit that was strictly observed. The Orléans Railway was affected less than most of the French railways during the First World War, and in the mid-1920s the company embarked upon a program of electrification that was intended to include the entire length of its two main lines, to Bordeaux and to its junction with the Midi Railway at Montauban, near Toulouse.

The system chosen was the French standard of 1,500 volts direct current from an overhead line, and in December 1926 the first section was brought into

operation, from Paris to Vierzon. This latter station was at the beginning of the hilly section of the Toulouse line. This diverged from the Bordeaux line at the junction of Les Aubrais (Orléans) and it meant that trains for Bordeaux and the south changed from electric to steam operation at Les Aubrais. Those responsible for steam locomotives working on the Orléans realized that with the powerful new electric locomotives at work and the acceleration of service that they made possible, unfavorable comparisons could well be made between the standards of train running north and south of Les Aubrais. At that time the very latest of the steam passenger locomotives in service were nearly 20 years old. Furthermore, the large Pacific engines had not come up to expectation and, when worked at maximum capacity, were not a great deal better than the much smaller Atlantics. So a most thorough research program was begun to try to pinpoint their deficiencies.

Chapelon and the Tours works

The work was entrusted to a young engineer named André Chapelon, and by 1929 one of the old Pacifics had been extensively rebuilt, to his recommendations, at the Tours works of the company. In tests out on the line it was shown that the capacity of the engine had been increased by no less than 50 percent. More engines of the type were rebuilt and it could soon be said that little if any difference could be discerned in the quality of the train running north and south of Les Aubrais. Steam, nevertheless, was fighting a rearguard action on the Orléans, because the policy of the company was to extend electrification southward, thereby displacing more steam locomotives. And when the amalgamation with the Midi Railway came, in 1934, steam operation was caught in a "pincer movement," because the main line of the Midi was electrified south of Bordeaux. But what had been done by the men of the

The Aquitaine is scheduled to run from Paris to Bordeaux nonstop, at an average speed of 150.8 km/h (94.3 mph). This heavy-weight train covers the distance in a very fast time of 3 hr 50 min.

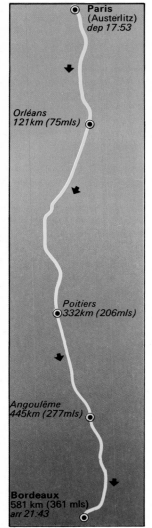

Paris (Austerlitz) dep 17:53

Orléans 121km (75mls)

Poitiers 332km (206mls)

Angoulême 445km (277mls)

Bordeaux 581 km (361 mls) arr 21:43

Right The Étendard, sister train of the Aquitaine, with the Capitole alongside.

Bordeaux is one of the largest French ports, and straddles major routes to Spain and Africa. It is also a tourist attraction: especially the twelfth-century church of Ste Croix.

Publicity photo of buffet car on the Aquitaine.

Orléans, at the Tours works, echoed around the railway world and was the pattern for many improvements in steam locomotive design in far distant lands such as the USA and Russia, as well as elsewhere in France and in Great Britain.

The Aquitaine's "flyers"

After the Second World War the rest of the former Orléans main lines were electrified, now under national ownership, and a great drive began toward the attainment of higher speeds. New electric locomotives were introduced and some thrilling high-speed trials conducted south of Bordeaux, where the record maximum speed of 329.6 km/h (206 mph) was attained on two successive trips. With the experience of these runs, and use of the same types of locomotive in general service on several different routes elsewhere in France, the present magnificent 8,000 hp electric locomotive was produced which has made practicable the very fast schedule worked to by the Aquitaine and other express trains on the Paris-Bordeaux route. Over a considerable proportion of the line, continuous running at 200 km/h (125 mph) is now permitted, and a remarkable high-speed train service is now provided. Until the autumn of 1976 it was considered very good going to cover the 580 km (360 miles) from Paris to Bordeaux in exactly 4 hr, that is an average speed of 145 km/h (90 mph); but in September of that year some further improvements were made.

Although there are many fast trains on this route the two outstanding "flyers" are the Étendard and the Aquitaine. Southbound the Étendard leaves Paris at 7:51 a.m. reaching Bordeaux in 4 hr 5 min with three intermediate stops – St-Pierre-des-Corps, Poitiers, and Angoulême. The successive start-to-stop average speeds are 150, 162.5, 140 and 123.5 km/h (93.8, 101.6, 87.5 and 77.2 mph). The Aquitaine, leaving at 5:53 p.m., goes down nonstop in 3 hr 50 min, averaging 150.8 km/h (94.3 mph). In the opposite direction the Aquitaine, leaving Bordeaux at 8:00 a.m., reaches Paris in 3 hr 59 min stopping at Angoulême and Poitiers, while the Étendard comes up nonstop in 3 hr 50 min arriving in Paris at 9:40 p.m. These trains are no lightweights. In some countries, notably West Germany, the fastest trains that are locomotive-hauled rather than fixed-unit consists like the Settebello, and certain of the TEE services for which the West German Federal

Railways provide the rolling stock, are restricted to limited consists; but the French have always specialized in hauling gargantuan loads, and a train like the Sud Express, which leaves Paris just after the Étendard has departed in the morning, may have a total load of up to 16 or 17 cars.

The Aquitaine and the Etendard, which are scheduled to run at 200 km/h (125 mph), are actually limited, though the limit is not a low one. They take a maximum of ten of the huge "Grand Confort" cars, which loaded with passengers and luggage weigh about 550 tons. It is not that the great CC 6500 class electric locomotives cannot take any more, at the very high speeds scheduled; it is that in so doing they would take too much electric current out of the overhead line. In this respect the Orléans line is paying the penalty of being a pioneer in electric traction in France. When this line was electrified in the mid-1920s, and had the wires extended farther south in the 1930s, there was no thought that such demands for power would be made as to haul a 550-ton train at 200 km/h (125 mph). The substations supplying the overhead power line were spaced at distances thought to be more than adequate for the heaviest demands foreseen at that time. That they are able to meet the needs of today is a tribute to the foresight of those who planned the electrification. But there is a limit.

Future acceleration

The accelerations of September 1977 do not represent the limit of point-to-point speed on this enterprising route, without exceeding the maximum speed of 200 km/h (125 mph) and with it the maximum demand for power. On the very first day of the new timetable the Aquitaine had to make an emergency stop on the first stage called for by signals, and reached Angoulême 6½ min late. No time was regained on the next section, on which the 113 km (70 miles) to Poitiers must be run in 45 min start-to-stop – an average of 149.6 km/h (93.5 mph). But on the final run up from Poitiers to Paris, 330 km (206 miles), allowed 135 min, not only was all the lost time regained, but the effect of four slight checks was absorbed, and the train arrived in Paris 2 min early. Allowing for the effect of those checks the net time from Poitiers was only 123¾ min – an average of 160 km/h (100 mph), and 11½ min better than the new accelerated schedule.

The Chief: America in style

The Atchison Topeka and Santa Fe is one of the largest railways in the USA, with a route length of more than 20,800 km (13,000 miles). Over its lengthy main line of 3,562 km (2,226 miles), from Chicago to Los Angeles, there used to run some of the most famous trains on the North American continent, such as the Fast Mail and the California Limited; but the queen of them all, and one of the world's greatest trains, was the Chief. In the days before and during the Second World War it was always popular with the most élite of travelers. Consequently heavy, it frequently had to be run in two sections. At the zenith of steam days on the Santa Fe, however, it ran in two sections only from Chicago to the West Coast – a Hudson type 4-6-4 over the more level eastern section of 1,595 km (991 miles) from Chicago to La Junta, Colorado, and then one of the mighty 4-8-4s of the 3765 or 3776 classes onward to Los Angeles.

The normal load of the Chief was 14 cars leading from the locomotive as follows: two mail storage cars, a railway post office, a combination baggage and dormitory lounge car, four sleeping cars, dining car, three sleeping cars, and an observation lounge car bringing up the rear. The journey time from Chicago to Los Angeles was nearly two days, and the accommodation and service *en route* were up to the finest American standards. In days before air travel became the prime mode of travel for wealthy patrons and businessmen, the standards set by the Atchison Topeka and Santa Fe were second to none on the railways of the world.

Seven states and fourteen crews

No fewer than seven states were passed on the journey to the west: in succession Illinois, Missouri, Kansas, Colorado, New Mexico, Arizona and California. Given such a cavalcade it was fortunate that some of the finest scenery was passed through in daylight. On the eastern end, with the Hudson-class locomotive, five separate engine crews were involved. Then from La Junta, with a 4-8-4 on the head end, nine different crews in succession were put on to work the train, making a total of 14 different crews on the entire two-day journey. Crews were changed at Fort Madison, Kansas City, Newton, Dodge City, La Junta, Raton, Las Vegas, Albuquerque, Gallup, Winslow, Seligman, Needles, and finally at Barstow before the train

finally ended its journey at Los Angeles. Because of its accessibility, the fuel used throughout from Chicago to Los Angeles was oil, and the locomotives were serviced twice on the route.

From La Junta westward the route crosses one mountain range after another, in majestic and often breathtaking scenery. First comes the Sangre de Cristo range, and the grade up to the Ratou Tunnel, 3.5 percent, is so severe that even the huge 4-8-4 locomotives had to take a "helper." Then comes fast downhill running and then another hard climb, from Las Vegas, New Mexico, to the crest of the Glorieta Range. Next, downhill into the Apache Canyon, along the old Santa Fe trail. It is "give and take" hard slogging for the locomotive all the way from La Junta until the summit of the Cajon Pass is reached in the early morning of the third day out from the start in Chicago. As an enthusiastic American observer has once recorded, "Often it seems they are doing the impossible, as they smash at long sustained grades at high speed, tip over high mountain passes, drift down, to attack a gleaming tangent (straight track) at 100 miles an hour."

New Mexico and Arizona

At Albuquerque, after 553 km (344 miles) of hard going, the locomotive was detached from the train briefly, and went to a bay in the neighboring roundhouse for servicing. Then she came back with the fourth crew of the journey in charge, and on a gradual ascending grade climbed to the top of the Continental Divide at an altitude of 2,209 m (7,248 ft). The ensuing descent toward Gallup, New Mexico, is one of the finest racing stretches of the whole route, and it was a regular thing for these enormous engines to cover 214 km (133 miles) here in two hours. Then to Winslow, Arizona, where the locomotive was serviced again, during a twenty-minute stop. It would be dark even in the summer by the time the train left again, and so it continued through the night and into California. In doing this type of work, with continuous hard steaming, nothing but the most intense and immaculate servicing by dedicated staff ensured the reliability demanded of the Santa Fe.

The diesel-hauled Super Chief was running by 1939. But although it was faster it never supplanted the Chief in

Left A memorable advertisement for the Chief.

Above Santa Fe's first California Limited, forerunner of the Chief, running into Los Angeles in the 1880s.

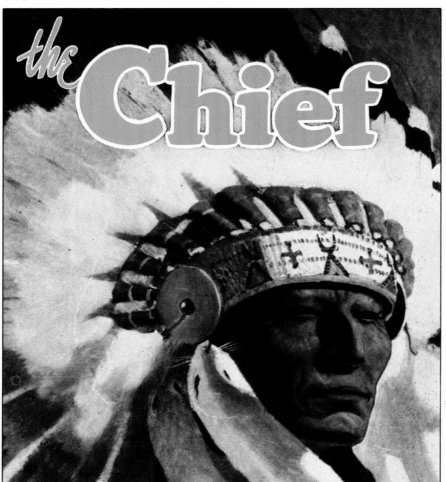

The Chief crossed seven states in its journey from Los Angeles to Chicago, and 14 crew changes were involved. The growth of the city of Los Angeles and its port was largely linked with the coming of the railways: today it is America's third greatest city.

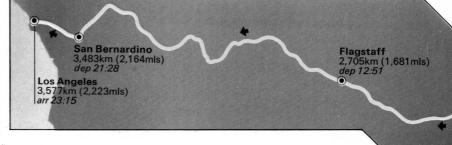

San Bernardino
3,483km (2,164mls)
dep 21:28

Los Angeles
3,577km (2,223mls)
arr 23:15

Flagstaff
2,705km (1,681mls)
dep 12:51

In the postwar era the Chief was diesel powered, and all Santa Fe diesels carried the device, *above*, emblazoned on their front. It has since been changed.

Below The Chief with cars that are the most familiar to this route.

popularity, until the great recession in American railway passenger travel began in the 1950s and the cream of the business passed to the airlines. Nevertheless, among older travelers the Chief of the Santa Fe is remembered with affection.

Super Chief and Southwest Limited

Today, under the auspices of Amtrak, its place has been taken by the Southwest Limited. With the aid of a trio of 3,000 hp diesel-electric locomotives, it runs from La Junta to Los Angeles, and the time is $5\frac{1}{2}$ hr faster than with steam. Two of those three locomotives work right through from Chicago; the third couples on at La Junta to help in the heavy-grade work over the western mountain ranges. There is much running at 137 to 145 km/h (85 to 90 mph) on the straight and level stretches. Diesel- or steam-hauled, it is a run that could scarcely be paralleled anywhere else in the world, both for its sustained interest for the railway historian and enthusiast, and for the variety and grandeur of its ever-changing scenery – some of the most dramatic in the entire continent.

Above The Southwest Limited, the modern Amtrak equivalent of the Chief, arrives at Los Angeles.

Chicago, a terminal point of the Chief, is the second city of the USA and claims to be the world's largest railway traffic center. The Super Chief began running in 1939 but the Chief retained its popularity until the 1950s.

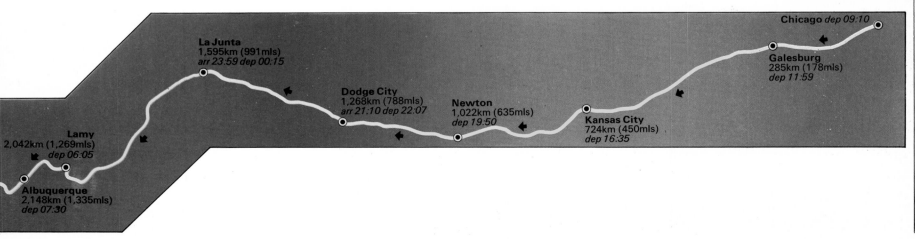

Chicago *dep 09:10*

Galesburg
285km (178mls)
dep 11:59

La Junta
1,595km (991mls)
arr 23:59 dep 00:15

Dodge City
1,268km (788mls)
arr 21:10 dep 22:07

Newton
1,022km (635mls)
dep 19:50

Kansas City
724km (450mls)
dep 16:35

Lamy
2,042km (1,269mls)
dep 06:05

Albuquerque
2,148km (1,335mls)
dep 07:30

The Blue Train: pride of South Africa

If one were asked to nominate a train in which the accommodation was the most luxurious ever offered to the traveling public, the Blue Train of the South African Railways would easily come first. The name would immediately remind English travelers of something much nearer home, because for some time before the South African Railways adopted the title the Paris, Lyon and Mediterranean had been running the *Train Bleu*, a nightly sleeping car express from Paris to the much-favored resorts on the Côte d'Azur. In South Africa the need for a luxury train from the Cape to the cities of the Transvaal came as part of the rehabilitation program at the conclusion of the Boer War. In 1903 the new service between Cape Town and Pretoria was put on, and even in those days the rolling stock was the height of luxury and ran in connection with the arrivals of the Union Castle mail steamers from England. Each train ran two days a week in each direction, leaving Cape Town at 10:45 a.m. and reaching Johannesburg at 4:30 p.m. on the following afternoon. At the time of its introduction it was operated jointly by the Cape Government Railway as far north as Kimberley, and there the Central South African Railway (CSAR) took over for the rest of the journey. Practically all the equipment of the CSAR was new, supplied from Great Britain.

After the Union

When the Union of South Africa was formed in 1910, and the previously independently worked railways of the Cape of Good Hope and of Natal amalgamated with the CSAR to form the South African Railways, the name of the luxury express running between Cape Town and Pretoria was initiated as the Union Limited. Although it remained first-class only, and required supplementary fares, there was an "all classes" express train running from Cape Town to the north on the five days that the Union Limited did not run, taking 39 hr to reach Johannesburg, with many more intermediate stops, against the 29¾ hr of the deluxe train. The Union Limited, despite its exclusive nature, became a most popular train requiring many more coaches. The locomotives grew in size from the smart Pacifics of the CSAR to giant 4-8-2s in the 1930s. Although the track gauge is no more than 1,067 mm (3 ft 6 in), physical conditions have enabled the locomotives to be built considerably wider and taller than those on the standard gauge railways of Great Britain. Speeds are not high by present-day standards, and with steam power the maximum permitted is 88.5 km/h (55 mph).

In April 1939 the name was changed to the Blue Train, this coinciding with the introduction of some magnificent new rolling stock which, unlike all other passenger car stock on the South African Railways, was painted blue. The new cars had clerestory roofs, and the upper panels were painted cream. The steam locomotives of the South African Railways had always been black, but black or not, the engines of the Union Limited, and later of the Blue Train, were always immaculately turned out. As to the modern rolling stock, the compartments are more like Royal lounges, or deluxe apartments on board ship, than the interior of trains available to the general public. They are upholstered in blue leather, and on the seats there are loose cushions. The compartments have writing tables and attractive headed notepaper, and available throughout the journey there is an excellent valet service. The dining car is sumptuously appointed, and at the rear end there is an observation car. The South African Railways sets store upon the public relations rendered by the traveling staff, and all those allocated to the Blue Train are specially selected. The train is now electrically hauled between Pretoria and Kimberley, and again between Beaufort West and Cape Town, by locomotives specially painted blue, in contrast to the standard russet color of nonsteam units on the SAR. Until fairly recently the central part of the journey was steam hauled, but now specially painted diesel-electric locomotives operate this section. The train now leaves Cape Town at 12 noon, and reaches Johannesburg in 24½ hr, an excellent overall average speed of 63 km/h (39 mph). Pretoria is reached at 2:00 p.m. On the southbound run, departure from Pretoria is at 10:00 a.m., arriving at Cape Town at 12 noon. The stops after Johannesburg are Klerksdorp, Kimberley, De Aar Junction, Beaufort West and Worcester.

Anniversary celebrations

In April 1969 the 30th anniversary of the Blue Train was celebrated in most spectacular fashion. At the suggestion of the Historical Transport Association of Johannesburg, a special anniversary run was organized, steam hauled throughout in both directions. Great pride has always been taken in the appearance and turnout of the main line steam locomotives of the South African Railways, and on this occasion a trophy was awarded to the crew of the best-prepared engine. The staging points for engine changing on this special occasion were the same as the normal passenger stops, except that in Cape Province engines were changed at Touwsrivier. Six locomotives were involved in each direction of operation and the competition between crews for the trophy produced some truly sensational efforts. It was not merely a question of polishing up the usual externals. The wheels, motion, and all the running gear were cleaned to watchmaker's standards, but the day's peak was attained when one of the huge 4-8-4s of Class 25 backed down on the train at Kimberley at nine o'clock at night and the great crowd assembled on the platform saw the interior of the engine cab, with not only all the paintwork of that usually dirty place immaculately clean, but every metal part burnished until the interior looked like a jeweler's shop. At every place on the journey where engines were changed, enthusiastic crowds were out in force to greet the train – even in the dead of night. That fantastic steam-hauled Blue Train will live in the memory of all who saw her – an experience to be treasured for a lifetime. Meanwhile the regular luxury train continues on its silent and effortless way.

Cape Town is the chief port of South Africa and the southern terminal of the South African railway network. The Blue Train originally ran as a link with the ships to Britain and had therefore to match the luxury available on board.

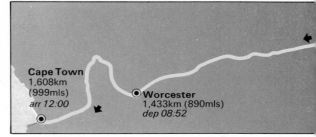

Cape Town
1,608km
(999mls)
arr 12:00

Worcester
1,433km (890mls)
dep 08:52

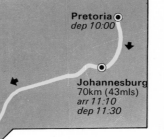

When the Blue Train was first electrified, it carried a bilingual headboard, *left*.

Before the rise of air travel finished the ocean liner, the Blue Train was an important link between the administrative capital, Pretoria, and the outside world, via the port at Cape Town. Pretoria is characterized by the Voortrekker Monument, to Dutch pioneers who first colonized the high veldt.

Pretoria
dep 10:00

Johannesburg
70km (43mls)
arr 11:10
dep 11:30

Klerksdorp
256km (159mls)
dep 14:39

Kimberley
563km (350mls)
arr 18:46 dep 19:11

De Aar
801km (498mls)
arr 22:16 dep 22:21

Beaufort West
1,064km (661mls)
arr 02:14
dep 02:39

Locomotives of the 25 class which once pulled the Blue Train, but which were superseded by diesel and electric power, and by a more modern "clean" image.

The modern Blue Train.

The modern Trans Natal near Durban, a great rival of the Blue Train.

The Canadian: transcontinental connection

The Canadian of Canadian Pacific Rail is indeed a train with a pedigree. Its predecessors take the history of travel in Canada back to the very dawn of transcontinental travel, and that is to the inception of the Dominion itself. The integration of the far-flung centers of early colonization into a unified community that was so soon to grow into a great nation depended entirely upon the provision of a railway line that would connect British Columbia and Vancouver Island, with the prairies, the cities of the St Lawrence basin, and with the maritime provinces. And when the great pioneers had found their way and built their line through the colossal barriers of the Rockies and the Selkirk ranges, and the last spike had been driven at Craigellachie on November 7, 1885, this extraordinary route had to be operated, 4,680 km (2,908 miles) of it, between Montreal and Vancouver.

Crack express

Across the length of the Canadian Pacific Railway the crack transcontinental express of the early 1900s, the Imperial Limited, made its stately way. It was not a fast train, and in the mountain passes of British Columbia, where some of the grades were as steep as 4 percent, it needed one locomotive to every two cars in the train. Very soon the burden of working this fearful incline, with a grade of 4.5 percent for 6.5 km (4 miles), had become excessive and in 1909 the tremendous task of easing it was undertaken by boring two spiral tunnels in the Swiss fashion, and reducing the grade to 2.2 percent. It was still, however, a single-track railway, and even though very much larger locomotives were introduced the weight of trains went on increasing, and by the beginning of the 1930s the need for triple headers was not unusual. The atmosphere in those single-track tunnels in the cab of the third of three hard-worked steam locomotives took some withstanding! By that time the crack transcontinental train was known as the Dominion, and the Canadian Pacific, in 1931, was running another, called the Canadian, not on this same route, which was then the fastest in the world. On the Montreal-Toronto run it covered the 200 km (124 miles) from Montreal West to Smith's Falls in 109 min. There was then fierce competition for the intercity traffic between the Canadian Pacific and the Canadian National Railways, which ended soon afterwards with a pooling agreement.

Vancouver Island, a natural west coast harbor, was the goal of the first Canadian transcontinental line to be built (the Canadian Pacific's) and was reached in 1887. A through traveler will have been in 4 time zones when he arrives after breakfast on the fourth day.

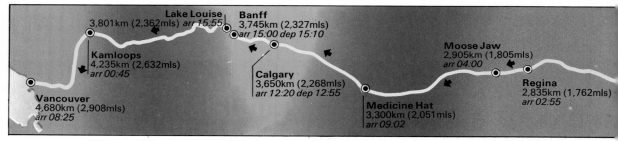

In the meanwhile the Dominion continued as the principal transcontinental train until 1955, when in the floodtide of postwar development a second train, consisting of splendid new stainless steel rolling stock, was put on. This train was named the Canadian and supplanted the Dominion as the premier service. Both continued, however, for another ten years on the Montreal/Toronto to Vancouver service; but after that declining traffic led to the withdrawal of the Dominion. Today the Canadian, diesel-hauled, leaves Montreal at 11:15 a.m. The Toronto section, which does not have so far to go, leaves at 3:30 p.m., and the two are combined at Sudbury, Ontario, leaving there at 10:25 p.m. It is a most luxurious train. The cars are of seven varieties. Coupled next to the locomotive is a baggage dormitory car, which includes living quarters for the dining and buffet car crews and the stewards. For although the locomotive crews are changed at each division point, the train crews are changed only once on the long journey, at Winnipeg. Then, in order going rearward from the locomotive come the deluxe coaches, providing seating for 60 passengers, followed by the scenic dome coach. This includes a buffet and snack lounge and the skyline coffee shop. The dining cars come next, and then there are the sleeping cars.

Finally at the rear end of the train is the special observation lounge, which includes an elevated dome portion, and a lower level stern-walk lounge buffet – a most satisfying car in which to ride. Except for the baggage car, and the 60-seater coaches, all cars on the Canadian are named, some with the prefix "Château" and others with the suffix "Manor." They are named after men famous in Canadian history, such as *Château Montcalm, Château Cadillac, Wolfe Manor* and *Dufferin Manor.*

The Canadian's Magnificent route

The route of the Canadian across the country varies in its scenic and historical interest; but apart from the tremendous scenery in the Rockies one of the most beautiful stretches – especially if the weather is fine – comes soon after breakfast time on the second day out from Montreal, when the train is making its way along the northern shores of Lake Superior. It was a terrible section to build, cutting a ledge in towering walls of rock rising sheer from the waters of the lake, working in a land where the best way of getting forward the necessary supplies was to bring them across the lake by water or by sledge during the winter months when the lake is always completely frozen over. Today the passenger can enjoy the ride as the

train rounds one bay after another, passes through tunnels in the solid rock, and it is not necessary to be in one of the domes to see the front and rear of the long train at the same time. At Thunder Bay, reached about lunchtime, the first change of time takes place, from Eastern to Central time. Winnipeg on the threshold of the prairies is not reached until late in the evening of the second day.

The richest of the prairie regions are passed in the night, and at Swift Current watches are put back a second time, when entering the region of Mountain Time. There are some long runs across the western prairies on the third day, in daylight from Swift Current to Medicine Hat, 236 km (147.5 miles), and then on into the province of Alberta and its capital city of Calgary. By that time the long, fascinating snow-capped range of the Rocky Mountains is already in sight. The train stops for half an hour at Calgary and for one dollar passengers may break their journey with a "lift" to the top of the station's Husky Tower, a Calgarian equivalent of the Post Office Tower in London, for a marvelous view of the city and the surrounding country. So back to the train and, with the shadows closing in, a dive into the mountains in earnest for the third night on the journey. Vancouver is reached about breakfast time on the fourth day.

The claim of the crest of the Canadian Pacific to "span the world," *left*, derives from the corporation's other interests in shipping and air travel.

Above Stopping point for the Canadian in the Prairies, here pulled by only two power units – see the doubling opposite.

The French-speaking city of Montreal is the world's largest inland port, due to the St Lawrence Seaway. It is the headquarters both of the Canadian Pacific, the operators of the Canadian, and also of the other major carrier, Canadian National.

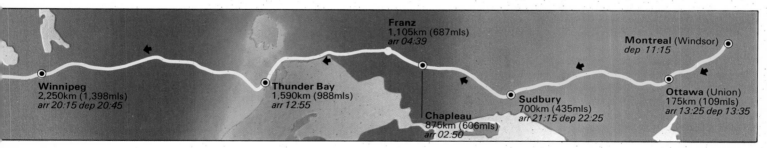

Franz
1,105km (687mls)
arr 04:39

Montreal (Windsor)
dep 11:15

Winnipeg
2,250km (1,398mls)
arr 20:15 dep 20:45

Thunder Bay
1,590km (988mls)
arr 12:55

Chapleau
875km (606mls)
arr 02:50

Sudbury
700km (435mls)
arr 21:15 dep 22:25

Ottawa (Union)
175km (109mls)
arr 13:25 dep 13:35

Above left The Canadian crossing typical landscape in the Rockies.

Right The Canadian at a stop in the Rockies, British Columbia. *Far right* The Canadian in the new paint scheme of VIA, a new cooperative operation of Canadian National and Canadian Pacific Railways.

The Rajdhani Express: India's fastest

In Imperial days there were several famous express trains crossing the Indian subcontinent, such as the Frontier Mail and the Imperial Indian Mail, from Bombay to Calcutta; but since independence the railway requirements of India have changed considerably, and one of the most important considerations has been to give improved and accelerated service without incurring heavy capital investment, or recurring capital charges. The outcome of much research work in the fine establishment of the Indian Railways in Lucknow has been the introduction of two Rajdhani Expresses, one running between New Delhi and Calcutta, the other from New Delhi to Bombay. One Rajdhani runs between New Delhi and Howrah, the great terminus on the right bank of the Ganges opposite Calcutta. This fine train, which runs twice a week in each direction, covers the 1,450 km (900 miles) in just over 16 hr, an average speed of 88.5 km/h (55 mph). It stops only at Kānpur and Mughalserai, and is classed as a deluxe train, conveying both first- and second-class passengers. A small supplement is charged for the speed of transit. Until recently a speed of 96 km/h (60 mph) was the maximum permissible with passenger trains on the broad gauge 1,676 mm (5 ft 6 in) lines in India; but the research establishment in Lucknow is now working to make possible speeds of 160 km/h (100 mph), and the Rajdhani Express

Diesel electric unit
hauls Rajdhani Express.

already runs at speeds of up to 120 km/h (75 mph) over long stretches of its journey. Eventually, overall journey times will be reduced considerably.

The design of the rolling stock is interesting. The train runs through the night, leaving New Delhi at 6:15 p.m. on the eastbound run, and Calcutta (Howrah) at 5:10 p.m. westbound. The coaches are fully air-conditioned throughout the sitting and sleeping accommodation. The "chair" cars each have 73 seats, and taking advantage of the wide gauge, these are arranged three on one side and two on the other side of the aisle. The price of a seat in one of the "chair" cars includes the cost of evening tea, dinner, early morning tea and breakfast, and meals are served airline style with boxes for every seat. The sleeping cars for travel, in which the fare is three times that in a "chair" car, each have three four-berth compartments, and three coupés with extra wide windows and sunk-in upper berths. There is an air-conditioned pantry car on the train, in which the excellent food prepared at base establishments is stored, hot or cold, until it is served at the appropriate meal times.

The other Rajdhani service between New Delhi and Bombay is a journey of 1,384 km (860 miles) the route lying through Kota and Vadodora Junction (Baroda). This is also a night service, but until now it has not been possible to schedule so high a speed as on the Delhi-Calcutta run. The southbound train leaves at 5:00 p.m. and reaches Bombay at 10:55 a.m., with stops at Ratlām and Baroda. The overall average is nevertheless the very good one of 77 km/h (48 mph) for this long run. The corresponding northbound train leaves Bombay at 3:30 p.m. Like the Rajdhani trains to and from Calcutta, the Bombay trains run twice a week in each direction.

The traditional steam
competitor of the Rajdhani
Express.

Bombay has been called
The "Gateway to India"
because of its fine
harbor; it is second only
to Calcutta as India's
leading port. Today its
population is approaching
six millions.

New Delhi, occupying an
almost central position in
the Indian subcontinent,
has been the capital of
India since 1931.

● **New Delhi**
dep 17:00

Mathura
141km (88mls)

Sawai Mādhopur
358km (222mls)

Kota
469km (291mls)

Ratlām
732km (455mls)
dep 02:28

Vadodara Junction
993km (617mls)
dep 06:07

Surat
1,122km(697mls)

Bombay
1,384km
(860mls)
arr 10:55

Decorative Indian steam.

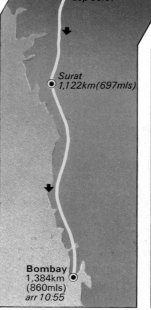

Atlas

ATLANTIC OCEAN

NORWEGIAN SEA

NORTH SEA

BALTIC SEA

MEDITERRANEAN SEA

Tyrrhenian Sea

Ionian Sea

Adriatic Sea

ICELAND
Reykjavik

FAERÖE ISLANDS (Den.)

SHETLAND ISLANDS
Lerwick

ORKNEY ISLANDS
Kirkwall

ROCKALL (U.K.)

Arctic Circle

NORWAY
Narvik
Trondheim
Bergen
Stavanger
Oslo

SWEDEN
Göteborg
Stockholm
Uppsala
Malmö

DENMARK
København
Odense
Ålborg
Århus

SCOTLAND
Glasgow
Edinburgh
Aberdeen
Dundee
Inverness

NORTHERN IRELAND
Belfast

IRELAND
Dublin
Cork
Limerick
Galway

ISLE OF MAN

UNITED KINGDOM
ENGLAND
WALES
Newcastle
Sunderland
Middlesbrough
Carlisle
Leeds
York
Kingston upon Hull
Liverpool
Manchester
Sheffield
Nottingham
Leicester
Birmingham
Coventry
Wolverhampton
Stoke
Derby
Blackpool
Norwich
Cambridge
Oxford
Bristol
Cardiff
Swansea
Newport
Southampton
Portsmouth
Brighton
Plymouth
Exeter
Reading
LONDON

LANDS' END
ISLES OF SCILLY

English Channel

NETHERLANDS
Amsterdam
's-Gravenhage
The Hague
Rotterdam
Utrecht
Eindhoven
Groningen

BELGIUM
Bruxelles
Antwerpen
Liège
Gent

LUXEMBOURG

FEDERAL REPUBLIC OF GERMANY
Hamburg
Bremen
Hannover
Dortmund
Essen
Düsseldorf
Köln
Bonn
Wuppertal
Münster
Bielefeld
Frankfurt
Wiesbaden
Mannheim
Karlsruhe
Stuttgart
Nürnberg
München
Augsburg
Freiburg
Kassel
Braunschweig
Lübeck
Kiel
Saarbrücken

GERMAN DEMOCRATIC REPUBLIC
BERLIN
Leipzig
Dresden
Magdeburg
Halle
Erfurt
Karl-Marx-Stadt
Rostock
Cottbus

POLAND
Szczecin
Gdańsk
Gdynia
Bydgoszcz
Poznań
Wrocław
Katowice
Częstochowa
Wałbrzych

CZECHOSLOVAKIA
Praha
Plzeň
Brno
Ostrava
Bratislava

AUSTRIA
Wien
Vienna
Graz
Linz
Salzburg
Innsbruck
Klagenfurt

SWITZERLAND
Zürich
Bern
Basel
Genève
Lausanne

FRANCE
PARIS
Marseille
Lyon
Toulouse
Nice
Nantes
Strasbourg
Bordeaux
Lille
Rennes
Le Havre
Rouen
Reims
Saint-Étienne
Grenoble
Clermont-Ferrand
Dijon
Nancy
Metz
Tours
Limoges
Angers
Le Mans
Orléans
Brest
Nîmes
Montpellier
Perpignan
Toulon
Avignon
Cherbourg

GUERNSEY (U.K.)
JERSEY

ANDORRA

SPAIN
Madrid
Barcelona
Valencia
Sevilla
Zaragoza
Málaga
Bilbao
Valladolid
Córdoba
Granada
Murcia
Alicante
Palma
Gijón
Oviedo
La Coruña
Vigo
Santander
Cádiz
Almería
Pamplona
Salamanca

PORTUGAL
Lisboa
Porto
Coimbra
Setúbal
Faro
Braga

ITALY
Roma
Milano
Napoli
Torino
Genova
Palermo
Bologna
Firenze
Catania
Bari
Venezia
Verona
Messina
Trieste
Brescia
Taranto
Padova
Reggio di Calabria
Modena
Parma
Livorno
Cagliari
Foggia
Salerno
La Spezia
Ancona
SAN MARINO
MONACO

CORSE CORSICA (Fr.)
Ajaccio
Bastia

SARDEGNA SARDINIA (It.)
Sassari

SICILIA SICILY

MALTA
Valletta

YUGOSLAVIA
Beograd
Zagreb
Ljubljana
Rijeka
Split
Sarajevo
Novi Sad
Mostar
Zadar

HUNGARY
Budapest
Pécs
Szeged
Szombathely

ISLAS BALEARES
BALEARIC ISLANDS
MALLORCA
MENORCA
IBIZA

MOROCCO
Casablanca
Rabat
Fès
Meknès
Tanger
Oujda
Safi
Essaouira

ALGERIA
Alger
Algiers
Oran
Constantine
Annaba
Mostaganem

TUNISIA
Tunis
Bizerte

ATLAS MOUNTAINS

Bay of Biscay

Skagerrak

Kattegat

Strait of Gibraltar
Gibraltar (U.K.)

PYRENEES

ALPS

CORDILLERA CANTABRICA

SIERRA NEVADA

CAP BON

Mi.
600
Km.
600
400
200
0

130

NORWAY

ATLANTIC OCEAN

NORTH SEA

SHETLAND ISLANDS

ORKNEY ISLANDS

OUTER HEBRIDES

ISLE OF LEWIS

ISLAND OF SKYE

The Minch

Little Minch

HIGHLAND

GRAMPIAN MOUNTAINS

MONADHLIATH MOUNTAINS

Inverness

Aberdeen

Dundee

Perth

GLASGOW

Edinburgh

Motherwell

Hamilton

Kilmarnock

Paisley

Greenock

Dumbarton

Falkirk

Dunfermline

CENTRAL

STRATHCLYDE

FIFE

LOTHIAN

BORDERS

DUMFRIES AND GALLOWAY

Carlisle

Newcastle upon Tyne

Gateshead

Sunderland

South Shields

Tynemouth

Hartlepool

Stockton

Middlesbrough

Bishop Auckland

Durham

Consett

Blyth

Morpeth

Berwick-upon-Tweed

NORTHUMBERLAND

SCOTLAND

ENGLAND

Kirkwall

Stromness

Wick

Thurso

Lerwick

Londonderry

Belfast

DONEGAL

SCALE 150 Mi.

150 Km.

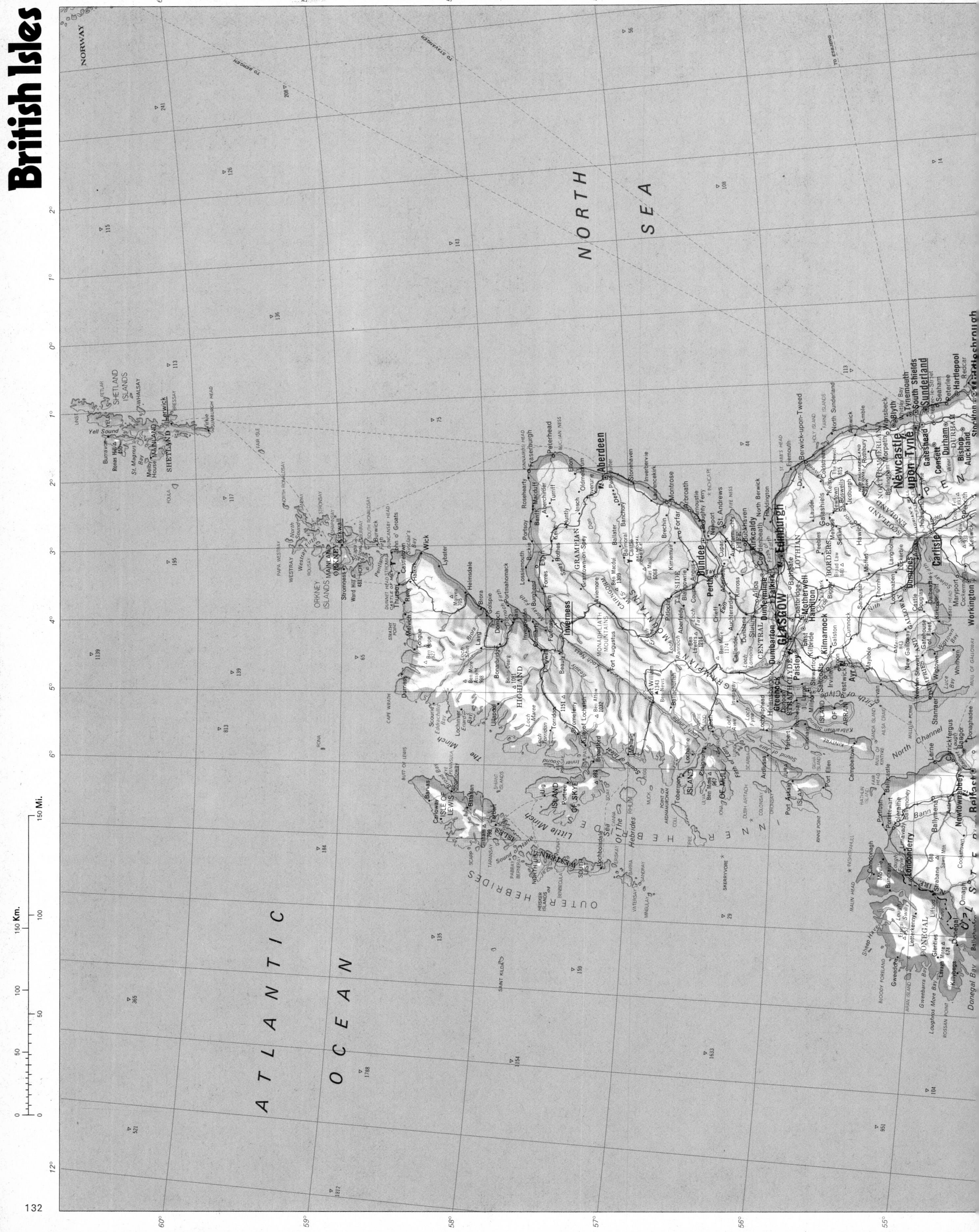

ATLANTIC

OCEAN

English Channel
La Manche

Bay of Biscay

PARIS

Rouen
Le Havre
Caen
Brest
Rennes
Nantes
Angers
Tours
Orléans
Le Mans
Poitiers
La Rochelle
Rochefort
Limoges
Clermont-Ferrand
Bordeaux
Bayonne
Biarritz
San Sebastián
Bilbao
Santander
Pau
Tarbes
Toulouse
Montpellier
Béziers
Narbonne
Perpignan
Carcassonne
Pamplona
Burgos
Zaragoza

Plymouth
Exeter
Torquay
Bournemouth
Southampton
Portsmouth
Brighton
Eastbourne
Hastings
Folkestone
Dover
Calais
Dunkerque
Boulogne-sur-Mer
Amiens
Beauvais
BRUXELLES
Lille
Roubaix
Valenciennes

GUERNSEY (U.K.)
St. Peter Port
JERSEY (U.K.)
St. Helier
CHANNEL ISLANDS

Cherbourg

134

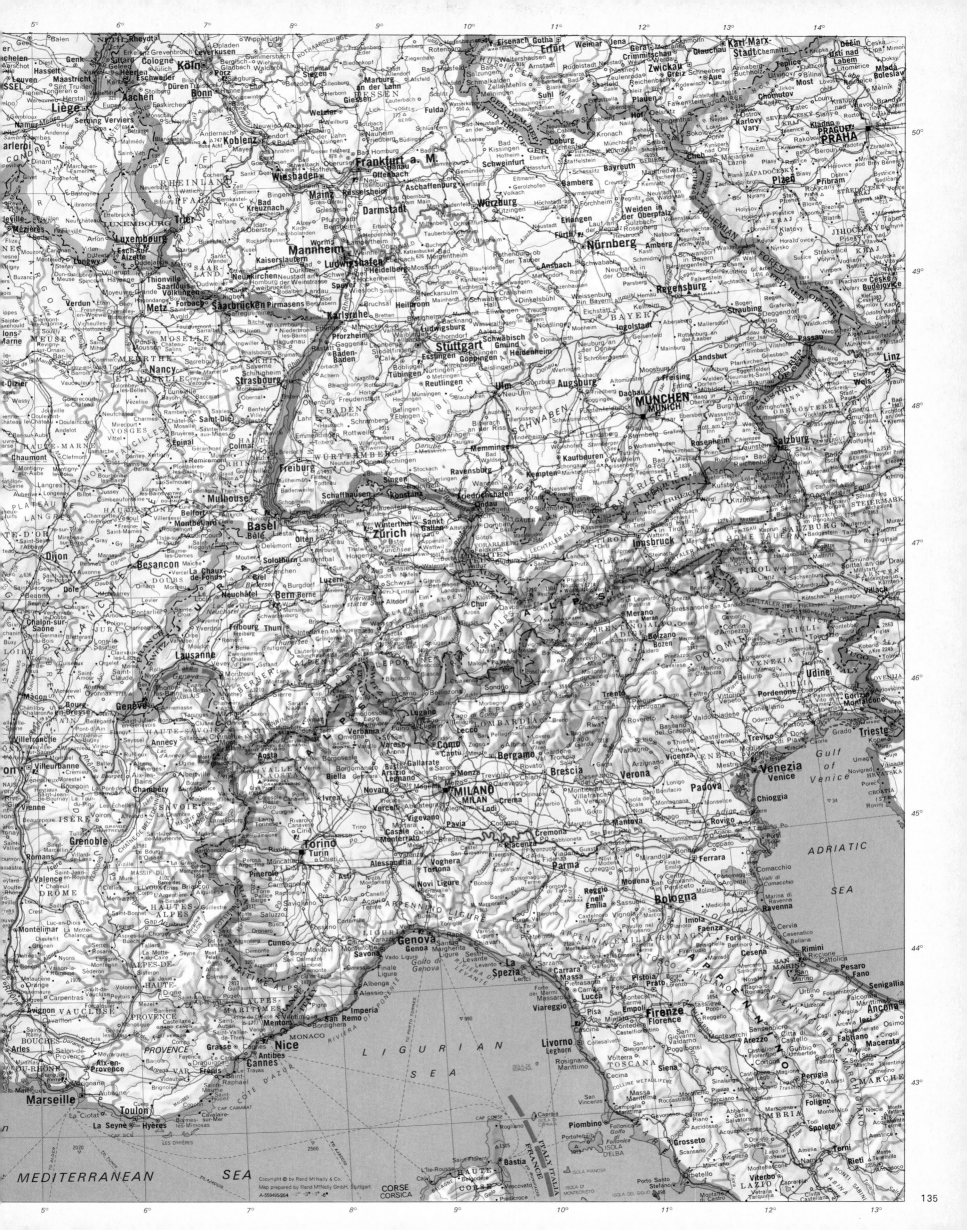

NORTH SEA

Deutsche Bucht

AMSTERDAM

Bremerhaven

Bremen

HAMBURG

Lübeck

Rostock

Schwerin

Rotterdam

Münster

Bielefeld

Hannover

Braunschweig

Magdeburg

Essen

Dortmund

Kassel

Halle

BRUXELLES

Düsseldorf

Köln

Bonn

Erfurt

Weimar

Frankfurt a. M.

Wiesbaden

Mainz

Luxembourg

Darmstadt

Würzburg

Mannheim

Nürnberg

Saarbrücken

Karlsruhe

Stuttgart

Regensburg

Strasbourg

Augsburg

Freiburg

MÜNCHEN

Basel

Zürich

Bern

Innsbruck

Genève

Lausanne

ADRIATIC SEA

LIGURIAN SEA

Gulf of Venice

BUDAPEST
WIEN VIENNA
Bratislava
MÜNCHEN MUNICH
Salzburg
Graz
Zagreb
Ljubljana
Trieste
Venezia Venice
MILANO MILAN
Torino Turin
Genova Genoa
Bologna
Firenze Florence
Ancona
Pescara
Split
Sarajevo
Mostar
Dubrovnik
Zadar
Rijeka
Pula
Udine
Verona
Padova
Brescia
Bergamo
Parma
Modena
Ravenna
Rimini
Pisa
Livorno Leghorn
La Spezia
Nice
Monaco
Basel Bâle
Zürich
Bern Berne
Lausanne
Innsbruck
Bolzano Bozen
Trento
Augsburg
Ulm
Freiburg
Mulhouse

CORSE CORSICA
Bastia

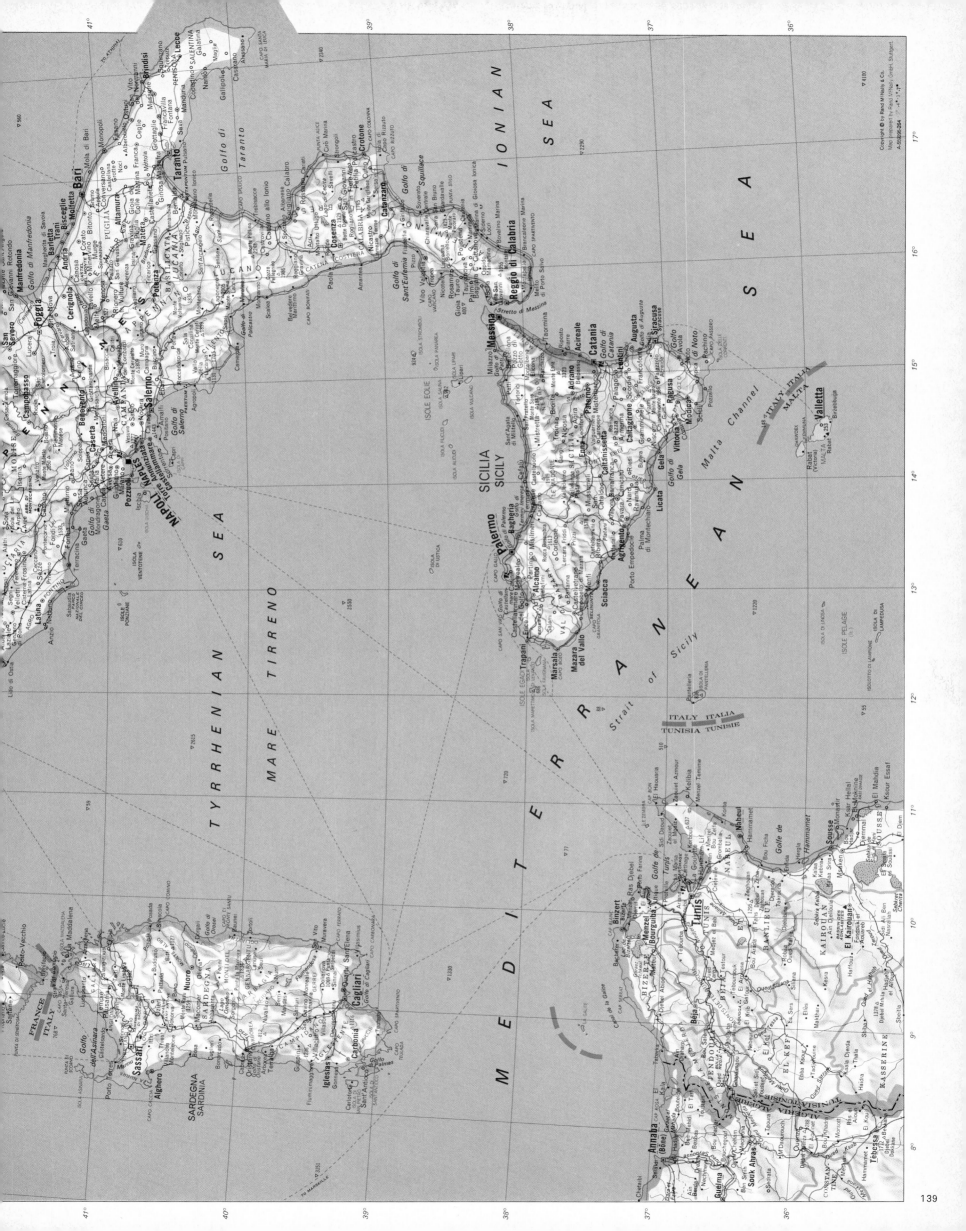

139

Northern Europe

Spain and Portugal

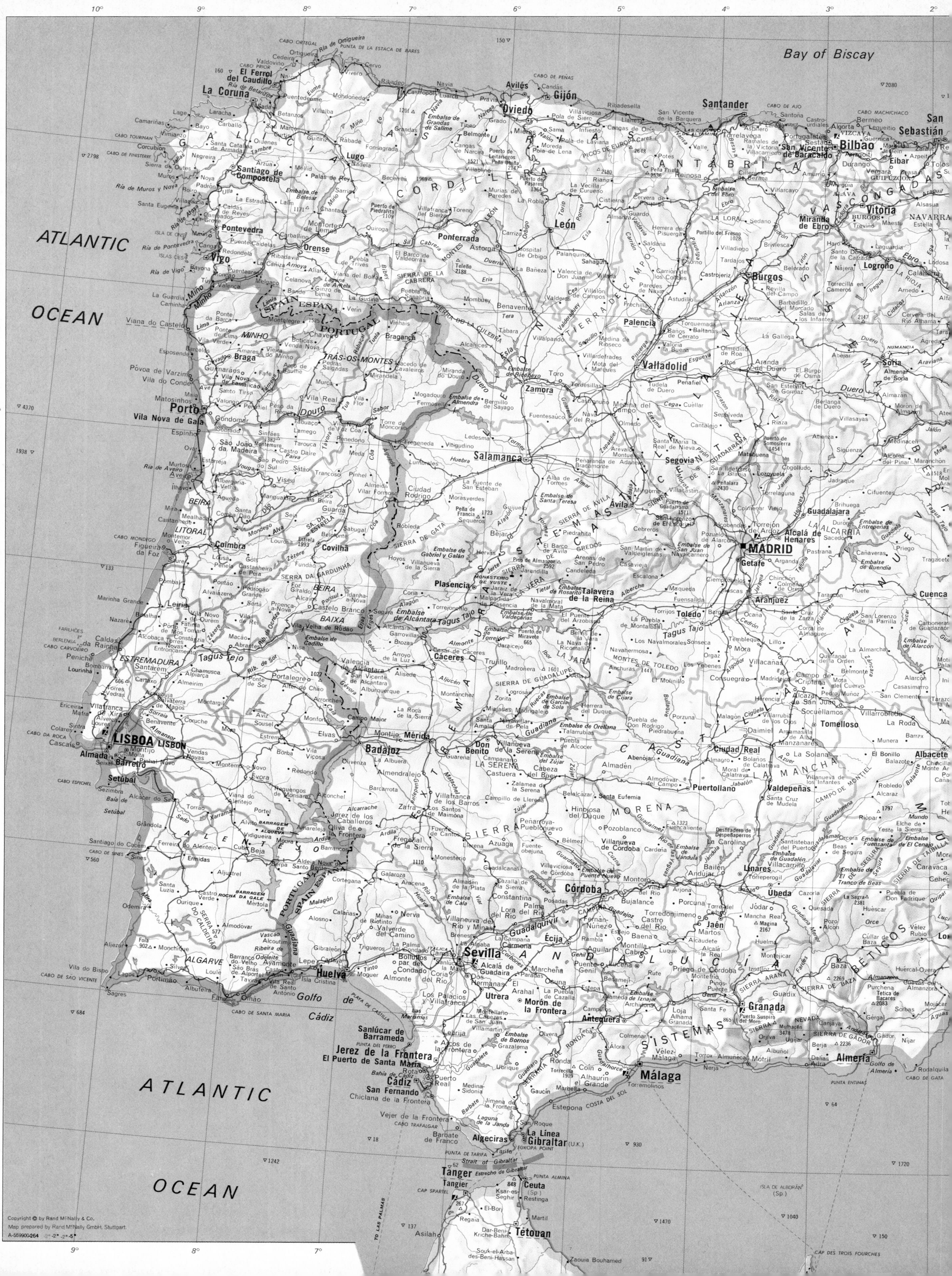

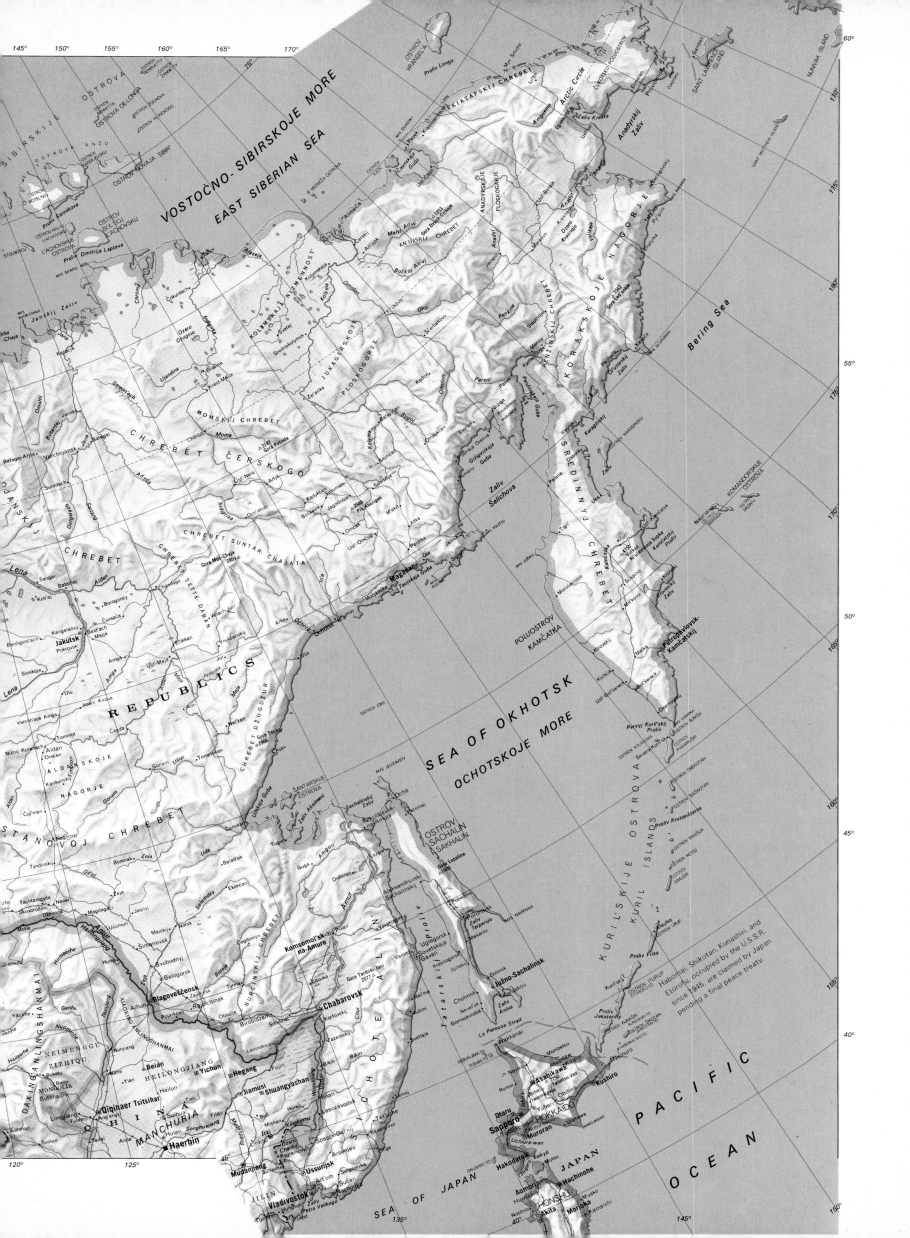

UNION OF SOVIET SOCIALIST REPUBLICS

KAZACHSKIJ MELKOSOPOCNIK

BETPAK-DALA

Ozero Balchaš

KAZACHSKAJA S.S.R.

CHREBET TARBAGATU

DZUNGARSKIJ ALATAU

Alma-Ata

Frunze

KIRGIZSKAJA S.S.R.

KIRGIZSKIJ CHREBET

TIEN SHAN

CHREBET KOKSAALATAU

Yining
Kuldja

Wulumuqi
Urumchi

ZHUANGAERPENDI

CHREBET TANNU-OLA

ROSSIJSKAJA S.F.S.R.

Ust'-Kamenogorsk

Irkutsk

MONGOL ALTAJN NURUU

CHANGAJN NURUU

M O N G O L I A

EDRENGIJN NURUU

GURVAN SAJCHAN UUL

G O B I

BEISHANMAI

Kashi
Kashgar

TADZ. S.S.R.

AFG.

PAK.

SINKIANG
XINJIANG WEIWUER ZIZHIQU

TALIMUPENDI

TAKLA MAKAN

Yarkand
Suoche

K U N L U N S H A N M A I

AERJINSHANMAI

KEKEXILISHANMAI

CHAIDAMUPENDI

QILIANSHANMAI

Yumen

Zhangye

GANSU

Yinchuan

NINGXIA HUIZU ZIZHIQU

Lanzhou

QINGHAI

Xining

Qinghai

X I Z A N G   Z I Z H I Q U

TIBET

GANGDISISHANMAI

TANGGULASHANMAI

BAYANKALASHANMAI

Lhasa
Lasa

H I M A L A Y A

NEPAL

Kathmandu

BHUTAN

Dhaulagiri

Mount Everest

Dehra Dūn

Meerut

Delhi

Lucknow

Kanpur

Allahabad

Varanasi
Benares

Patna

I N D I A

VINDHYA RANGE

Jabalpur

Raipur

Jamshedpur

Howrah

CALCUTTA

BANGLADESH

Dacca

Narayanganj

Khulna

Chittagong

Cuttack

Vishākhapatnam

Rājahmundry

EASTERN GHATS

B A Y   O F   B E N G A L

CHIN HILLS

B U R M A

ARAKAN YOMA

PEGU YOMA

Mandalay

Sittwe
Akyab

Mount Victoria

Pegu

Henzada

THAILAND

Chiang Mai

Doi Inthanon

LAOS

Louangphrabang

Viangchan

VIETNAM

Ha-noi

Hai-phong

Nam-dinh

Vinh

SICHUAN

Chengdu

Nanchong

CHONGQING

Yibin

Zunyi

GUIZHOU

Guiyang

Anshun

YUNNAN

Kunming

Gejiú
Koklu

Mengzi

Mi.
600

Km.
600

400

200

148

SEA OF OKHOTSK

SEA OF JAPAN

EAST CHINA SEA

PACIFIC OCEAN

PHILIPPINE SEA

SOUTH CHINA SEA

Copyright © by Rand McNally & Co.
Map prepared by Esselte Map Service AB, Stockholm
A-569700-264

149

PACIFIC OCEAN

Hachinohe
Morioka
KITAKAMI-SANCHI
Aomori
Hirosaki
Noshiro
TSUGARU-HANTO
HOKKAIDO
Akita
Sakata
KYURYO
DEWA
Tsuruoka
Niigata
Sado
Sado-Kaikyo
SENDAI
Ishinomaki
MIYAGI
Sendai
Shiogama
Yonezawa
Yamagata
Fukushima
Koriyama
ABUKUMA
Iwaki (Taira)
Hitachi
Mito
IBARAKI
TOCHIGI
Utsunomiya
Nikko
GUMMA
Maebashi
Takasaki
SAITAMA
Kawagoe
TOKYO
Yokohama
Kawasaki
Chiba
BOSO-HANTO
HONSHU
Nagano
Ueda
Matsumoto
Kofu
HIDA
Toyama
Kanazawa
Komatsu
Nagaoka
Sanjo

Wakkanai
La Pérouse Strait
Sōya-kaikyō
U.S.S.R.
JAPAN
NIHON
OSTROV SACHALIN / SACHALIN / SAKHALIN
SEA OF OKHOTSK
KURIL'SKIJE OSTROVA / CHISHIMA RETTŌ / KURIL ISLANDS
OSTROV KUNAŠIR / KUNASHIRI-TŌ
U.S.S.R. / S.S.R.
JAPAN / NIHON
Nemuro
Nemuro Strait
Kushiro
KONSEN-DAICHI
TOKACHI-HEIYA
Obihiro
HIDAKA-SAMMYAKU
KITAMI-SANCHI
Kitami
Asahikawa
HOKKAIDO
ISHIKARI
TESHIO-SANCHI
YUBARI-SANCHI
Yubari
Otaru
Sapporo
Tomakomai
Muroran
Hakodate
OSHIMA-HANTO
SEA OF JAPAN / NIHON-KAI
PACIFIC OCEAN
HONSHU
Hachinohe
Aomori
SHIMOKITA-HANTO
Tsugaru-kaikyō

Hidatsu, Enkotan, Kunashiri, occupied by the U.S.S.R. and Ecotoroku since 1945, are claimed by Japan pending a final peace treaty settlement.

150 Mi.
150 Km.

150

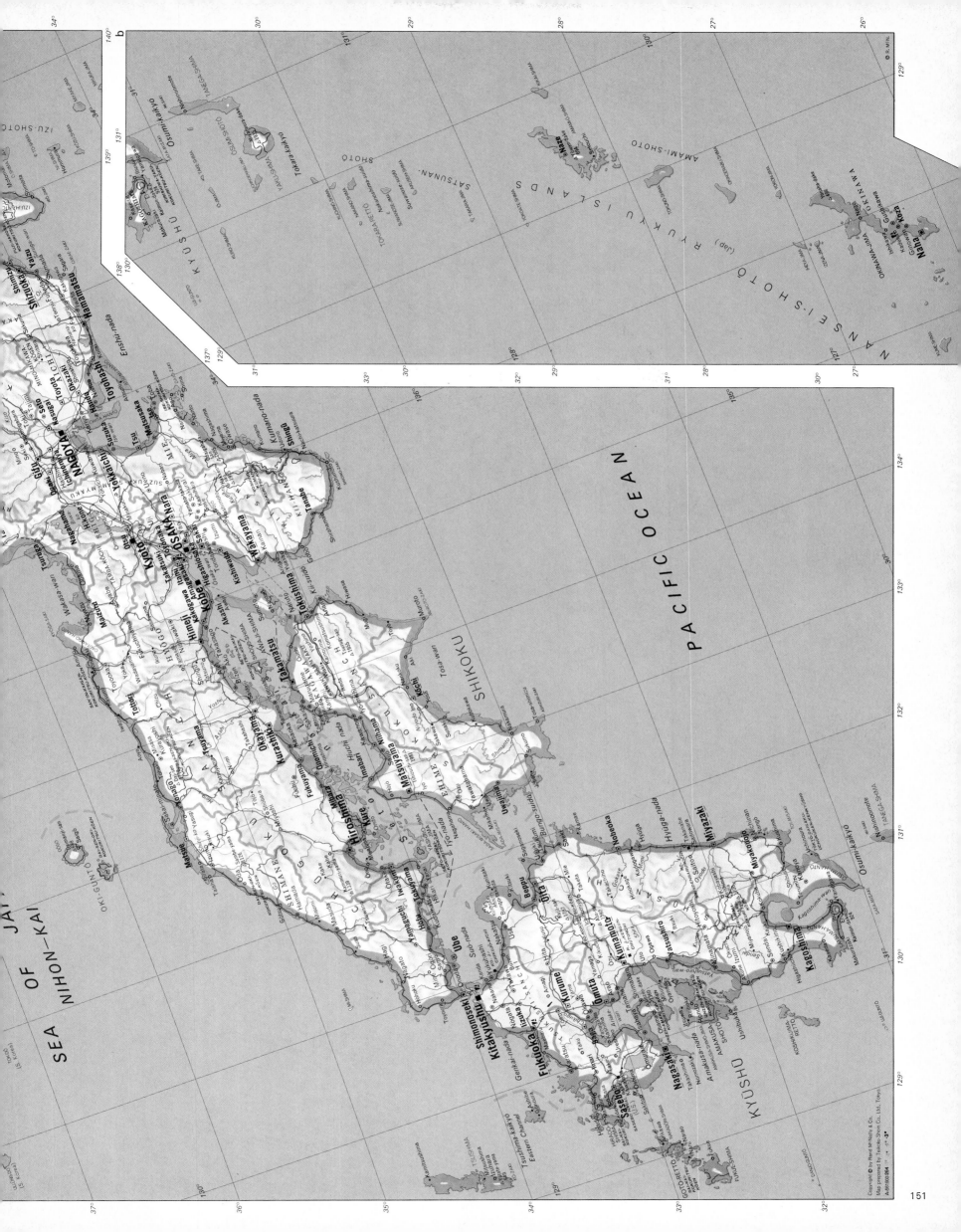

SEA OF JAPAN
NIHON-KAI

PACIFIC OCEAN

NANSEI-SHOTO RYUKYU ISLANDS (Jap.)

KYUSHU

SHIKOKU

NAGOYA

KYOTO
OSAKA
Kobe
Himeji

Okayama
Kurashiki

Hiroshima
Kure

Matsuyama

Takamatsu
Tokushima

Tottori
Matsue

Shimonoseki
Kitakyushu

Fukuoka

Nagasaki
Sasebo

Kumamoto
Kurume
Ōmuta

Ōita
Beppu

Miyazaki
Miyakonojō

Kagoshima

Naze

Naha
Koza

Shizuoka
Hamamatsu

Yokkaichi

Wakayama

151

BANGLADESH
Chittagong
Cox's Bazar
INDIA
Imphyo
Falam
Kalewa
Haka
Bawdwin
Namhu
Lashio
Hsipaw
Mandalay
Maymyo
Monywa
Sagaing
Shwebo
YUNNAN
Gejiu Kaikiu
Simao
Honghe Yuanjiang
Lanshui
CHINA
GUANGXI
Nanning
Wuzhou
Xijiang
GUANGDONG
GUANGZHOU
CANTON
Chaoan
Foshan
Dongguan
Jiangmen
Huiyang
Shantou
Swatow

BURMA
CHIN HILLS
Mount Victoria
3053
Pakokku
Meiktila
Myingyan
Taunggyi
Inle Lake
Mong Hsat
Keng Tung
LAOS
Muang Sing
Muang Ngoy
Xam Nua
HANOI
Hai-phong
Nam-dinh
Gulf of Tonkin
Haikou
HAINANDAO

Sittwe (Akyab)
ARAKAN YOMA
Henzada
Prome (Pyé)
Toungoo
Pyinmana
Chiang Mai
Lampang
Phrae
Luangphrabang
Xiangkhoang
VIETNAM
Vinh

BAY OF BENGAL
Bassein
RANGOON
Syriam
Pegu
Moulmein
Gulf of Martaban
THAILAND
Sukhothai
Phitsanulok
Khon Kaen
Nakhon Phanom
Savannakhet
Hue
Da-nang

ANDAMAN SEA
Tavoy
KRUNG THEP
BANGKOK
Nakhon Ratchasima
Ubon Ratchathani
CAMBODIA
Tonlé Sab
Stung Treng
Lac-giao
Nha-trang

Gulf of Thailand
PHNUM PENH
THANH-PHO HO CHI MINH (SAI-GON)
Can-tho

SOUTH CHINA SEA

MALAYSIA
MALAYA
Kuala Lumpur
SINGAPORE
SUMATERA
SUMATRA
Palembang
Medan
BORNEO
KALIMANTAN
Pontianak
Banjarmasin
BRUNEI
Bandar Seri Begawan
Kuching

INDONESIA
LAUT JAWA
JAVA SEA
JAKARTA
BANDUNG
Semarang
SURABAYA
Yogyakarta
Surakarta

INDIAN OCEAN

CHRISTMAS ISLAND (Austr.)

Copyright © by Rand McNally & Co.
Map prepared by Esselte Map Service AB, Stockholm
152
A-569600-264

India and Pakistan

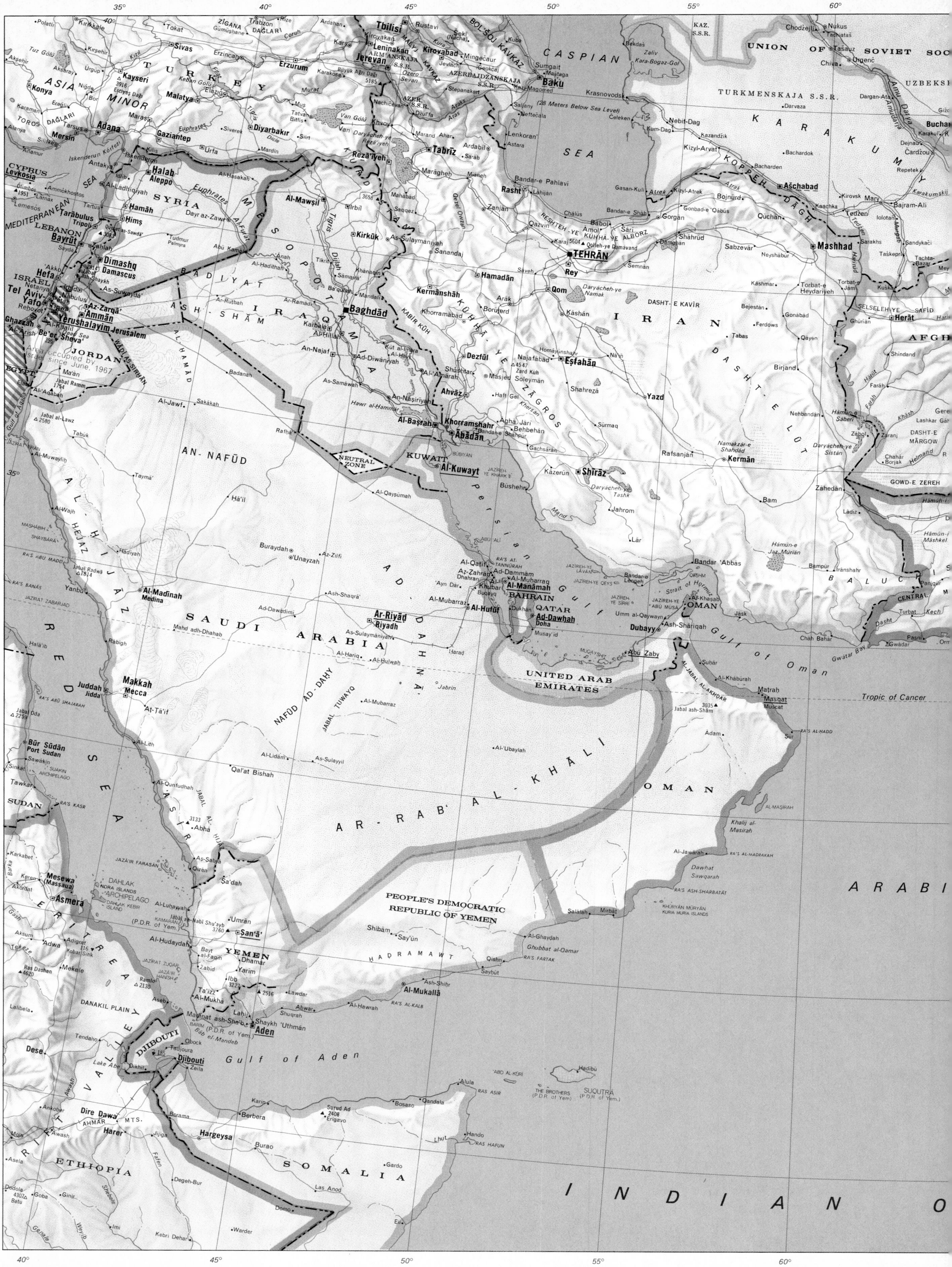

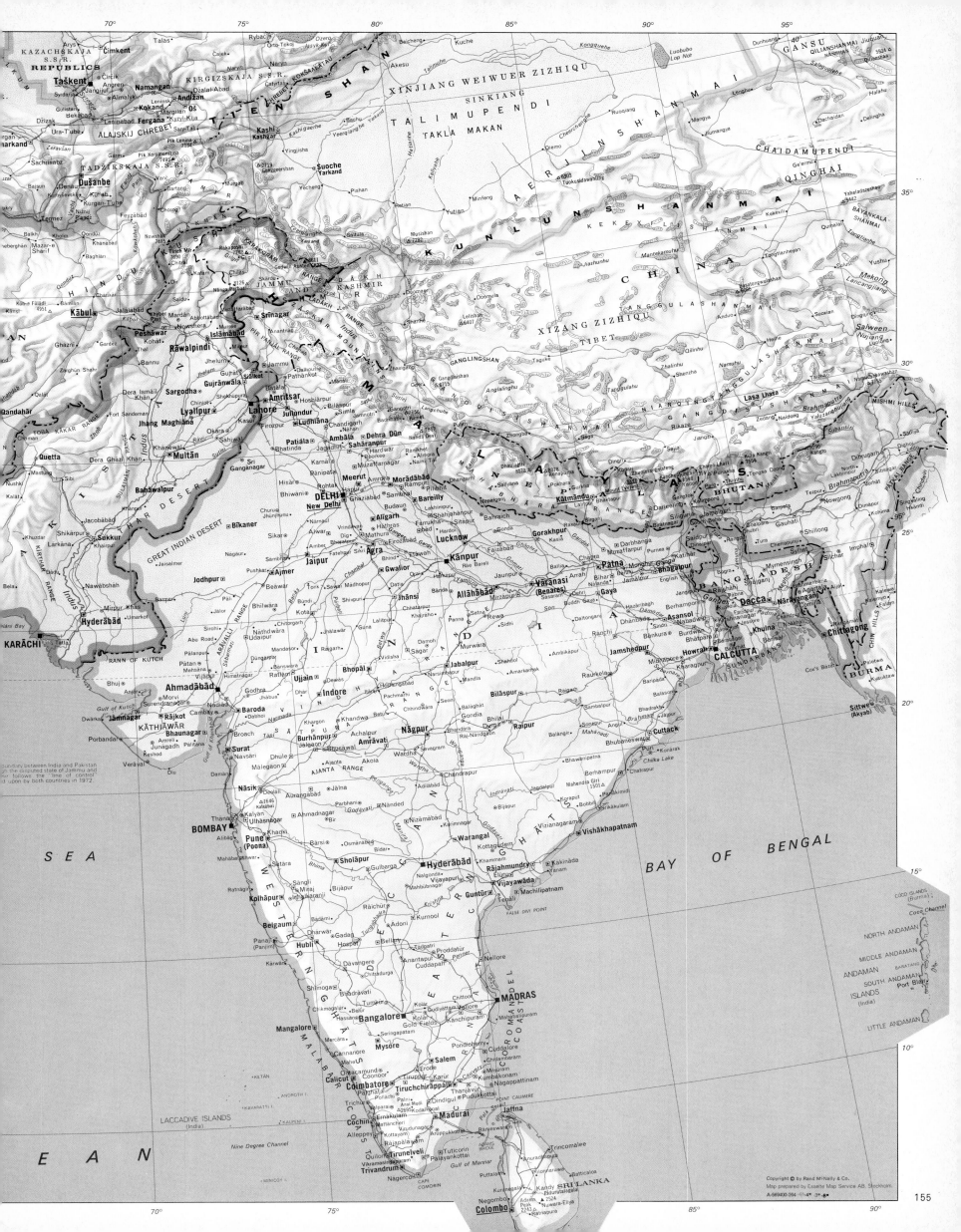

ARQUIPÉLAGO DA MADEIRA
MADEIRA ISLANDS
(Portugal)
PORTO SANTO
Funchal
MADEIRA

ILHAS SELVAGENS
(Port.)

ISLAS CANARIAS
CANARY ISLANDS
(Spain)
LA PALMA
Santa Cruz de la Palma
Pico de Teide
Santa Cruz de Tenerife
GOMERA
HERRO
LANZAROTE
Arrecife
Las Palmas de Gran Canaria
FUERTEVENTURA
GRAN CANARIA
CAP JUBY

SPAIN
MÁLAGA
Algeciras
Tanger
Gibraltar (U.K.)
Ceuta (Sp.)
Strait of Gibraltar
Tétouan
Asilah
Larache
Al-Hoceima
Melilla
Nador
Oujda
Kenitra
Rabat
Salé
Meknès
Fès
Casablanca
Dar-el-Beïda
El-Jadida
Mohammedia
MOROCCO
Safi
Settat
Khouribga
Essaouira
Marrakech
HAUT ATLAS
4165
Jbel Toubkal
ANTI ATLAS
Agadir
Ouarzazate
CAP RHIR
Tiznit
ATLAS
Béchar
Sidi Ifni
IFNI
Tarfaya
HAMADA DU DRA
Béni Abbès

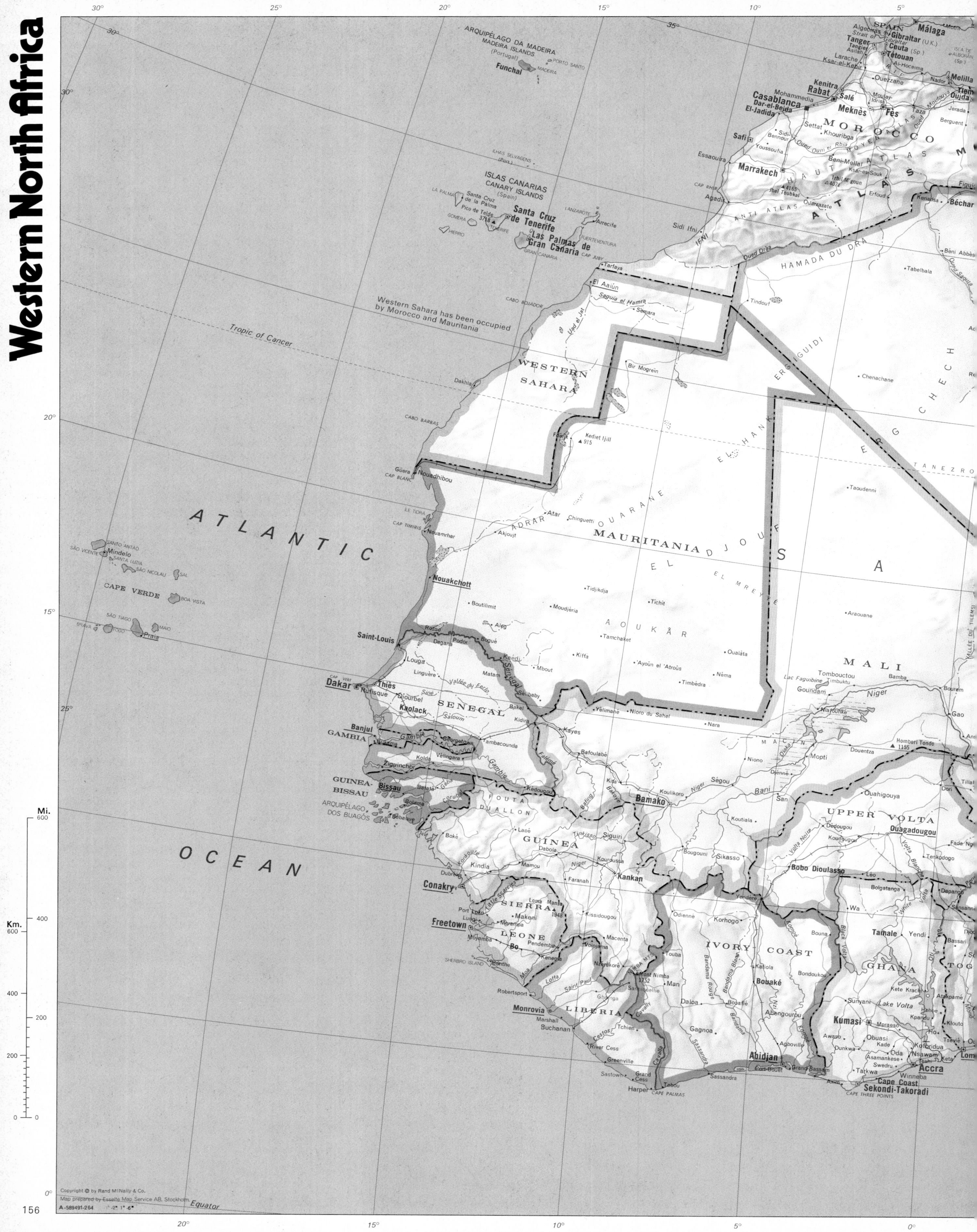

WESTERN SAHARA
El Aaiún
Saguia el Hamra
Samara
Bir Mogreïn
CABO BOJADOR
Dakhla
CABO BARBAS
Güera
Nouadhibou
CAP BLANC
Kediet Ijill
915
Faa

Western Sahara has been occupied
by Morocco and Mauritania

Tropic of Cancer

ATLANTIC

OCEAN

ILE TIDRA
CAP TIMIRIS
Atar
Chinguetti
Akjoujt
ADRAR
Nouamrhar
Boutilimit
Nouakchott
Tidjikdja
Moudjéria
MAURITANIA
AOUKÂR
Tichit
EL MREYE
EL HANK
OUARANE
DJOUF
Araouane
Tamchaket
Kiffa
'Ayoûn el 'Atroûs
Oualâta
Néma
Timbédra
Tombouctou
Goundam
MALI
Niger
Bamba
Bourem
Gao
Homberi Tondo
1155

Saint-Louis
Rosso
Dagana
Podor
Bogué
Kaédi
Aleg
Mbout
SENEGAL
Louga
Linguère
Matam
Sénégal
Sélibaby
Yélimané
Nioro du Sahel
Nara
CAP VERT
Dakar
Thiès
Rufisque
Diourbel
Kaolack
Saloum
Bakel
Kidira
Kayes
Bafoulabé
Niono
Banjul
GAMBIA
Gambia
Tambacounda
Kolda
Vélingara
Kita
Koulikoro
Niger
Ségou
Bani
San
Mopti
Djenné
Douentza
MACINA

GUINEA-BISSAU
Bissau
Bolama
ARQUIPÉLAGO DOS BIJAGÓS
FOUTA DJALLON
Labé
Kédougou
Siguiri
Koutiala
Sikasso
Bougouni
UPPER VOLTA
Ouahigouya
Dédougou
Koudougou
Ouagadougou

Boké
GUINEA
Dabola
Mamou
Kindia
Kankan
Bobo Dioulasso
Léo
Tenkodogo
Conakry
Faranah
Kissidougou
Dinguiraye
Kouroussa
SIERRA
Loma Mtns.
1948
LEONE
Makeni
Odienné
Korhogo
Bouna
Wa
Bolgatanga
Dapango
Freetown
Kenema
Bo
Beyla
Macenta
Man
IVORY COAST
GHANA
Tamale
Yendi
Bassari
SHERBRO ISLAND
Bonthe
Voinjama
Mont Nimba
1752
Katiola
Bouaké
Sunyani
Lake Volta
Robertsport
LIBERIA
Ganta
Daloa
Bondoukou
Kumasi
Obuasi
Koforidua
Monrovia
Marshall
Buchanan
Gagnoa
Abengourou
Awaso
Dunkwa
TOGO
River Cess
Greenville
Abidjan
Grand Bassam
Accra
Cape Coast
Sekondi-Takoradi
Harper
CAPE PALMAS
Sassandra
CAPE THREE POINTS

CAPE VERDE
SANTO ANTÃO
Mindelo
SÃO VICENTE
SANTA LUZIA
SÃO NICOLAU
SAL
BOA VISTA
MAIO
SÃO TIAGO
BRAVA
FOGO
Praia

Equator

Mi.
600
400
200
0

Km.
600
400
200
0

Eastern North Africa

MEDITERRANEAN SEA

IONIAN SEA

Palermo Messina Reggio di Calabria
Marsala Trapani Monte Etna 3290 ITALY
Caltanissetta Catania
SICILIA SICILY Siracusa
Ragusa CAPO PASSERO

Pátrai Athínai Piraiévs GREECE TURKEY
PELOPÓNNISOS KIKLADHES RHODOS
Kritikón Pélagos KARPATHOS Iráklion KRITI CYPRUS

TUNISIA
Alger Algiers Blida Tizi-Ouzou Skikda Annaba Bône Tunis
El Asnam Miliana Bejaïa Constantine Bizerte Nabeul Hammamet
Mostaganem Mascara Sétif Guelma El Kef Sousse El Moknine
ATLAS TELLIEN Batna El Kairouan Sfax
Saïda Bou Saada Tébessa El Kasserine
ATLAS MOUNTAINS Biskra Gafsa Golfe de Gabès
ATLAS SAHARIEN Chott el Fedjadj Gabès ILE DE DJERBA
Laghouat Oued Djedi Médenine

ALGERIA
GRAND ERG OCCIDENTAL GRAND ERG ORIENTAL
Hassi R'Mel Ghardaïa El Oued Touggourt
Ouargla Hassi Messaoud Nalūt Yafran
El Goléa Ghudāmis Daraj
PLATEAU DU TADEMAIT PLATEAU DU TINRHERT
In Salah Ohanet In Amenas
Aoulef Zaouia el Kahla Edjeleh Illizi
TASSILI N'AJJER Ghāt
Arak AHAGGAR Djanet

LIBYA
Tarābulus Tripoli Al-Khums Zliten Misrātah
Zuwārah Zāwiyah Al-'Azīzīyah Tarhūnah
Remada Gharyān Qasr Bani Walid
Mizdah Surt Zāwiyat al-Bayda' Darnah
Khalīj Surt Al-Marj Banghāzī
Sulūq Bīr al-Hukayyim Ajdābiyah
TARĀBULUS TRIPOLITANIA Al-Uqaylah BARQAH CYRENAICA
Al-Qaryah ash-Shargīyah Al-Jaghbūb
Sawknah Marādah Awjilah Al-'Irq
JABAL AS-SAWDĀ Zillah Waha Siwah
Dahra 42 Waha
Brach AL-HARŪJ AL-ASWAD
Awbāri Sabhah FAZZĀN FEZZAN
Marzūq Tarbū Bīr al-Harash
Sardalas Sārir Nerastro
Idehan Marzūq SARĪR TIBASTI
Al-Qatrūn Wāw al-Kabīr
Djado Aozou Ma'tan Bishārah

EGYPT
Al-Iskandarīyah Alexandria Damanhūr Tanta
Matrūh As-Sallūm Shibīn al-Kawm Az-Zaqāzīq
MUNKHAFAD AL-QATTĀRAH AL-QĀHIRAH CAIRO Al-Jīzah
Birkat Qārūn AL-FAYYŪM Banī Suwayf
AS-SAHRĀ AL-GHARBĪYAH WESTERN DESERT
Al-Minyā Mallawī Dayrūt Samālūt
Al-Wāhāt al-Farāfirah Qasr al-Farāfirah
Al-Wāhāt ad Dākhilah Al-Khārijah Bāris
NUBIAN DESERT LIBYAN DESERT
Jabal al-'Uwaynāt 1934 Wāhāt Salīmah
Bīr Misāhah NUBĀT AL JILF AL-KABĪR

Tropic of Cancer

ADRAR DES IFORAS In Guezzam
Tahat 3003 Tamanrasset Djebel Teleriheba 2455
Mont Gréboun 2000 Pic Tousside 3315 Bette 2286
Chirfa Bardai TIBESTI
Séguédine Zouar Emi Koussi 3415
Ouallene Oum Chalouba Ounianga Kébir Al-Jawf Al-Khandaq

MALI
Ménaka

NIGER
SAHARA
AÏR AZAOUAK Iferouane In-Gall Agadez
MONTS BAGZANE Bilma
GRAND ERG DE BILMA BODELE
Tahoua Tanout BODELE
Iléla Dogondoutchi TÉNÉRÉ
VALLÉE DE L'AZAOUAK VALLÉE DE L'AZAOUAK
Dallol Bosso Dallol Maouri Birni Nkoni Koro Toro

CHAD
ENNEDI Fada Largeau DÉPRESSION DU MOURDI
Malha Wells Jabal Marrah 3088
Abéché Al-Junaynah Al-Fāshir
Ati Mongo An-Nuhūd Al-Ubayyid
Moussoro Abou Deïa Nyala Al-Udayyah
Massenya Am Timan Al-Muglad Kāduqlī
Mao Bahr el Ghazal
Lake Chad Lac Tchad (281)
Ndjamena (Fort-Lamy)
Kukawa Dikwa Chari Bongor Birao Bahr al-'Arab
Maroua Yagoua Pala Kélo Sarh Gordil
Garoua Doba Koumra Ouanda Djallé Kafia Kingi

NIGERIA
Sokoto Katsina Zamfara Gusau Kano Hadejia Nguru Azare
Talata Mafara Kaura Namoda Zaria Nguigmi Potiskum
Maradi Tessaoua Zinder Gouré Maiduguri
Rima Kontagora Kaduna Bauchi Gombe
Malanville Minna Jos Kumo
Kontagora BENUE Benue
Parakou Bida Keffi Lafia Makurdi
BENIN Shaki Ilorin Ila Panyam Gashaka
Ogbomosho Iseyin Oyo Ede Oshogbo Okene Nsukka
Ibadan Abeokuta Ife Ikerre Owo Ondo Enugu
Mushin Ijebu-Ode Onitsha Afikpo
Lagos Benin City Sapele Aba Calabar
Warri Owerri Port Harcourt
Bight of Benin Bight of Biafra

CAMEROON
Dimlang 2042 Hoséré Batandji 2049 Ngaoundéré
Yola Jada Tibati Betaré Oya
Garoua Mamfe Bamenda Foumban Meiganga
Kumba Dschang Batouri Bertoua
Mont Cameroun 4070 Douala Yaoundé Abong Mbang
Victoria Edéa N'yong Ebolowa
MALABO Kribi Sangha

CENTRAL AFRICAN EMPIRE
Bozoum Bossangoa Bambari Bria Yalinga
Bouar Berbérati Bangui Bambari Kotto
Nola Mbaïki Bimbo Bangassou
Bétaré Oya Bossembélé   Bamingui Ouadda
CHAÎNE DES MONGOS Ndélé Raga

ZAIRE
Libenge Gemena Buta Aketi
Bondo Titule Bomokandi Isiro Mungbere
Businga Lisala Congo Uele

EQUAT. GUINEA
SAO TOME AND PRINCIPE Santo António Rio Benito
MACÍAS NGUEMA BIYOGO EQUAT. GUINEA San Carlos
Bata GABON Oyem Bitam

Gulf of Guinea

CONGO
Impfondo Ouésso

158

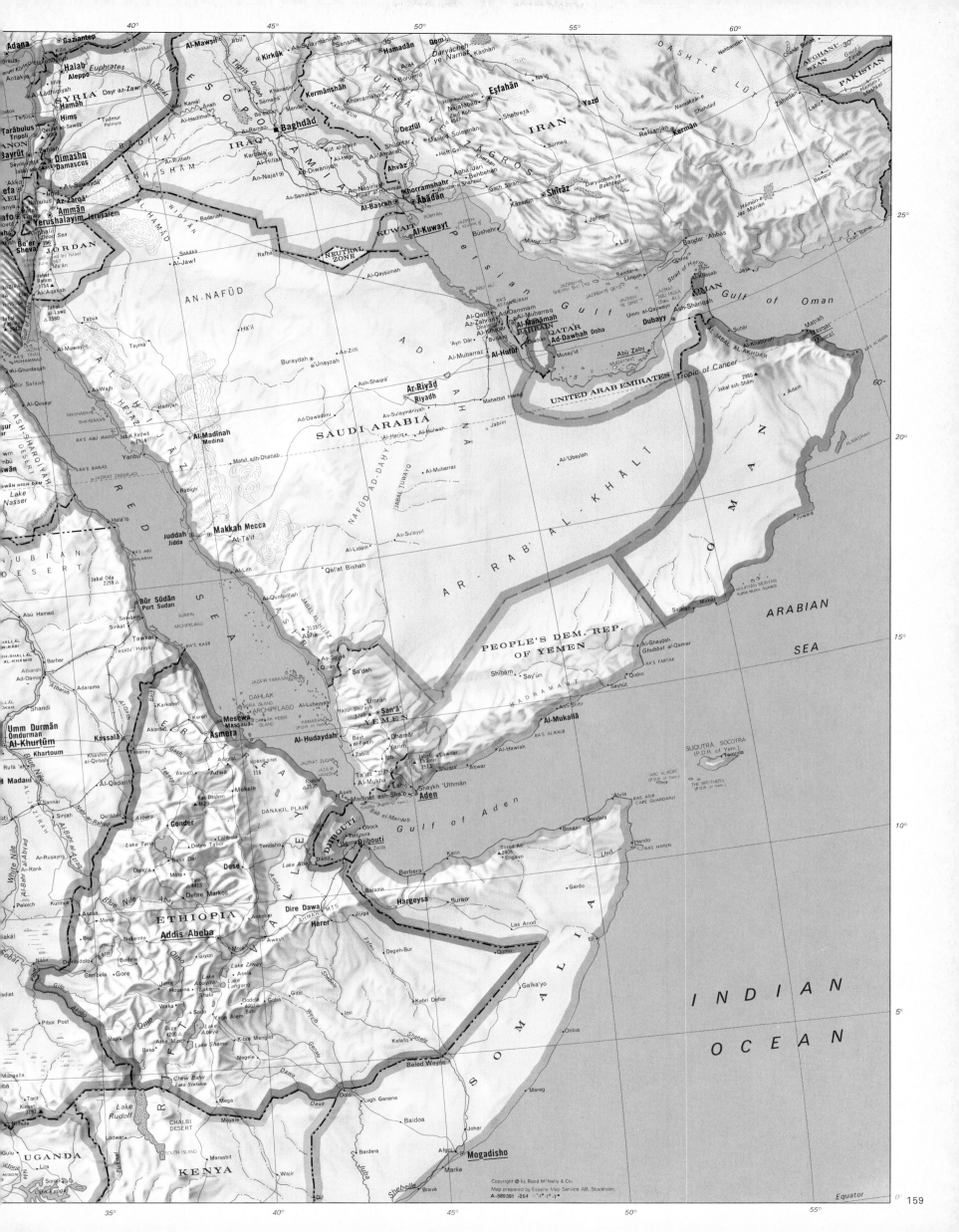

Southern Africa

ATLANTIC

OCEAN

The United Nations declared an end to the
mandate of South Africa over South West
Africa in October, 1966. Administration of the
territory by South Africa is not recognized
by the United Nations.

Tropic of Capricorn

INDIAN OCEAN

Equator 0°

SOMALIA

KENYA
Nairobi

Mombasa

TANZANIA
Zanzibar
Dar-es-Salaam

5°

SEYCHELLES
PRASLIN
ISLAND ◦ LA DIGUE
SILHOUETTE ◦ Victoria
MAHÉ ISLAND

AMIRANTE ISLANDS
(Sey.) ◦ ÎLE DESROCHES
(Sey.) ◦ PLATTE ISLAND (Sey.)

COETIVY ISLAND
(Sey.)

◦ ALPHONSE ISLAND (Sey.)

◦ PROVIDENCE ISLAND
(Sey.)

ALDABRA ISLANDS
(Sey.) SAINT PIERRE ISLAND
(Sey.)
COSMOLEDO GROUP
(Sey.) ◦ CERF ISLAND
(Sey.) 10°
ASSUMPTION ISLAND
(Sey.) ASTOVE ISLAND
(Sey.) ◦ FARQUHAR GROUP
(Sey.)

◦ AGALEGA ISLANDS
(Mauritius)

ÎLES GLORIEUSES
(Mad.)
CAP D'AMBRE
GRANDE COMORE CAP
Moroni ◦ SAINT-SÉBASTIEN Diégo-Suarez
COMORO ISLANDS
Fomboni MOHELI ◦ Mutsamudu
ANJOUAN BANC DU GEYSER
MAYOTTE ◦ Dzaoudzi NOSY MITSIO
(Fr.) NOSSI-BÉ Amblobe
Hell-Ville Ambanja Vohémar
Ambatondrazaka MASSIF DU
Maromokotro ▲ 2876
NOSY LAVA TSARATANANA
Analalava Antsohihy Doany Sambava
Baie de Narinda Bealanana Andapa
Befandriana Antalaha
Baie de la Mahajamba CAP EST
Majunga Port-Bergé PRESQU'ÎLE
Soalala Marovoay MASOALA
CAP SAINT-ANDRÉ Lac Mandritsara
ÎLE CHESTERFIELD Kinkony Mampikony TROMELIN
Besalampy Maevatanana Tsaratanana (Fr.)
ÎLE JUAN DE NOVA Andriamena ÎLE SAINTE-MARIE
Tambohorano Ambodifototra
ÎLES BARREN Lac Alaotra Fénérive
Morafenobe Ankazobe
Maintirano Tamatave 15°
Ankazobe Brickaville
Ankavandra Tsiroanomandidy Antananarivo
MADAGASCAR Vatomandry
Belo Ambatolampy
Miandrivazo ANKARATRA Antsirabe Mahanoro
Tsiribihina Malaimbandy
Morondava Mahabo Ambositra Nosy Varika
Port Louis Mahébourg
Mandabe Manjary Curepipe
Mandabe Manja MAURITIUS
Manja Ambalavao
Mangoky Beroroha Fianarantsoa Le Port Saint-Denis 20°
Ankazoabo Saint-Paul RÉUNION
Morombe ▲ Pic Boby Manakara Saint-Pierre (Fr.)
CAP SAINT-VINCENT 2658
Ihosy MASCARENE
Tuléar Betroka Farafangana ISLANDS
Betioky Vangaindrano
Midongy Sud Tropic of Capricorn
Ampanihy Bekily
Androka Amboyombe Fort-Dauphin
Tsihombe Ambovombe
CAP SAINTE-MARIE 25°

MOZAMBIQUE
Beira

INDIAN OCEAN 30°

161

Canada

PACIFIC

OCEAN

UNITED STATES

CANADA

MEXICO

BRITISH COLUMBIA
ALBERTA
SASKATCHEWAN
MANITOBA
WASHINGTON
OREGON
IDAHO
MONTANA
NORTH DAKOTA
SOUTH DAKOTA
WYOMING
NEBRASKA
NEVADA
UTAH
COLORADO
KANSAS
CALIFORNIA
ARIZONA
NEW MEXICO
OKLAHOMA
TEXAS

VANCOUVER ISLAND

GREAT BASIN

ROCKY MOUNTAINS
SIERRA NEVADA
COAST RANGES
CASCADE RANGE
SALMON RIVER MOUNTAINS

Tropic of Cancer

Edmonton
Calgary
Saskatoon
Regina
Winnipeg
Vancouver
Victoria
Seattle
Tacoma
Olympia
Spokane
Portland
Salem
Eugene
Boise
Great Falls
Helena
Butte
Billings
Bismarck
Rapid City
Aberdeen
SAN FRANCISCO
Oakland
San Jose
Sacramento
Stockton
Modesto
Reno
Fresno
Bakersfield
Salt Lake City
Ogden
Provo
Denver
Aurora
Colorado Springs
Pueblo
LOS ANGELES
Long Beach
Santa Ana
Anaheim
Riverside
San Bernardino
Pasadena
Santa Barbara
Ventura
Lancaster
San Diego
Tijuana
Mexicali
Oceanside
Las Vegas
Phoenix
Mesa
Scottsdale
Tempe
Tucson
Flagstaff
Albuquerque
Santa Fe
Las Cruces
El Paso
Ciudad Juárez
Roswell
Lubbock
Amarillo
Oklahoma City
Wichita
Wichita Falls
Fort Worth
Abilene
Odessa
Midland
San Angelo
Austin
San Antonio
Laredo
Nuevo Laredo
Monterrey
Torreón
Saltillo
Chihuahua
Hermosillo
Ciudad Obregón
Culiacán
Durango
Mazatlán
La Paz
Tepic
Guadalajara
Aguascalientes
San Luis Potosí
León

ISLA DE GUADALUPE (Mex.)
ISLA CEDROS
BAJA CALIFORNIA
GOLFO DE CALIFORNIA
SIERRA MADRE OCCIDENTAL
SIERRA MADRE ORIENTAL

Mount Whitney
Mount Shasta
Boundary Peak 4006
Humphreys Peak
Wheeler Peak 4011
Mount Elbert 4399

Rio Grande
Colorado
Columbia
Snake
Missouri
Yellowstone

Copyright © by Rand McNally & Co.
Map prepared by Rand McNally & Co.
A-620500-364

Mi. 600
Km. 600

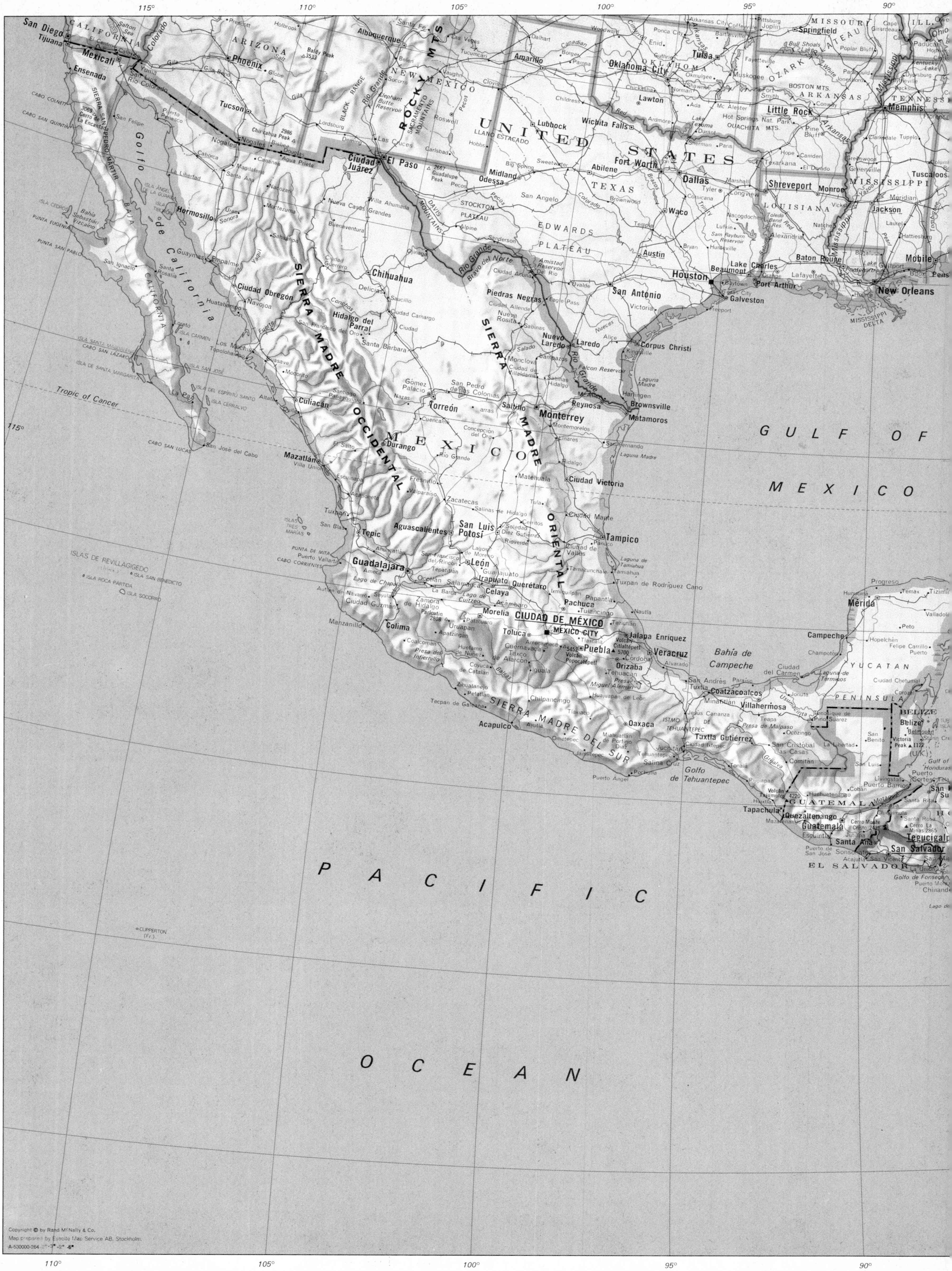

115° 110° 105° 100° 95° 90°

UNITED STATES

MISSOURI
Springfield
ILL
OKLAHOMA
Oklahoma City
Tulsa
ARKANSAS
Little Rock
TENNESSEE
Memphis
MISSISSIPPI
Jackson
LOUISIANA
Shreveport
Monroe
Baton Rouge
New Orleans
Mobile

ARIZONA
Phoenix
Tucson
NEW MEXICO
Albuquerque
TEXAS
El Paso
Dallas
Fort Worth
Waco
Austin
San Antonio
Houston
Galveston
Corpus Christi
Brownsville

CALIFORNIA
San Diego
Tijuana
Mexicali
Ensenada
Hermosillo
Ciudad Juárez

ROCKY MTS.

Golfo de California

BAJA CALIFORNIA

Guaymas
Ciudad Obregón
Los Mochis
La Paz
CABO SAN LUCAS
San José del Cabo
Mazatlán

SIERRA MADRE OCCIDENTAL
Chihuahua
Hidalgo del Parral
Durango
Culiacán
Torreón
Gómez Palacio
Saltillo
Monterrey
Nuevo Laredo
Laredo
Matamoros
Reynosa

Tropic of Cancer

MEXICO

SIERRA MADRE ORIENTAL

Ciudad Victoria
Tampico
San Luis Potosí
Aguascalientes
Tepic
Guadalajara
León
Irapuato
Celaya
Querétaro
Pachuca
Toluca
CIUDAD DE MÉXICO
MEXICO CITY
Puebla
Veracruz
Orizaba
Morelia
Colima
Manzanillo
Acapulco

SIERRA MADRE DEL SUR

Oaxaca
Tuxtla Gutiérrez
Puerto Ángel
Golfo de Tehuantepec
ISTMO DE TEHUANTEPEC
Coatzacoalcos
Villahermosa

GULF OF MEXICO
Bahía de Campeche
Ciudad del Carmen
Campeche
Mérida
Progreso
YUCATAN PENINSULA
BELIZE
Belize

GUATEMALA
Guatemala
Quezaltenango
Tapachula
EL SALVADOR
San Salvador
Santa Ana
Tegucigalpa

PACIFIC OCEAN

Mi.
Km.

Copyright © by Rand McNally & Co.
Map prepared by Esselte Map Service AB, Stockholm.

166

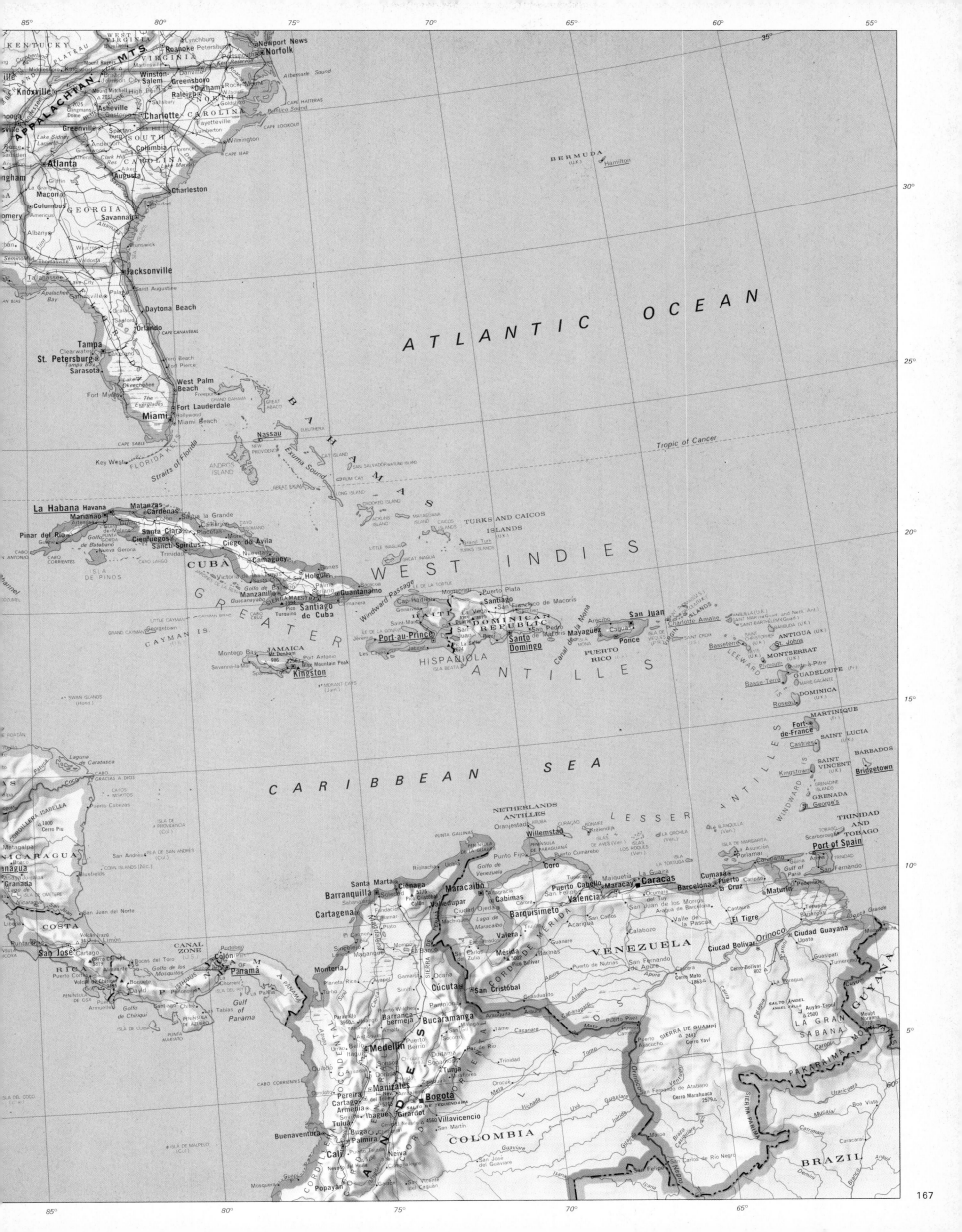

Northern South America

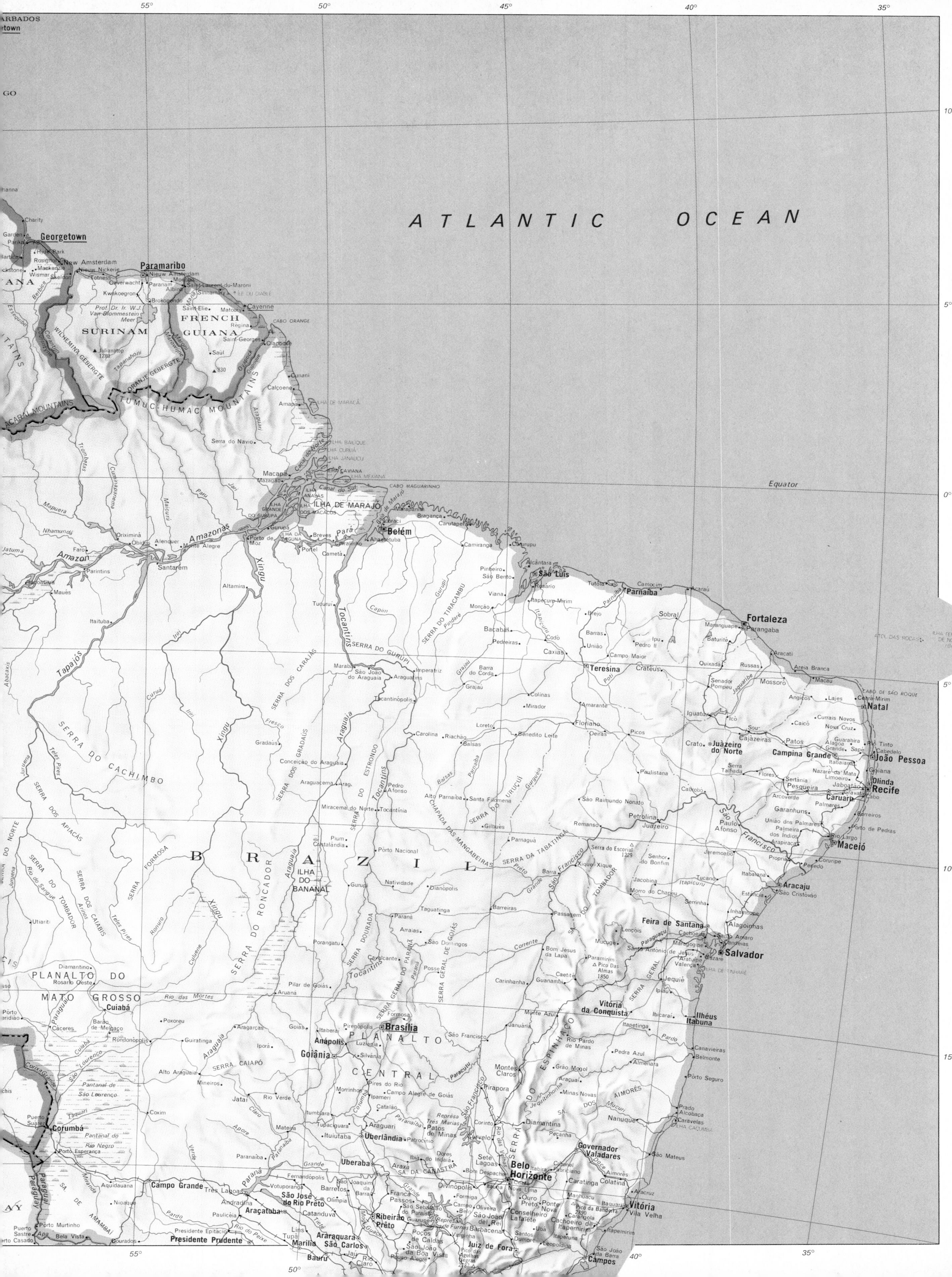

ATLANTIC OCEAN

BARBADOS
town

Georgetown
New Amsterdam
Paramaribo
Nieuw Nickerie
Nieuw Amsterdam
Saint-Laurent-du-Maroni
ÎLE DU DIABLE
Cayenne

FRENCH
GUIANA

SURINAM

Prof. Dr. Ir. W.J.
Van Blommestein
Meer

Juliantop
1280

CABO ORANGE

Regina
Saint-Georges
Saül

WILHELMINA GEBERGTE
ORANJE-GEBERGTE

TUMUC-HUMAC MOUNTAINS

ACARAI MOUNTAINS

Oriximiná
Óbidos
Amazonas
Amazon
Parintins
Maués
Santarém

Macapá
ILHA DE MARAJÓ

Belém

Gurupá
Pará
Abaeté

Cametá
Altamira
Itaituba

Tucuruí

São Luís
São Bento
Parnaíba
Fortaleza
Sobral
Teresina
Viana
Bacabal
Codó
Caxias
Pedreiras
Colinas
Mirador
Crateús
Quixadá
Russas
Mossoró
Macau
Areia Branca
Natal
Currais Novos
Nova Cruz
Caicó

BRAZIL

Carolina
Riachão
Balsas
Floriano
Oeiras
Picos
Amarante
Crato
Juàzeiro
do Norte
Cajàzeiras
Patos
Campina Grande
João Pessoa
Olinda
Recife
Caruaru

SERRA DO CACHIMBO

PLANALTO DO
MATO GROSSO

Cuiabá

Corumbá

Campo Grande

São José
do Rio Prêto

Presidente Prudente

Brasília
Anápolis
Goiânia

PLANALTO

CENTRAL

Uberlândia
Uberaba

Belo
Horizonte

Feira de Santana
Salvador

Vitória
da Conquista

Ilhéus
Itabuna

Governador
Valadares

Vitória
Vila Velha

Campos

Juiz de Fora

Equator

Maceió
Aracaju

Petrolina
Juàzeiro

São Francisco

SERRA DO ESPINHAÇO

Diamantina
Montes
Claros

169

PACIFIC

OCEAN

CHILE

ARGENTINA

BOLIVIA

PAR

Tropic of Capricorn

Antofagasta

Salta

San Miguel de Tucumán

Catamarca

La Rioja

Santiago del Estero

Asunción

Resistencia

Corrientes

Córdoba

Santa Fe

Paraná

Concordia

San Juan

Mendoza

Valparaíso

Viña del Mar

SANTIAGO

Rosario

BUENOS AIRES

Rancagua

San Rafael

Talca

Chillán

Talcahuano

Concepción

Temuco

Valdivia

Osorno

Puerto Montt

ARGENTINA

Bahía Blanca

Neuquén

PATAGONIA

Comodoro Rivadavia

Golfo San Jorge

PENÍNSULA VALDÉS

Golfo San Matías

Golfo Nuevo

Trelew

Rawson

Río Gallegos

Punta Arenas

Estrecho de Magallanes

TIERRA DEL FUEGO

CABO DE HORNOS

FALKLAND ISLANDS (U.K.)

WEST FALKLAND

ISLAS JUAN FERNÁNDEZ (Chile)

ISLA SAN FÉLIX (Chile)

ISLA SAN AMBROSIO (Chile)

ISLA DE CHILOÉ

ARCHIPIÉLAGO DE LOS CHONOS

PENÍNSULA DE TAITAO

ISLA WELLINGTON

PENÍNSULA VALDÉS

Mi. 600

Km. 600

Copyright © by Rand McNally & Co.
Map prepared by Esselte Map Service AB, Stockholm

170

A-549200-284

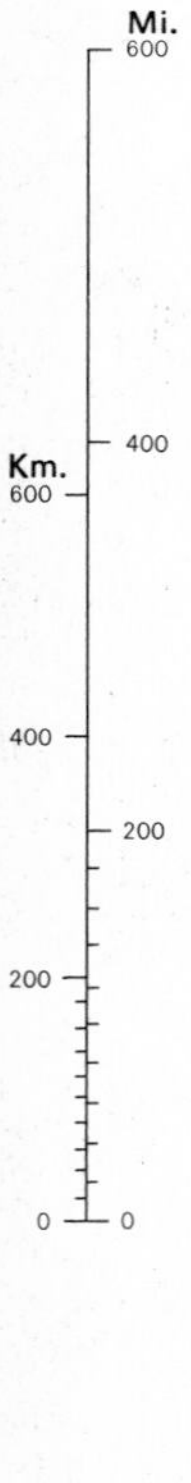

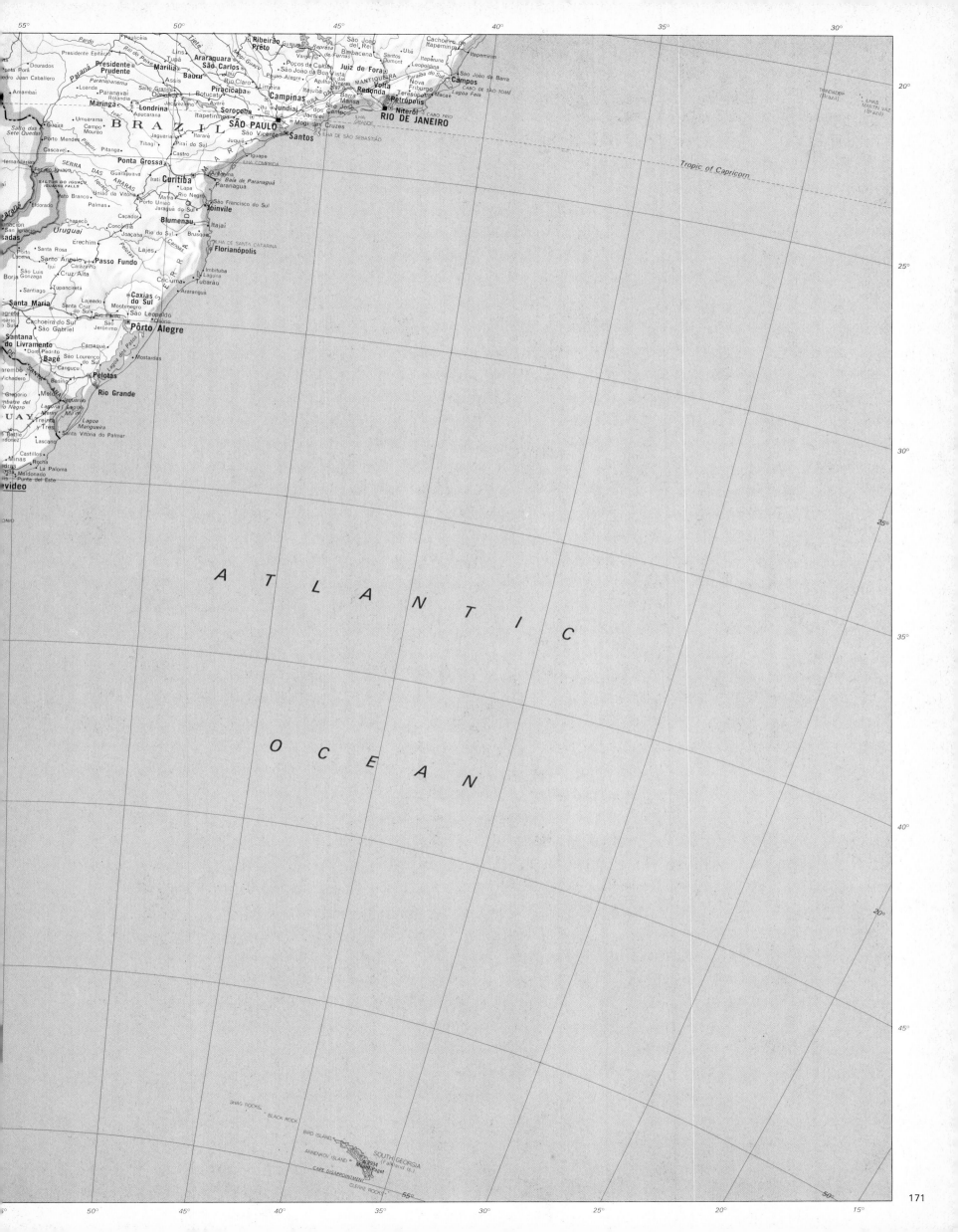

ATLANTIC

OCEAN

171

INDONESIA

G. Slamet 3428
Tasikmalaya Magelang Madjun Kediri Malang Jember
Cilacap Yogyakarta Surakarta Blitar Banjuwangi BALI Singaraja
JAWA JAVA Denpasar LOMBOK Mataram Praja SUMBAWA SUMBAWA Basan
NUSA LESSER SUNDA ISLANDS TENGGARA
Waikabubak Waingapu Laut Sawu
SUMBA Savu Sea
Baing PULAU SEMAU
PULAU SAWU PULAU ROTI
TIMOR Soe
Kupang

Timor
Sea

HIBERNA REEF
ASHMORE ISLANDS CARTER ISLAND (Austl.)

MELVILLE ISLAND CAPE CROKER
BATHURST ISLAND
Van Diemen Gulf
Beagle Gulf Clarence Strait
POINT BLAZE Darwin
Palm Jungle
ARNHEM
Pine Creek
Daly

CAPE LONDONDERRY
Joseph Bonaparte Gulf
BONAPARTE ARCHIPELAGO
Admiralty Gulf
York Sound
BROWSE ISLAND
SCOTT REEF
ADÈLE ISLAND BEAGLE REEF
BUCCANEER ARCHIPELAGO
Collier Bay Yampi Sound
CAPE LEVEQUE
King Sound Derby
Broome

Katherine
Victoria River Downs
Wyndham Kununurra Lake Argyle
KIMBERLEY PLATEAU
Mount Ord 936
Fitzroy Crossing
Halls Creek
Gordon Downs
Wave Hill
Newcastle Waters
Victoria

INDIAN

OCEAN

ROWLEY SHOALS

CAPE LATOUCHE TREVILLE
La Grange
EIGHTY MILE BEACH

NORTHERN

TERRITORY

Gregory Lake
TANAMI DESERT
Barrow

GREAT SANDY DESERT
Shay Gap
Port Hedland Roebourne
DAMPIER ARCHIPELAGO Dampier
MONTEBELLO ISLANDS
BARROW ISLAND
Marble Bar
De Grey
Nullagine
Lake Dora (Dry) Lake Auld (Dry)
Lake Wills Lake White (Dry)
Lake Mackay (Dry Salt Lake)
Mount Leisler 901 Mount Zeil 1511

MUIRON ISLANDS
NORTH WEST CAPE Onslow Pannawonica
Exmouth Gulf
Forth
HAMERSLEY RANGE Wittenoom
Mount Brockman 1129 1235 Mount Bruce
Tom Price Paraburdoo Newman
Ashburton
POINT CLOATES

Lake Disappointment
Savory
Lake Macdonald (Dry) MACDONN

WESTERN

GIBSON DESERT
906 Mount Essendon
Lake Neale
Lake Amadeus (Dry)

Tropic of Capricorn
105°
CAPE CUVIER
Geographe Channel Carnarvon
BERNIER ISLAND
OCHRE ISLAND
Naturaliste Channel Shark Bay
DIRK HARTOG ISLAND
STEEP POINT
Lyons
Lake Macleod Mount Augustus 1105
Gascoyne
Woorame Wooramel
Murchison

AUST

Mount Olga 1069 Ayers Rock 867
Mount Aloysius 1085
1439 Mount Woodroffe

AUSTRALIA

Peak Hill
ROBINSON RANGES
Meekatharra
Wiluna
Lake Carnegie (Dry)
Lake Gillen (Dry)
Lake Wells (Dry)

GREAT VICTORIA DESERT
SOU
Lake Maurice (Dry)

25°
Nannine
Cue
Lake Austin (Dry) Sandstone
Boogardie Mount Magnet
Yalgoo Northampton
Mullewa
HOUTMAN ABROLHOS Geraldton
Dongara
Tipree Springs
GREEN HEAD
Moora
Dalwallinu
Bonnie Rock
Bencubbin
Bullfinch
Southern Cross

Agnew
Mount Redcliffe 576
Leonora Malcolm
Laverton
Leinster
Lake Carey (Dry Salt Lake)
Menzies
Lake Ballard Lake Raeside (Dry)
Lake Minigwal (Dry)
Yeo Lake (Dry)

Mongers Lake
Lake Barlee (Dry Salt Lake)
Lake Moore

Kalgoorlie Boulder
Coolgardie
Kanowna
Zanthus
Haig
Rawlinna
Forrest Deakin
NULLARBOR PLAIN
Eucla
CAPE ADIEU
SAINT PETER

Marahinga
Ooldea

Kangwna

Machins
Stirling Perth
Fremantle
Northam
York Kellerberrin
Beverley
Brookton
Pinjarra
DARLING RANGE
Merredin
Hyden
Narrogin
Wagin
Newdegate
Nyabing
Katanning
Gnowangerup
Pingelly

Lake Lefroy (Dry)
Lake Cowan (Dry Salt Lake)
Norseman
Lake Dundas (Dry)
Lake Johnston (Dry)
Ravensthorpe
Hopetoun
POINT CULVER

Esperance
Esperance Bay
ARCHIPELAGO OF THE RECHERCHE
CAPE ARID

Great Australian Bight

Eyre

INVES

Bunbury
Geographe Bay
CAPE NATURALISTE Busselton
Collie Budgetown
Augusta
Manjimup Bridgetown
CAPE LEEUWIN Pemberton
Denmark
POINT D'ENTRECASTEAUX Deewars
WEST CAPE HOWE
Bluff Knoll 1096 Mount Barker
Albany
CAPE VANCOUVER
King George Sound
HOOD POINT
CAPE KNOB

INDIAN OCE

Copyright © by Rand McNally & Co.
Map prepared by Esselte Map Service AB, Stockholm
172
A-590200-264

Mi.
600
Km.
600

Indian Ocean
Ara

NORTHE

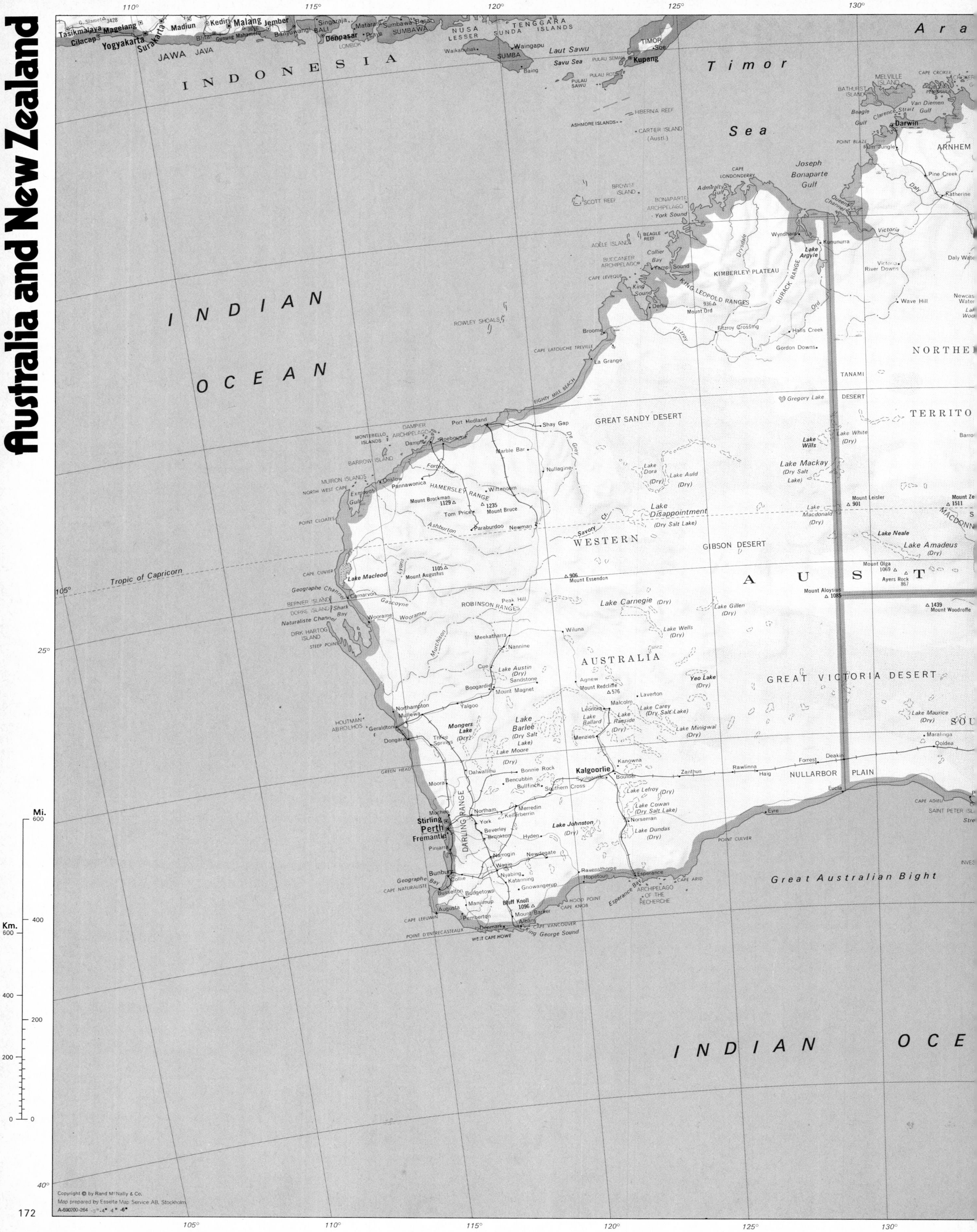

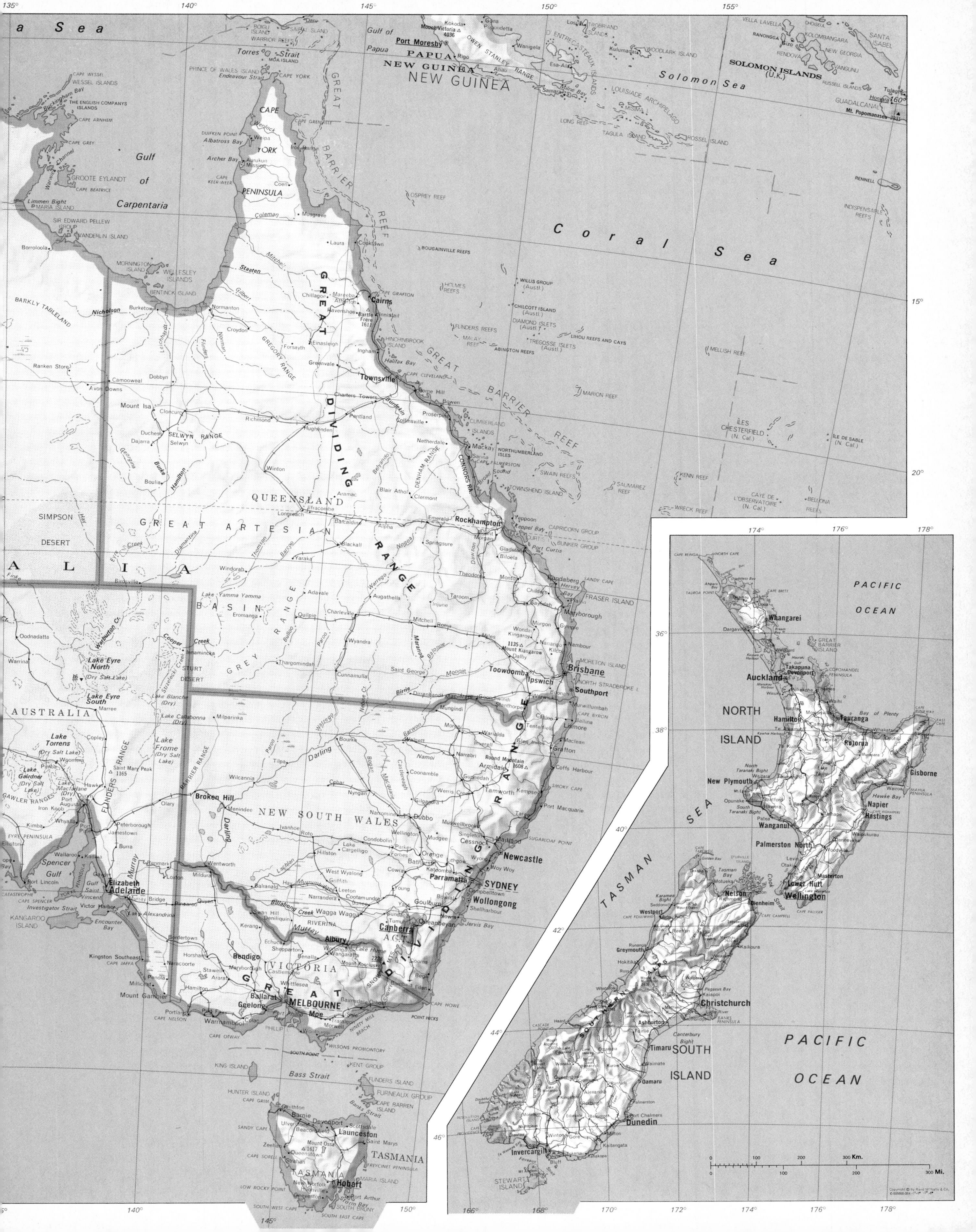

a Sea

Gulf of Carpentaria

NEW GUINEA
PAPUA NEW GUINEA
Port Moresby
Papua

Coral Sea

Solomon Sea
SOLOMON ISLANDS (U.K.)
GUADALCANAL

CAPE YORK PENINSULA
GREAT DIVIDING RANGE

QUEENSLAND
GREAT ARTESIAN BASIN

Cairns
Townsville
Charters Towers
Mount Isa
Cloncurry
Winton
Longreach
Barcaldine
Emerald
Rockhampton
Gladstone
Bundaberg
Maryborough
Gympie
Toowoomba
Ipswich
Brisbane
Southport

NEW SOUTH WALES
GREAT DIVIDING RANGE

Broken Hill
Bourke
Dubbo
Tamworth
Armidale
Grafton
Coffs Harbour
Port Macquarie
Newcastle
Parramatta
SYDNEY
Wollongong
Canberra
A.C.T.
Goulburn
Wagga Wagga
Albury

SOUTH AUSTRALIA
Lake Eyre North
Lake Eyre South
Lake Torrens
Lake Gairdner
Lake Frome
FLINDERS RANGES
Spencer Gulf
Adelaide
Elizabeth
KANGAROO ISLAND

VICTORIA
GREAT DIVIDING RANGE
Bendigo
Ballarat
Geelong
MELBOURNE
Warrnambool

Bass Strait

TASMANIA
Launceston
Hobart

SIMPSON DESERT
STURT DESERT
GREY RANGE
BARKLY TABLELAND

Gulf of Carpentaria
GROOTE EYLANDT
Borroloola

AUSTRALIA

New Zealand (inset)

PACIFIC OCEAN

NORTH ISLAND
Whangarei
Auckland
Hamilton
Tauranga
Rotorua
New Plymouth
Gisborne
Napier
Hastings
Wanganui
Palmerston North
Masterton
Lower Hutt
Wellington

TASMAN SEA

SOUTH ISLAND
SOUTHERN ALPS
Nelson
Blenheim
Westport
Greymouth
Hokitika
Christchurch
Ashburton
Timaru
Oamaru
Dunedin
Invercargill
STEWART ISLAND

PACIFIC OCEAN

0 100 200 300 Km.
0 100 200 300 Mi.

Copyright © by Rand McNally & Co.

Legend

Legend to Maps

Transportation

┣━━━┿━━━┫	Railway
─────────	Primary Road
─────────	Secondary Road
─────────	Minor Road, Trail
✈	Airport
─────────	Navigable Canal
──────────	Ferry

Inhabited Localities

1:3,000,000
1:6,000,000
- • 0—10,000
- ○ 10,000—25,000
- ⊚ 25,000—100,000
- ⊡ 100,000—250,000
- ▣ 250,000—1,000,000
- ■ >1,000,000

1:12,000,000
- • 0—50,000
- ⊚ 50,000—100,000
- ⊡ 100,000—250,000
- ▣ 250,000—1,000,000
- ■ >1,000,000

Urban Area (area of continuous industrial, commercial, and residential development)

Capitals of Political Units

BUDAPEST	Independent Nation
Luanda	Dependency (Colony, protectorate, etc.)
Villarica	State, Province, etc.
White Plains	County, Oblast, etc.

Political Boundaries

International (First-order political unit)

Demarcated, Undemarcated, and Administrative
Disputed de jure
Indefinite or Undefined

Internal

State, Province, etc. (Second-order political unit)

County, Oblast, etc. (Third-order political unit)

Miscellaneous Cultural Features

- ▲ Point of Interest (Battlefield, cave, historical site, etc.)
- ⚲ Church, Monastery
- ∴ Ruins
- ⌇ Castle

Hydrographic Features

- Intermittent Stream
- Rapids, Falls
- Reef
- *Tuz Gölü* Salt Lake
- *The Everglades* Swamp
- Glacier — SEWARD GLACIER
- Intermittent Lake, Reservoir
- Dry Lake Bed

Topographic Features

Mt. Kenya △ 5199	Elevation Above Sea Level
76	Elevation Below Sea Level
Mount Cook ▲ 3764	Highest Elevation in Country
133	Lowest Elevation in Country
Khyber Pass ≍ 1067	Mountain Pass

Elevations and depths are given in meters

Highest Elevation and Lowest Elevation of a continent are underlined

Country Comparisons

The figures listed below cover all countries in the world with a railway system. Direct comparison is made between major railway statistics and the basic area and population data for the country concerned. Figures usually relate to the state system, but where this does not exist, or where the level of private ownership is significant, this position is reflected. Metric values are given, *with American equivalents in italic*. Information is based on United Nations and Rand McNally sources, supplemented by other available material.

Information is set out under country headings, as follows:

Capital
A Area – km² *miles²*
B Population
C Route length (km *miles*) per 10,000 km² *10,000 miles²*
D Route length (km *miles*) per 10,000 population
E Net ton km *miles* per capita
F Passenger km *miles* per capita

Information not available marked n/a

Albania
Tiranë
A 28,748 *11,100*
B 2,520,000
C 101.6 *164*
D 1.2 *0.7*
E n/a
F n/a

Algeria
Algiers
A 2,381,741 *919,595*
B 17,045,000
C 16.6 *26.6*
D 2.3 *1.4*
E 11.2 *7*
F 62.1 *38.8*

Angola
Luanda
A 1,246,700 *481,353*
B 6,090,000
C 18 *29.1*
D 3.7 *2.3*
E 732.3 *457.7*
F 68.6 *42.9*

Argentina
Buenos Aires
A 2,776,889 *1,072,162*
B 25,550,000
C 144.1 *233.3*
D 15.7 *9.8*
E 418 *261.3*
F 563.1 *352*

Australia
Canberra
A 7,686,849 *2,967,909*
B 13,645,000
C 55.9 *90.5*
D 31.5 *19.7*
E 2,183.7 *1,364.8*
F n/a

Austria
Vienna
A 83,849 *32,374*
B 7,745,000
C 695.2 *1,125.3*
D 7.5 *4.7*
E 1,360.4 *850.2*
F 863 *539.4*

B

Bangladesh
Dacca
A 142,775 *55,126*
B 77,650,000
C 200.2 *324*
D 0.4 *0.2*
E 5 *3.1*
F 26.7 *16.7*

Belgium
Brussels
A 30,513 *11,781*
B 9,865,000
C 1,353.8 *2,911.9*
D 284.9 *178.1*
E 672.7 *420.4*
F 832 *520*

Benin
Porto Novo
A 112,622 *43,484*
B 3,180,000
C 51.4 *82.6*
D 1.8 *1.1*
E 39.8 *24.8*
F 30.4 *19*

Bolivia
Sucre and La Paz
A 1,098,581 *424,164*
B 5,715,000
C 32.6 *52.8*
D 6.3 *3.9*
E 63.9 *39.9*
F 47.2 *34.9*

Brazil
Brasília
A 8,511,965 *3,286,487*
B 108,640,000
C 75.8 *122.6*
D 5.9 *3.7*
E 393 *245.6*
F 97.6 *61*

Bulgaria
Sofia
A 110,912 *42,823*
B 8,765,000
C 386.8 *626.1*
D 4.9 *3.1*
E 1,945.5 *1,215.9*
F 855.7 *534.8*

Burma
Rangoon
A 678,033 *261,790*
B 31,415,000
C 45.7 *74*
D 1 *0.6*
E 13.4 *8.4*
F 90.6 *56.6*

C

Cambodia
Phnum Pénh
A 181,035 *69,898*
B 8,215,000
C 35.8 *58*
D 0.8 *0.5*
E 1.2 *0.7*
F 6.6 *4.1*

Cameroon
Yaoundé
A 475,442 *183,569*
B 6,450,000
C 24.7 *39.6*
D 1.8 *1.1*
E 827.9 *517.4*
F 40.9 *25.6*

Canada
Ottawa
A 9,976,139 *3,851,809*
B 22,975,000
C 70.9 *114.8*
D 30.8 *19.3*
E 8,583.9 *5,365*
F 127.5 *79.7*

Chile
Santiago
A 756,945 *292,258*
B 10,685,000
C 120.2 *194.6*
D 8.5 *5.3*
E 180.8 *113*
F 196.5 *122.8*

China[1]
Peking
A 9,561,000 *3,691,500*
B 845,300,000
C 57.5 *93.1*
D 0.7 *0.4*
E 356.1 *222.6*
F n/a

Colombia
Bogotá
A 1,138,914 *439,737*
B 21,960,000
C 30.2 *48.6*
D 1.6 *1*
E 56.8 *35.5*
F 23.3 *14.5*

Congo
Brazzaville
A 342,000 *132,000*
B 1,360,000
C 23.2 *37.6*
D 5.8 *3.7*
E 373.2 *233.3*
F 180.9 *113.1*

Costa Rica
San José
A 50,900 *19,650*
B 1,990,000
C n/a
D n/a
E n/a
F n/a

Cuba
Havana
A 114,524 *44,218*
B 9,340,000
C 441.2 *714.2*
D 5.4 *3.4*
E 173.1 *108.2*
F 101.3 *63.3*

Czechoslovakia
Prague
A 127,876 *49,373*
B 14,875,000
C 1,042.4 *1,677.6*
D 9 *5.6*
E 4,755.6 *2,972.3*
F 1,241.5 *776*

D

Denmark
Copenhagen
A 43,069 *16,629*
B 5,100,000
C 577.1 *933.9*
D 4.9 *3*
E 416.5 *260.3*
F 637.6 *398.5*

Dominican Republic
Santo Domingo
A 48,734 *18,816*
B 4,760,000
C 57.5[1] *92.5*[1]
D 0.6[1] *0.4*[1]
E n/a
F n/a

E

Ecuador
Quito
A 283,561 *109,483*
B 6,615,000
C 39.5 *63.6*
D 1.7 *1.1*
E 7 *4.4*
F 9.2 *5.7*

Egypt[2]
Cairo
A 1,002,000 *386,900*
B 38,045,000
C 45 *72.9*
D 1.2 *0.7*
E 67.3 *42.1*
F 190.8 *119.2*

Eire
Dublin
A 70,285 *27,137*
B 3,165,000
C 311.4 *504.1*
D 6.9 *4.3*
E 179.1 *111.9*
F 253 *158.1*

El Salvador
San Salvador
A 21,393 *8,260*
B 4,152,000
C 289.8 *466.1*
D 1.5 *0.9*
E n/a
F n/a

Ethiopia
Addis Ababā
A 1,221,900 *471,778*
B 28,265,000
C 6.4 *10.3*
D 0.3 *0.2*
E 8.6 *5.4*
F 3.8 *2.4*

Finland
Helsinki
A 337,032 *130,129*
B 4,710,000
C 176.7 *286.1*
D 12.6 *7.9*
E 1,388.5 *867.8*
F 665 *415.6*

France
Paris
A 543,998 *210,039*
B 52,930,000
C 639.7 *1,035.5*
D 6.6 *4.1*
E 1,294.3 *808.9*
F 966.7 *604.2*

Germany, East
East Berlin
A 108,178 *41,768*
B 17,365,000
C 1,329.7 *2,152.4*
D 8.3 *5.2*
E 2,983.2 *1,864.5*
F 1,286.7 *804.2*

Germany, West
Bonn
A 248,533 *95,959*
B 62,650,000
C 1,157.6 *1,873.9*
D 4.6 *2.9*
E 945.1 *590.7*
F 612.2 *382.6*

Ghana
Accra
A 238,537 *92,100*
B 9,990,000
C 40 *64.3*
D 1 *0.6*
E 30.5 *19.1*
F 52.1 *32.5*

Greece
Athens
A 131,944 *50,944*
B 9,010,000
C 194.2 *314.5*
D 2.8 *1.8*
E 103.4 *64.6*
F 172.3 *107.7*

Guatemala
Guatemala
A 108,889 *42,042*
B 5,920,000
C 83.9 *135.9*
D 1.5 *1*
E 17.9 *11.2*
F n/a

Guinea
Conakry
A 245,857 *94,926*
B 4,460,000
C 38.2 *61.8*
D 2.1 *1.3*
E n/a
F n/a

H

Honduras
Tegucigalpa
A 112,088 *43,277*
B 3,150,000
C 46.6[1] *75.4[1]*
D 1.7[1] *1[1]*
E n/a
F n/a

Hong Kong
Hong Kong
A 1,034 *399*
B 4,385,000
C 324 *526.3*
D 0.1 *0.05*
E 10.6 *6.6*
F 57.2 *35.7*

Hungary
Budapest
A 93,032 *35,920*
B 10,510,000
C 867.9 *1,404.8*
D 7.7 *4.8*
E 2,145.4 *1,340.9*
F 1,271.9 *795*

I

India
New Delhi
A 3,183,643 *1,229,210*
B 604,000,000
C 189.4 *306.6*
D 1 *0.6*
E 236.9 *148.1*
F 223.1 *139.4*

Indonesia
Djakarta
A 1,950,963 *753,271*
B 133,840,000
C 35.7 *57.8*
D 0.5 *0.3*
E 7.2 *4.5*
F 26.3 *16.5*

Iran
Tehrān
A 1,648,000 *636,300*
B 33,365,000
C 28 *45.3*
D 1.4 *0.9*
E 160.2 *100.1*
F 67.9 *42.5*

Iraq
Baghdād
A 434,924 *167,925*
B 11,300,000
C 58.1 *94.1*
D 2.2 *1.4*
E 151.1 *94.4*
F 56 *35*

Israel[2]
Jerusalem
A 20,770 *8,019*
B 3,480,000
C 287.9 *466.4*
D 1.7 *1.1*
E 133.3 *83.3*
F 92.8 *58*

Italy
Rome
A 301,250 *116,313*
B 56,060,000
C 531.6 *860.5*
D 2.9 *1.8*
E 296.9 *185.6*
F 699.5 *437.2*

Ivory Coast[3]
Abidjan
A 322,463 *124,504*
B 6,795,000
C 19.7 *31.7*
D 0.9 *0.6*
E 34.3 *21.5*
F 73.3 *45.8*

J

Jamaica
Kingston
A 10,962 *4,232*
B 2,035,000
C 301 *484.4*
D 1.6 *1*
E 76.7 *47.9*
F 31.4 *19.7*

Japan
Tōkyō
A 372,197 *143,706*
B 111,680,000
C 721.8 *1,168.4*
D 2.4 *1.5*
E 428.5 *267.8*
F 2,875.1 *1,797*

Jordan[2]
'Ammān
A 97,740 *37,738*
B 3,430,000
C 51.2 *82.1*
D 1.5 *0.9*
E 8.2 *5.1*
F n/a

K

Kenya[4]
Nairobi
A 582,644 *224,960*
B 13,550,000
C 33.4 *53.8*
D 1.5 *0.9*
E 120.9 *75.6*
F 40.2 *25.1*

Korea, North[5]
P'yŏngyang
A 120,538 *46,540*
B 16,035,000
C 317.3 *513.8*
D 2.4 *1.5*
E n/a
F n/a

Korea, South[5]
Seoul
A 98,477 *38,022*
B 34,290,000
C 259.8 *420.4*
D 0.7 *0.5*
E 276.8 *173*
F 405.2 *253.3*

L

Lebanon
Beirut
A 10,230 *3,950*
B 3,485,000
C 404.7 *655.7*
D 1.2 *0.7*
E 12.1 *7.5*
F 0.6 *0.3*

Liberia
Monrovia
A 111,369 *43,000*
B 1,730,000
C 44.3 *71.6*
D 2.8 *1.8*
E 2,303[6] *1,439.3[6]*
F n/a

Luxembourg
Luxembourg
A 2,586 *998*
B 335,000
C 1,048 *1,693.4*
D 8.1 *5*
E 1,869.9 *1,168.7*
F 877.6 *548.5*

M

Malagasy Republic
Tananarive
A 587,041 *226,658*
B 9,025,000
C 15 *24.7*
D 1 *0.6*
E 31.8 *19.9*
F 27.5 *17.2*

Malawi
Lilongwe
A 118,484 *45,747*
B 5,070,000
C 47.8 *77*
D 1.1 *0.7*
E 43 *26.9*
F 12.1 *7.5*

Malaysia
Kuala Lumpur
A 332,633 *128,430*
B 12,180,000
C 54.1 *87.6*
D 1.5 *0.9*
E 959.3 *599.6*
F 51.7 *32.3*

Mali
Bamako
A 1,239,710 *478,655*
B 5,810,000
C 5.2 *8.3*
D 1.1 *0.7*
E 28.7 *17.9*
F 17.2 *10.8*

Mauritania
Nouakchott
A 1,030,700 *397,950*
B 1,340,000
C 6.3 *10.2*
D 4.9 *3*
E 5,080.6 *3,175.4*
F n/a

Mexico
Mexico City
A 1,972,546 *761,604*
B 61,040,000
C 87.5 *141.7*
D 2.8 *1.8*
E 533.2 *333.2*
F 68.8 *43*

Mongolia
Ulan Bator
A 1,565,000 *604,200*
B 1,460,000
C 9.1 *14.7*
D 9.8 *6.1*
E 1,583.6 *989.7*
F 142.5 *89*

Morocco
Rabat
A 446,550 *172,415*
B 17,785,000
C 45.4 *73.1*
D 1.1 *0.7*
E 176.1 *110.1*
F 49.1 *30.7*

Mozambique[7]
Maputo
A 783,763 *303,771*
B 9,380,000
C 49 *79.1*
D 4.1 *2.6*
E 232.8 *145.5*
F 22.4 *14*

N

Nepal
Kāthmāndu
A 140,797 *54,362*
B 12,705,000
C 4.5 *7.2*
D 0.05 *0.03*
E n/a
F n/a

Netherlands
Amsterdam
A 40,844 *15,770*
B 13,695,000
C 691.7 *1,119.8*
D 2.1 *1.3*
E 19.4 *12.1*
F 605.5 *378.4*

New Zealand
Wellington
A 268,675 *103,736*
B 3,120,000
C 178.5 *289*
D 15.4 *9.6*
E 1,266.7 *791.7*
F 2,045.8 *1,278.6*

Nicaragua
Managua
A 130,000 *50,200*
B 2,185,000
C 24.5 *39.2*
D 1.5 *0.9*
E 76.9 *48.1*
F 153.8 *96.1*

Nigeria
Lagos
A 923,768 *356,669*
B 75,080,000
C 38.1 *61.7*
D 0.5 *0.3*
E 18 *11.2*
F 13.6 *8.5*

Norway
Oslo
A 323,878 *125,050*
B 4,040,000
C 130.9 *212*
D 10.5 *6.6*
E 343.1 *214.4*
F 246.5 *154.1*

P

Pakistan
Islāmābād
A 895,496 *345,753*
B 72,000,000
C 98.4 *159.2*
D 1.2 *0.8*
E 120.7 *75.4*
F 178.7 *111.7*

Panama
Panamá
A 75,651 *29,209*
B 1,485,000
C 58.3 *90*
D 3 *1.8*
E n/a
F n/a

Paraguay
Ascunción
A 406,752 *157,048*
B 2,755,000
C 12.2 *19.6*
D 1.8 *1.1*
E 11.8 *7.4*
F 97.9 *61.2*

Peru
Lima
A 1,285,216 *496,224*
B 16,080,000
C 16.8 *27.2*
D 1.3 *0.8*
E 45.7 *28.6*
F 16.8 *10.5*

Philippines
Manila
A 300,000 *115,831*
B 43,300,000
C 39.2 *63.5*
D 0.3 *0.2*
E 1.5 *0.9*
F 22.2 *13.9*

Poland
Warsaw
A 312,677 *120,725*
B 34,175,000
C 760.1 *1,230.4*
D 7 *4.3*
E 3,829.1 *2,393.2*
F 1,252.5 *782.8*

Portugal
Lisbon
A 92,082 *35,553*
B 9,110,000
C 387.3 *627.4*
D 3.9 *2.4*
E 93.9 *58.7*
F 59.3 *37*

R

Rhodesia
Salisbury
A 390,580 *150,804*
B 6,405,000
C 86.2 *139.5*
D 5.3 *3.3*
E 992.7 *620.4*
F n/a

Romania
Bucharest
A 237,500 *91,699*
B 21,220,000
C 460.7 *745.7*
D 5.2 *3.2*
E 3,053.7 *1,908.6*
F 1,055.8 *659.9*

S

Saudi Arabia
Riyadh
A 2,149,690 *830,000*
B 9,105,000
C 2.8 *4.6*
D 0.7 *0.4*
E 172.2 *107.7*
F 0.007 *0.005*

Senegal
Dakar
A 196,722 *75,955*
B 4,480,000
C 52.5 *84.5*
D 2.3 *1.4*
E 65.2 *40.8*
F 50.7 *31.7*

South Africa[8]
Cape Town and Pretoria
A 1,222,161 *471,879*
B 25,815,000
C 109.6 *176.2*
D 8.4 *5.2*
E 2,552.6 *1,595.3*
F n/a

South West Africa[8]
Windhoek
A 823,168 *317,827*
B 870,000
C 109.6 *176.2*
D 8.4 *5.2*
E 2,552.6 *1,595.3*
F n/a

Spain
Madrid
A 504,750 *194,885*
B 35,765,000
C 282.4 *483*
D 4 *2.6*
E 301 *188.1*
F 466.4 *291.5*

Sri Lanka
Colombo
A 65,610 *25,332*
B 14,250,000
C 233.8 *378.4*
D 1.1 *0.7*
E 20.8 *13*
F 203.8 *127.4*

Sudan
Khartoum
A 2,505,813 *967,500*
B 14,790,000
C 19.1 *30.9*
D 3.2 *2*
E 146 *91.3*
F n/a

Surinam
Paramaribo
A 163,265 *63,037*
B 430,000
C 5.3 *8.4*
D 2 *1.2*
E n/a
F n/a

Swaziland
Mbabane
A 17,366 *6,705*
B 500,000
C 126.1 *214.3*
D 4.4 *2.7*
E 1,058.8 *661.7*
F n/a

Sweden
Stockholm
A 449,750 *173,649*
B 8,190,000
C 256.7 *415.6*
D 14.1 *8.8*
E 1,887.2 *1,179.5*
F 654.9 *409.3*

Switzerland[9]
Bern
A 41,288 *15,941*
B 6,410,000
C 708.9 *1,147.4*
D 2.3 *1.4*
E 881.7 *551.1*
F 1,267.4 *792.1*

Syria[2]
Damascus
A 185,180 *71,498*
B 7,460,000
C 100.2 *162.1*
D 2.5 *1.6*
E 21 *13.2*
F 13.5 *8.5*

T

Taiwan
T'aipei
A 35,961 *13,885*
B 16,305,000
C 280.2 *453.5*
D 0.6 *0.4*
E 165.6 *103.5*
F 515.9 *322.4*

Tanzania[4, 10]
Dar es Salaam
A 945,087 *364,900*
B 15,330,000
C 33.4 *53.8*
D 1.5 *0.9*
E 120.9 *75.6*
F 40.2 *25.1*

Thailand
Bangkok
A 514,000 *198,500*
B 42,860,000
C 73.2 *118.5*
D 0.9 *0.5*
E 58.4 *36.5*
F 131.3 *82.1*

Togo
Lomé
A 56,000 *21,600*
B 2,240,000
C 78.9 *127.3*
D 2 *1.2*
E 2,396.4 *1,497.8*
F 34.6 *18.7*

Tunisia
Tunis
A 164,150 *63,379*
B 5,905,000
C 127.3 *206*
D 3.5 *2.2*
E 216.2 *135.1*
F 108.5 *67.8*

Turkey
Ankara
A 780,576 *301,382*
B 39,675,000
C 66.3 *107.3*
D 1.3 *0.8*
E 171.5 *107.2*
F 119.2 *74.5*

Uganda[4]
Kampala
A 235,886 *91,076*
B 11,705,000
C 33.4 *53.8*
D 1.5 *0.9*
E 120.9 *75.6*
F 40.2 *25.1*

United Kingdom
London
A 244,013 *94,214*
B 57,605,000
C 752.8 *1,218.6*
D 3.2 *2*
E 384.5[11] *204.3*[11]
F 692.8[11] *433*[11]

Upper Volta[3]
Ouagadougou
A 274,200 *105,800*
B 6,115,000
C 19.7 *31.7*
D 0.9 *0.6*
E 34.3 *21.5*
F 73.3 *45.8*

Uruguay
Montevideo
A 177,508 *68,536*
B 2,780,000
C 169.5 *272.3*
D 10.8 *6.7*
E 86 *53.7*
F 127 *79.4*

USA[12]
Washington, DC
A 9,519,617 *3,675,545*
B 214,580,000
C 335.2 *542.5*
D 14.9 *9.3*
E 5,135 *3,209.4*
F 73.2 *45.8*

USSR
Moscow
A 22,274,900 *8,600,350*
B 255,520,000
C 62.1 *100.5*
D 5.4 *3.4*
E 12,914.8 *8,071.8*
F 1,223.1 *764.4*

V

Venezuela
Caracas
A 912,050 *352,144*
B 12,185,000
C 1.9 *3.1*
D 0.14 *0.09*
E 1.2 *0.8*
F 3.4 *2.2*

Vietnam[1, 13]
Ha-noi
A 332,559 *128,402*
B 46,430,000
C 66.2 *107.1*
D 4,738.3 *2,961.4*
E 0.04 *0.03*
F 3.7 *2.3*

Y

Yugoslavia
Belgrade
A 255,804 *98,766*
B 21,465,000
C 406.5 *658*
D 4.8 *3*
E 978.9 *611.8*
F 460.1 *287.6*

Z

Zaire
Kinshasa
A 2,345,409 *905,567*
B 25,205,000
C 22.4 *36.2*
D 2.1 *1.3*
E 119.7 *74.8*
F 17.7 *11.1*

Zambia[10]
Lusaka
A 752,614 *290,586*
B 4,960,000
C 13.8 *22.3*
D 2.1 *1.3*
E 183.3 *114.6*
F n/a

Notes
1 Estimated figures
2 Figures do not reflect changes in 1967
3 Upper Volta and Ivory Coast railway data combined
4 Kenya, Tanzania and Uganda railway data combined (East African Railways)
5 Demilitarized zone, 1,252 km² (487 miles²), not included
6 Standard gauge only
7 Figures are pre-independence
8 South Africa and South West Africa railway data combined
9 State system only
10 Tazara line excluded
11 Excluding Northern Ireland
12 Class I railways only
13 South Vietnam only

Railway Systems

Europe: Scandinavia

Railways were a European invention and, with the exception of Albania, a comprehensive system has been developed in every country. The extent of the commitment to railways has been shown twice this century, by the rapid and thorough repair of the damage inflicted in the course of the two world wars. From an early date, most governments took control of the railways, and attempts were made to unify gauges and to create a truly continental network that transcended national boundaries. Today, gauge-changing facilities are necessary only at the borders of Finland, USSR and Spain. This unification made possible the introduction, at the end of the last century, of international trains, the Orient Express being the most famous. Although the luxuriousness of such trains is now but a memory, their decline has been compensated for by dramatic increases in speed.

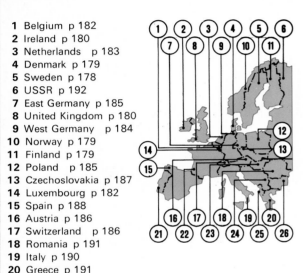

On pages 178–208, DATA PANELS appear for all countries owning a railway system. Those omitted have either closed all their railways, or have yet to open one, or have their lines worked by someone else. The data panels summarize the principal railway assets of each country. In some cases, such information is unobtainable, or the most recent available statistics may not reflect the contemporary situation.

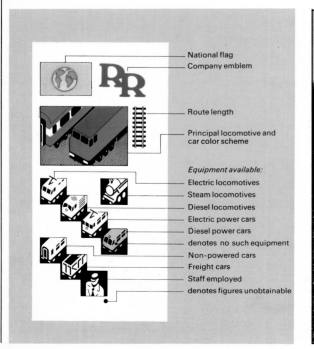

National flag
Company emblem
Route length
Principal locomotive and car color scheme

Equipment available:
Electric locomotives
Steam locomotives
Diesel locomotives
Electric power cars
Diesel power cars
— denotes no such equipment
Non-powered cars
Freight cars
Staff employed
— denotes figures unobtainable

SWEDEN *Statens Jarnvagar (SJ)*

The Swedish railway system began in 1849 with a narrow gauge line 8 km (5 miles) long between Fryksta and Klarälven, using horse-drawn trains; but the main line network and the state-owned system dates from 1856. Today the Swedish State Railways (*Statens Jarnvagar*) operates more than 90 percent of the total traffic and has a route length of approximately 11,200 km (7,000 miles). More than half of this is electrified. There are several railways in Sweden that are still privately owned, notably the Grängesberg-Oxelösund, which has a main line 296 km (185 miles) long. This is an east-west route threading its way from the coast at Oxelösund through the picturesque lake country to the west of Stockholm. It is entirely electrified, though its experiments with a non-condensing steam turbine locomotive in 1932 led to the building of similar, but much larger, locomotives in Great Britain and the USA. From Stockholm, headquarters of the state system, main lines run westward to Charlottenberg, on the Norwegian frontier, and southward to Gothenburg and Malmö, and it is over these two latter routes that fast express trains are operated. Northward from Stockholm the main line runs through Uppsala, to the junction of Ånge, where there is a large mechanized classification yard for dealing with traffic coming eastward from Trondheim in Norway. The main line continues to Boden, where it intersects the important northwest-to-southeast ore-carrying line of the Riksgransen Railway that comes across the Arctic Circle, from Narvik, via the Norwegian State Railways, to the port of Luleå on the Gulf of Bothnia. Except where the Swedish railways approach the mountainous Norwegian frontier, more than a third of the lines are carried over generally level track. Another 20 percent is on grades no steeper than 0.5 percent. The rail gauge is the standard European, carried on ties of impregnated wood. This gauge permits the operation of several important international train services. There is a train ferry between Helsingborg and Helsingør in Denmark, and a through sleeping car express runs between Stockholm and Hamburg, by way of Copenhagen.

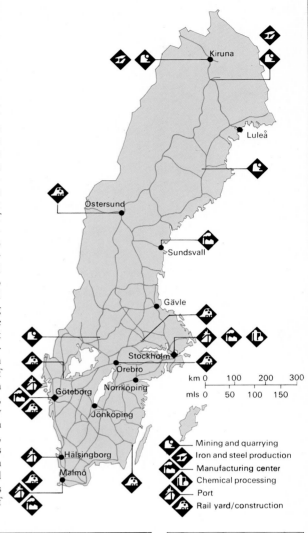

Mining and quarrying
Iron and steel production
Manufacturing center
Chemical processing
Port
Rail yard/construction

Sweden

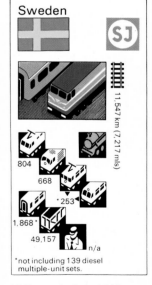

11,547 km (7,217 mls)
804
668
253
1,868*
49,157
n/a

*not including 139 diesel multiple-unit sets.

All figures include 182 km state-owned 891 mm gauge line, and 300 km of a privately owned passenger-carrying line. Privately owned freight-only lines are omitted from all totals.

Above left A Swedish electric locomotive. *Above right* The East Södermanland narrow gauge railway. *Left* Near Ragunda in winter at −30°C.

NORWAY *Norges Statsbaner (NSB)*

The Norwegian railways, of which the first section was opened in 1854, have the particular fascination of being operated for the most part in exceedingly rugged country, subject to great extremes of climate. In striking contrast to Sweden, less than 6 percent of the total length of about 4,480 km (2,800 miles) is on grades of less than 1 percent. More than three quarters of the total is on truly mountain grades of 2.5 percent to 1.5 percent. Until the Second World War the very severe Dombas line, forming the main route from Oslo to Trondheim, was worked by some of the most powerful steam locomotives in Europe. The principal main lines are electrified, but the line from Trondheim northward across the Arctic Circle to Boden is diesel-powered. This line was opened as recently as 1962. In the far north, the line from Narvik to the Swedish frontier is completely isolated from the rest of the Norwegian State Railways system, but forms part of the important iron ore route into northern Sweden. The fastest trains in Norway are those following the southern coastline from Oslo, south to Kristiansand and then northwest to Stavanger. This runs on easier grades than the great mountain routes from Oslo to Bergen and Oslo to Trondheim, and the Stavanger Express covers the 592 km (370 miles) from Oslo in 8 hr, including ten stops. The special Sorlands Express, which serves Kristiansand only, makes the run of 352 km (220 miles) in 4½ hr, nonstop from Oslo, an average speed of almost 80 km/h (50 mph). The Norwegian railways must be one of the very few, anywhere in the world, to be completely equipped throughout with a system of color light signaling.

Norway

4,241 km (2,651 mls)

158
170
94 50
911
8,929 18,052

*not including 29 electric multiple-unit sets.

The 39 km of line to the northern town of Narvik is separated from the rest of the network and worked as a part of the Swedish system.

Below Electric train at Flamsdalen, Norway.

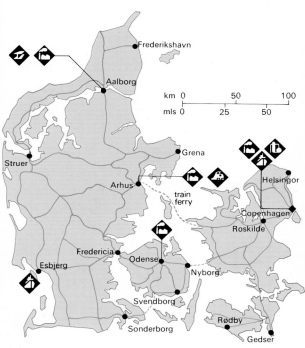

DENMARK *Danske Statsbaner (DSB)*

The geographical structure of Denmark, with some of its most important and populous areas on islands, naturally presented special problems when it came to building up an efficient railway network. The first section was that from Copenhagen to Roskilde, opened in 1847. It involved the construction of larger bridges to provide transit between the islands. In certain cases the distances were too great for bridges, and train and car ferry services evolved. No fewer than four of the train ferries involve international cooperation: Rødby-Fehmarn, with the Federal Railway of West Germany; Gedser-Warnemünde, with the State Railway of East Germany; and Copenhagen-Malmö and Helsingør-Helsingborg, with the Swedish railways. It is only in the Copenhagen suburban area that electric power is used in Denmark. The principal main line services are worked either by diesel-electric locomotives or diesel-railcars. The internal fast trains are the Intercity (IC) regular interval services and the "Lyntog," or lightning diesel trains, which are high-speed diesel railcar sets, having limited accommodation. There are a few steam locomotives still in service.

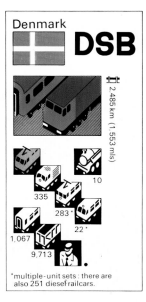

Denmark DSB

2,485 km (1,553 mls)

10
335
283*
22*
1,067
9,713

*multiple-unit sets: there are also 251 diesel railcars.

FINLAND *Valtionrautatiet (VR)*

From their inception in 1862, the Finnish State Railways, because of the long eastern frontier, have been oriented toward those of Russia rather than those of the rest of Europe. The rail gauge is 1,524 mm (5 ft), although at Tornio, in the far north, there are interchange facilities with the standard gauge Swedish system. Each day from Helsinki there is a through express with sleeping cars, one for Leningrad and one for Moscow, the departure times being arranged to provide arrivals in the Russian cities at around 9:00 a.m. Finland is subject to extremes of climate, and the railways are efficiently operated in the depths of the sub-Arctic winters. Although there is a general transition to diesel traction, the Finnish railway still operates a number of modern steam locomotives, and upward of 150 more steam locomotives are held in reserve. There are ferry services across the Baltic between Helsinki and Lübeck and between Naantali and Stockholm.

All the figures include 486 km of privately owned passenger-carrying lines. The state system has no steam engines.

Finnish lines are built to Russia's gauge of 1,524 mm, necessitating transfer facilities at Tornio where the Swedish system is met.

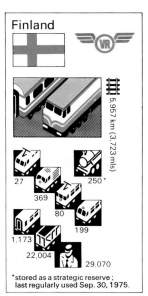

Finland

5,957 km (3,723 mls)

27 250*
369
80
199
1,173
22,004 29.070

*stored as a strategic reserve; last regularly used Sep. 30, 1975.

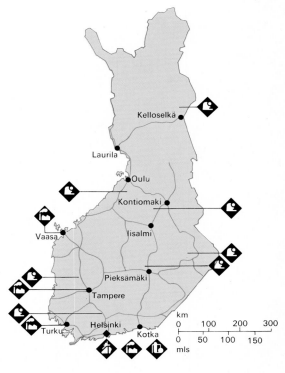

United Kingdom and Ireland

IRELAND *Coras Iompair Eireann (CIE)*

The railways in this now politically divided land originated in the same way as those of Great Britain and were subject to the surveillance of the Board of Trade at Westminster. In a rural and unprosperous country there was, however, not the same opportunity for intense railway development. Trunk routes were constructed from Dublin to Cork, to Galway, to Wicklow and Wexford, and to Belfast; and this latter, the Great Northern, had the distinction of becoming an international main line, operating on both Eire and Northern Ireland after the partition in 1922. The cross-country connections were also important, serving Waterford and Limerick, while in the north the Belfast and Northern Counties (to Londonderry) was a busy and prosperous concern, later taken over by the English Midland Railway.

Because of the need to provide transportation in rural areas where a full-scale main line railway would not pay, in a series of "Light Railway Acts" Parliament authorized the construction of many narrow gauge lines. These lines later became of much interest to the seekers after the unusual in railway practice, from the picturesque steam locomotives used to the happy, leisurely ways of doing business. In 1925 the railways of Eire were merged. The Great Northern, because of its international character, remained untouched; but all other lines were merged into a new Great Southern system, still under private ownership. In 1945 it was nationalized as Coras Iompair Eireann, and in 1958 also took over that portion of the former Great Northern Railway situated in Eire.

Ireland

₂,189 km (1,368 mls)

221
382   39
6,700

The data panel figures refer only to Republic of Ireland. N. Ireland, although a province of the United Kingdom, has a system independent of British Rail and built to the Irish broad gauge of 1,600 mm. A freight service from Londonderry to the Republic is worked by CIE locomotives. Car totals for Northern Ireland Railways – the system's title – are not in the data panels either for Ireland or for the UK. The latest available figures for NIR are: 6 diesel locomotives, 87 diesel-powered cars, 67 other coach units, 31 freight cars and 1,229 staff to work 357 route-km.

Mining and quarrying
Iron and steel production
Manufacturing center
Oil refining
Chemical processing
Port
Rail yard/construction
Tourist center

km 0   50   100   150   200
mls 0   50   100

A modern Irish express in familiar countryside.

BR Class 40 hauling Glasgow-Leeds express near Bingley.

UNITED KINGDOM *British Rail*

The intricate railway network of Great Britain developed in a series of privately originated, and quite unconnected, local projects. Although there were men of vision like George Stephenson, who looked forward to a time when the whole country would be provided with railways, there was no overall planning, and no attempt at coordination by the governments of the day. Parliament exercised control only to the extent that the fixed equipment and rolling stock had to satisfy the examination of inspecting officers appointed by the Board of Trade. From the success of the pioneer enterprises like the Stockton and Darlington, the Liverpool and Manchester, and the Newcastle and Carlisle, the earliest trunk lines were projected, including the London and Birmingham, the North Midland (Derby to Leeds) and the Great Western (London to Bristol), and from these the nationwide system developed. Success led to an immense proliferation of new schemes, some quite spurious and with no solid financial backing. There were many proposals for amalgamation, but while Parliament looked favorably upon mergers – lengthwise as it were, as that of the London and Birmingham with northern companies that brought the line from London to Lancaster and Carlisle under a single management – any merging of competitive routes was vetoed, because it was felt that the existence of competitive facilities would be in the interest of the traveling public.

By the 1880s there were three independent routes from London to Scotland, each providing a lavish train service to Edinburgh from London, and two out of the three serving Glasgow. There were three competitive routes from London to Manchester, and five different ways of traveling from England and Wales to Ireland. There was competition between London and Plymouth, London and Portsmouth, and London and the Kentish resorts and packet stations. But the network as it grew up could be criticized for the way in which attention became focused upon London. While cross-country routes existed, the train services operated were for the most part slow and unattractive. The exception was between Liverpool and Manchester, where two rivals to the original line of 1830 were built, and a swarm of fast express trains ran throughout the day on all three routes. With no competition except from canals, freight traffic became heavy, and it was handled in relatively small four-wheeled wagons at slow speed. Small consignments could be sent from one end of the country to the other. Remote country stations all had their freight sidings, at which goods of all descriptions could be brought for dispatch, or collected, by private conveyances.

The early years of the twentieth century in Great Britain saw the heights of railway preeminence as carriers of all kinds; but already there were signs of dissatisfaction, particularly with the freight service. Nevertheless, despite the steeply rising cost of coal – almost the only form of locomotive fuel – and rising costs of other services, the private railways were prosperous throughout Britain. At the outbreak of the First World War in 1914 there were 16 systems, with tracks extending from the Channel ports to Wick and Thurso, from East Anglia to Penzance, together with a number of active and prosperous companies with local services such as the great coal carriers in the valleys of South Wales, the Furness, and the Hull and Barnsley. During the war all the British railways were brought under government control, and in 1921 legislation was imposed upon them by Parliament, forming the whole network into four group companies. The ownership was still entirely private, but the company amalgamations, and the composition of each group, was laid down by Act of Parliament. The era of the "Big Four" – Great Western, Southern, London Midland and Scottish, London and North Eastern – began on January 1, 1923.

The "grouped" companies carried on through a period of extreme financial difficulty and increasingly severe competition from highway haulers. Legislation governing the fixing of rates and fares remained unchanged from the days of unchallenged railway monopoly in transport and handicapped the "grouped" railways in their fight for traffic. Fortunately the managements saw to it that maintenance of track and rolling stock was kept at the highest level, and the railways, once again under government control, were able to render a great national service in the Second World War. Less than three years after its conclusion, as from January 1, 1948, the British railways were nationalized. Since that time a considerable reduction in total track mileage has been made, by elimination of one-time competitive routes and closing of unprofitable branch lines. The last British Rail steam train ran in 1967 and the first High Speed Train was introduced in 1976.

Above British Rail train hauled by Peak class diesel on the wall at Dawlish.

Below The British Rail diesel electric High Speed Train (HST), holder of the world record.

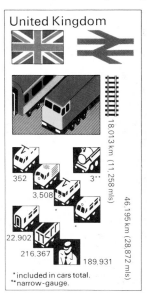

United Kingdom

18.013 km (11,258 mls)

46,195 km (28,872 mls)

352   3**

3,508

22,902

216,367   189,931

*included in cars total.
**narrow-gauge.

UK totals refer only to British Rail and exclude several major networks, eg National Coal Board lines and the London Underground (subway).

Belgium and Luxembourg

BELGIUM *Société Nationale des Chemins de Fer Belges (SNCB)*

Belgium was the first country in the world to have a railway system that from the outset was almost entirely state owned. The principle of state ownership was accepted by an Act of Parliament passed as long ago as 1834, and the railway system in the country was planned as a coordinated network. It grew to be one of the busiest and most intense to be found anywhere, reckoned on the basis of route distance per square kilometer of territory served. Belgium has a high proportion of intensely industrialized areas, comparable to the English Black Country, and frequent service of fast passenger trains coupled with ample freight facilities became necessary at an early stage of development.

But while the demands of Belgium itself have always been heavy, the geographical situation of the country makes it an important connecting link in many international train services. Historically Belgium has been called the "cockpit" of Europe; from the railway point of view it does form a general crossroads. While the original network was planned to have all the main lines radiating from Brussels, not all the international trains of today pass through the capital. The crack trains from Paris to the Rhineland take a route to the south, passing through Charleroi, Namur and Liège to enter West Germany at Aachen, and there is a busy electrified main line diverging eastward from the principal north to south line at

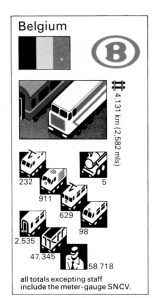

Belgium

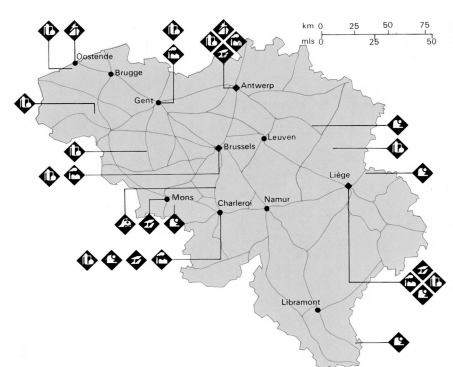

Belgium retains 221 km of secondary railways, a feature which has largely disappeared in Europe. A reason for its survival is that most are electrified.

Mechelen, and passing through Louvain and Landen to reach Liège.

It was not until comparatively recent times that through international trains like those from the Dutch cities to Paris, or those from Ostend to West Germany, or the Luxembourg line, could pass through Brussels without reversal of direction at some point. Today there is an underground main line through the heart of the city connecting the Nord and Midi stations, and a prestige train like the Étoile du Nord Pullman from Amsterdam to Paris passes beneath the city center. It is the same with the sleeping car express that leaves Ostend about 9:00 p.m., and carries through sections for Swiss resorts and for Milan.

Because of its geographical position at a railway crossroads in western Europe, and the intensity of the internal traffic of the country, which developed well before the end of the nineteenth century, the technical equipment of the Belgian railways rapidly became some of the most sophisticated outside Great Britain. Comprehensive signaling was installed at large centers such as Antwerp, Gent and Liège, in addition to those around Brussels, and these units incorporate full interlocking. Steam power has now been entirely eliminated, and roughly one third of the total route covered is electrified. The system used differs from those of all the neighboring countries, as they do from each other; but modern methods of interchange at the international frontiers are swift and efficient, and in some cases performed without the train stopping, thus speeding up services considerably.

Above New Belgian EMU.
Right Brussels Midi Station.

LUXEMBOURG *Société Nationale des Chemins de Fer Luxembourgeois (CFL)*

One of the most important international routes is that running southeast from Brussels, and making its way through very mountainous country to enter Luxembourg at Arlon. Until 1946 there were several privately owned railways in the Grand Duchy, but in April of that year all the railways were taken over by a new company – the Luxembourg National Railways. The stock was split between the Luxembourg government, 51 percent, and the Belgian and French governments, 24.5 percent each. The system consists of a north to south line and an east-west system intersecting the former at Luxembourg city. Much of the latter is electrified, but most of the international north to south route is worked by diesel locomotives. The total route length in the Grand Duchy is only about 264 km (165 miles), half of which is electrified. Luxembourg city is itself a most important railway center, at the meeting point of five international routes. The southwest is part of the Luxembourg-Lorraine iron mining region and is well served by the Grand Duchy's railways, which are concentrated in the south.

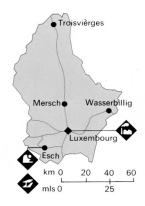

Luxembourg

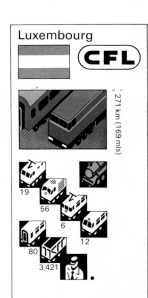

Luxembourg's position is important astride European routes; the French and Belgian governments each appoint five members to the Board, and each contributes 24.5% of the company's capital.

Netherlands

NETHERLANDS *N.V. Nederlandse Spoorwegen (NS)*

In the Netherlands railways were built, and are maintained today, in physical conditions that are not paralleled anywhere in the world. Except on the eastern frontiers the countryside is flat, and intersected by an elaborate system of inland waterways: but the ground is soft and spongy, and anything but ideal for sustaining the weight and pounding effect of heavy, fast, railway traffic. The existence of a frequent and efficient service is a tribute to the excellence of the civil engineers' maintenance of the track and of the formation beneath it. Until January 1938 there were a number of independent railways in Holland, one owned by the state and the rest private; but in that year full merging took place, and the consolidated organization took the title of Netherlands Railways.

Although the tasks of the original companies lay, to quite a large extent, in providing international services, the growth of industry and commerce in Holland has led to the development of a different pattern of activity today. In the nineteenth century the close connection between the royal houses of Great Britain and Imperial Germany invested the mail service between England and Germany with great importance, while the prevailing fashion for wealthy English families to patronize the spas of south Germany sustained another prestige service, as with the Anglo-German mails through Holland. The steam locomotives on most of the Dutch railways were almost without exception built in Great Britain.

The growth of railways in Holland in the nineteenth century was in many ways similar to that in Britain. Companies were promoted and lines built in direct competition with one another, and there was during this early period no attempt by the state to coerce, or squeeze, the private companies out of the picture. One could, for example, travel from Rotterdam to Amsterdam either by the Holland Railway, via Delft and The Hague, or by the Dutch Rhenish Railway via Utrecht. There were rivals, each with their own packet stations for the cross-channel business from England. The State Railway ran to Flushing, whence there were sailings at first to Queenborough in the Isle of Sheppey and later to Folkestone, and against this the Dutch Rhenish Railway worked in connection with the steamers from the Hook of Holland to Harwich. Both these rivals were deeply concerned in the Anglo-German traffic; yet small as Holland is, the State Railway did not carry this traffic right across the country to the German frontier. At Boxtel they interchanged to yet another private railway, the North Brabant German, which although entirely Dutch-owned, ran for a considerable distance into Germany to reach Wesel. The Dutch Rhenish, as its name suggests, went as far as the Rhine, to Arnhem. Another interesting private line was the Netherlands Central, which ran from Utrecht northeastward through Amersfoort to Zwolle. The central station at Utrecht at times had the colorful glamor of some great English junctions, because there could be seen the bright green locomotives of the State Railway, the Indian reds of the Rhenish, the dark green of the Holland Railway, and the bright yellow of the Netherlands Central. It is interesting that the first major amalgamation of railways in Holland did not concern the state system but was between two of the private concerns, the Holland Railway and the Dutch Rhenish. Travelers with experience of railways in many parts of the world were quick to notice one significant difference between the largely private railways of Holland and the nationally owned railways of Belgium: in the nineteenth century the Dutch were much more efficient.

High density, high speed

Today the network of passenger train service in Holland is provided by a system of fast, closely integrated electric multiple-unit trains, so timed that if a through train is not provided between the towns or cities that a passenger wishes to visit, there are connections at intermediate points where the change of trains involves a wait of no more than a few minutes. Obviously in the operation of such a pattern of service a high standard of punctuality is essential, and this is ensured by a comprehensive system of train dispatching, coupled with the automatic operation of the major junctions. The equipment is programed to operate in accordance with the planned schedule, and it is

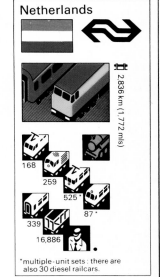

The route total includes 11 km of line scheduled for 1977 (Den Haag-Zoetermeer). A 55 km line is being built for 1982 completion: Amsterdam-Leiden via Schipol Airport.

Netherlands

2,836 km (1,772 mls)

168
259
525
87*
339
16,886

*multiple-unit sets: there are also 30 diesel railcars.

Oil refining
Mining and quarrying
Iron and steel production
Manufacturing center
Chemical processing
Port
Rail yard/construction

Above Rotterdam station. *Right* Amsterdam station.

only in the event of irregularities or late running that the men in the control centers have to intervene.

Not all the Dutch railway network is electrified. Routes on which the traffic density is less are worked by diesel multiple-unit set trains. There are a number of international express trains that originate in Holland, such as the Rheingold, with sections from both Amsterdam and the Hook of Holland running south through the Rhineland to Switzerland, and other trains for north and northwest Germany. These are hauled by electric locomotives, of the same type that are used for the freight trains. Amid all this modern operation, however, the enthusiast should break his journey at Utrecht to visit the magnificent Transport Museum, where the origins and development of railways in the Netherlands can be studied from pictures, maps, models and full-size preserved examples of locomotives and rolling stock.

West Germany

WEST GERMANY *Deutsche Bundesbahn (DB)*

The railways of Germany, like those of Great Britain, began as a large number of independent, unconnected private enterprises. They developed at a time when Germany itself did not yet exist as a single coordinated state. The first was in Bavaria in 1835, from Nürnberg to Fürth. Gradually, however, the various lines were taken over by the states in which they ran, and many of them came under the control of Prussia. Their origins could be discerned from the names of the "Administrations" they carried, such as "Magdeburg," "Right Rhine," "Breslau" and "Hannover." After the war with France in 1870–1, Bismarck tried to amalgamate all the railways of Germany under one imperial control. He failed because the southern states, like Saxony, Bavaria and Baden-Württemberg, stood out strongly against such a merger. The annexation of most of the French provinces of Alsace and Lorraine after the war included the French railway of that name. It was thoroughly Germanized, being renamed Imperial Elsass-Lothringen, controlled directly by Prussia. Its operation changed from the French practice of running on the left-hand track to the German right-hand running. At the new frontier point between Nancy and Strasborg, special junctions were laid in to facilitate the transfer. When the provinces were restored to France after the First World War, the junction layout was not altered (it remains unchanged today) and they retained their own state-controlled railways until after the end of the First World War. Nevertheless the railways of Germany tended to be focused upon the imperial capital, Berlin, as those of Great

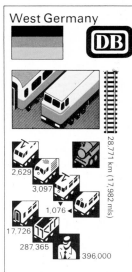
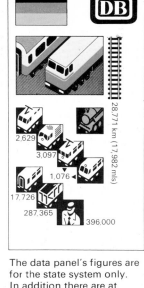

West Germany

The data panel's figures are for the state system only. In addition there are at least 180 private railways with another 4,600 km.

Below TEE train running alongside the Rhine.

Mining and quarrying
Iron and steel production
Manufacturing center
Oil refining
Chemical processing
Grain processing
Port
Rail yard/construction

Britain were upon London. The great complexity and proliferation of routes in the Ruhr and the Rhineland corresponded in some respect to the situation in Britain at that time, especially in Lancashire, Yorkshire and the North Midlands.

One administration

In 1920 the state railways were brought into a single administration, the *Deutsche Reichsbahn*, and under this organization great improvements were made in technology and in the services offered, both nationally and internationally. Until that time German railways in general had not been renowned either for convenience of scheduling or for the speed of passenger trains; but under the *Reichsbahn* organization they gradually stepped into the very front rank of speed, particularly with the diesel railcar trains of the 1930s. Much of the system suffered severe damage during the Second World War and, before any appreciable steps had been taken towards reconstruction, the partition of the former Reich into two separate and ideologically contrasting states of West and East Germany, in 1945, immediately changed the significance of the railways. The *Deutsche Bundesbahn*, operating in West Germany, was faced with providing service in a state that was very largely cut off from the former imperial capital, and the traffic pattern became very largely one of "north and south," with main routes toward Berlin confined to those from Hamburg, Hannover, Bebra, and Nürnberg.

A great deal of rethinking was necessary to adapt the railway organization to this new pattern. In addition to the main route up the valley of the Rhine, a popular tourist route, the line running roughly parallel to the frontier with East Germany, from Nürnberg northward through Würzburg, Bebra. Göttingen to Hannover and Hamburg, became of great importance. There developed also a much closer liaison with the railways in the countries of the West, with freely-used interchange points with the Dutch, Belgian and French railways, and operation of an increasing number of international express train services. In imperial days Germany had sought to reduce to a minimum railway connections with France and Belgium. Her purpose had been to secure a preponderance of traffic from England to east and south European business and holiday centers. But now, all that is changed. Frankfurt is the headquarters of the *Deutsche Bundesbahn*, and the very picturesque valley of the Rhine, with its lofty heights, vineyards, and many medieval castles, provides an intensely used artery for railway traffic. There are double-tracked main lines on both banks and frequent connections by bridges from one bank to the other. It is a fascinating run by train, but the volume of both passenger and freight traffic can perhaps be appreciated most by taking a trip on one of the many pleasure steamers cruising on the river. From such an unusual railway-spotting vantage point, the enthusiast receives a dramatic impression of the *Deutsche Bundesbahn* in action.

Krupp stock running up Rhine valley.

East Germany and Poland

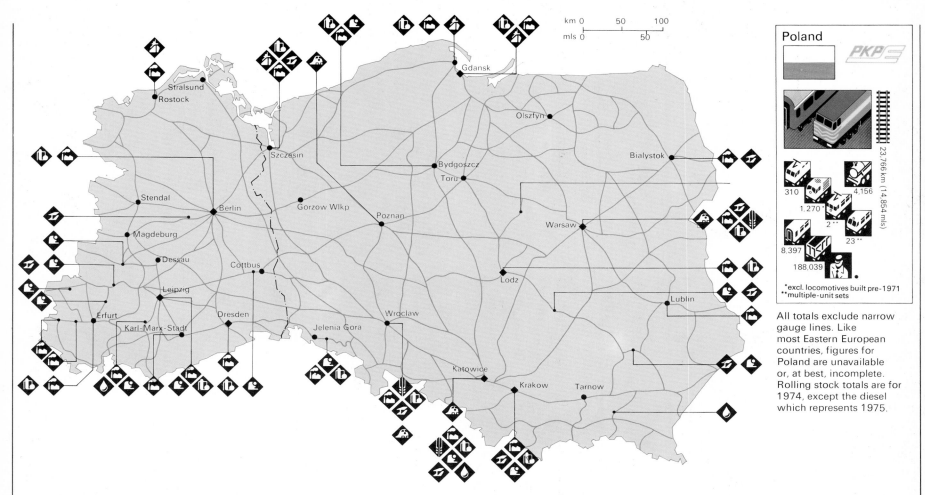

Poland
PKP
23,766 km (14,854 mls)
310   4,156
1,270
2**   23**
8,397
188,039
*excl. locomotives built pre-1971
**multiple-unit sets

All totals exclude narrow gauge lines. Like most Eastern European countries, figures for Poland are unavailable or, at best, incomplete. Rolling stock totals are for 1974, except the diesel which represents 1975.

EAST GERMANY *Deutsche Reichsbahn (DR)*

The state railway of East Germany retains much of the radial layout of earlier days, with Berlin as the focal point. It has, however, only about half the route length as the system of West Germany. Its services are coordinated more with those of Poland and Czechoslovakia than with the West. Apart from the connections mentioned in the section dealing with West Germany, the radiating main lines from Berlin are those going east to Warsaw and beyond to the frontier with the USSR, southeast to Prague, and south to the West German frontier and onward to Munich. Additionally, there are two routes going north from Berlin, which diverge at Neustrelitz. They lead to the train ferry ports of Warnemünde and Sassnitz, respectively, and over them through train services are operated to Copenhagen and to Stockholm. While the modernization of motive power has progressed rapidly in West Germany, and there are no longer any steam locomotives remaining in regular service, less than 1,600 km (1,000 miles) of the East German system are electrified as yet, and many steam locomotives remain. The international set-up in Berlin has to some extent simplified the railway terminal arrangements, which at one time included many stations belonging to the formerly independent companies. Today only a single route, known as the *Stadtbahn*, passes from West into East Berlin. Arriving in the International zone from the west, the stations reached are first Charlottenburg and then Zoo; after passing into East Berlin there is first Friedrichstrasse and then Ost, prior to reaching the complicated set of junctions by which *Reichsbahn* trains can proceed to the Baltic ferry ports, Warsaw, Leipzig and Dresden.

An ex-*Deutsche Reichsbahn* 2-10-0 Kriegslok waits to leave Opole, Poland, for Nysa.

POLAND *Polskie Koleje Panstwowe (PKP)*

The Polish State Railways has one of the most complicated histories imaginable. Firstly, when railways were first constructed in eastern Europe, Poland, as an independent country, did not exist at all. The territory was divided up between Germany and Russia, and remained so until 1919. The first railways – which were initiated as long ago as 1835, though not actually brought into service until several years later – were sponsored by those countries to suit their own needs. As a result those in what could be termed the German and Austrian sectors were built on the European standard gauge, and those in the Russian sector on the 1,524 mm (5 ft) gauge. The Austrians built a line to connect Warsaw with Vienna, while the Russians constructed a line north from Warsaw to join up with the Grand Russian Railway. This provided a through route to St Petersburg (Leningrad). By 1862 Warsaw was connected by rail to St Petersburg, to Vienna, and with the Prussian railway system, and therefore with systems throughout western Europe.

During the First World War the Russian part of Poland was overrun by German and Austrian forces, and after the war the lines in these territories were converted to the standard gauge. The establishment of the new independent state of Poland – including the highly strategic "Polish Corridor" to the Baltic at Danzig, cutting East Prussia from the rest of Germany – brought railway, as well as political, problems. This was particularly true in the operation of through trains from the west to Königsberg (Chojna). In the meantime the Polish State Railways were extensively modernized, only to suffer appalling destruction during the Second World War. One of the most important improvements had been to equip all the freight rolling stock with continuous automatic air brakes, and to install much color light signaling. Both advances were contained in contracts placed in Great Britain – all unhappily to have little lasting effect. A total of 46 percent of all tunnels and bridges, 600 steam locomotives, and 60,000 cars were destroyed. Today, although there are still some 4,000 steam locomotives at work in Poland, rapid progress is being made toward electrification, and by reason of its geographical position the Polish State Railways has a great significance for transit traffic traveling westward from other countries of eastern Europe, and equally for traffic from western Europe.

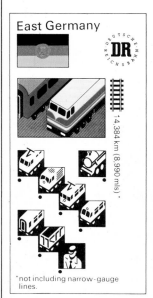

East Germany
DR
DEUTSCHE REICHSBAHN
14,384 km (8,990 mls)*
*not including narrow-gauge lines.

Route length is about half West Germany's, omitting 352 km of narrow-gauge lines. 10% of routes are electrified and steam will survive into the 1980s.

Switzerland and Austria

SWITZERLAND *Schweizerische Bundesbahnen (SBB)*

The railways of Switzerland, most of which are nationalized, can be divided into two distinct geographical groups. There is the close, intensely used network in the broad valleys linking up Zürich, Basel, Luzern, Lausanne, and Bern with a series of fast intercity electric trains; and then there are the great mountain routes. The mountain routes are famed for some of the most spectacular railway engineering in the world, with many examples of spiral track locations, viaducts of breathtaking height, and some of the longest tunnels ever driven beneath mountain ranges. But in the mountain routes, too, there are distinct subdivisions. There are those like the Gotthard, the Lötschberg and the Simplon, that are teeming arteries of heavy north-south international traffic, and others built on the meter gauge to provide access to some of the more remote resorts. It was soon after the establishment of the Swiss Confederation in 1848 that the government invited Robert Stephenson to submit proposals for a national railway system. At that time only one railway had been built, connecting Zürich with Basel. Stephenson proposed a main line from Zürich through fairly level country to Lausanne and Geneva, and this is the extremely busy line that forms the internal backbone of Switzerland's railway operation today.

Crossing the Alps

It was when railway connections with the neighboring states were started that the Alpine ranges had to be crossed. The Gotthard route was the first, heading south from the twin central "springboards" of Zürich and Luzern, beneath the historic mountain pass into the Italian-speaking canton of the Ticino, and from there through Como to Milan. To obtain an acceptable grade for steam locomotives – even though this had to be 2.7 percent the technique of spiral tunneling in the mountain sides was adopted for the first time ever. The great Gotthard Tunnel was opened in 1882. The approach to the Simplon Tunnel, opened in 1906, does not involve such dramatic engineering because the former Jura-Simplon Railway followed the valley of the Rhône from the head of Lake Geneva, near Montreux. The Gotthard and the Jura-Simplon lines are now part of the Swiss Federal Railways. But at Brig, at the eastern entrance to the Simplon Tunnel, the line into Italy is joined by the greatest of the private railways of Switzerland, the Bern-Lötschberg-Simplon. This mammoth enterprise has tunneled under the mighty ranges of the Bernese Oberland and provided some truly spectacular sights for the traveler on the ascent to the Lötschberg Tunnel from Spiez on the lake of Thun, and perhaps even more awe-inspiring views on the descent into the Rhône valley.

Finally, there is the magnificently engineered meter gauge Rhaetian Railway, leading from Chur to the famous Alpine resorts of Pontresina and St Moritz in the Upper Engadine. The Albula Line, as it is otherwise known, is also spectacular in the sharpness of its curves and for the speed and smoothness with which they are negotiated, often on the edge of towering precipices.

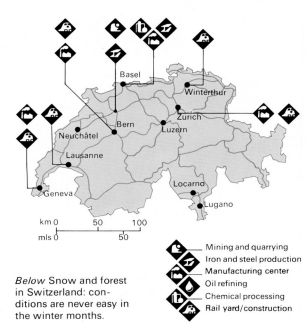

km 0   50   100
mls 0   50

Mining and quarrying
Iron and steel production
Manufacturing center
Oil refining
Chemical processing
Rail yard/construction

Below Snow and forest in Switzerland: conditions are never easy in the winter months.

The figures for Austria, *below,* exclude privately owned lines even though 646 route-km carry passengers. The state system's remaining steam locos are all narrow-gauge (ÖBB has 454 route-km of narrow gauge lines).

AUSTRIA *Österreichische Bundesbahnen (ÖBB)*

The city of Vienna, once a great imperial capital, was the focal point of a remarkable system of railways, and it is surprising to recall not only that at one time there were seven trunk routes radiating from the city, but that these belonged to five different companies. Competing for the traffic to Prague and southeast Germany were the Austrian North Western and the Imperial Royal Austrian State – which were state-owned – and the Austro-Hungarian State, which despite its name was privately owned. To the west, the Imperial Royal had the field to itself, but to the northeast of Vienna, the Kaiser Ferdinand's Northern (state-owned) provided the main link to Warsaw. The Southern, which was privately owned, ran to the shores of the Adriatic at Trieste, which was then in Austrian territory. After the general breakup of the Austro-Hungarian Empire at the end of the First World War, the republic of Austria was left with the one-time Imperial Royal line to Salzburg and the west, and the interesting Southern line, leading over the famous Semmering Pass on to the province of Styria. The construction of this line by the celebrated Karl Ghega was one of the epics of early railway building. In the 1840s, with no modern aids such as aerial surveys to act as a guide, the surveying had to be done entirely from ground level, and on the northern approach to the pass the land is just a wild confusion of crags, ravines and steep slopes. There is no ordered geographical pattern, and to make things worse for the pioneers the slopes were all thickly wooded. How Ghega managed to contrive a line on a steadily ascending grade of 2.5 percent is a marvel; and when he had done it no one believed that any locomotive would ever be able to climb that grade. But it was done, and for 100 years steam worked all the traffic.

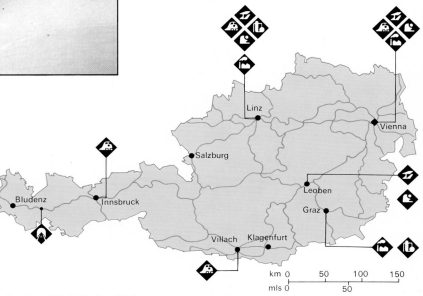

km 0   50   100   150
mls 0   50

Austrian class 52 2-10-0 at Hieflau.

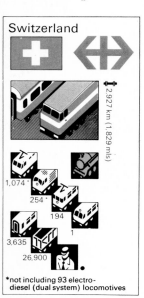

Switzerland, *left,* has the highest track length per capita in the world, though this is not apparent from the data panel figures, which are for the state system only. Another 2,165 km, 45%, of railways are privately owned. Two of these are: the Bern-Lötschberg-Simplon Railway, which conveys international trains through its 14 km Lötschberg Tunnel; and the Rhaetian Railway, a meter-gauge system with 363 route-km covering the canton of the Grisons.

Switzerland

2,927 km (1,829 mls)

1,074
254
194
1
3,635
26,900

*not including 93 electro-diesel (dual system) locomotives

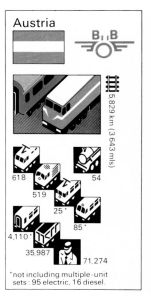

Austria

B B

5,829 km (3,643 mls)

618   54
519
25*
85*
4,110
35,987   71,274

*not including multiple-unit sets: 95 electric, 16 diesel.

Czechoslovakia and Hungary

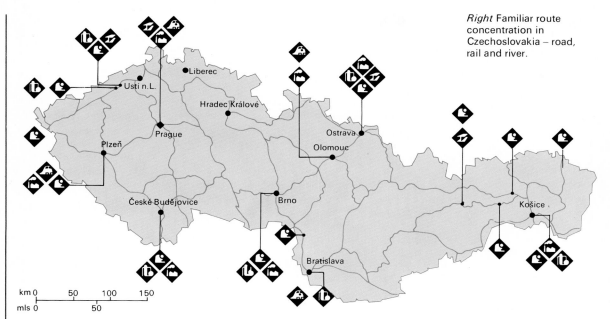

Right Familiar route concentration in Czechoslovakia – road, rail and river.

CZECHOSLOVAKIA *Československé Státni Dráhy (ČSD)*

When the state of Czechoslovakia was set up under the provisions of the Treaty of Versailles after the First World War, the rationalizing of the railway system was a matter of some urgency and difficulty. The provinces of Bohemia, Moravia and Silesia had formerly belonged to Austria, with railways focused upon Vienna and Prague, while the province of Slovakia had belonged to Hungary, with its railways directed toward Budapest. From 1924, therefore, the policy of the ČSD had to make provision for better west-to-east communication within the new country. No less than 160 km (100 miles) of new main line was constructed in the late 1920s. About 240 km (150 miles) of previously single-tracked secondary line was converted to double track and brought up to full main line standards. In the Second World War the ČSD was severely damaged, and after the war it was necessary to repair many tunnels and bridges, while more than 1,920 km (1,200 miles) of line had to be renewed. Many new lines have been built subsequently, and conversion to electric power is proceeding steadily, including the principal west-east line throughout the country. Out of a total of some 12,800 km (8,000 miles) of route, about 2,400 km (1,500 miles) are electrified. At the same time many steam locomotives remain in use, including some of the most advanced modern design. The main lines from the west, entering the country at Cheb from West Germany, and Děčín from East Germany, join up at Prague and continue east through Přerov. Here the line from Vienna to Warsaw intersects and proceeds eastward through Žilina to the border station with Soviet Russia at Čierna. From Prague southward to Vienna the main line today is that of the former Imperial Royal Austrian State Railway, entering the present Austria at Gmünd.

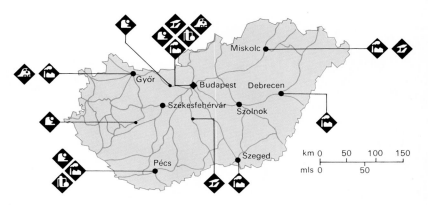

Czechoslovakia

ČSD

13.330 km (8.283 mls)

715*   2,907
1,077*
88
10,835   991
136,150
208,533

*excludes 1,200 locomotives, diesel and electric, bought 1970–1975

The rolling stock figures are for 1968. By the end of the 1970–75 Plan, 25% of the system should be electrified; 1,200 new locomotives were bought and 5% of traffic remained steam-hauled.

Double header pulling mixed freight through dramatic scenery in Czechoslovakia.

HUNGARY *Magyar Államvasutak (MAV)*

In imperial days there were three separate railways operating in Hungary, roughly one-third of the system being state-owned. The privately owned lines were the Austro-Hungarian State (despite its name) and the Austrian Southern. Budapest was very much the center of all railway activities. The Hungarian State, and the Austro-Hungarian State, were in direct competition for the traffic between Budapest and Vienna, one on each side of the River Danube. But today, although both routes still exist, the northerly one – the former Austro-Hungarian – is no longer competitive; it forms the most easterly section of the main line between Budapest and Prague. From Budapest the Hungarian State had three routes striking out to the north and east, but one of the most important was that running south to Belgrade. Until the First World War the River Danube marked the frontier between Hungary and Serbia, as it was then known. The third railway entering Budapest was the Austrian Southern, from the southwest. This made a junction with the line over the Semmering Pass from Vienna, and provided a through route from Budapest to Trieste. Because of the changing of state boundaries after the First World War, the extent of the Hungarian State Railways has been reduced from the original route length of 9,120 km (5,700 miles), a merger of the three separate railways, to 7,840 km (4,900 miles) today. Since the end of the Second World War, considerable progress has been made with electrification, and the circular railway in Budapest, 19 km (12 miles) long, is also electrified. Although the railways of Hungary use the European standard gauge, the loading gauge is much taller. Hungarian steam locomotives are often built to the maximum possible heights, and like those of Austria they seem immense compared with those of western Europe. But, as everywhere else, steam power is gradually being superseded, though many locomotives still remain in service. The now withdrawn Orient Express originally turned south from Budapest to serve Belgrade and eventually Constantinople.

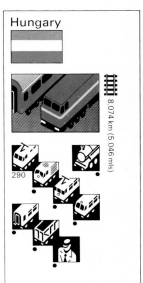

Hungary

8.074 km (5.046 mls)

290

Almost no figures are available for Hungary. About 16% of the system is electrified. The route length includes 35 km built to the Russian gauge of 1,524 mm, and 329 km of 760 mm gauge. Two classes of narrow gauge diesel locomotive exist.

Portugal and Spain

PORTUGAL *Companhia dos Caminhos de Ferro Portugueses (CP)*

The first railway in Portugal was opened in 1856 between Lisbon and Carregado, and the national network, amounting eventually to 3,520 km (2,200 miles) of route, was built up under private enterprise. The principal main line within the country connected Lisbon with Oporto, and had a connection running northward into Spain and continuing to Corunna. Important west-east international routes provide connections from Lisbon to Madrid, Barcelona and Seville, while a more northerly line reaching the Spanish frontier at Vilar Formoso, is used by trains providing the international service between Lisbon and Paris. These routes are laid to the Portuguese broad gauge standard of 1,665 mm (5 ft 5½ in). Until 1926 the lines at present worked were roughly half private and half state-owned, and then the government handed over, by lease, its own lines to the private company. In 1947, however, the whole concern was brought directly under the Ministry of Communications though remaining company operated, and in 1951 the government granted the company a 50-year concession to work the lines previously leased.

Narrow gauge steam

A feature of Portuguese railways of great interest to enthusiasts and photographers is the system of narrow gauge feeder lines in the north. There is a series of branches extending northward into the frontier regions from the Oporto-Barca d'Alva broad gauge main line, and on these the meter gauge trains are worked by historically interesting and immaculately maintained steam locomotives. On the broad gauge lines steam operation finally ended in March 1977. In the Lisbon suburban area, and on the main line northward toward Oporto, electrification is in progress, using the same system – 25,000 volts alternating current at 50 cycles – as standardized in Great Britain and France, while on other routes extensive use is now being made of diesel electric locomotives on long distance and international trains, and railcars for local branch line work. On the narrow gauge lines steam locomotives are still used for some of the work, though diesel railcars, diesel locomotives, and some gasoline-driven railcars, have been introduced.

Braga, Portugal, two switching engines.

SPAIN *Red Nacional de los Ferrocarriles Españoles (RENFE)*

Railway operation in Spain began in 1848 under rather curious circumstances. Before this 29 km (18 mile) length of line between Barcelona and Mataro had been built, a Royal decree of 1845 had insisted on extensive state intervention, and among other things demanded the adoption of a wider gauge than the European standard of 1,435 mm (4 ft 8½ in). It is thought that this was influenced by the work of I. K. Brunel in England; and while Spain had the same gauge – or nearly the same – as Portugal, 1,674 mm against 1,665 mm, there developed a major confrontation at the French frontier, that still remains today. From that beginning, Spanish railway construction, dependent upon foreign capital and the need for foreign advisers, progressed slowly. Major companies incorporated later were the Northern, in 1858, to build a line from Madrid to Irun; the Madrid, Zaragoza and Alicante in 1857, and the Andalusian Railway. All suffered in due course from lack of staple traffics, the difficulties of operating in mountainous country, and the imposition of low rates for both freight and passenger business. Unable to renew their assets they went into decline. In 1924 a convention in Madrid, signed by the state and the companies, provided for the supply of state capital for railway restoration and authorized the establishment of more realistic rates. This latter condition was not however fulfilled, and despite the infusion of state capital the railways were in poor shape when the Civil War broke out in 1936.

The Civil War and after

The destruction was widespread and severe. More than a thousand locomotives – over half the total stock – were destroyed, and many bridges, tunnels and lengths of track damaged. After the war the government took control of the railways, and in 1943 purchased the whole of the stock of the previous private companies, and an autonomous corporation, nominally independent of the government, was set up to operate the railways. This was named *Red Nacional de los Ferrocarriles Españoles*. Under this unified management great progress has been made in rebuilding and reequipping the Spanish railways. Many sections were electrified; others were changed from steam to diesel power. One of the most important developments has been the construction of the new direct line from Madrid to Burgos via Aranda, avoiding the long westward detour via Avila, Medina del Campo and Valladolid and saving a total of 120 km (75 miles) on the journey between Madrid and the French frontier.

Figures for CP's multiple-unit trains have proved impossible to obtain. The route length includes 759 km of meter gauge. Portugal's last steam engines are all narrow gauge: the last broad gauge steamers ran in 1977.

RENFE owns only broad (1,676 mm) gauge lines; another government agency FEVE operates (without owning) 1,757 km of narrow gauge lines. All totals include these lines, but exclude other privately owned railways.

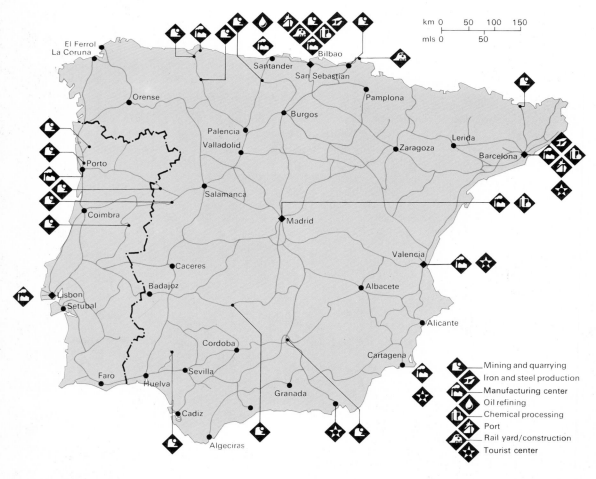

Mining and quarrying
Iron and steel production
Manufacturing center
Oil refining
Chemical processing
Port
Rail yard/construction
Tourist center

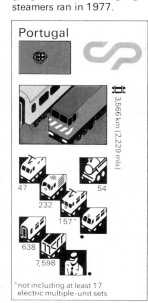

Portugal **cp**
3,566 km (2,229 mls)
47 · 54
232
157 ·
638
7,598

*not including at least 17 electric multiple-unit sets

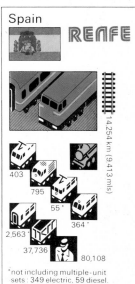

Spain **RENFE**
14,254 km (9,413 mls)
403 · 795
55 ·
2,563 · 364
37,736
80,108

*not including multiple-unit sets: 349 electric, 59 diesel.

France

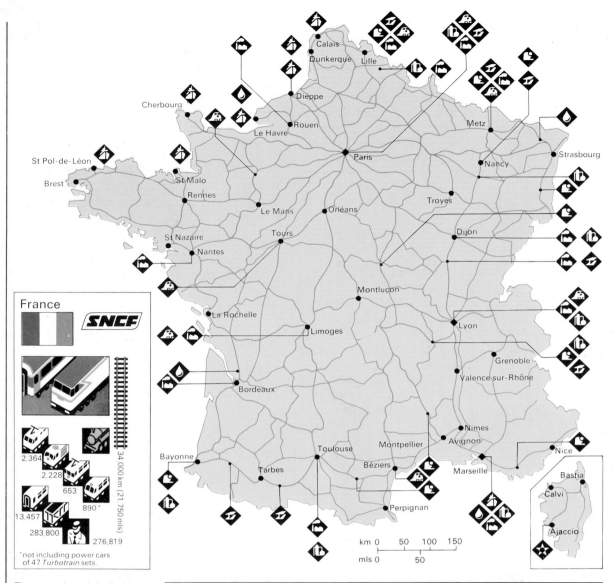

France

SNCF

2,364
2,228
653
890*

34,000 km (21,750 mls)

13,457
283,800
276,819

*not including power cars
of 47 *Turbotrain* sets.

The route length includes
the new 13.4 km line to
Roissy Airport but shows
only SNCF lines. Excluded
are the remains of a once-
extensive network of
secondary lines – about
975 km meter gauge, and
1,125 km standard, still
exist. The freight total
includes private stock.

Right A night train
departs, Paris. *Below
left* Font Romeu, La
Tour de Carol system.
Below right Steam
French style.

FRANCE Société Nationale des Chemins de fer Français (SNCF)

Railways in France began, as in Great Britain, with local mineral lines using horses for power, but at a very early stage in the development the government, seeing what was happening with unbridled competition in other places, divided the whole country into a number of clearly defined geographical regions, and gave the pioneer railway companies concessions to build only within those limits. In this way it was hoped that wasteful competition and unnecessary proliferation of routes would be avoided. The individual companies, of which there were originally seven, held concessions due to terminate in the 1930s, and during the intervening period the dividends paid to their shareholders were guaranteed by the government. Five out of the original seven continued in this manner until nationalization in 1937, but the Western was seriously affected by the establishment of the French State Railways, in 1878, which brought competition into Western territory and so contravened the original conception. The Paris-Orléans Railway was also affected, though not to such a serious extent. The other four original railways remained in almost exclusive possession of their allotted territories. These companies were the Northern, Eastern, Paris, Lyon, and Mediterranean, the Southern (Midi) and the Alsace-Lorraine.

Nineteenth-century complacency

The monopolies these companies held tended to generate policies lacking in enterprise, and train services in the nineteenth century were relatively poor. The exception was the Paris-Orléans, which did become affected by competition. At both Bordeaux and Toulouse it handed over traffic for the south to the Midi, which also received similar traffic from the PLM. The Midi was encouraged to favor the Orléans traffic for the better service from the north provided by that company. Before the general mergers of 1937-8, the Paris-Orléans and the Midi had themselves merged, in 1934. Competition between the state-owned system, the État, and the Western Railway led to the absorption of the latter in 1908. Of the original companies the Alsace-Lorraine was profoundly affected by the Franco-Prussian War of 1870-1, after which most of the territory in which it operated was annexed by Germany. For a period of 48 years until 1919 it was controlled and operated by Prussia, and its equipment changed to correspond with standard German practice.

Era of speed and efficiency

The *Société Nationale des Chemins de fer Français* was set up in January 1938; but long before this act of nationalization all of the individual French railways had thrown off their nineteenth-century complacency and were between them providing some of the fastest and most efficient train services in the whole of Europe. From the experience of invasion, in 1870 and again in 1914, there was reluctance to electrify any of the lines leading to the eastern frontier, and development in this respect had come first on the Paris-Orléans and on the Midi railways, in the 1920s. In the Second World War the greatest destruction took place not at the time of the general overrunning of the country by Nazi forces in 1940, but just prior to the reentry of Allied forces in 1944, when systematic strategic bombing to hinder the movement of troops led to the almost complete disruption of the entire railway network and much destruction of rolling stock.

Since the war recovery has been remarkable. The lines to the eastern frontier have been electrified and fast services inaugurated, but the highest speeds so far are run on the former Paris-Orléans lines up to a maximum of 200 km/h (125 mph) with heavy luxury express trains. The greatest development, however, is now in course of construction, namely the new high-speed line between Paris and Lyon, on which speeds up to 300 km/h (185 mph) will be run, by special TGV (*très grande vitesse*) electric trains. The new line is being built roughly parallel to the former PLM main line, though passing somewhat to the west of Dijon. It is planned that when the new route comes into operation in the early 1980s the journey time between Paris and Lyon, now 3 hr 44 min, will be reduced to 2 hr. Thus, since the end of the war, France has become a world leader in railway innovation.

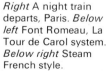

Italy, Yugoslavia, Albania

ITALY *Ferrovie dello Stato-Italia (FS)*

Although the first railway in Italy was built in 1839, and various other projects followed, there was no co-ordination, because at that time Italy had not been unified as a single country. Lombardy was then occupied by Austria. The Dukedom of Tuscany and the Papal States were then independent. After the union of 1861 plans were drawn up for a national network, and from the various independent and unconnected lines five companies were set up: the Upper Italian, operating in Lombardy and Piedmont; the Roman, taking over lines in Tuscany and the Papal States; the Southern, working east of the Apennine mountains; the Royal Sardinian, in Calabria; and the Victor Emmanuel Railway in Sicily. In 1885 a further merging took place into three private companies, and finally between 1905 and 1907 all came under the control of the state.

Italy was one of the first countries to introduce main line electric power, on the line between Genoa and the French frontier at Ventigmiglia and on the steeply graded Giovi Incline, but the system adopted did not prove adaptable to heavy modern traffic, and the lines were reequipped. During the Fascist era notable strides were made towards the improvement of the national network. The piecemeal nature of the original buildup, at a time when reliance had to be placed on foreign capital, resulted in many important routes being sharply curved and constructed so as to minimize initial costs. While the main lines eastward from Milan to Venice, and from Milan through Bologna to Rimini and Ancona, were straight and capable of use by fast trains, the important route from Bologna to Florence and Rome was extremely sinuous and heavily graded. In the Fascist era a new direct line was built from Bologna to Florence, involving a great new tunnel through the Apennine range 19 km (12 miles) long, and opened in 1934. Another great project was the building of a new high-speed direct line between Rome and Naples, running near to the coast for much of the way, and avoiding use of the old inland route that was so unsuitable for fast running operations.

These improvements left the old line between Florence and Rome as the only remaining section of the route between Milan and Naples in the old style. In mountainous country it was perhaps the most difficult of all to operate. Eventually the decision was taken to build a new direct line regardless of the natural obstacles. It has involved some tremendous engineering feats, great viaducts and long tunnels, in fact nearly one-third of the entire distance of 257 km (160 miles) from Florence to Rome is in tunnel. The end-to-end average speed of the fastest trains is planned to be no less than 177 km/h (110 mph), with a maximum of about 250 km/h (155 mph). This high-speed line will take much of the traffic burden off the old route.

YUGOSLAVIA *Jugoslovenske Železnice (JŽ)*

The state of Yugoslavia, created after the end of the First World War, inherited a mixed collection of railways. There had been groups of lines in Croatia and Slovenia, the lines of the former Serbian State Railways, and meter gauge lines, and some even narrower in Bosnia, Herzogovina and Dalmatia. The first aim of the Yugoslav government was to establish the northwest to southeast link from Ljubljana through Belgrade to Caribrod (now Dimitrovgrad), as an international main line. Today Belgrade is a focal point of main routes from Austria and Italy in the west, Hungary in the north, and Greece and Turkey in the east. While it is no longer possible to travel through in one car from Paris to Istanbul, the Simplon Express from Paris to Belgrade connects there with the Marmara Express, and also the Athens Express. The Republic of Yugoslavia is divided into six socialist republics, and in 1954 the railways introduced workers' self-government, so that the Community of Yugoslav Railways lost the title of State. There are five Railway Transport Enterprises, or regional headquarters, in Belgrade, Zagreb, Ljubljana, Sarajevo and Skopje. The coordinating authority is in Belgrade.

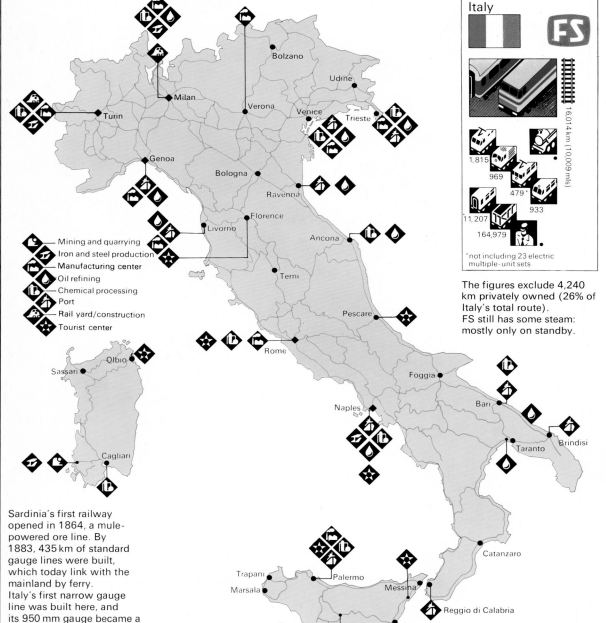

Mining and quarrying
Iron and steel production
Manufacturing center
Oil refining
Chemical processing
Port
Rail yard/construction
Tourist center

Sardinia's first railway opened in 1864, a mule-powered ore line. By 1883, 435 km of standard gauge lines were built, which today link with the mainland by ferry.
Italy's first narrow gauge line was built here, and its 950 mm gauge became a standard throughout Italy. About 1,050 km were opened, the last as late as 1932.

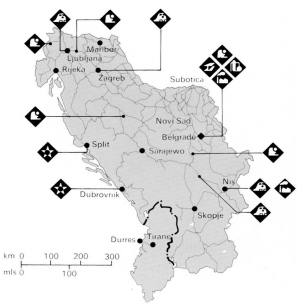

Italy

16,014 km (10,009 mls)

1,815
969
479*
933
11,207
164,979

*not including 23 electric multiple-unit sets

The figures exclude 4,240 km privately owned (26% of Italy's total route).
FS still has some steam: mostly only on standby.

The route length figure is from 1973 and includes 1,045 km of narrow gauge, some having been closed subsequently. By 1985 it is hoped that 35% of the system will be electrified. The last steam locomotive is due to be phased out in 1980.

Albania's first railway was opened in 1947, and the system is still expanding: at present a link is being built to Bar (Yugoslavia). Steam locomotives are 2-8-2 Polish tanks, while CKD (the Czech manufacturer) recently supplied three classes of diesels.

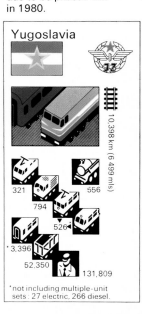

Yugoslavia

10,398 km (6,499 mls)

321
556
794
526
3,396
52,350
131,809

*not including multiple-unit sets : 27 electric, 266 diesel.

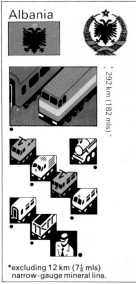

Albania

292 km (182 mls)*

*excluding 12 km (7½ mls) narrow-gauge mineral line.

Romania, Bulgaria, Greece

ROMANIA *Caile Ferate Romane (CFR)*
The first railway in Romania, built in 1869, was the result of a concession granted to two Englishmen, John Barkley and John Staniforth, and connected Bucharest with the Danubian port of Giurgiu, 72 km (45 miles) distant. But building and operating railways by private enterprise did not last long and in 1888 all railways in Romania became state owned. Although the rail gauge is the European standard, there is a short length of mixed gauge, with three rails, to provide access for the Russian standard gauge of 1,524 mm (5 ft 0 in). The total route length on standard gauge is 10,100 km (6,300 miles). The principal route into Romania from the west enters the country from Budapest at Apiscopia Bihor, and links up with a more southerly route at Teius. Bucharest, the former eastern terminus of the Orient Express, is a major railway center, lines running north to cross the Russian border at Ungeny, and east to the Black Sea port of Constantza.

BULGARIA *Bulgarski Durzhavni Železnitsi (BDŽ)*
For a relatively small country railway construction in Bulgaria began on quite a large scale, with a main line 225 km (139 miles) long from the Danubian port of Ruschuk to Varna on the Black Sea, in 1866. A still greater milestone, however, was the completion of the international main line across the country from Dragoman on the present Yugoslav frontier, through Sofia to Svilengrad, and providing the all-rail route of the Orient Express to Constantinople. King Boris of Bulgaria was a keen railway enthusiast and frequently drove the steam locomotives of fast trains. Today more than half the total route of 4,300 km (2,700 miles) is electrified, and the rest is operated by diesel traction and steam locomotives.

Steam train waiting in a Bulgarian station.

GREECE *Organismos Siderodromon Ellados (ΣΕ)*
It is remarkable in view of its ancient civilization that Greece should have been one of the most backward of European countries to adopt modern means of communication in the form of railways, and, still more remarkable perhaps that the country was not connected to the rest of Europe by rail until 1916. One of the first railways in Greece was indeed directed away rather than toward Europe, and came from a concession granted to a company called the Piraeus, Athens and Peloponnesus to build a line across the isthmus of Corinth and into the Peloponnesus. It was built on the meter gauge, and by the turn of the century had a total route length of about 800 km (500 miles). It passed through Athens to reach the port of Piraeus.

The standard gauge main line from Piraeus and Athens to the north was opened in sections between 1904 and 1909 to Papapouli. At that time its limit was the Turco-Greek frontier; but at the Treaty of Bucharest, following the Balkan war of 1913, the frontiers were redrawn, and the borders of Greece were pushed northward to those of Serbia and Bulgaria. This brought the Thessaly Railway into Greek territory, and in 1916 the link was made between Papapouli and Platy. This enabled railcar services to be established between Athens and other European cities. In 1962 all railways in Greece were amalgamated under the title of Hellenic Railways, and in 1971 these railways were set up as a state-owned company with the title of Hellenic Railways Organization Ltd.

Romania

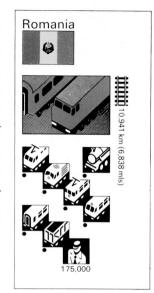

10,941 km (6,838 mls)

175,000

Few figures are available for Romania, *above*, or Bulgaria, *below*. Both retain some steam locomotives, though both are electrifying. The route totals of both countries include narrow gauge lines.

Bulgaria

BDZ

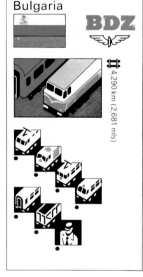

4,290 km (2,681 mls)

The route total, *below*, includes 2 narrow gauges. The rolling stock figures are for those in service by end 1975. Mid-1976, OSE had 74 steam locomotives, of all 3 gauges, on hand: most were stored.

Greece

ΣΕ

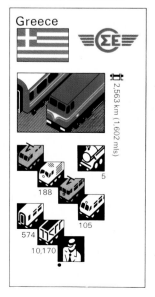

2,563 km (1,602 mls)

5
188
105
574
10,170

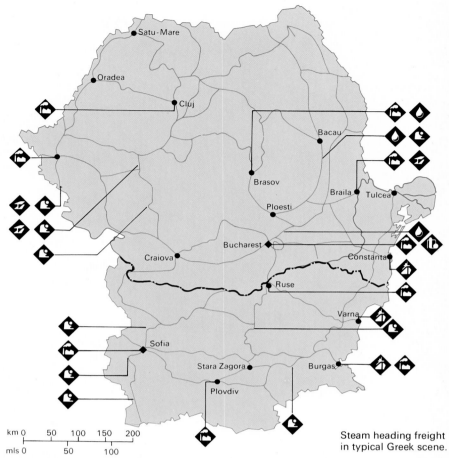

km 0   50   100   150   200
mls 0   50   100

Steam heading freight in typical Greek scene.

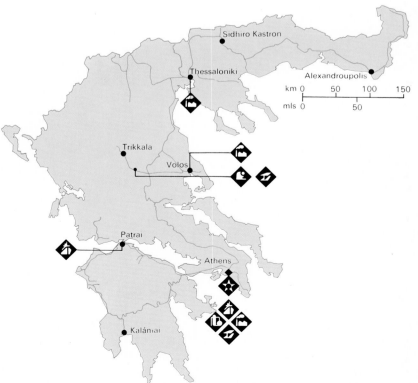

km 0   50   100   150
mls 0   50

191

USSR

USSR *Soviet Railways (SZD)*

The railways of Soviet Russia represent the largest single railway system in the world. They extend from the Polish frontier to Vladivostok, a distance of some 10,000 km (6,300 miles), and from the White Sea in the north to Turkestan. The first public railway was opened in 1836 with British locomotives from both Stephenson and Hackworth, and from a modest beginning great expansion followed the completion of the main line between Moscow and Leningrad (then St Petersburg) in 1851. By 1913 the railway network consisted of no fewer than 25 state lines and 13 private lines; but although then the largest system in Europe there was little coordination between individual companies and strategically the lines were built with the emphasis on the southern frontiers, toward Afghanistan and India rather than the west.

After the Revolution

The almost ledgendary Trans-Siberian line was still under construction at the turn of the century, though communication between Moscow and Vladivostok had been established by shipping passengers and goods by ferry across Lake Baikal, until the line was completed, blasted out of the solid rock along the shores of the lake. The absence of good railways in the European provinces of Russia was in part responsible for the collapse of the military position in the First World War. After the Revolution of 1917 the railways were nationalized and great efforts made towards reconstruction. It was realized that efficient communication was the first essential of the new state, and by the 1930s the railway system had been so modernized that from being a serious liability it had been advanced to become one of the greatest assets to the national economy. Although a great deal of damage was done to the lines in the war zones in 1941–4, reconstruction and development continued and today the route length is more than 128,000 km (80,000 miles), of which more than 32,000 km (20,000 miles) is electrified, including the Trans-Siberian line as far east as China. In nonelectrified areas there is a general move to replace steam locomotives by diesel, and a new high-speed line has been inaugurated between Moscow and Leningrad on which speeds of 200 km/h (125 mph) are projected.

Russian steam heading Trans-Siberian, with familiar decoration.

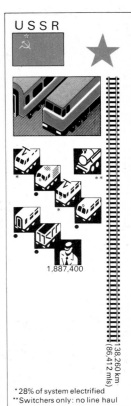

USSR

* 28% of system electrified
** Switchers only: no line haul

1,887,400

138,260 km
(86,412 mls)

Although few USSR data are available, they do admit to "achievements": 28% of the system is electrified and steam may end in 1980. In 1975 alone, USSR bought 389 electric and 1,108 diesel locomotives.

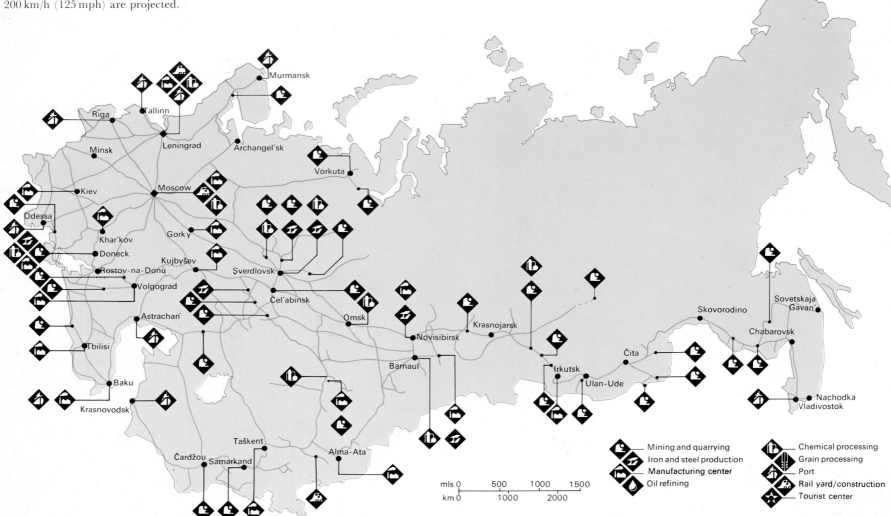

Mining and quarrying
Iron and steel production
Manufacturing center
Oil refining
Chemical processing
Grain processing
Port
Rail yard/construction
Tourist center

mls 0   500   1000   1500
km 0   1000   2000

Asia: Turkey and Middle East 1

Asia has some of the oldest, and some of the most modern, trains in the world. It is thought that China is still building steam locomotives, and India has 8,000. However, the Japanese opened their *Shinkansen* line in 1964; over a major trunk route, trains are run at a frequency usually associated with commuter lines at speeds up to 210 km/h (130 mph). Asia is a varied mixture of rich and poor, of countries which were once colonies and those which were left to develop their own rail system in the national, rather than the colonizing power's, interest. As a result, Asia's lines are a multiplicity of gauges, some countries own systems much more comprehensive than others, and the completion of a through route from Paris to Peking, although a serious proposal (see page 94), is many years away from realization.

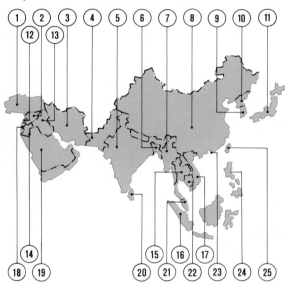

1 Turkey p 193
2 Syria p 193
3 Iran p 194
4 Pakistan p 195
5 India p 194
6 Bangladesh p 194
7 Burma p 194
8 China p 195
9 South Korea p 195
10 North Korea p 195
11 Japan p 196
12 Lebanon p 193
13 Iraq p 194
14 Jordan p 193
15 Thailand p 196
16 Indonesia p 196
17 Vietnam p 195
18 Israel p 193
19 Saudi Arabia p 194
20 Sri Lanka p 194
21 Malaysia p 196
22 Cambodia p 196
23 Hong Kong p 195
24 Philippines p 195
25 Taiwan p 195

TURKEY *Turkish State Railways (TCDD)*

The old Ottoman Empire straddled the Bosporus, and the Turkish railway system consisted of little more than the route of the Orient Express in Europe, and about 4,000 km (2,500 miles) of route in Asia Minor, independent, unconnected and serving local areas. After the Balkan War of 1913, however, Turkey was left with no more than a foothold in Europe, while her association with the Central Powers in the First World War, and involvement in their collapse, left the country and its railways in very poor shape. While under strong German influence a railway had been built through Asia Minor to connect Constantinople with Baghdād, completed in 1918, the starting-point of the modern railway system of Turkey was the proclamation of the republic in October 1923 and the move of the capital city from Constantinople to Ankara – then little more than a remote settlement. A well-balanced system of railways being essential to build up the economy of the country, plans were prepared for a fully integrated network in Asia Minor. In 1927 the "General Management of the Railways and Harbors of the Republic of Turkey" (TCDD) was set up and since then the railway length has virtually doubled. Ankara was placed on the principal main line from Istanbul to the Iraqi and Soviet frontiers, although the route of the Taurus Express, from Istanbul to Baghdād, is that of the German-sponsored line built earlier. In mountainous country the Turkish railways of today follow the winding river valleys and cross high mountain passes.

Israel

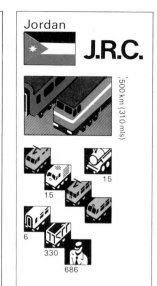

598 km (374 mls)

55
107
2,168
1,860

Israel's lines are now all standard gauge, though the first (1890) was meter and the second, 1,050 mm (Haifa-Dera'a, Syria: now closed, it included 80 km below sea level). Middle East politics have isolated Israel: before 1948, trains ran to Egypt, Lebanon and Jordan via Dera'a. The system within Israel is expanding.

Jordan

J.R.C.

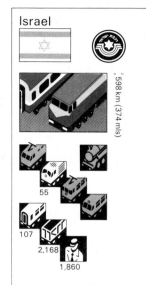

500 km (310 mls)

15
15
6
330
686

Jordan's first train ran in 1904, as part of the Turkish-inspired Pilgrim's Railway (Damascus-Medina). The line was damaged in 1918, and fell into disuse south of Ma'an. Part was refurbished in connection with the new Aqaba line (opened 1975). Steam locomotives and passenger trains are only found north of Amman.

Lebanon

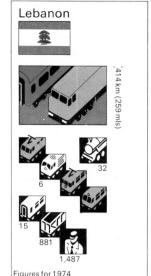

414 km (259 mls)

32
6
15
881
1,487

Figures for 1974

Lebanon was carved out of the Turkish empire with no regard to the existing rail system. Running inland from Beirut (with 32 km of rack rail) is part of the 1,050 mm Damascus line. Others are standard gauge, but the junction of the system is in Syria. All lines were closed by the civil war and have not yet reopened.

Syria

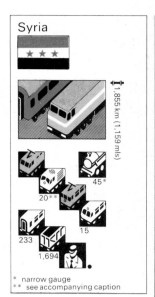

1,855 km (1,159 mls)

45*
20**
233
15
1,694

* narrow gauge
** see accompanying caption

The diesel locomotive figure is unreliable: recently, standard gauge steam has ended and the route-km has doubled (expansion in the north). Syria has two systems: 1,050 mm linking Damascus with Lebanon and Jordan; in the north, a standard gauge system links Hims/Aleppo with Lebanon and Turkey, soon reaching Damascus.

A 2-10-0 near Siringo in Turkey.

The route figure includes 47.5 km of line scheduled to open in 1977. Rolling stock totals are 1974 and rather out of date: 300 more diesels should be delivered before 1978.

Turkey

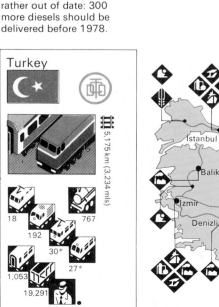

5,175 km (3,234 mls)

18
767
192
30*
27*
1,053
19,291

* multiple-unit sets: excludes 25 diesel railcars

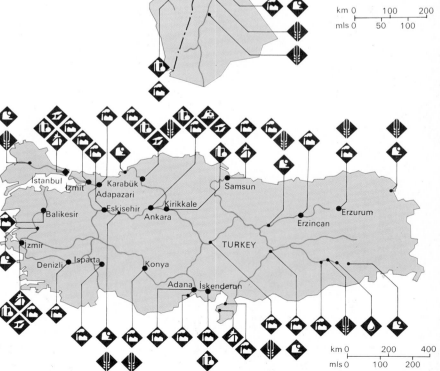

km 0   100   200
mls 0   50   100

km 0   200   400
mls 0   100   200

Middle East 11 and India

INDIA *Indian Government Railways*

The railways of India as a basic national network were planned by the Marquis of Dalhousie when Governor-General in the early 1850s. The plan was to develop trade routes connecting the seaports of Calcutta, Bombay and Madras, and to provide good communication from the ports to the North-West Frontier, where the greatest military danger was thought to lie. From 1853 when the first railway was constructed from Bombay the main line network was built on the 1,676 mm (5 ft 6 in) gauge recommended by Dalhousie; but later, when many more lines were found necessary and the cost of construction was high, the government agreed to the establishment of a system of feeder lines on the meter gauge. Railway building in India and what is now Pakistan involved some tremendous feats of civil engineering, in crossing the range of the Western Ghats eastward from Bombay, in crossing the great rivers Indus and Ganges, and in carrying strategic lines of communication into the mountain ranges of the North-West Frontier.

In imperial days the railways of India were household names in transport and engineering circles: Great Indian Peninsula; Bombay, Baroda and Central India; Madras and Southern Mahratta; East Indian; Bengal Nagpur; Eastern Bengal; and above all "His Exalted Highness the Nizam's Guaranteed State Railway." Some of the railways were state-owned, others were operated by private companies holding concessions and certain financial guarantees. When the concessions ended they were brought under government control. After the granting of independence to India and Pakistan the railways were nationalized, and the railways of India are operated in nine territorial zones: Northern, Western, Central, Southern, Eastern, North Eastern, South Eastern, North-East Frontier and South Central. Since independence great strides have been made towards the provision of all rolling stock and technical services by indigenous manufacture and technology.

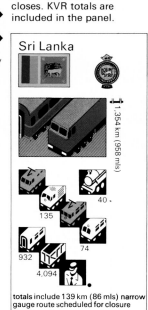

The Bangladesh Railway originated as an integral part of the Bengal-Assam Railway, which was arbitrarily divided at the Partition of India and Pakistan in 1947. Further, administrative, upheaval came in 1973 in the wake of the civil war which created a separate Bangladesh. The system is built to both Indian gauges: about a third is broad (1,676 mm) gauge, the rest meter.

km
0 100   300   500
0 100   200   300
mls

Sri Lanka's first railway opened in 1865 to the Indian 1,676 mm gauge. This will soon be the only gauge, if the 762 mm Kelani Valley Railway closes. KVR totals are included in the panel.

Railway construction began in Iraq, *below right*, in 1902, part of the Berlin-Baghdad project, seen as a standard gauge through route. After the British invasion of 1914 Basra-Baghdad was built with surplus meter gauge equipment from India, and Iraq has a similar mileage now of both gauges.

Below: Saudi Arabia's first railway now lies derelict, damaged by Lawrence of Arabia in 1918. Trains got to Tabūk from Jordan in 1906, and reached Medina in 1908. The line now working opened in 1951, built by ARAMCO as one of the conditions of their oil exploration licence.

India

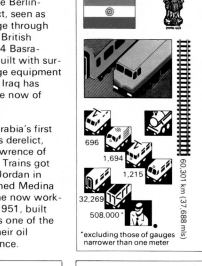

696
1,694
1,215
32,269
508,000
60,301 km (37,688 mls)

*excluding those of gauges narrower than one meter

Indian railways, *left*, have 4 different gauges. The broad gauge (1,676 mm) is used for 30,274 route-km and the meter gauge for 25,551 km. Two narrower gauges of 762 mm and 610 mm account for 4,476 route-km (7½% of the total). The freight figure therefore need increasing by the same percentage.

Mining and quarrying
Iron and steel production
Manufacturing center
Oil refining
Chemical processing
Grain processing
Port
Rail yard/construction

Sri Lanka

1,354 km (958 mls)
40
135
932
74
4,094

totals include 139 km (86 mls) narrow gauge route scheduled for closure

Bangladesh

2,858 km (1,786 mls)
337
178
4
1,204
18,882

Iran, *below*, acquired its first line in 1916, built by the Russians from their frontier to Tabriz. It was 1,524 mm gauge until 1958. The Trans-Iranian Railway (Persian Gulf-Caspian Sea) was opened throughout only in 1938. The link to Turkey was completed in 1971. A 10-to-25 Year Development Plan, drawn so it can be proceeded with as fast or slowly as required, calls for another 9,500 km to be built – twice as much as the country owns now. One line planned is a link to Pakistan Railways, whose system extends over their border to Zāhedān (where gauge-changing facilities will be needed). A section of this line, from Zarand to Kermān, opened in 1977. The plan also proposes extensive electrification. The first line being done is the original one to the Russian frontier, but no details are yet available of the progress made.

The Bangladesh Railway originated as an integral part of the Bengal-Assam Railway, which was arbitrarily divided at the Partition of India and Pakistan in 1947.

Burmese Railways, *left*, own the longest double-track meter-gauge line anywhere (the 220 km north from Rangoon). The first line opened in 1877: all were built by the government of India, from which Burma separated in 1937. Few recent figures are available. A 1975 estimate gives 200 steam and more than 50 diesels at Rangoon depot alone. The remaining steam locomotives include Garratts for the 4 percent grade of the Lashio line.

Saudi Arabia

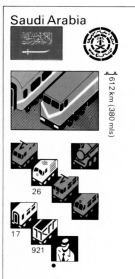

612 km (380 mls)
26
17
921

Iraq

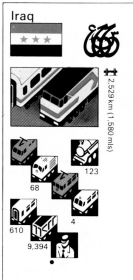

123
68
4
610
9,394
2,529 km (1,580 mls)

Iran

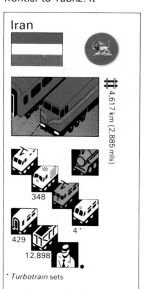

348
4*
429
12,898
4,617 km (2,885 mls)

* *Turbotrain sets*

Burma

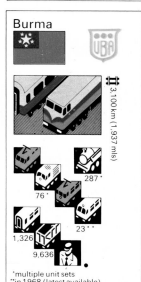

287*
76*
23**
1,326
9,636
3,100 km (1,937 mls)

*multiple unit sets
**in 1968 (latest available)

Pakistan and Far East 1

PAKISTAN *Pakistan Railways (PR)*

The first line in Pakistan was the 173 km (108 mile) Scinde Railway between Karāchi and Kotri, opened in 1861. It was promoted because of the hazardous navigation along the lower Indus. By 1865, a route had been completed via Amritsar to Delhi, the capital of British India, but it still included a 912 km (570 mile) river voyage. Thus began the North Western Railway, which became the largest railway company on the Indian subcontinent. Divided by the 1947 Partition of India, the major portion became what is now Pakistan Railways. The countryside presents extraordinary challenges. One line crosses the Sind desert, another climbs above the snowline. The Quetta route climbs 1,524 m (5,000 ft) in 80 km (50 miles). Above all, the railway is plagued by the capricious flooding of the River Indus, despite much magnificent bridge building by the original engineers.

Pakistan

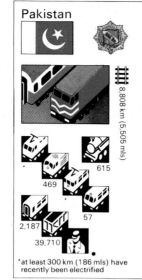

*at least 300 km (186 mls) have recently been electrified

km
0 100   300   500

0   100   200   300
mls

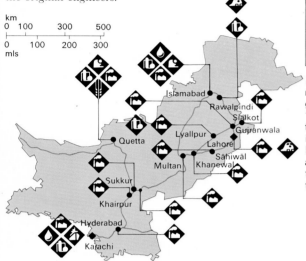

Like India, Pakistan's railways were built to 4 gauges, but 88% is 1,676 mm gauge. The line from Lahore to Khānewāl is electrified, but no locomotive figures are available (and the steam total may refer to before this line was electrified).

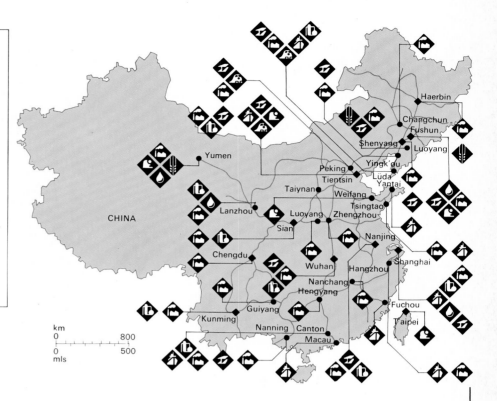

CHINA

km
0   800
0   500
mls

Vietnam

About 2,210 km of meter gauge lines were opened in Vietnam, the first in 1885. However, the system suffered extensively in years of warfare and at present it is planned to rebuild only 1,680 km. Through services between Hanoi and Saigon only reopened in January 1977.

Most of the Philippines' lines are on Luzon, the main island, where the first railway was opened in 1892 by the English Manila Railroad Co. Ownership was acquired by the government in 1917. The totals include the 116 km Phividec Railway on another island, Panay.

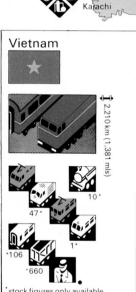

* stock figures only available for what was S Vietnam

Philippines

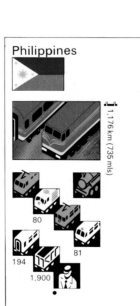

CHINA *Chinese Republic Railways*

It is only 100 years since a railway line opened in China, but the possibilities of development were soon exploited by foreign investors and building accelerated, particularly after the war with Japan in 1894. From 1908 all foreign contracts had to give complete administrative control to the government, and the formation of the republic led to a degree of consolidation of the railways with the establishment of central control in 1915.

At the time of the Japanese invasion of Manchuria in 1931, total route length reached 14,436 km (9,022 miles), but in the period following over 6,000 km (3,728 miles) was ceded to the Japanese. This led to a divided development of the area with the national government attempting to build new lines to compensate for their losses to the Japanese in the northeast. The two systems were reunited following the Japanese surrender in 1945.

Postwar development until 1960 was heavily assisted by the USSR, particularly after the establishment of the People's Republic in 1949. It was in this period that the link between Peking and Ulan-Ude in Russia via Ulan Bator was completed, thus cutting 2,400 km off the old Trans-Siberian route to Europe via Haerbin.

Since the split with the USSR the Chinese have forged ahead with railway expansion, tackling difficult terrain with great determination, and a doubling of the present route length is envisaged in the next few years. The whole network is extremely well maintained, the main source of power still being based on steam; but diesel and electric traction are increasing in importance.

Figures for China's railways are virtually non-existent. It is thought that steam locomotives are still being built, though dieselization has begun and at least 675 km are electrified.

China

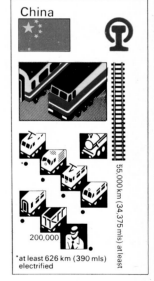

*at least 626 km (390 mls) electrified

South Korea

Korea's first line was opened in 1899, and 6,400 km were developed during the Japanese annexation, 1910–45. At partition in 1948, network and stock were divided by 2:1, N Korea getting the greater share. In the war of 1950–3 much damage was done, but S Korea is rapidly updating its share and is building 600 km of new lines. Details for N Korea are not known: those in the panel were devised by subtracting from the 1945 totals for the whole of Korea the amounts left to the South after partition.

North Korea

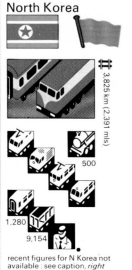

recent figures for N Korea not available: see caption, right

Hong Kong

Hong Kong's railway opened in 1910, the British section of the Kowloon-Canton line. The rest is now part of China's system, though cars still cross the frontier. Hong Kong is building a separate mass transit line.

Taiwan's first train ran in 1891. Recently its 1,067 mm gauge was adopted for all lines, the 176 km East Line built to 762 mm gauge in 1939, currently being converted. The electric locomotives were bought for the West Line electrification plan for 1977. An 82 km link line joining these two will open in 1978. The totals exclude 2,838 km of government-owned plantation lines.

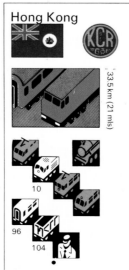

Taiwan

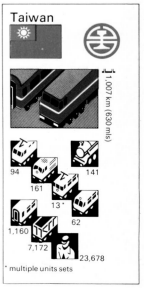

* multiple units sets

Far East 11

JAPAN *Japanese National Railways (JNR)*
There could not be a greater contrast between the leisurely, almost primitive beginnings of the Japanese railway system in 1872 and the tremendous volume of passenger traffic carried at equally tremendous speed on the *Shinkansen* high-speed lines of today. With British advisers and mechanical engineers, the first lines were constructed on a meandering 1,067 mm (3 ft 6 in) gauge track along the coast from Tōkyō to Yokohama. The first railways suited the temperament of the people of those days, in being quite unable to hurry. Eventually a narrow gauge system was extended across the country, built by both the government and private enterprise. The mountainous nature of the country called for some heavy engineering works and confirmed the original choice of a narrow gauge. When the government nationalized the 17 major private railway companies in 1906, it made itself the owner of 6,407 km (4,004 miles) of route. From an early reliance upon foreigners, the Japanese railways had quickly become self-sufficient, and a high standard of engineering was established.

A major consideration in any railway building was to take every possible precaution against the effect of earthquakes, but in spite of this much of the system, particularly the lines around Tōkyō and Yokohama, suffered terribly in the catastrophic earthquake of September 1923. Accompanied by a tidal wave and fires, it destroyed much of those two great cities. However, reconstruction was rapid, and by the early 1930s the traffic on busier parts of the system was approaching saturation point.

Plans were then made for the building of a new high-

speed line, using the European standard gauge, to provide for through traffic on the most congested line (that between Tōkyō, Nagoya, Kyōto and Osaka). It was not to be a mere duplication of the existing line, but was entirely new and virtually straight in order to permit far higher speeds. The limit on existing lines was then 100 km/h (62 mph).

Development of this plan was interrupted by the Second World War, in the later stages of which the Japanese railways were severely damaged by aerial attack. Such setbacks delayed the opening of the first of the new high-speed, or *Shinkansen*, lines until 1964. Its engineering is spectacular, carrying the tracks straight through or across any obstacle, and permitting speeds of 210 km/h (130 mph) continuously. It has set the pattern not only for extensions in Japan, but also for new lines in Italy, France and West Germany. The *Shinkansen* was originally intended to be a general-purpose railway, but its popularity has proved so great that it is used exclusively for passenger traffic. Indeed, despite the fact that 90 *Shinkansen* trains leave Tōkyō every day for the south, the commuter services are badly oversaturated and the building of new high-speed lines under way.

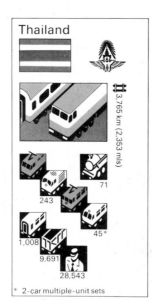

Thailand

3,765 km (2,353 mls)

71
243
13
45*
1,008
9,691
28,543

* 2-car multiple-unit sets

Thailand's first line was begun in 1891, to standard gauge. But meter gauge was used for the south line, begun 1898, to link with Malaya. Burma also chose this gauge and it was decided to convert the first gauge, finishing in 1930.

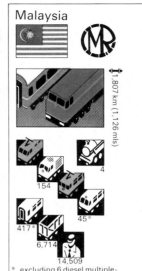

Kampuchea

649 km (406 mls)

24
13
4
4
4
680

Figures are not available from the present Cambodian regime, and it is not known whether the system is working: it was badly damaged in the war. The line to Kompong Som was wrecked only four months after its 1969 opening.

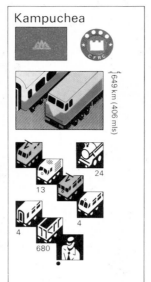

Malaysia

1,807 km (1,126 mls)

4
154
45*
417*
6,714
14,509

* excluding 6 diesel multiple-unit sets

Railways in Malaya began in 1885. By 1918 the 787 km West Coast line from Thailand to Singapore was complete except for the Johore Strait causeway. The East Coast line was completed in 1931, providing another route to Thailand. The totals include the Sabah State Railway, built 1896–1905 by the British North Borneo Co. (Sabah was N Borneo until 1963).

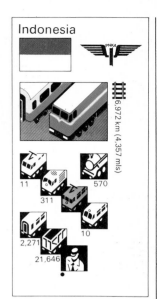

Indonesia

6,972 km (4,357 mls)

11
570
311
2,271
10
21,646

Indonesia's railways are built to 3 gauges. The widest is now 1,067 mm: during the last war the Japanese narrowed the standard gauge lines. The first 26 km line opened in 1864. Java has since acquired a comprehensive network but Sumatra has only 3 isolated systems. In recent years Indonesia has become famous among enthusiasts for its steam locomotives.

Japan

26,866 km (16,791 mls)

2,171
8**
2,150
28,659
8,599
125,844
502,000

* includes trailer cars
** no steam on state system

The Japan figures include 146 privately-owned lines (hence the steam locomotives). The totals are for the end of 1974.

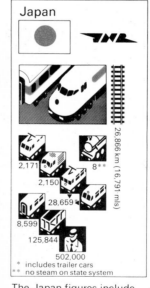

The unmistakable *Shinkansen* trains of Japan.

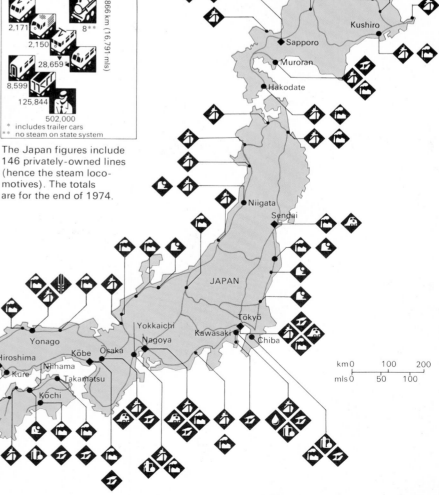

Africa: northeast

The development of the African rail network up to the present time can be divided into two distinct phases. The first was as an aid to colonial exploitation and expansion by several European powers, notably Britain and France. The colonial experience left Africa with a series of lines running inland from the coast: only in southern Africa were lines joined up into the semblance of a network.

The second phase began at independence. Railways were seen as a means of binding together countries which in some cases were little more than loose amalgamations of tribal areas. Separate lines were linked to form a national railway system, branch lines were built and attempts have been made to extend the railway into parts of the country not previously served.

A third, future, stage is the creation of a pan-African rail network. This can be said to have begun with the vision of Cecil Rhodes, who foresaw a line running the length of the continent, from the Cape to Cairo. Rhodes' legacy is the fact that most of the railways in southern Africa were built to the same 1,067 mm (3 ft 6 in) gauge, and several countries are now linked together. In the 1920s, a through service operated from Cape Town to Bukama, at the upper limit of navigation on the River Congo. Southern African politics at present preclude such services, but in theory it would be possible for trains from Cape Town to travel to Kindu (Zaire); to Lobito, Angola's main port; and to Dar-es-Salaam, the capital of Tanzania.

The 1,860 km (1,162 mile) line from Zambia to Dar-es-Salaam was a major undertaking, only completed in 1975. Gabon, which emerged from the colonial era without any railways, is now building a line of 695 km (434 miles). The first section should open in 1978. Thus in Africa at least, railways are still regarded as a vital part of a nation's infrastructure.

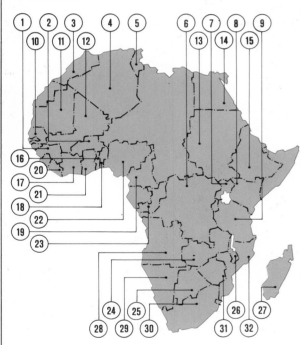

1	Guinea	p 198
2	Upper Volta	p 198
3	Morocco	p 198
4	Algeria	p 198
5	Tunisia	p 198
6	Zaire	p 199
7	Uganda *see* EAR	p 200
8	Kenya *see* EAR	p 200
9	Tanzania *see* EAR	p 200
10	Senegal	p 198
11	Mauritania	p 198
12	Mali	p 198
13	Sudan	p 197
14	Egypt	p 197
15	Ethiopia	p 197
16	Togo	p 199
17	Ivory Coast	p 198
18	Benin	p 199
19	Cameroon	p 199
20	Liberia	p 198
21	Ghana	p 199
22	Nigeria	p 199
23	Congo	p 199
24	Zambia	p 200
25	Botswana (South Africa)	p 201
26	Malawi	p 200
27	Malagasy Republic	p 200
28	Angola	p 199
29	S. W. Africa (South Africa)	p 201
30	South Africa	p 201
31	Rhodesia	p 201
32	Mozambique	p 201

EGYPT *Egyptian Republic Railways*

Although much of Egypt appears to be far from the railway, most of the population is confined to the delta and Nile valley. These inhabited areas are as well served by rail as many densely populated areas of Europe.

As early as 1834, a railway was proposed from Alexandria to Suez as a means of expediting the Indian mails. Work on such a line began in 1851 with Robert Stephenson as engineer: Cairo was reached in 1856 and Suez in 1858 (though the stretch across the desert was made unnecessary by the opening of the Suez Canal, and was dismantled 20 years later). Stephenson's appointment was no doubt responsible for the standard gauge being used on the Egyptian railways.

The system developed in two separate groups, the comprehensive network in the delta, and the Upper Egypt (or Nile valley) railway. The two were not linked at Cairo until 1898. South of Luxor, the Upper Egypt line was 1,067 mm (3 ft 6 in) gauge (standardized in 1926). At Shellal steamers waited to convey passengers to Sudan, and this line's completion in 1898 was seen as a link in Rhodes' envisaged Cape to Cairo route.

The two world wars internationalized the system further. By 1918, Egyptian stock could be seen in Jerusalem. During the Second World War, the north coast line reached Tobruk (Libya); and Egypt was linked with Europe when the Lebanese coastal railway was completed. Political turmoil in the Middle East since the end of the Second World War has prevented any through services from being developed.

Egypt

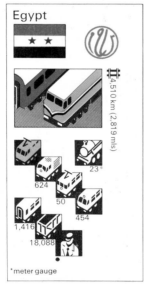

The steam locomotives all belong to the Basse Egypt Railway, a meter-gauge system of 253 route-km based at Mansura. Serving the delta is the 750 mm Egyptian Delta Light Railway, once 950 route-km but being replaced by buses. EDLR totals are therefore not included in the data panel.

*meter gauge

Due to the civil war, few trains are now running in Ethiopia. The 950 mm gauge Northern Railway closed in 1976; mid-1977, the southern line was cut between Dire Dawa and Djibouti.

Ethiopia

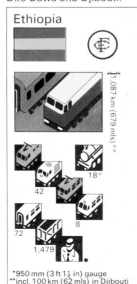

*950 mm (3 ft 1½ in) gauge
**incl. 100 km (62 mls) in Djibouti

SUDAN *Sudan Railways*

The first railway in Sudan opened in 1875, as a means of circumnavigating a waterfall on the Nile. Running south from Wādī Halfā', it eventually extended 270 km (168 miles) to Kerma. It was essentially a military railway, used by the government of Egypt (first Turkish, then British) to intervene in Sudan. Rendered unnecessary by later developments, it was closed in 1905. It was built to the same 1,067 mm (3 ft 6 in) gauge as lines then under construction in the Cape, and these two decisions undoubtedly influenced the choice of gauge for many African railways and may have sparked the idea of a Cape to Cairo line. The first of the present lines is also of military origin, built by General Kitchener across the Nubian desert to Khartoum during his campaign against the Mahdist revolt (1897–9). Kitchener was certainly aware that his line might form a part of the Cape to Cairo route and insisted upon equipment of 1,067 mm (3 ft 6 in) gauge.

The next quarter century saw the north effectively opened up. Trains reached the Red Sea in 1905, Al-Ubayid in 1912 and Kassalā in 1924. The south had to be more patient: the branch south from Sennar opened in 1954, and the first trains did not reach Wāw until late in 1961. Even now the system is regarded as incomplete, as at present the provincial capital of Jūbā has only the railways-operated White Nile steamer service. Since cotton and cottonseed are the principal cash crops of Sudan, accounting for 60 percent of the country's export earnings, the Gezira Light Railway serving the cotton fields is of great importance.

The staff figure includes those operating the river steamers over routes totaling 3,480 km. All totals exclude the 600 mm Gezira Light Railway: more than 800 km of track used only when picking cotton.

Sudan

* only about half are active

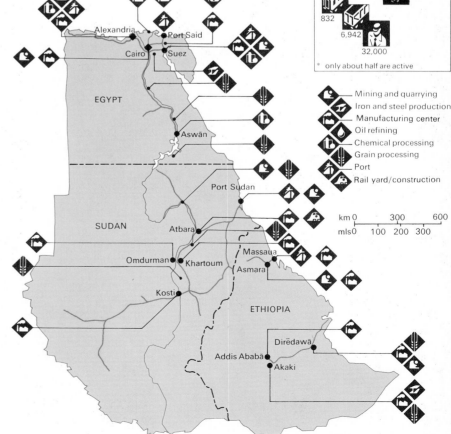

- Mining and quarrying
- Iron and steel production
- Manufacturing center
- Oil refining
- Chemical processing
- Grain processing
- Port
- Rail yard/construction

km 0   300   600
mls 0   100 200 300

West Africa

ALGERIA *Société Nationale des Chemins de Fer Algériens (SNCFA)*
The first line in Algeria in 1862 and from 1863 was worked by the French Paris, Lyon and Mediterranean Railway. The PLM acquired other lines in Algeria, including some leased from the French Colonial Department. Two other major railway companies were established: the Algerian State Railway extending from Tunisia to Algiers, with a subcenter at Oran including the 1,055 mm (3 ft 5⅜ in) gauge line south to Colomb-Béchar in the desert; and the Algerian Western Railway, worked by the PLM from 1922. In 1933 a joint administration was set up, the *CF Algériens*, but with what was now the French state railway still involved as major partner. In 1939 came financial autonomy and the present name was adopted. The line along the coast is standard. Bulk traffic transport on Algeria's railways is assuming increasing importance due to the extensive exploitation of mineral deposits. Most lines running inland are narrow gauge. Exceptions are the Touggourt branch, standardized in 1957 when oil was discovered, and the line to Djebel Onk, built to exploit phosphate deposits (part is Algeria's only electric line).

Algeria

3,942 km (2,450 mls)

60
356
75
618
12,833

Algeria totals include all items ordered during the 5 Year Plan which ended in 1977. There are two major gauges, standard and 1,055 mm, as well as 120 km of meter gauge. 600 mm gauge military lines were the first in Morocco. Totaling 1,888 km, in 1915 they opened to the public. All have been converted to standard gauge, the first by 1923. The first electric line was opened in 1927. An Algerian line extended into what is now Tunisia in 1876. Thus the lines NW of Tunis are standard gauge. In 1897 a meter gauge line was built to exploit the phosphates at Gafsa. Today three-quarters of the system is meter gauge.

Morocco

2,029 km (1,261 mls)

194*
122
299
10,883

* 41% of the system electrified

Tunisia

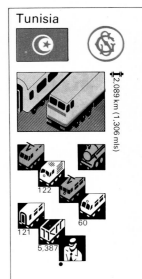

2,089 km (1,306 mls)

122
60
121
5,387

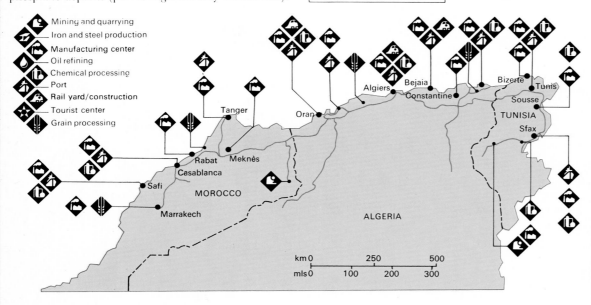

Mining and quarrying
Iron and steel production
Manufacturing center
Oil refining
Chemical processing
Port
Rail yard/construction
Tourist center
Grain processing

Tanger
Oran
Algiers Bejaia Bizerte Tunis
Constantine Sousse
Rabat Meknès TUNISIA
Casablanca Sfax
Safi
MOROCCO ALGERIA
Marrakech

km 0   250   500
mls 0   100   200   300

Dakar-Bamako train, Senegal.

Mauritania

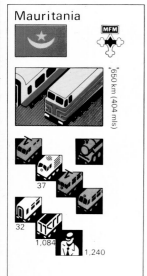

650 km (404 mls)

37
32
1,084
1,240

Senegal

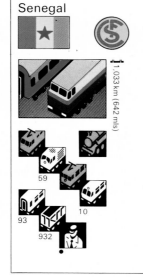

1,033 km (642 mls)

59
93
10
932

Mali

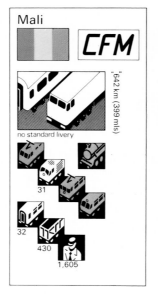

CFM

642 km (399 mls)

no standard livery

31
32
430
1,605

Guinea

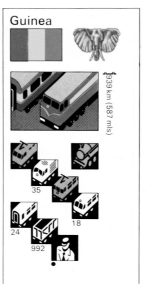

939 km (587 mls)

35
24
18
992

Liberia

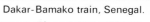

493 km (308 mls)

no standard livery

39
2
18
1,043

Ivory Coast and Upper Volta

RAN

1,173 km (730 mls)

68
178
18
1,277

Mauritania's railway was opened in 1963, to ship out iron ore discovered at Fdérik. Passengers are also carried. The line is standard gauge, with an odd L-shaped route caused by the need to avoid the Spanish Sahara: this added an extra 80 route-km. At Choum, where the line turns north, is a tunnel almost 2 km long. Shifting sand constantly threatens to bury 80 km of the line.

Until the dissolution of the Federation of Mali in 1960, the lines in Senegal and Mali were part of one company, known since 1933 as the Dakar-Niger line. It was built in 4 stages by the French colonial administration to facilitate penetration of the Senegal River valley. The first line linked the mouth of the navigable Senegal River with Dakar's deep-water harbor. This

line, Senegal's first, opened in 1885. The next stage linked the upper limit of the Senegal navigation (at Kayes) with the Niger at Koulikoro. Begun in 1881 but not completed until 1904, this was Mali's first line. In 1924 a link between the 2 lines was opened. Since then, several branches have opened in Senegal, but there has been no railway building.

A meter gauge line was begun in 1900. By 1914 it had reached Kankan. Construction was due to begin in 1975 on the 1,200 km standard gauge Trans-Guinea Railway, replacing some of this meter gauge. Progress made so far is unknown, and only meter gauge totals are included here (so excluding the 134 km CF de Boké, opened in 1973 with 15 diesel locomotives).

There are 3 railways in Liberia, all engaged with the mining of iron ore. All run inland from a suitable port, and the only 2 which meet (at the same port, Monrovia) are of different gauges. The first was opened in 1951, to 1,067 mm gauge. The 2 later lines, 348 km, are standard gauge, the southernmost being built for trains of 14,000 tons capacity.

The meter gauge Ivory Coast Railway (sometimes called the CF Abidjan-Niger) runs inland from Abidjan to the capital of Upper Volta. Despite serving 2 countries, it is one administrative unit. The first stretch opened in 1904, but trains did not enter Upper Volta until 1934, and Ouagadougou until 1954. The line has been fully diesel since 1956.

Central Africa 1

Ghana

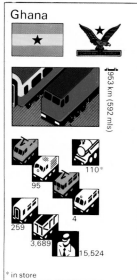

Railway equipment first arrived in Ghana in 1873 when the British governor Garnet Wolseley decided it might help him to win an Ashanti war. But he managed without, and it was not until gold was discovered that a railway was considered. Construction began from Sekondi in 1898, reaching Tarkwa in 1901 after great hardships. The line got to Kumasi in 1903. Another from the capital Accra inland was begun in 1909. It finally reached Kumasi in 1923, completing a circuitous route of 583 km. A more direct route from Sekondi to Accra, via Achiasi, was completed in 1956.

953 km (592 mls)

95   110*

259   4

3,689   15,524

* in store

Togo

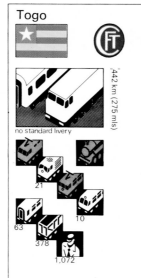

442 km (275 mls)

no standard livery

21   11

63   10

378

1,072

Benin

579 km (359 mls)

no standard livery

11   11

28   11

387

1,588

Cameroon

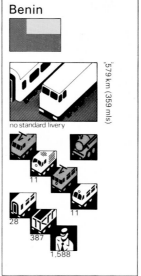

1,173 km (727 mls)

81   11

80   11

1,243

3,094

Congo

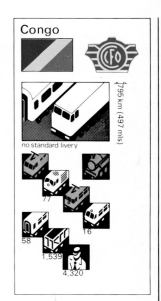

795 km (497 mls)

no standard livery

77

58   16

1,539

4,320

Benin and Togo have similar systems opened at about the same time (*circa* 1905). Both are meter gauge; both are fully dieselized with equipment resembling that in so many other former French colonies (though Togo was German until 1914).

Cameroon's meter gauge system was begun in 1906 by the German colonial administration. After the 1914–18 War, the French extended it to Yaoundé. Since independence it has been extended another 633 km, reaching Ngaoundéré in 1974.

Zaire

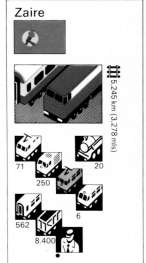

5,245 km (3,278 mls)

71   20

250

6

562

8,400

ZAIRE AND CONGO *Chemin de Fer Congo-Océan (CFCO)*
Société Nationale des Chemins de Fer Zairois (SNCZ)

Railways in Zaire and Congo make better sense if considered with the rivers which still form an integral part of the area's transport system. Zaire's first line opened in 1898 around the rapids which keep ocean-going ships below Matadi. It linked Matadi with Kinshasa, terminus of river services up the Congo, and Kasai. Congo's main railway is a similar line on the other side of the river, completed in 1934. Transport up the Congo was improved by lines around two other obstacles: from Kisangani to Ubundu, and from Kindu to Kongolo. From there the river is navigable to Bukama. Rails reached Bukama from southern Africa in 1919, and these connections were seen as part of the Cape to Cairo route. The Congo River lines were built by a company formed in 1902 to build the missing link from the Congo to the Nile. Today such a route is partly supplied by the 600 mm (1 ft 11⅝ in) gauge Vicicongo line running west from Aketi.

Angola

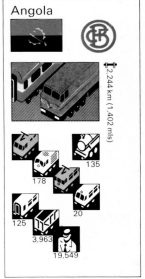

2,244 km (1,402 mls)

135

178

192   4

125   3,963

19,549

NIGERIA *Nigerian Railway Corporation*

Nigeria's earliest lines were built as separate entities and only joined up as an afterthought. Some of them were built as 762 mm (2 ft 6 in) gauge light railways, but these have all eventually been superseded by railways of 1,067 mm (3 ft 6 in) gauge.

Railway construction began near Lagos in 1896. By the time it reached Ibadan, 192 km (120 miles) inland, work was almost complete on a light railway linking the administrative center of Zungeru to the head of navigation on the Kaduna River (1901). The main line reached Jebba in 1909, but its pace had proved too slow for the new High Commissioner of Northern Nigeria, Sir Percy Girouard (one of Africa's foremost railwaymen: previously he had been Director of Sudan Railways, President of Egyptian Railways Board, and Director of Railways during the Boer War). He began a line from the Niger River port of Baro north toward Kano. It opened throughout in 1911; the original line did not meet it until 1912. Work on the Eastern Railway began in 1913. It reached its initial objective – the coal near Enugu – in 1916, but did not join up with the other lines until 1926.

The last line built was the Maiduguri Extension, completed in 1964. However, an ambitious scheme contained in the Third National Development Plan (1975–80) envisages most or all of the 1,067 mm (3 ft 6 in) gauge lines being replaced by standard gauge lines. Work was scheduled to begin in 1977.

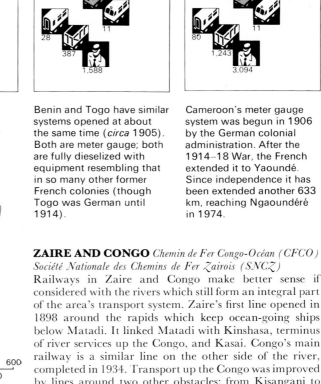

Nigeria

3,523 km (2,202 mls)

133*

189   4

655

6,979

* in 1974 : other totals for 1976

Since the Bauchi Light Railway, which ran from Zaria to Jos, closed in 1957, all Nigeria's lines have been of the 1,067 mm gauge. However, work was due to begin in 1977 on the plan to convert the entire network to standard gauge.

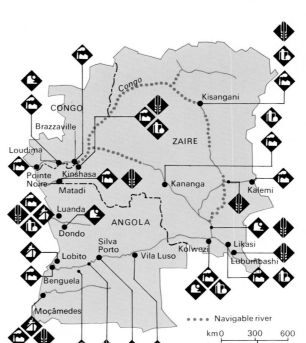

... Navigable river

Angola has 4 unconnected railways, each running inland from a port. Only the line from Porto Amboim is not 1,067 mm gauge, though the Luanda State Railways were regauged in the 1960s. The most important line is the Benguela, begun in 1903: it meets the Zaire system at Dilolo. But the still-smoldering civil war has stopped through traffic.

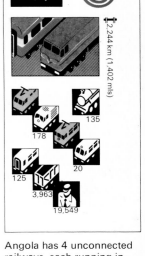

Central Africa 11

EAST AFRICAN RAILWAYS

In 1948, Tanganyika Railways and the Kenya and Uganda Railway amalgamated to form East African Railways. While the union was effective under British influence, differences between the governments arising since independence caused such difficulties that EAR has again separated into its two constituent parts.

Unusually for former British possessions in Africa, EAR operates on the meter gauge. In Tanzania's case this is because most of the lines were built by the Germans, whose colony it was until the First World War. The Kenya and Uganda Railway seems to have been built to this gauge owing to a series of misunderstandings because no one in Britain wanted it built, seeing it as a mad imperialist venture on which the expenditure of public money was unjustified. Finally, grudgingly, it was built to meter gauge because cheap second-hand equipment would be available from India.

The first line in the area was the 600 mm (1 ft 11⅝ in) gauge, 96 km (60 mile), Central African Railway. It was later taken up and relaid as a tramway in Mombasa. The first of the present lines was started from Tanga in 1891, but it was only 40 km (25 miles) from the coast in 1896 when building began at Mombasa. In 1901 Lake Victoria was reached, in 1914 Lake Tanganyika. Kampala's first train arrived in 1931, Pakwach's in 1964. All these lines were built originally to aid the area's agricultural and industrial development.

Tazara Railway

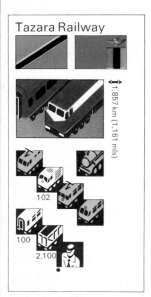

1,857 km (1,161 mls)

102
100
2,100

Zambia

ZR

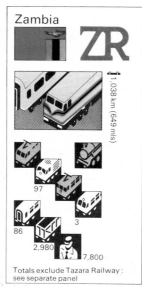

1,038 km (649 mls)

97
3
86
2,980
7,800

Totals exclude Tazara Railway: see separate panel

TAZARA RAILWAY *Tanzania Zambia Railway Authority*
The Tazara Railway links Zambia Railways with Dar-es-Salaam, 970 km (600 miles) lying in Tanzania and 890 km (550 miles) in Zambia. It is run as a single entity and has therefore been kept separate from the other totals for these countries. Built with generous technical and financial assistance from China, its successful completion has without doubt earned China enormous prestige in Africa. China provided 25,000 men, one-third of the workforce, and an interest-free loan of $420 million with generous repayment terms. It is the largest railway construction project completed since the Second World War. The line is built to Zambia's 1,067 mm (3 ft 6 in) gauge and was completed in 1975. Over one million tons of freight was carried by the line in its first year of operation.

For Tanzania, the line will develop the neglected southwest, enabling vast coal and iron ore deposits to be exploited. Zambia sees the line as an essential link to that part of Africa with which she feels sympathetic. Before the Tazara line was opened, all her routes led south, and events have conspired to make her wish it had been built much earlier: Rhodesia's unilateral declaration of independence in 1965 closed the Victoria Falls route, and the Angolan civil war has seriously disrupted Benguela Railway traffic since 1975.

One 16 km (10 mile) section between Mlimba and Makambako in Tanzania contains 30 percent of all earthworks, bridges and tunnels on the line, including Irangi No. 3 tunnel, which attains a length of almost 2.5 km (1.5 miles).

Kenya, Uganda and Tanzania

EAR

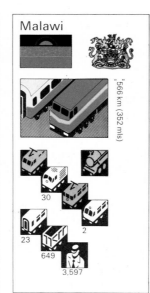

5,895 km (3,663 mls)

235
192
536
17,000
43,539

Totals exclude Tazara Railway: see separate panel

Malawi

566 km (352 mls)

30
2
23
649
3,597

The East African unified rail system is at present being dismembered, after 28 years, because of disagreements between owning governments. Normal services between Tanzania and Kenya ceased in 1974, and Lake Victoria car ferries stopped early in 1976. No figures for the individual countries are available yet.

Zambia Railways formed in 1967 when the Rhodesia Railways Unitary System split. Before, the lines were part of Rhodesia Railways administered from Bulawayo. The dividing point was the center of the Victoria Falls bridge. The first line opened in Zambia in July 1905, though the bridge was not opened until September: it was built with equipment swung across the gorge on a cableway. Before 1910, the rails were at Zaire's border. One of the line's main functions is to transport the copper belt's production, though when opened it was seen as part of the Cape to Cairo route.

Malawi's first line opened in 1908 and the system is still expanding. Since 1970 it has linked 2 separate Mozambique lines, and data panel totals do not include the 112 km Salima-Lilongwe line due to open before 1978. Malawi Railways operates the Lake Nyasa steamer service.

Malagasy's first line was opened in 1903 by the French colonial administration. The development of the northern system of lines was completed in 1923. In 1934 an isolated line opened, running inland from the port of Manakara. A 253 km line to link this to the others has been begun.

Malagasy

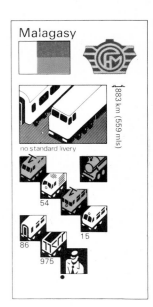

883 km (559 mls)

no standard livery

54
15
86
975

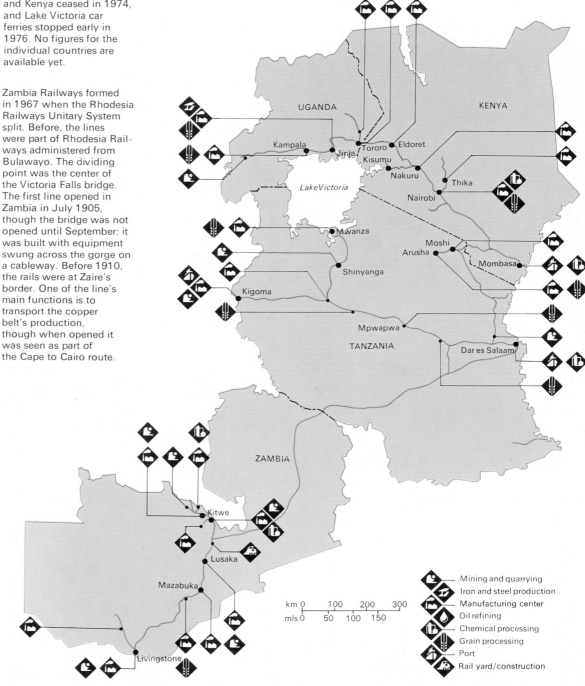

UGANDA
Kampala
Jinja
Tororo
Kisumu
Eldoret
Nakuru
Nairobi
Thika
Lake Victoria
Mwanza
Moshi
Arusha
Mombasa
KENYA
Shinyanga
Kigoma
Mpwapwa
TANZANIA
Dar es Salaam
ZAMBIA
Kitwe
Lusaka
Mazabuka
Livingstone

km 0   100   200   300
mls 0   50   100   150

Mining and quarrying
Iron and steel production
Manufacturing center
Oil refining
Chemical processing
Grain processing
Port
Rail yard/construction

Southern Africa

SOUTH AFRICA *South African Railways (SAR)*
The closely knit, efficient network of the South African Railways began as a series of individual and unconnected enterprises at a time when the whole land south of the Zambesi River was entirely pastoral and being slowly colonized by Europeans whose aims extended no further than farming. Short lines were pioneered inland from Cape Town and Port Elizabeth. Mountain ranges inland, and the experiences of those who had taken part in the Great Trek, had suggested that there was little to be gained by carrying the rails further inland, until, in 1869, there came the sensational discovery of diamonds in great quantity at Kimberley. Even then, railway construction did not proceed rapidly. For one thing there was the question of gauge to be settled. The Cape Town and Wellington Railway had set out on the standard gauge, but when it came to carrying the line northward to the diamond mines, and the severe terrain of the Hex River Pass had to be dealt with, the government's consulting engineer, William G. Brounger, recommended 1,067 mm (3 ft 6 in) as the standard for Cape Province. It was then that the race to connect up Kimberley with Cape Town began in earnest, while a rival line driving inland from Port Elizabeth had the same objective. Railways were the only alternative to the primitive carts used by the pioneer trekkers. Something more reliable had to be used in conveying the precious diamonds to ports from which they could be shipped to Europe.

The gold race
An even more dramatic change came over the whole South African scene in 1886, when gold was discovered on the Witwatersrand. By a strange twist of irony this discovery, which transformed the entire economic and financial structure of South Africa, was made at the very place where the peace-loving pastoral farmers of the south had ended their trek in search of a place where they could settle and till the land. From that resting place rose Johannesburg. At the very start there was a railway race, not between trains, but between two rival organizations seeking to be first in connecting the gold fields with the sea. One was the British, under the dashing leadership of Cecil Rhodes, pressing ahead with the extension of the Cape Government Railway northward from Kimberley. The other was the Dutch coming westward from Lourenço Marques (now Maputo) in Portuguese East Africa. Due to Rhodes' tenacity and diplomacy, the first train from the south steamed into Johannesburg in September 1892, nearly three years ahead of the Dutch. In the British colony of Natal, also, railways were being pushed inland from Durban, and these came prominently into the picture as military targets during the Boer War. After the end of the war much was done to consolidate railway working in the four states that were eventually brought together in the Union of South Africa in 1910. In the period between the end of the war and the Union, the Cape Government and the Natal Government Railways carried on as previously, while the lines in the two former Boer republics operated under the name of the Central South African Railways. The three organizations were finally merged to form the South African Railways shortly after the establishment of the Union.

Since 1910 the system has developed into one of the greatest in the world, operating entirely on the 1,067 mm (3 ft 6 in) gauge. In recent years great progress has been made with electrification at both ends of the system. The busy suburban area of Cape Town, and the main line as far north as Wellington, is so equipped, while the intense network around Johannesburg is a natural place for its advantages to be exploited to the full. At the same time extensive use is still being made of steam. The South African Railways, with the cooperation of British firms, developed the steam locomotive to its highest degree on the 1,067 mm (3 ft 6 in) gauge, and it is still being maintained to high standards. Except on the Blue Train, most motive power is steam in the central part of the system south of Kimberley and north of Beaufort West. The system now includes, however, the railways in the former German colony of South West Africa, where near-desert conditions and absence of water have favored the introduction of diesel-electric locomotives on the line running north from De Aar Junction to Windhoek.

4-8-2 moving coal trucks at Wankie Colliery, Rhodesia.

Mozambique

There are 6 lines in Mozambique, linking ports with the interior. Since 1970, 2 of the major ones are linked via Malawi, and plans exist to join them to the southern Maputo system. The first was begun in 1892 by a contractor under pressure from Cecil Rhodes to open a line from Rhodesia to the sea quickly. Beira-Umtali was complete by 1898 and widened to 1,067 mm in 1900. Today only the line from João Belo is not this gauge. Mozambique also runs the 224 km Swaziland railway, opened in 1964.

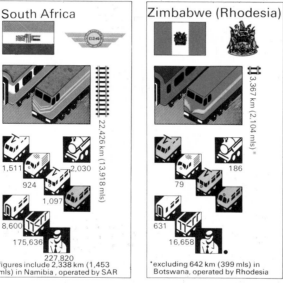

Rhodesia's first line opened to Bulawayo, 1897. In 1899 Umtali-Salisbury opened, and when the two were joined in 1902, 3,256 km of continuous railway existed from Cape Town to Beira. The system was to continue north from Gwelo to Lake Tanganyika, but it was diverted to the Wankie coalfield and so crossed into what is now Zambia at Victoria Falls. Until 1967, the Zambian lines were run from Bulawayo as part of Rhodesia Railways. RR has operated the Botswana line since 1966.

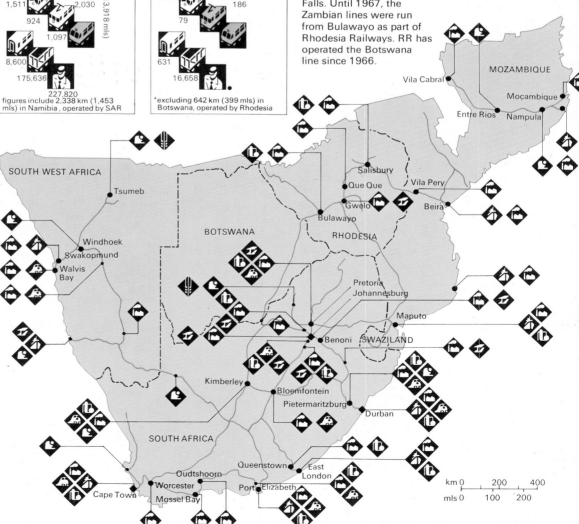

Canada and United States

CANADA

Railway development in Canada began along the line of the St. Lawrence River, with the Grand Trunk, authorized in 1852 and incorporating some earlier projects. It knew no international frontiers. When its first line was completed it ran from Sarnia through Toronto and Montreal to Portland, Maine, and by this provided a means of communication with Europe during the winter months when the St. Lawrence estuary was frozen over. At its western end it came to penetrate into the USA. It was, however, thought desirable to have a line to an Atlantic port that was independent of the USA, particularly as relations had not been entirely amicable since the War of Independence; and thus was born the concept of the "Intercolonial Railway," connecting Montreal with the maritime provinces of New Brunswick and Nova Scotia. After much discussion, extending over more than 20 years, the Intercolonial was authorized, and was built by that great engineer Sandford Fleming, who later made the first surveys for the Canadian Pacific. The undertaking to build a railway connecting British Columbia with the eastern provinces was contained in an agreement signed in Ottawa in July 1870, and Fleming's first surveys led the federal government to decide that the line should pass through the main range of the Rocky Mountains by way of the Yellowhead Pass.

Although some contracts were let for the western end of the line, eastward from Vancouver, progress of the work under government control was slow and unsatisfactory, and it was not until ten years after the signing of the Ottawa agreement of 1870 that the work was put on a sound business footing. An agreement was signed in England in September 1880 between the government and a syndicate of Canadian businessmen, the work of construction being handed over to a company to be formed by the syndicate. The "big four" of this arrangement were George Stephen, Donald A. Smith (afterwards Lord Strathcoma), R. B. Angus, and a fiery entrepreneur named J. J. Hill. It was the last mentioned who made perhaps the greatest contribution of all, because he brought in, as general manager, that most outstanding of railwaymen, W. C. van Horne, then an American citizen. The line across Canada was completed in November 1885, with the driving of the last spike at Craigellachie, in the Rockies of British Columbia.

The success of the Canadian Pacific in developing the prairie regions – as King George V, when Prince of Wales, said in a speech made in London in May 1908 – ". . . it helped to make a nation," led to the building of competitive lines. Although when it came to the actual construction, the Canadian Pacific did not go through the Yellowhead Pass, but took the shorter, yet far more difficult Kicking Horse Pass, its two rivals from Winnipeg to Pacific tidewater both went through the Yellowhead, alongside each other, the Canadian Northern to come

abreast of the Canadian Pacific in the canyons west of Kamloops and eventually to reach Vancouver, and the Grand Trunk Pacific to continue northwestward through absolutely virgin country to Prince Rupert. Both these railroads, and the lines connecting with them from the east at Winnipeg, fell into financial difficulties and were kept going during the First World War by substantial government loans. All these diverse lines were finally amalgamated with the Grand Trunk and the Intercolonial in 1922 to form the huge Canadian National Railways, publicly owned but working alongside the privately owned Canadian Pacific.

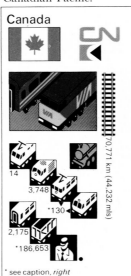

Canada

The great majority of the powered rolling stock is diesel. A few are electric, and there are also 10 Turbotrain sets. The freight total excludes 17,700 privately owned. The figures are for 1973, the latest available.

70,771 km (44,232 mls)

14
3,748
*130
2,175
*186,653

* see caption, *right*

Below Streaking through the Rockies.

Bottom Toronto sunset.

USA

In the USA railways began with projects to connect the Atlantic seaports with the rich valley of the Ohio River, between which lay densely wooded mountain ranges of the Alleghenies and the Appalachians. The Baltimore and Ohio, dating from 1827, and the Chesapeake and Ohio by their names indicate the extent of their first activities. Another famous early line was the Pennsylvania, from Pittsburgh over the Alleghenies to Atlantic tidewater at Philadelphia. West of the mountains a considerable network began to develop from Chicago and St. Louis down the valley of the Mississippi. This was one of the main battle areas in the Civil War, and the railways came to play a major part in the conflict. It was during the war that Abraham Lincoln realized the importance of having communication with the west coast and ordered the hasty completion of the partly finished lines of the Union Pacific and Central Pacific, to meet in the famous "gold spike" ceremony at Promontory, Utah, in 1869. In the meantime the great proliferation of lines radiating from Chicago earned that city its title of the greatest railway center in the world.

Famous Routes

In main lines alone, running southwest and west there are no fewer than four different routes to Kansas City and beyond – those of the Illinois Central Gulf, the Sante Fe, the Rock Island and the Burlington; while to Omaha, en route to the far west, there are five routes all covering different tracts of the intervening country. Due northward, jockeying for position as it were beside the shores of Lake Michigan, are the Chicago and North Western and the Chicago and Milwaukee, St. Paul and Pacific, once steam rivals in a high-speed passenger service. From the east, crowding around the head of the lake, come the Baltimore and Ohio, the New York Central, the Pennsylvania and other great names, with the Wabash, the Monon, and the Illinois Central coming up from the south.

The discovery of gold in the Colorado Rockies, coupled with the extreme difficulty of the terrain, led to the building of a network of narrow gauge lines, weaving their ways through seemingly impossible mountain gorges. One of the most famous of these, remaining today as a major standard gauge artery through this region, is the Denver and Rio Grande Western. Two other routes to the west coast were the Atchison, Topeka and Santa Fé, from Chicago, through Kansas City and Albuquerque to Los Angeles, and the Great Northern, from St. Paul running just south of the Canadian border and rivaling the Canadian Pacific to Spokane and Seattle. But the Great Northern did not have the territory south of the US border to itself. From Minneapolis westward there were two other routes, those of the Northern Pacific and of the Chicago, Milwaukee, St. Paul and Pacific. All three by diverse routes made their way to Spokane and then through the highly picturesque Cascade Range to the west coast. Today the Great Northern and the Northern Pacific are included in the Burlington Northern Railroad, running in a degree of competition with the Milwaukee. Connecting the cities of the west coast and continuing south alongside the Mexican border to New Orleans was the Southern Pacific.

Into the twentieth century

Towards the end of the nineteenth century railways covered the entire United States, and the numerous private companies entered the new century on a great wave of confidence and prosperity. A huge manufacturing industry had grown up to supply the needs of the railways in locomotives, passenger and freight cars, signaling and track equipment. Few of the railway companies built their own, though some, like the Pennsylvania, had extensive research facilities. Names like the New York Central, Union Pacific, Norfolk and Western, Erie, Louisville and Nashville, quite apart from the great pioneers, became household words in the world of transport. Delegations from celebrated railways in Europe traveled to the USA to study methods; and although exuberance and over-confidence sometimes led to bad accidents and serious loss of life, a tremendous bank of experience in operation was being built up, of which the benefit was reaped in later years.

Mining and quarrying
Iron and steel production
Manufacturing center
Oil refining
Chemical processing
Grain processing
Port
Rail yard/construction
Tourist center

America's railways are divided into Class I and Class II roads. Class I are those with annual operating revenues which exceed $10m. There were 52 in 1977, owning 96% of America's lines. Figures are for Class I only.

USA
Amtrak

216   7
27,350
1,590
230
6,471
1,331,705
482,882
* excluding cabooses

319,058 km (199,411 mls)

km
0   200   400   600

0   100   200   300
mls

Below left Rio Grande-Durango 473 on turntable.

The railways of the USA compared with those at the scene of conflict were very little affected by the First World War, although in 1917 – almost nine months after the USA declared war on the Axis powers – Woodrow Wilson put the whole system under government control, a measure that was to be enforced for over two years.

American railways entered on the period between the two world wars with renewed strength and for a short period were moderately successful. It was then that serious competition from the increasing use of road transport began to appear, although because of the sometimes great distances involved it was at first not as serious a threat as that seen in such countries as Britain. But the period of the great slump of the 1930s struck hard, leading to a decline in equipment and manpower. Despite these setbacks many spectacular new services, using diesel power, were introduced.

The Second World War, on two fronts, made tremendous demands, particularly to the Pacific coast, and modern signaling technology was applied toward securing a greater traffic of trains on single-line track. Both steam and diesel locomotives were called upon for outstanding feats, not only of power output but of aggregate distances traveled per month. In the immediate postwar era British engineers went to the USA to learn how it had been done. But the great recession soon started. With the rapid

development of internal airlines it became unfashionable to travel by train. Patronage of great express trains of international fame, such as The Twentieth Century Limited, languished; postal traffic was transferred to the air, and a train like the Fast Mail of the Santa Fe found itself with no business at all, and long-distance trucking on state subsidized highways began to supersede the freight train. Several famous railways went bankrupt. Others wished to discontinue altogether their unprofitable passenger business. This the federal government would not allow, and in 1971 the National Railroad Passenger Corporation (Amtrak) was set up, to support the operation

of intercity passenger trains with federal funds. This provided a network of main line passenger services, while in the meantime, with greatly improved technology and immense drive, the railways themselves began to win back much of the freight traffic lost to the roads. There have been major mergers of companies and much pruning of hitherto redundant services. The largest of the mergers has been that of Conrail, in 1976, a grouping of six bankrupt eastern railways, supported by a large loan from the federal government. This group includes such previous giants as the Pennsylvania and the New York Central, the financial plight of which is enough to show the severity of the recession suffered by the American railways generally after the end of the Second World War.

Today, besides the activities of Amtrak, the principal accent is upon freight, in which the American railway have developed to an unparalleled extent the technology of handling huge loads at medium-high speed. At the points of traffic concentration all the latest classification yards are fully computerized, while the operations over entire railways, like the Southern at Atlanta, are monitored from a single operations center, through remotely controlled color light signaling and radio communication with train crews. The art of handling such great trains at speed, and particularly on steep grades, has become a highly developed science.

Central America

Central America may be divided into two parts: Mexico, and the rest, for Mexico alone has acquired a nationwide network, originally inspired by engineers and capital from the USA. In the rest of Central America, interest has concentrated on routes across the isthmus and none of these have been developed into adequate national rail systems. This can be attributed in part to the difficult terrain which makes railway construction so difficult and in part to the climate which compounds these difficulties, the torrential rain leading to frequent washouts. But, generally speaking, the railways here, like those in Africa, have been built by outside interests for purposes of exploitation rather than national development.

The first Central American railway was built to provide transport across the isthmus. The Panama Railroad, which opened in 1855, saved so much time and money by cutting out the voyage around Cape Horn that it was able to charge passengers $25 for the 77 km (48 mile) journey. Another proposal was for a "Ship Railway," with six lines of rails which would carry ships bodily across the isthmus. More recently, some banana-growing states have had lines built by the United Fruit Company of Boston and the Standard Fruit Company of New Orleans, as the best means of facilitating the immediate shipment that this kind of fruit requires.

Mining and quarrying
Iron and steel production
Manufacturing center
Oil refining
Chemical processing
Grain processing
Port
Rail yard/construction

km
0   200   400   600
0   100   200   300
mls

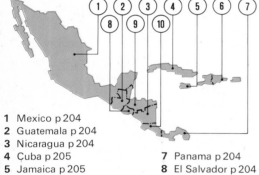

1 Mexico p 204
2 Guatemala p 204
3 Nicaragua p 204
4 Cuba p 205
5 Jamaica p 205
6 Dominican Republic p 205
7 Panama p 204
8 El Salvador p 204
9 Honduras p 204
10 Costa Rica p 204

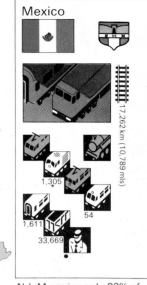

Mexico

17,262 km (10,789 mls)

1,305
54
1,611
33,669

NdeM carries only 82% of all rail traffic. Figures include other lines which own cars. The last steam and only electric locomotives work ore lines.

MEXICO *FC Nacionales de Mexico (N de M)*
Mexico's first train ran in 1850, but the bulk of the present extensive network was constructed in the 20 years after 1880. During that time, 12,300 km (7,687 miles) were built. Most lines are standard gauge, but the nationalized system N de M operates 450 km (280 miles) of 914 mm (3 ft) narrow gauge.

The creation of N de M began in 1908 with the merging of the National Rail Road of Mexico with the Mexican Central Railway. Other railways have been acquired since, but at least two large lines remain independently managed, and N de M can claim to comprise only 71 percent of the Mexican railway system.

The largest of the independents is the FC del Pacifico, once a subsidiary of the USA's Southern Pacific. It stretches 2,140 km (1,330 miles) from Guadalajara to the US border. Incorporated in 1909, this company opened throughout only in 1927.

Guatemala

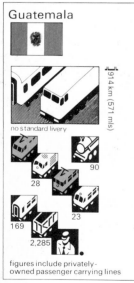

914 km (571 mls)

no standard livery

90
28
169
23
2,285

figures include privately-owned passenger carrying lines

The main rail network in Guatemala belongs to the International Railways of Central America, one of whose lines crosses into El Salvador (where it has been nationalized). This company formed in 1904, though Guatemala's first train had run in 1880. Totals include 95 km owned bu a subsidiary of the American United Fruit Co. Lines are 914 mm gauge.

Honduras

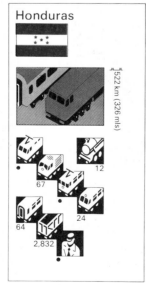

522 km (326 mls)

12
67
24
64
2,832

Honduras's route total is unreliable, because only one quarter of the lines are owned by the government: the others belong to American fruit-growing companies (though all have passenger services). One of the private railways is built to 914 mm gauge, the rest (just over half of the total) to 1,067 mm. Honduras's first train ran in 1869.

El Salvador

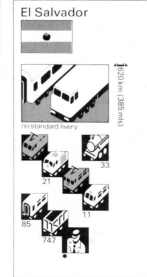

620 km (385 mls)

no standard livery

33
11
85
747

Ferrocarriles Nacional El Salvador were established in 1975 with the merger of 2 lines previously nationalized. The larger section was part of International Railways of Central America until 1974 (still operating in Guatemala). Steam locomotives may not now be working, as the government was hoping to upgrade the San Salvador-Acajutla line by mid-1976.

Nicaragua

318 km (197 mls)

no standard livery

9
10
4 *
1
194
663

* multiple unit sets : there are also 2 gasoline railcars

The only railway of any importance in Nicaragua is the *FC del Pacifico*, both owned and operated by the government. The initial section, from Corinto to Chinandega, was opened in 1881. The line was finished in 1903, though Granada, the inland terminal, had been linked to the railhead since 1886 by a lake steamer service. The gauge is 1,067 mm.

Costa Rica

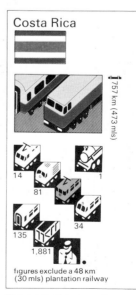

757 km (473 mls)

14
1
81
135
34
1,881

figures exclude a 48 km (30 mls) plantation railway

The original concession for a Costa Rican railway was granted in 1871, but it was not finished until 1890. Running from the Caribbean port of Limón to San José, it connects with the electrified Pacific Railroad to form a route from sea to sea. The Pacific opened in 1910 and was electrified in 1930. Isolated in the south is the FC del Sur.

Panama

441 km (263 mls)

51
1
49
29
1,817
880

Panama has 3 independent lines. The first opened in 1855, a predecessor of the Canal as a means of crossing the Isthmus. It is 1,524 mm gauge.
In 1914 a line was begun from the Pacific port of Armuelles, intended to be part of an intercontinental Mexico-Argentina line.
In the NW a line owned by an American company runs 48 km into Costa Rica.

Caribbean and South America 1

Jamaica

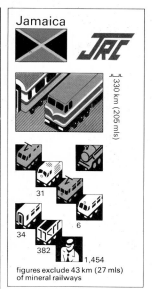

330 km (205 mls)

31

34   6

382

1,454

figures exclude 43 km (27 mls)
of mineral railways

Dominican Republic

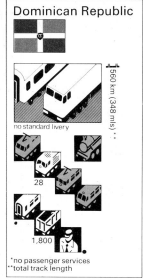

560 km (348 mls)**

no standard livery*

28

6

1,800

*no passenger services
**total track length

Cuba

4,425 km (2,750 mls)

170

*excl. 9,441 km (5,866 mls) sugar
lines **at least 11 km (7 mls) electric

Jamaica's first train ran
in 1845, on the first-ever
British colonial railway.
Now the bauxite industry
provides most traffic (and
2 mine companies own more
cars than the state).
Dominica's railways
suffer from road compet-
ition: passenger services
have ended and the narrow
gauge government lines
may have shut completely.
Cuba has the densest
system in the Caribbean,
but information is sparse.
The diesel total is
a minimum, representing
known orders only. The
vast network of sugar
industry lines is only
used 100 days a year.

Railway construction in South America started very late,
as it was dependent upon the availability of foreign capital
and was adversely affected by the lack of political stability.
However, most of the network now existing was completed
by 1930. Because many of the countries had closer ties with
Europe and the USA than with each other, South America
appears like a group of islands: the separate hinterlands of
each port and their railway lines are often isolated from
each other except by sea. One result has been that a
profusion of gauges was used, at least nine existing in
substantial route lengths being found on the continent. But
much of South America's traffic is still of the mine-to-port
pattern and the lack of interregional trade has not yet
made the break-of-gauge the acute problem it has been in,
for example, Australia. The decision of Paraguay to alter
its gauge in 1911, to make through working with
Argentina possible, was an isolated early example of a
change which may become increasingly common in the
next decade as South America progresses toward the
creation of a standardized rail system that will eventually
cover the whole of the continent and became a major aid to
economic growth.

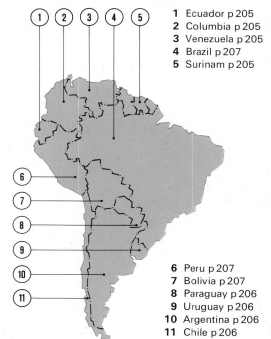

COLOMBIA *Ferrocarriles Nacionales de Colombia (FCN)*
Although Colombia is the third most populous country in
South America, its railway system is somewhat inadequate. Partly this is due to the mountains which divide
the country into several regions between which transport
of any kind has always been difficult. Partly it is due to
political upheavals which culminated in civil war in 1899;
foreign capital was difficult to attract, and the few lines
which were built cost the government dear. As a result, a
national rail system was a long time forming, and Bogotá,
the capital, was for long of secondary importance to the
city of Cali, which was first in acquiring an outlet to the
sea. To this day, the link between Bogotá and the Pacific
port of Buenaventura is extremely circuitous, and the
missing 110 km (69 miles) of the direct route, from Ibagué
to Armenia, is no more than a project. An attempt to build
it started in 1913 but was finally abandoned in 1930. The
Atlantic line was not completed until 1961.

ECUADOR *Empresa de Nacional de Ferrocarriles del Estado*
Railways arrived in Ecuador in 1871, when the line from
Guayaquil up to Quito, the capital, was begun.
Geographical and financial difficulties ensured that it was
not finished until 1908. Although its 3,609 m (11,841 ft)
summit is not high by South American standards, it is one
of the more dramatic Andean lines. The total curvature of
the line amounts to 16,000 degrees, the equivalent of
45 complete circles; many have a radius of only 60.35 m
(198 ft). Between Sibambe and Palmira, the line climbs
1,433 m (4,700 ft) in only 35 km (22 miles), on an actual
grade of 5.5 percent; compensating for the curvature, this
equals a straight 6.6 percent. It is entirely adhesion worked
and accounts for 40 percent of Ecuador's route length.
Making a junction with it are two other 1,067 mm (3 ft
6 in) gauge lines, and there are also two isolated narrower
gauged lines on the coast, at Bahía and Puerto Bolívar.
Much of the equipment in use on the G & Q is very old.

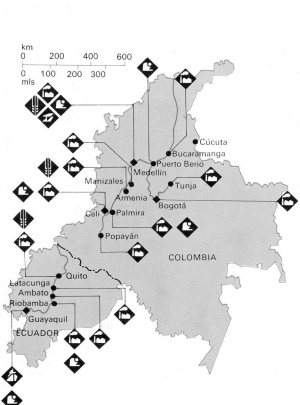

km
0   200   400   600

0   100   200   300
mls

Cúcuta
Bucaramanga
Puerto Berío
Medellín
Manizales
Armenia   Tunja
Cali   Palmira
Bogotá
Popayán
COLOMBIA

Quito
Latacunga
Ambato
Riobamba
Guayaquil
ECUADOR

Colombia

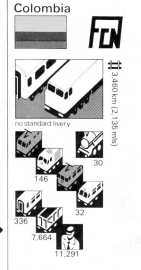

3,460 km (2,135 mls)

no standard livery

30

146

32

336

7,664

11,291

The stock totals for
Colombia must be treated
with caution, for the
sources are unreliable,
particularly about
the extent of dieseliz-
ation. The long-drawn-out
process of nationaliz-
ation (it was started in
1901 and only completed
in 1962) has enabled the
gauge of Colombia's lines
to be made uniform at
914 mm.

Venezuela

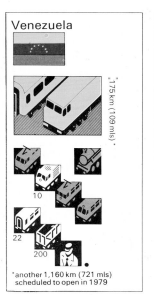

175 km (109 mls)*

146

22

200

*another 1,160 km (721 mls)
scheduled to open in 1979

Venezuela's first line was
begun in 1873. About 1,000
km of narrow gauge lines
were built by 1894 but
all have now closed, the
last in 1967. The govern-
ment is now building a
standard gauge network,
which should extend to
1,339 km in 1979. There
are also 3 mineral
lines totaling 96 route-
km (and not included in
the data panel figures).

Ecuador

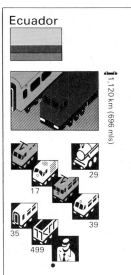

1,120 km (696 mls)

29

17

35   39

499

The Ecuador totals are for
the nationalized railways
and exclude several sugar
plantation lines. Included
are four 1,067 mm gauge
lines (one of which is an
isolated 25 km at Puerto
Bolívar) and two separate
750 mm lines totaling
96 km. The main system is
under 3 divisional man-
agements: Guayaquil-Quito,
the Cuenca branch, and the
San Lorenzo line.

Surinam

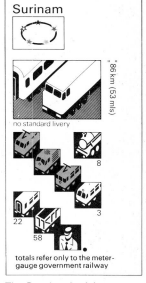

86 km (53 mls)

no standard livery

8

22   3

58

totals refer only to the meter-
gauge government railway

The Dutch colonial government thought railways were
unnecessary in Surinam
because of the waterways,
but eventually opened a
meter gauge line from
Onverwacht to Brownsweg.
It may close because of
road competition (which
has already happened in
neighbouring Guyana), but
70 km of standard gauge
will soon open to service
bauxite mines in the west.

South America 11

CHILE *Empresa de Los Ferrocarriles del Estado (FFCCE)*
Chile claims that the line from Caldera to Copiapó, which opened in 1852, is the oldest in South America. It was not the first, however: that honor goes to a now-defunct railway in Guyana. The Caldera line was built by the American William Wheelwright to exploit the silver and copper ores of Atacama Province. Chile's mineral wealth stimulated many of the early railways. The government became involved from an early date, through having to step in to keep open lines whose economic justification (a mine) had closed. In 1873, the Organic Law for Railway Operation was passed. It established the state railway administration and a plan for a national railway construction policy. The plan envisaged a north-south trunk line through the Central Valley, with cross branches to the coast and to the foothills of the Andes. Today, Chile's rail system conforms very closely to the ideas established by this Law. When it was passed, there existed 950 km (594 miles) of government-owned, and 1,254 km (784 miles) of privately-owned, lines. However, it was not intended to be a vehicle for the nationalization of the railways, and today almost 1,900 km (1,187 miles) of line are still in private ownership. The largest such line is the Antofagasta (Chili) and Bolivia Railway, which operates a meter gauge line over the Andes with a weekly through train to the Bolivian capital, La Paz. It is one of the most financially successful of the Andean lines. Three other lines cross the Andes, including the Arica-La Paz Railway which is isolated from the rest of the Chilean system.

Argentina – traditional steam.

ARGENTINA *Ferrocarriles Argentinos (FA)*
The construction of Argentina's first line began in 1855, built by the English engineer William Bragge using equipment originally destined for the Crimean War which was of the broad gauge of 1,676 mm (5 ft 6 in). The first section opened in 1857. The broad gauge, however accidentally established, was used for all early lines and almost 23,000 km (14,375 miles) now exist. But in 1872, the meter gauge was chosen for the line from Córdoba to Tucumán: it has grown into a system of 13,461 km (8,413 miles). In 1874, the East Argentina Railway chose the standard gauge, and the country now has 3,086 km (1,929 miles) of it. However, there are few problems with breaks of gauge: nearly all the lines were built to facilitate the export of agricultural produce, and nearly all the original railways, of whatever gauge, had access to the port of Buenos Aires, from which the Argentine system spreads like a gigantic fan. Much of the traffic still flows in this pattern, radiating from Buenos Aires. The British maintained their early interest in the development of Argentina's railways, and by the 1920s about 70 percent were British owned. Much of the equipment is still very British in appearance. The railways were nationalized in 1947. Today the state system is divided into six lines, each named after an army general. Four of these lines are broad gauge, and there is one standard 1,676 mm (5 ft 6 in) and one meter.

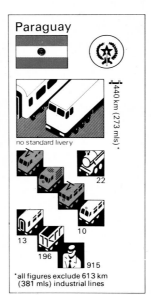

Chile

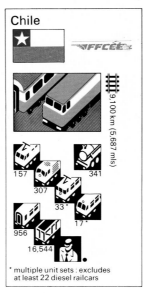

‡9,100 km (5,687 mls)

no standard livery

157   341
307
33
17
956
16,544

* multiple unit sets : excludes at least 22 diesel railcars

Chile's figures include privately owned passenger carrying lines. Of the 5 gauges, the commonest are 1,676 mm and meter.

Paraguay

‡440 km (273 mls)*

22
13   10
196   915

*all figures exclude 613 km (381 mls) industrial lines

Paraguay has 4 separate railways, but only 1 caters for passengers, the PCAL (see right): so the totals are for this line only, although it operates only 42% of the country's total railway route length.

PARAGUAY *FC Presidente Carlos Antonio Lopez (PCAL)*
The first section of what is now the PCAL, from Asuncíon to Paraguarí, was built to a 1,676 mm (5 ft 6 in) broad gauge by British engineers employed by the government, and opened in 1861. Political upheavals delayed further construction until after 1889, when the Paraguay Central Railway Company was formed in London and continued construction under government guarantee. Rails finally reached Encarnación in 1911, across the River Paraná from the Argentine North Eastern Railway. To permit through traffic (carried on a train ferry), the Paraguayan system was converted to the Argentinian line's standard gauge in the same year. Little has changed since. The government bought out the British company in 1961 and it was given its present name in 1964. But the only sign of the modern era is the ten railcars purchased in 1971.

URUGUAY *Administración de Ferrocarriles del Estado*
Most of Uruguay consists of rolling plains. Even the hills in the north do not rise above 610 m (2,000 ft). In this easy countryside was built a comprehensive network, one of the densest national systems in South America, mostly by British interests and mostly between 1865 and 1915. The first line was opened in 1872, by a company which four years later became the Central Uruguay Railway and which grew into one of the three groups owning Uruguay's railways when all were nationalized in 1952. Projects are under way to extend the present system and three new lines are planned.

Uruguay's lines are all standard gauge, reducing the usefulness of the connections with railways in Brazil: all Brazil's lines at the border are meter.

Uruguay

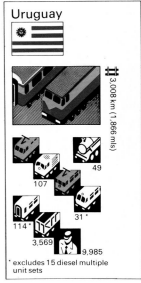

‡3,008 km (1,866 mls)

49
107
31*
114
3,569   9,985

* excludes 15 diesel multiple unit sets

Argentina

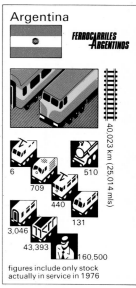

‡40,023 km (25,014 mls)

6   510
709
440   131
3,046
43,393   160,500

figures include only stock actually in service in 1976

A new, military, administration took over FA in April 1976 and discovered that half of the diesel-electric fleet was out of service due to a shortage of spare parts. The stock totals are for those in service at end 1976.

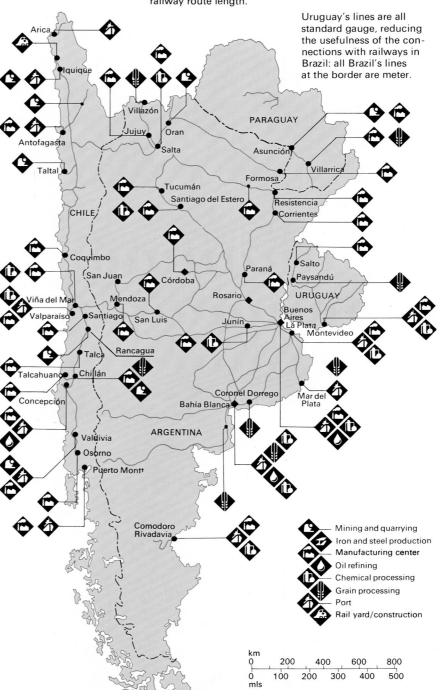

Arica
Iquique
Villazón
Jujuy   Oran
Antofagasta   Salta
Taltal
Tucumán
CHILE   Santiago del Estero
Coquimbo
San Juan
Córdoba
Viña del Mar   Mendoza
Valparaíso   Santiago   San Luis
Talca   Rancagua
Talcahuano   Chillán
Concepción
Valdivia
Osorno
Puerto Montt
ARGENTINA
Comodoro Rivadavia

PARAGUAY
Asunción
Formosa   Villarrica
Resistencia
Corrientes
Paraná   Salto
Paysandú
Rosario   URUGUAY
Buenos Aires
Junín   La Plata
Montevideo
Coronel Dorrego   Mar del Plata
Bahía Blanca

Mining and quarrying
Iron and steel production
Manufacturing center
Oil refining
Chemical processing
Grain processing
Port
Rail yard/construction

km
0   200   400   600   800
0   100   200   300   400   500
mls

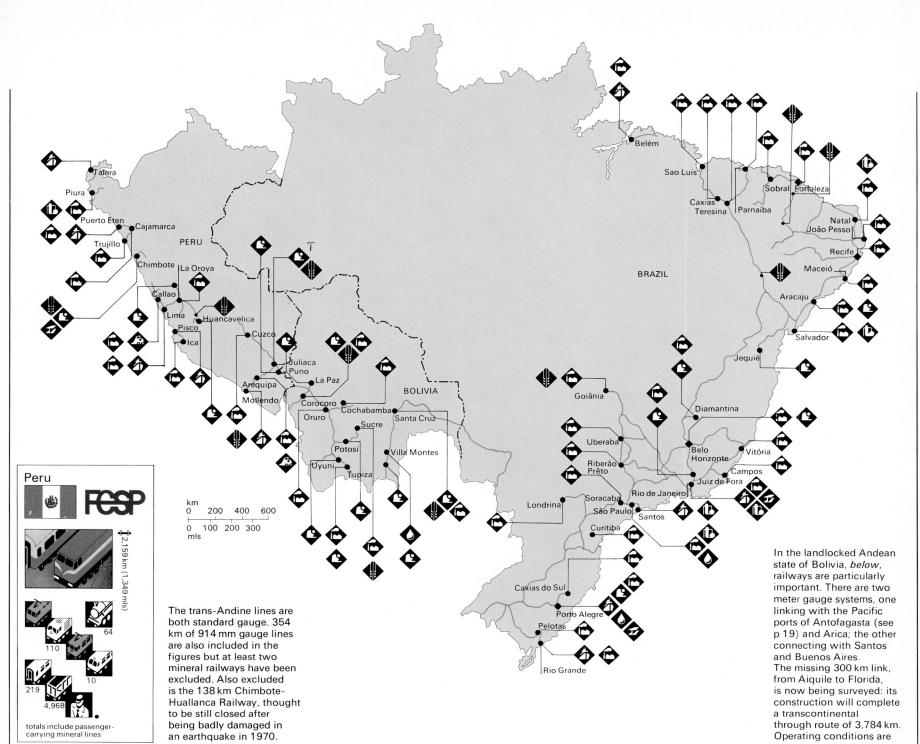

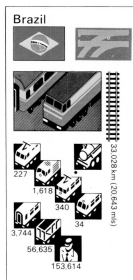

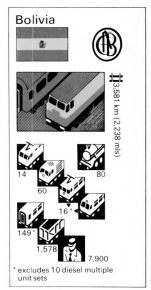

The trans-Andine lines are both standard gauge. 354 km of 914 mm gauge lines are also included in the figures but at least two mineral railways have been excluded. Also excluded is the 138 km Chimbote-Huallanca Railway, thought to be still closed after being badly damaged in an earthquake in 1970.

In the landlocked Andean state of Bolivia, *below*, railways are particularly important. There are two meter gauge systems, one linking with the Pacific ports of Antofagasta (see p 19) and Arica; the other connecting with Santos and Buenos Aires. The missing 300 km link, from Aiquile to Florida, is now being surveyed: its construction will complete a transcontinental through route of 3,784 km. Operating conditions are

PERU *Empresa Nacional de Ferrocarriles del Peru (ENAFER-PERU)*

The railways of Peru are lines running inland from ports, some to serve sugar plantations and two to assault the Andes. But however dramatic the achievement of operating over the Andes, Peru has nothing approaching a rail network. Since 1972, though, the railways have been nationalized, and present government plans would do much to expand the system. A coastal line from Nazca north through Lima to Chimbote, and the joining of the trans-Andean lines by building from Cuzco to Huancayo, are the major proposals. The latter is hardly new, as it was first surveyed in 1907. At present only the two Andean lines are of much importance. Both were built by the American engineer Henry Meiggs, though he died before the more spectacular, the Peru Central, was completed. It climbs 4,783 m (15,693 ft) with a ruling 4.5 percent grade between stations on the upper section. It is adhesion worked throughout (see also page 19). A mineral siding off this line rises to the highest altitude ever achieved by a railway. At Oroya is the junction for the erstwhile Cerro de Pasco Railway, whose lowest point is 3,740 m (12,272 ft) above sea level and which advertised itself as "a railway on the roof of the world." Only just eclipsed by these achievements is Meiggs's other line, the Southern. It connects the coast with Lake Titicaca, where the railway runs a steamer service at 3,818 m (12,526 ft) – the highest navigation in the world. This single-line track depends on freight traffic for its survival, although the expanding tourist trade is giving it a new importance.

BRAZIL *Rede Ferroviaria Federal SA (RFFSA)*

The geography of Brazil has been a great obstacle to railway development, and this vast country of over 8 million sq km (3 million sq miles) has only 33,000 km (20,625 miles) of railway. Ninety percent of the total is to be found within 480 km (300 miles) of the coast. This reluctance to penetrate the interior stems from the difficulty of ascending the steep scarp on to the interior plateau, and the neglect from which the Amazon basin has suffered until only very recently. The escarpment exercised the talents of several early engineers, including Robert Stephenson, who produced a report for a projected line from Santos to the interior as early as 1839. The English engineer James Brunlees produced a spectacular solution in the 1850s: the São Paulo Railway ascended on an incline 8.5 km (5.3 miles) long, with cable haulage on a grade of 10 percent. In Amazonia, the first attempt to build a line, in 1878, was defeated by fever. It was promoted for a traditional nineteenth-century reason, to go around a set of rapids blocking navigation of the River Madeira. After the discovery of quinine it was retackled, successfully this time, in 1908. This railway is the only one in the vast Amazonia region. Only recently has Brazil realized the economic potential of the interior. The government made a dramatic gesture to publicize the possibilities by creating a new capital 960 km (600 miles) inland in 1960. A new line was completed to Brasília in 1968, and during a Five Year Plan ending in 1979, the government is attempting to construct another 2,500 km (1,560 miles) of line and to some extent standardized gauges.

The RFFSA system owns less than 80 % of Brazil's lines: the railways in the state of São Paulo are managed independently, and the totals also include 1,000 km of other independent passenger lines.

severe. The first diesels found the rarefied atmosphere indigestible, and had to be supercharged and have the brake compressors enlarged. The line down to La Paz is adhesion worked with electric power on a grade of 7 percent.

Australia and New Zealand

AUSTRALIA *Australian National Railways*

Railways in Australia began when the separate states were sparsely settled colonies in which matters of transport were controlled by the War Office in London. Work began with local enterprises in Melbourne (1854), Sydney (1855) and Adelaide (1855), but at an early date all were taken over by their respective state governments. In London concern was felt that all these independent projects should be built to the same gauge, but through intransigence and lack of communication New South Wales adopted the European standard while Victoria and South Australia adopted the Irish broad gauge standard of 1,600 mm (5 ft 3 in). In Queensland and Western Australia, which were thought at first to be beyond any unified state system, the 1,067 mm (3 ft 6 in) gauge was adopted to enable a greater length to be built for a given capital outlay. When the Commonwealth of Australia was set up in 1901 an inducement offered to Western Australia was that a line of railway would be built across the Nullarbor Plain to connect the state with those farther east. For this line, with a view to future standardization, the European standard gauge was chosen. It was not however until 1970, when the construction of further standard gauge lines was complete, that it became possible to travel without change of cars

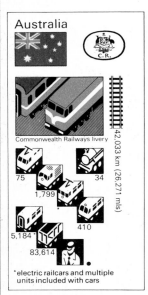

Christchurch to Greymouth railcar crossing Rough Creek just before arriving at Arthur's Pass.

from one side of the continent to the other, between Sydney and Perth, Western Australia.

The great conurbations of Sydney and Melbourne, with nearly half the total population of Australia concentrated around the two cities, led to the electrification of the suburban lines at an early date. In Sydney preparations had begun even before the First World War, but the system was greatly developed with the opening of the Sydney Harbour Bridge in 1932, and the opening in 1956 of the Circular Quay Loop on the underground line. In Melbourne, where at the great Flinders Street station all the passenger traffic is worked by multiple-unit electric trains, work is now in progress on a quadruple-tracked underground loop, which is planned to spread the traffic flow more evenly around the city center. The new tracks will have a capacity of 24 trains an hour and the station will be able to handle up to 130,000 passengers an hour.

One of the most important recent developments in Australian railway working has been the establishment of a number of long single-purpose mineral lines. Some of these, such as the iron ore run from Koolyanobbing, near Kalgoorlie, to the port of Kwinana, near Fremantle, and the coal runs in Queensland, are over state railway tracks; but in northwestern Australia great industrial organizations, such as Hamersley Iron, have built their own railways to act as a giant conveyor belt from the mines to the port of shipment. These special railways have been built to carry a clearly defined tonnage of ores every day and the traffic regulation is thereby simplified from that necessary, for example, on the Western Australia main line, where the lengthy ore trains have to be accommodated amid an otherwise mixed traffic, including some prestige passenger trains like the transcontinental Indian Pacific.

The color scheme shown here is that of the Australian National Railways. There are 4 other major rail transport organizations, run by individual states. The totals exclude almost 1,000 km of standard gauge mineral lines, the largest of which, the 382 km Hamersley Iron Railway owns 47 diesel locomotives. There are 3 track gauges: 1,600 mm gauge with 24 % of the total route length; standard gauge with 34 %; and 1,067 mm narrow gauge with 42 %. Small amounts of narrower gauges remain, including the 762 mm gauge Puffing Billy Railway retained by the Victoria Government Railways for tourists.

NEW ZEALAND *New Zealand Government Railways*

Early local railway enterprises in New Zealand, all in the South Island, had resulted in the construction of no more than 74 km (46 miles) of line being opened to traffic by 1870; but in that year Julius Vogel, Colonial Treasurer, in a notable immigration and public works scheme, put forward proposals for construction of some 2,400 km (1,500 miles) of "cheap" railway to open up the country. The idea was that as the traffic grew so the railways would be improved. As a result, by 1880, 1,891 km (1,182 miles) of track had been laid and opened to traffic, including the 590 km (369 mile) South Island trunk line between Christchurch and Invercargill. In the North Island progress was slower, due to the central mountainous country; but by 1886 there was a 400 km (250 mile) line between Wellington and New Plymouth, run by the Manawatu Company. The North Island Main Trunk line, 682 km (426 miles) long between Wellington and Auckland, was not completed until 1908, including the famous Raurimu spiral, referred to in detail on page 98. In the South Island, the Otago Central line, providing a connection "over the garden wall," as it was jocularly described, between Dunedin, Alexandra and Cromwell, was a somewhat protracted enterprise running through very rugged mountain country. Begun in 1877, it was not finally opened throughout until 1921. In 1923 Westland was connected with Canterbury through the Otira Tunnel, but it was not until 1945 that the link between Christchurch and the present ferry port of Picton was completed. In the 1950s several new lines were built to tap large man-made forests in the North Island, and from 1968 onward great improvements have been made in many areas to shorten distances, ease grades and reduce curvature on the "cheap" railways built under the 1870 plan.

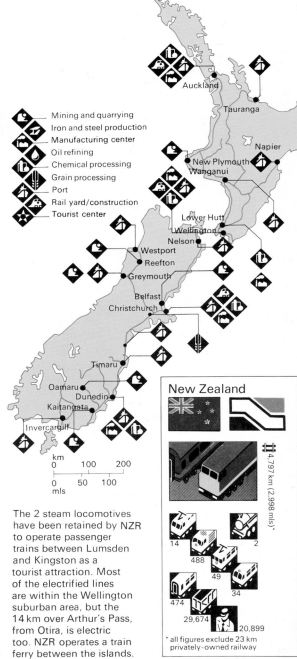

The 2 steam locomotives have been retained by NZR to operate passenger trains between Lumsden and Kingston as a tourist attraction. Most of the electrified lines are within the Wellington suburban area, but the 14 km over Arthur's Pass, from Otira, is electric too. NZR operates a train ferry between the islands.

Reference

Chronology

1801 Surrey Iron Railway incorporated and sanctioned by Parliament

1813 William Chapman patents

1803 Surrey Iron Railway, first public freight line in world

1800 Richard Trevithick constructs low-pressure steam engine

1815 First American railwa

1806 Swansea and Mumbles Railway

1814 George Stephenson

1804 Oystermouth (Swansea and Mumbles) Railway incorporated

1803 Trevithick builds first steam rail locomotive for passengers

1807 Experiment with sail power on Swansea and Mumbles Railway

1807 Swansea and Mumbles Railway carries first fare-paying passengers

1812 Scotland

1808 Wrought-iron rails introduced in Cumberland

1812 First commercial use of steam locomotiv

1812 Introduction of spring-loaded safety val

1807 Abolition of slave trade in British Empire

1801 Trevithick constructs first steam-powered road vehicle for passengers

1815 Humphry Davy invents

1801 First submarine *Nautilus* produced

1815 Battle of Waterloo·

Inaugurations

Locomotive engineering landmarks

Railway disasters

Other railway events

World events

Who's Who

The biography section aims to be a concise guide to the originators of most of the more familiar features of railway practice as it has developed over the last 150 years. It does not claim to be a comprehensive "Who was who" of the whole world of railways. It includes only those who were innovators and pioneers, and an example may help to illustrate our intention. Charles Beyer is included, the man who founded the locomotive building firm of Beyer Peacock, because of the revolutionary design of engines for which the firm became famous (the Beyer Garratt double engine); but James Kitson, who founded a locomotive works at Leeds in 1839 which also exported worldwide, is not mentioned because there was nothing in any way novel about his enterprise – just good solid business acumen.

The majority of the people mentioned therefore belong to the latter half of the nineteenth century. Partly this is because many of the standard features of even a modern railway system had emerged by 1900; partly it is because the identity of individuals is nowadays often submerged in that of the vast corporations which supply most of the needs of the railway industry today. Now, it is firms rather than individuals who tend to get the credit for a new achievement: identifying those individuals responsible for the technical developments incorporated in a modern diesel locomotive is almost impossible.

ABT, Roman (1850–1933) Swiss engineer, invented perhaps the most widely used rack railway system: 1,695 km (1,059 miles) were installed 1884–1929.
ADAMS, William Bridges (1797–1872) Invented the steam railcar, founded the Fairchild Works, Bow, London, where he built them. His rail brake anticipated that developed later by Fell (q.v.).
ALLPORT, Sir James (1811–92) The champion of cheap travel in the UK. As general manager, he had all Midland Railway trains carry third-class passengers from 1872, in cars which set new standards of accommodation. Until then, cheap travelers had been scorned, and carried only on some trains.
ARROL, Sir William (1839–1913) Scottish bridge contractor who founded the Dalmarnock Works and was knighted after his completion of the Forth Bridge in 1890.

BAIRD, Matthew (1817–77) Sole proprietor of the USA's Baldwin loco-

Arrol

motive works after 1866. Pioneer of spark arresters and the firebrick arch.
BAKER, Sir Benjamin (1840–1907) English civil engineer who designed the cantilever system for the Forth Bridge. Engineered most of the early London Underground subways.
BALDWIN, Matthias William (1795–1866) Founder of the Baldwin works, Philadelphia, which built almost 75,000 steam locomotives.
BARLOW, William Henry (1812–1902) Chief civil engineer to the Midland Railway (England) after 1844. He took out several

patents for right of way, including one in 1849 much used on the GWR. He designed London's St Pancras station train shed, and the second Tay Bridge (the longest in Europe).
BEHN-ESCHENBURG, Hans (1864–1938) Electrical engineer who rose to be managing director of the Swiss firm Maschinenfabrik Oerlikon, which pioneered railway electrification. Introduced the first practical single-phase traction motor (1904).
BELPAIRE, Alfred Jules (1820–93) Belgian who introduced his famous firebox in 1860, achieving greater efficiency from low-grade fuels.
BERKLEY, James (1819–62) Englishman who in 1849 became chief engineer of the Great Indian Peninsula Railway, inventing the zig-zag technique to lessen the grades on that company's two main lines over the Ghats.
BEYER, Charles Frederick (1813–76) A German who in 1843 became chief

Baldwin

designer of locomotives with the English firm Sharp Roberts & Co. In 1853 he was co-founder of the Beyer Peacock locomotive firm, Manchester.
von BORRIES, August (1852–1906) Pioneer of compound steam locomotives; chief mechanical engineer to the Prussian State Railways (1875–1902).
BOUCH, Sir Thomas (1822–1880) English civil engineer with a reputation for paring costs to the bone: the first Tay Bridge, which he built, collapsed only a year after its opening.

820   **1825**   **1830**   **1835**   **1840**   **1845**

omotive truck   **1825** Stockton and Darlington Railway, first public railway to use steam from outset   **1839** East Germany   **1844** Switzerland

Austrian Empire **1827**   Irish Republic **1834**   **1835** First attempts to propel railway cars by electric batteries   **1846** Hungary

arter granted   Liverpool and Manchester Railway **1830**   **1833** Two killed in first passenger train accident in USA   **1845** Jamaica

nstructs first practical steam locomotive   **1827** Marc Séguin constructs first locomotive with multi-tubular boiler   **1839** Italy

France (St Etienne-Andrézieux) **1828**   Walschaert develops his valve gear **1844**

Stephenson's *Rocket* wins Rainhill trials **1829**   First major disaster: 53 killed on Versailles-Paris express **1842**   Denmark **1847**

Crampton introduces driving wheels behind firebox to support larger boiler **1845**   **1846** Yugoslavia

Baltimore and Ohio Railway founded **1828**   **1835** World's first nationalized railway system — Belgium

Delaware and Hudson's gravity railway **1829**   USSR **1836**   **1837** Cuba   **1842** Poland

1830 Baltimore and Ohio Railway, first passenger and freight railway in USA   Spain **1848**

West Germany **1835**   Pneumatic brake invented by James Nasmyth **1844**

Middleton colliery railway, England   Semaphore signals first used for railways at New Cross, England **1841**

Leeds, England   **1830** First regular steam passenger service in England (Canterbury)

Compound steam engine developed by William M'Naught **1845**

1820 Bedlington Iron Works granted patent for production of rolled rails.   Canada **1836**   **1838** Austria   British Guiana **1848**

1839 Netherlands

1831 US fireman killed in boiler explosion   **1839** Czechoslovakia

er's safety lamp

Introduction of Morse telegraph between Baltimore and Washington **1844**

1839 Charles Goodyear discovers process of rubber vulcanization

---

du BOUSQUET, Gaston (1839–1910) Chief engineer to France's Northern Railway from 1890. His compound Atlantic of 1900 set the style for many French locomotives.
BOVERI, Walter (1865–1921) German engineer and co-founder of Brown Boveri & Co in 1891, the Swiss manufacturers of railway electrification equipment.
BRADSHAW, George (1801–53) Published a schedule for Britain's railways, 1839. From December 1841 it was *Bradshaw's Monthly Railway Guide* and was last published in June 1961.
BRANDT, John (1785–1860) Credited by many with the classic American 4-4-0 design.
BRASSEY, Thomas (1805–70) The greatest English railway contractor. He built lines in Europe, Canada, Australia, Argentina and India besides Britain. Brassey's contracts amounted to 3,820km (2,374 miles) altogether.
BROWN, Charles

(1827–1905) English founder of the Swiss Locomotive and Machine Works (SLM) at Winterthur in 1871. His son, Charles E. L. Brown, became a pioneer of railway electrification and co-founder of the Swiss firm Brown Boveri & Co.
BRUNEL, Isambard Kingdom (1806–59) Brilliant civil engineer whose excursions into the realms of mechanical engineering were either spectacular failures or touched with genius. When only twenty-seven he was appointed Engineer to the Great Western Railway. His controversial use of a 2,134 mm (7 ft) broad gauge, and a grade profile that was compared to a billiard table, made the GWR by far the fastest of the early railways, though this was not achieved until Brunel relinquished the design of the locomotives to Gooch (q.v.)
BULLEID, Oliver Vaughan Snell (1881–1970) Born in New Zealand. Made chief mechanical engineer of

Brunel

England's Southern Railway in 1937. He was a steam engineer in a world abandoning steam engines and many of his innovations did not have a chance to prove themselves.
BURY, Edward (1794–1858) Owner of a workshop in Liverpool, where he built his first locomotive in 1829. Originated bar frames (much used in the USA) in 1830. His locomotives had a very distinctive large copper firebox.

CAPROTTI, Arturo (1881–1938) Italian

engineer, designer of a locomotive valve gear first used in 1921.
CHAPELON, André (b. 1892) Seen by many as the greatest locomotive designer ever. He rose to be head of the French Railways' Department of Steam Locomotive Studies. In 1926, he designed with Kylala the Kylchap double blast-pipe. His main achievement lay in vastly increasing the thermodynamic efficiency of his steam locomotives by streamlining internal steam passages.
CHURCHWARD, George Jackson (1857–1933) Chief mechanical engineer to the Great Western Railway and perhaps the greatest British locomotive engineer. His design sources were international: the high boiler pressures were an idea of de Glehn (q.v.); from America came the front end design with the long travel valves and the tapered boiler; and he used Belpaire's (q.v.) firebox. In 1902 he built the first successful British 4-6-0.

CONRAD, Frederik Willem (1800–69) Appointed engineer director of the Dutch Railway Co in 1839 because his earlier work with waterways and dykes was considered an asset when building a railway through the Dutch countryside.
COOK, Thomas (1809–92) Founded the travel firm, the unlooked-for result of an excursion he ran in 1841. The firm was greatly expanded by his son J. M. Cook, who was sole manager after 1878.
CRAMPTON, Thomas Russell (1816–88) Englishman who patented a locomotive design in 1843. It was used more in France and Germany than in England.
CROCKER, Charles (1822–88) American in charge of the construction of the Central Pacific Railroad (1863–9). Responsible for merging the CP with the Southern Pacific in 1884.

DALHOUSIE, Lord (1812–60) Became President of the Board of

Trade in 1845, during England's "Railway Mania," when he formed opinions about the desirability of government control of railway construction. Prime Minister Peel refused, but Dalhousie pursued such ideas in India when appointed Governor-General. His 1853 Minute on the railways of India recommended a speedy introduction of railways throughout India, to be built by private enterprise under government supervision.
DIESEL, Rudolph (1858–1913) French born, German educated inventor. Did not in fact have much to do with the application of his engine unit to rail traction. The first diesel engines went into ships, starting 1903. The first diesel locomotive was built at the Swiss Sulzer works in 1913.
DODGE, Grenville Mellen (1831–1916) American civil engineer, surveyed nearly 97,000 km (60,000 miles) of rail routes. In 1866 became chief

Chronology

1850	1855	1860	1865	1870

1850 Mexico

1856 Portugal

1859 First Pullman sleeping car put into service in USA

1869 Honduras

1853 India

1856 Sweden

1861 Pakistan

1865 Sri Lanka

1872 Japan

1851 Peru

1854 Australia

1859 Luxembourg

1863 New Zealand

1869 American transcontinental railway

1851 J.E.McConnell produces *Bloomer* express engine

1861 Paraguay

1864 Indonesia

1869 Romania

1873 Boliv

1850 Thomas Rogers introduces taper boiler, USA

1862 Bangladesh

1867 Railway through Brenner Pass completed

1851 First all-steel tires for locomotive wheels produced, Germany

1862 Finland

1869 Uruguay

1872

1850 Britannia Bridge across Menai Straits opened

1860 South Africa

1871 Mont Cenis Tun

1851 Longest stretch of railway completed — 725 klm (450 miles), New York to Dunkirk, Lake Erie

1871 Ecuador

1850 Stephenson's cast iron railway, Newcastle

1860 Belpaire's firebox introduced

1866 Bulgaria

1852 Chile

1855 Panama

1863 Introduction of narrow gauge steam locomotive

1854 Brazil

1857 First steel rail made and laid at Derby

1854 Egypt

1857 Argentina

1862 Algeria

1869 Greece

1854 Norway

1856 Interlocking of signals and points patented by John Saxby

1856 Turkey

1859 First oil well drilled in USA

1857 Indian Mutiny

1865 Assassination of Abraham Lincoln

1855 Tungsten steel developed

1853 Outbreak of Crimean War

1859 Steamroller invented

1867 Manufacture of bicycles begins

Who's Who

engineer to Union Pacific Railroad.

DREW, Daniel (1797–1879) American financier whose manipulation of railway stock brought disaster not riches: bankrupted himself by 1876.

EDMONDSON, Thomas (1792–1851) Englishman who in 1837 invented the card railway ticket and date press that have become standard throughout the world.

EIFFEL, Alexandre Gustave (1832–1923) French bridge builder whose wrought and cast iron constructions can be found in France, Spain and Portugal.

FAIRBAIRN, Sir William (1789–1874) Founder in 1817 of the firm which became Fairbairn & Sons in Manchester, building almost 1,000 bridges and 400 locomotives.

FAVRE, Louis (1826–79) Swiss builder of the St Gotthard tunnel (inside which he died) and first to use spiral tunnels as a means of gaining height.

Favre

FELL, John Barraclough (1815–1902) English inventor of a center-rail friction drive system for extra adhesion. First in use 1868. Used on New Zealand's Rimutaka Incline, 1878–1955, it permitted a grade of 7 percent.

FLEMING, Sir Sandford (1827–1915) Born in Scotland, became engineer to the Canadian Pacific Railway in 1871.

FOTHERGILL-COOKE, Sir William (1806–79) Patented the railway electric telegraph in 1837. His 1842 publication *Telegraphic Railways or the Single Way* led to the

introduction of block signaling.

FOWLER, Sir John (1817–98) English civil engineer of the Metropolitan Railway and the Forth Bridge.

FOX, Sir Douglas Charles (1810–74) Civil engineer and contractor who built many of the larger English train sheds. He pioneered narrow gauge railways in India.

GARRATT, Herbert William (1864–1913) Became locomotive superintendent to Central Argentina Railway, 1892. Worked on other railways in S. America, Cuba, Nigeria and Australia before returning to UK in 1906. In 1907 he patented his articulated locomotive design. Almost 2,000 were built by Beyer Peacock in Manchester.

GHEGA, Karl Ritter (1802–60) In 1836, made engineer on Austria's first steam-powered railway. His great achievement was the engineering of the fearsomely graded

de Glehn

Semmering Railway (1848–54).

GIFFARD, Henri (1825–82) French inventor of the injector (to feed water into the boiler against pressure). First used in 1859.

de GLEHN, Alfred George (1848–1936) His work on compound locomotives as technical head of the French firm of Société Alsacienne was very influential. The first 4-cylinder de Glehn compound was made in 1886, and the last in 1929.

GÖLSDORF, Karl (1861–1916) Locomotive engineer to Austrian State

Railways from 1893. He introduced the 2-6-2 and 2-6-4 wheel arrangements into Europe and his numbering system was much copied. His most important innovation was a simple, reliable, starting gear for compound locomotives, widely used in Europe and America.

GOOCH, Sir Daniel (1816–89) First locomotive superintendent, and later the chairman, of England's Great Western Railway. Designer of the magnificent locomotives which symbolized the GWR in its broad gauge era.

GOULD, Jay (1836–92) One of the great American railroad magnates whose controversial activities were of much public interest in the era after the Civil War.

GREATHEAD, James Henry (1844–96) Inventor of the Greathead shield tunneling device. Engineer to the world's first electric underground subway (the City and South London Railway, opened 1890).

GRESLEY, Sir Nigel (1876–1941) Became chief mechanical engineer of

Gresley

England's Great Northern Railway, 1911. As CME to its successor the London and North Eastern Railway, he designed the *Mallard*, world speed record holder for a steam locomotive, 203 km/h (126 mph).

HACKWORTH, Timothy (1786–1850) Responsible for the establishment of the works of the Stockton and Darlington Railway, where he originated many of the features which became standard steam locomotive practice.

HASWELL, John (1812–97) Scottish engineer who settled in

875   **1880**   **1885**   **1890**   **1895**

874 Colombia

1875 Sudan

1876 International Sleeping Car Company founded

1877 Burma

1876 Tunisia

estinghouse perfects automatic railway air brake

Alps opened

1878 Tay Bridge opened

1877 Venezuela

1879 Electric locomotive exhibited in Berlin by E. W. von Siemens

1879 Tay Bridge collapse in Scotland results in 78 deaths

1881 Nicaragua

1883 Electric power inaugurated on Giant's Causeway railway — first to use hydroelectric power

1881 Canadian Pacific Railway Company founded

1881 First public electric railway, Berlin

1882 El Salvador

1880 Guatemala

1883 China   **1886** Angola

1882 Gotthard Tunnel and railway opened

1885 Vietnam

1886 4-cylinder de Glehn compound locomotive introduced

1887 Mallet's articulated locomotive constructed

1886 Mozambique

1885 Senegal

1886 Severn Tunnel opened

1887 Present Tay Bridge opened

1888 Ethiopia

1885 Malaysia

1884 Parsons invents first practical steam turbine engine

1886 Canadian Pacific Railway

1890 Costa Rica

1890 Israel

Multiple-unit train invented, USA **1897**

1889 British Railways Regulations alter signaling laws

1889 80 killed due to signaling error at Armagh, Ireland

1892 British rail gauge size standardized

1892 Philippines

1893 Botswana

1893 Thailand

Schmidt's high-degree superheater developed **1898**

1891 Trans-Siberian Railway construction begins

1895 Lebanon

1895 South West Africa

1891 Taiwan   **1894** Tanzania

1892 Cape-Johannesburg railway

1895 Syria

1893 Diesel designs his internal combustion engine

1897 Kenya

1897 Rhodesia

1897 Uganda

Korea **1899**

1898 Zaire

1879 Zulu War

1876 Bell invents telephone

1888 Electric motor constructed

1885 Karl Benz builds single-cylinder engine for motor car

1893 Henry Ford builds his first car

Zeppelin builds airship **1898**

Vienna where in 1837 he designed a locomotive works of which he became manager. In 1851 he produced the first European 8-coupled locomotive.

HAWKSHAW, Sir John (1811–91) Civil engineer, undertook many heavy projects in nineteenth-century Britain. The first to prove that a 2 percent grade was not the limit for adhesion worked inclines.

HOWE, William (1814–79) In 1842, invented the valve gear known as Stephenson's link motion.

HUBER, Peter Emil (1836–1915) Pioneer of Swiss railway electrification. The Bern-Lötschberg-Simplon line, which opened in 1913, was electrified from the outset to his specifications (15,000 volts AC at $16\frac{2}{3}$ cycles per sec). This system was used on lines in Germany, Austria and Scandinavia.

HUDSON, George (1800–71) Early railway magnate who rose to be mayor of York and to control a network of 1,600 km (1,000 miles) of

Jessop

lines in the north of England. His questionable means of financing led to his downfall.

HUNTINGTON, C. P. (1821–1900) American railroad magnate and unscrupulous financier. One of the four men who formed the Central Pacific Railroad Co in 1861 (called the Big Four). To disguise the enormous profits made at the government's expense out of its construction, the CP's books were later burned. In 1865, the same quartet formed the Southern Pacific Railroad by merging lines they controlled in the

south, Huntington becoming vice-president.

JANNEY, Eli Hamilton (1831–1912) Inventor of an automatic coupler made standard throughout the USA from 1888.

JESSOP, William (1745–1814) Civil engineer responsible for the Surrey Iron Railway, the horse-drawn line that was England's first public railway. He was the first to think of edge rails.

KANDO, Kalman (1869–1931) Became managing director of the Hungarian firm of Ganz and Partners. One of the few outstanding individuals (as opposed to firms) in the history of electric traction. From 1902, he electrified mountain lines in Italy. In 1915 he built the first locomotive to run on electricity at the industrial (high) frequency now used.

KETTERING, Charles (1876–1958) Chief engineer from 1922 of the firm later renamed General Motors. He and his son Eugene have done much to

create the modern diesel locomotive.

von KRAUSS, Georg (1826–1906) In 1866, he founded his locomotive firm at Munich, Germany. Another factory was later opened at Linz, Austria.

LIST, Friedrich (1789–1847) Engineer to the first German line (Fürth-Nürnberg, 1835). His plans for a pan-Germanic rail network were ridiculed and he committed suicide.

LOCKE, Joseph (1805–60) English civil engineer, who built lines cheaply with steep grades and no tunnels. He introduced the bullhead rail, which became standard on all of Britain's railways for 100 years.

LOMONOSSOF, George Vladimir (1876–1952) Became chief mechanical engineer to the Tashkent Railway, 1908. Later president of the Locomotive Research Bureau, and deputy director-general of Russian Railways. As president of the Russian War Railway Mission to the

USA, he was responsible for designing and ordering 2,000 locomotives.

LOREE, Loener Fresnel (1858–1940) Came to exert a strong influence on USA railway affairs due to his excellent management of the Delaware and Hudson Railroad during his 31-year presidency.

MALLET, Anatole (1837–1919) Swiss born, French educated engineer, patented his articulated locomotive in 1884. The design was particularly developed in the USA.

MARSH, Sylvester (1803–84) Built the first mountain rack railway (up Mt Washington, USA: opened 1869). Used a rack system like that patented by Riggenbach in 1863.

MEIGGS, Henry (1811–77) Moved from New York to Chile in 1854, where he started railway building. From 1867, engineer and contractor, Peru Central Railway: an extraordinary engineering feat which goes over the world's highest railway summit.

Meiggs

MILHOLLAND, James (1812–75) American locomotive engineer who developed a coal burning firebox in 1855.

MORGAN, John Pierpont (1837–1913) US banker with an interest in railways. He and his partners controlled 29,000 km (18,125 miles) of lines in the south, enabling him to induce many companies to agree to common rates and avoid ruinous competition.

MURRAY, Matthew (1765–1826) Built the first "commercially successful locomotive" for the Middleton Colliery line at Leeds (UK), in 1812.

Chronology

1900	1905	1910	1915	1920	1925	1930	1935

1900 Surinam
1906 Saudi Arabia
1916 Iran
1929 Swansea and Mumbles Railway electrifie

1904 Ivory Coast
1910 Trans-Andine Railway
1928 London-Edinburgh line, longest nonstop

1902 Iraq
1909 Cameroon
1915 More than 600 killed near Guadalajara when train plunges into gorge
1932 Sydney Harbour Bridg

1901 Mombasa-Lake Victoria railway
1911 Morocco
1917 Out of control train near Modane, France — at least 543 killed
1934 Congo

1905 Benin
1910 Guinea
1927 Great Moffat Tunnel in Rocky Mountains opene

1901 Nigeria
1908 Malawi
1913 First diesel locomotive constructed, Switzerland
1929 Cascade railway tunnel completed —

1903 Malagasy Republic
1917 Trans-Siberian Railway
1934 Upper Volt

1904 First practical single-phase traction motor introduced
1931 Turkestan-Siberia (Turksib

1901 Ghana
1909 First Garratt locomotives built
193

1904 Mali
1910 Hong Kong
1917 Trans-Australian Railway

1905 Togo
1915 Multiple crash on Caledonian Railway causes 227 deaths
1930 Cambodia

1904 Jordan
1915 Kalman Kando builds first high-frequency electric locomotive
1931 First trans-African railway,

1905 Zambia
1917 Quebec railway bridge completed — 549 m (600 yds) long
1936

1904 Railway tunnel constructed under Hudson River

1906 Railway Nationalization Law, Japan

1906 Simplon Tunnel in Alps opened

1908 Ford Model 'T' produced
1918 First World War ends
1929 Wall Street crash
19

1903 Wright brothers successfully fly powered airplane
1917 Russian Revolution
1926 USA develops liquid-fuel rocket
1937 Fran

1901 First Mercedes car constructed
1914 Outbreak of First World War
1923 Aeroflot airline founded, USSR
1936 Spanish Ci

Who's Who

Nagelmackers

NAGELMACKERS, George (1845–1905) Belgian who founded the Wagons-Lits company in 1869 (Compagnie Internationale des Wagons-Lits et des Grands Express Européens): it inaugurated the Orient Express and other famous luxury expresses.
NORRIS, William (1802–67) Locomotive manufacturer in Philadelphia who refined and developed Jervis's 4-2-0 arrangement. Often called "Norris engines," they became an early American standard also used in Britain.

PAGET, Sir Cecil (1874–1933) Organizational genius who created the pattern of operating of the London Midland and Scottish Railway after the Grouping in 1923, and applied by British Rail after the 1948 nationalization.
PAULING, George (1853–1919) Engineer and contractor often associated with lines promoted by Rhodes (q.v.) in southern Africa.
PEASE, Edward (1767–1858) The first man ever to invest a substantial amount of money in what today could be called a railway. He was the promoter of the Stockton and Darlington line, and appointed George Stephenson (q.v.) its chief engineer. Together, they founded the locomotive building firm of Robert Stephenson & Co.
PULLMAN, George Mortimer (1831–97) American who founded the Pullman Car Company in 1867. The crowded squalor of his cars caused Pullman's attempts to break

Ramsbottom

into the European market to be defeated by consumer resistance and Nagelmackers' (q.v.) superior product.

RAMSBOTTOM, John (1814–92) Chief mechanical engineer of England's London and North Western Railway from 1862. Invented a safety valve named after him. Pioneered water troughs. Installed a Bessemer steel plant at Crewe in 1864, which led to the replacement of wrought iron by steel as the material for rails.
RHODES, Cecil John (1853–1902) English colonialist who in his struggles to gain control of southern Africa realized the unifying force of the railway. Railway promoter with a sense of the theatrical: proposed the Cape to Cairo route; wanted the Victoria Falls bridge built so that the spray would wet the cars (which it does).
ROGERS, Thomas (1792–1856) founder of Rogers Locomotive Works, 1837. Introduced the taper boiler in 1850.

SAXBY, John (1821–1913) English signaling pioneer who in 1871 invented his famous interlocking frame.
SCHMIDT, Wilhelm (1859–1924) German who developed a widely used high-degree superheater first tried out on the Prussian State Railways in 1898.
SEGUIN, Marc (1786–1875) First to build a locomotive in France (1827), using the multi-tubular boiler he had patented in 1826.

Von Siemens

SHAY, Ephraim (1839–1916) Invented the Shay geared locomotive, most popular of three geared locomotive designs made in America for temporary lines with steep grades.
von SIEMENS, Ernst Werner (1816–92) German who exhibited what was really the world's first electric railway in Berlin in 1879. He built the electrified Giant's Causeway Tramway in Ireland (opened 1883).
SPOONER, Charles Easton (1818–89) Pioneered narrow gauge steam power, which he introduced onto the Welsh

600 mm gauge Festiniog Railway in 1863.
SPRAGUE, F. J. (1857–1934) American pioneer of electric traction who invented the multiple-unit train in 1897.
STANIER, Sir William (1876–1965) As chief mechanical engineer to England's London Midland and Scottish Railway, he developed a remarkably standardized fleet of locomotives drawing on GWR practice, where he had been apprenticed under Churchward (q.v.). His 2-8-0 freight locomotive was adopted as a standard during the Second World War.
STANLEY, Albert, Lord Ashfield (1874–1948) After gaining experience in the USA (where he superintended Detroit's tramways, 1901–3), he returned to the UK and was the man behind the establishment of the present London Transport system.
STEPHENSON, George (1781–1848) Son of a fireman at Wylam Colliery in the north of England

| 1940 | 1945 | 1950 | 1955 | 1960 | 1965 | 1970 | 1975 |

1947 Albania

British Rail Advanced Passenger Train begins track trials **1972**

world   **1964** High-speed Tokaido line, Japan

ustralia, opened   Turbotrain introduced in France **1974**

1944 About 500 passengers suffocate by fumes in Italian tunnel   **1964** Swaziland

1954 Volcanic eruption in New Zealand causes railway bridge collapse — 149 die

ngest in North America   **1952** 112 killed in double collision at Harrow, England   **1967** Derailment at Hither Green, England — 47 killed

1948 British Railways nationalized   Last journey of Orient Express (Paris-Istanbul) **1977**

ilway   Tazara line, Africa — Kapiri Mposhi-Dar es Salaam, 1,859 km (1,155 miles) **1976**

ongolia   Amtrak begins operation of long-distance passenger railways, USA **1971**

In Argentina, 236 die as a result of signaling irregularities **1970**

nguela-Katalanga   **1951** Liberia   **1960** Withdrawal of steam from Canadian National Railways

ondon-Paris through trains   Experimental paved concrete track introduced near Nottingham **1970**

1961 Trans-Siberian Railway electrified, Moscow-Irkutsk

1955 Reorganization of British Railways   **1968** End of steam on British Railways

New world rail speed record, 408 km/h (255 mph) established in USA **1974**

1957 Trans-Europe Express introduced   **1968** Nanking-Pukou Bridge, China, opened

1963 Mauritania

econd World War declared

hittle builds jet engine   **1947** First supersonic flight by US airplane   **1958** USA launches first moon rocket

ar begins   **1945** Second World War ends   **1956** Suez Canal crisis   **1966** First spacecraft soft-lands on moon

---

George Stephenson

who rose to become engineer to many early railways. His most important achievement was proving the capabilities of steam traction at the 1829 Rainhill Trial, which led to the choice of steam power for the first major public railway, the Liverpool-Manchester line opened in 1830 (which Stephenson engineered).
STEPHENSON, Robert (1803–59) Really a civil engineer, but put in charge of his father George's (q.v.) locomotive works at Newcastle in 1823: the firm took his name. In 1833, he engineered the London and

Birmingham Railway. Remembered for his tubular bridges, developed with Fairbairn (q.v.).
STEVENS, Robert Livingston (1787–1856) President and chief engineer of the USA's Camden and Amboy Railroad in 1830. Pioneer of much typical American railway practice, for example the cowcatcher.
SYKES, William (1840–1917) Englishman who patented the Lock & Block interlocking signal system in 1875. His son Joseph, who joined his signaling works in 1896, pioneered electric signaling.

TREVITHICK, Richard (1771–1833) Builder of pumping engines and the first to use high-pressure steam. Built a locomotive in 1803, the first to haul a load on rails (on the Coalbrookdale wagon-way). Ruined financially by Peru's revolution (where he had gone in 1817 to install mine engines).
VAN HORNE, Sir William Cornelius (1843–1915)
TYER, Edward

Trevithick

(1830–1912) English inventor of the electric tablet system in 1878, for the safe working of single-line railways.

VANDERBILT, Cornelius (1794–1877) Made a fortune in steamboats. Sold out at age 67 and invested in railways. Gained control of the New York Central in 1867. When he died, he was worth $100 million. The revelation of such wealth staggered America: his was the first modern-scale fortune.
VAN HORNE, Sir William Cornelius (1843–1915) Started as telegraph

operator with Illinois Central Railroad. Rose to be president of the Canadian Pacific in 1888 after having much to do with its construction.
VAUCLAIN, Samuel Matthews (1856–1940) Worked 51 years for Baldwin, the USA locomotive firm, of which he became chairman in 1929. Invented the Vauclain system of locomotive compounding in 1889: Baldwins built 2,000 such locomotives.
VIGNOLES, Charles Blacker (1793–1875) Irish born early railway civil engineer. Built Ireland's first

Van Horne

line (Dublin-Kingstown), 1832–4. In 1837 he introduced the flat-bottomed rail, now standard throughout the world. Later worked on lines in England, Russia, Switzerland and Poland.

WALSCHAERT, Egide (1820–1901) Belgian inventor in 1844 of one of the most efficient valve gears ever.
WESTINGHOUSE, George (1846–1914) American inventor of the compressed-air brake in 1868. He refined it in a further patent of 1871, making its application in an emergency, automatic.
WHISTLER, George Washington (1800–49) American civil engineer responsible for Russia's 1,524 mm (5 ft) gauge. When working on the Moscow–St Petersburg line from 1842, he used the gauge then found on railways around his birthplace in the South.
WHITTON, John (1819–98) Englishman who was chief engineer to New South Wales

Walschaert

Government Railways, 1856–1890. Responsible for the Great Zig-Zag Railway over the Blue Mountains.
WINAN, Ross (1796–1877) Originator of the American camel-back locomotive in the 1850s. The driver sat in a separate cab over the center of the boiler.
WORSDELL, Nathaniel (1809–96) In 1837 invented an apparatus for picking up mailbags at speed, when he was car superintendent of the Liverpool and Manchester Railway.

Glossary

A

Adhesion Maintenance of contact between wheel and rail through friction.
Air brake Brake operated by compressed air.
Alco (American Locomotive Company) US *locomotive* builder.
Alternating current (ac) Electric current whose direction is regularly reversed; in normal use in industry.
Alternator *Dynamo* producing *alternating* rather than *direct current*.
Amtrak (National Railroad Passenger Corporation) Nationwide US passenger carrying railway organization inaugurated in 1971.
Antislip Device which detects, and automatically corrects, sliding or skidding of the wheels when braking by momentarily reducing the braking force.
Armature Rotating part of a *dynamo*.
Articulated locomotive One which has two independent sets of frames, hinged or joined by a pivot, with independent groups of wheels driven by separate cylinders.
ATC (Automatic Train Control) Applied to any form of automatic engineer assistance, including total automatic control.
Atlantic locomotive Steam *locomotive* with 4-4-2 wheel arrangement.
ATO (Automatic Train Operation) Automatic regulation or operation of trains as applied on certain single-track railways.

B

Ballast Material, eg crushed granite or slag, in which are bedded the *ties* carrying the track, to distribute the load of passing traffic, prevent track movement and provide drainage.
Blast pipe Vertical pipe evacuating steam and waste products from the cylinders into the atmosphere, designed to create a partial vacuum in the *smokebox* and improve the drafting for the fire.
Block signaling System whereby only one train is permitted in each predetermined section of line at a time.
Boiler Part of *locomotive* in which steam is produced under pressure by the combustion of fuel in a *firebox* surrounded by water.
Box car Covered freight car.
Brake horsepower Horsepower is a unit showing the rate at which work is done, originally defined as the weight a horse could raise 1 ft in 1 second – 550 lb (250 kg). The electrical equivalent is 746 watts. At the output shaft of an engine or motor, it is termed brake horsepower, indicating the power needed to stop the shaft from turning.
Brakeman Guard
Brake shoe Standard braking system whereby a block is applied to the edge of a rotating drum or wheel.

C

Cable railway One on which trains are hauled by a cable attached to a stationary winding engine; usually used only on short, steeply graded sections of line.
Caboose Conductor and brakeman's car on end of freight train.
Camshaft Rotating shaft on which shaped bodies (cams) are fixed to operate inlet and outlet valves of a *diesel engine* via a pushrod.
Cant *Superelevation*.
Cardan shaft Shaft with universal or cardan joint at one or both ends.
Catenary Cable in overhead electrification system which supports contact or conductor wire.
Chaired track Track on which rail is held in place on *ties* by iron or steel sockets (chair).
Circuit breaker Automatic switch to make or break an electric circuit.
Classification yard Large area devoted to multiple track siding network used for sorting freight into complete trains. Particularly important in USA for high-load long distance running.
Clerestory roof Old-fashioned roof design with small windows and ventilators in slightly raised section running down center of roof.
Color light signal Fixed signal with red, yellow and green lights displayed as required – similar to road traffic signal.
Commutator Ring-shaped fitting connected to the *armature* of a *dynamo*, and bearing on to the brushes.
Compounding In steam *locomotives*: use of steam twice, first in a high-pressure cylinder, then in a larger, low-pressure cylinder, before exhausting it. Although intended as an economy measure, often necessitated more careful maintenance than "simple" locomotives.
Compression stroke Upward movement of piston into a cylinder which results in compression of air mixture in the cylinder.
Compressor Machine which increases air pressure by reducing the volume taken up by the air.
Conrail (Consolidated Rail Corporation) US railway organization established in 1976 to operate six bankrupt *railroads* in the northeast.
Consist Composition or makeup of a train.
Container Large box, with or without roof, which can be easily lifted from a flat freight car and placed on a road transporter, plane or ship.
Conversions Metric to US:
1 mm = 0.0393701 in
1 cm = 0.393701 in
1 m = 1.09361 yd
1 km = 0.621371 mile
US to Metric:
1 in = 25.4 mm
1 in = 2.54 cm
1 ft = 0.3048 m
1 yd = 0.9144 m
1 mile = 1.609344 km
Coupler Means by which vehicles are linked together.
Creep Gradual forward movement of rails as a result of recurrent pressure from passing vehicles.
Crosshead Bar or metal block joining piston rod to connecting rod of a steam *locomotive*.
Crossing Intersection of two railway lines on the same level, enabling a vehicle to pass across another line.
CTC (Centralized Traffic Control) System of working signals from a central panel by remote control.
Cut Group of cars coupled together in a *classification yard*.
Cut and fill technique (*also* Cut and cover) Method of tunneling where a trench is dug, lines laid and the whole then roofed over.
Cutoff (1) Shortcut or bypass route. (2) Point in the piston stroke when steam is stopped from entering the cylinder of a steam engine.
Cutting Open excavation for a railway through hilly terrain.

D

Dead man's throttle Automatic lever in a *locomotive* kept depressed by engineer. If released as in the event of an accident to the engineer, automatically cuts off power and applies brakes.
Dead section Part of conductor in electric railway circuit which is not supplied with power.
Deck Floor of *locomotive*.
Diaphragm Flexible connection between two cars to provide access.
Diesel engine Internal combustion engine in which compressed air in a cylinder reaches a temperature high enough to ignite the fuel subsequently injected.
Direct current (dc) Electric current which always flows in one direction. Used in early railway electrification schemes, but now being superseded by *alternating current*.
DMU Diesel *multiple unit*.
Double head Two steam *locomotives* working together to draw a train.
Drawbar Form of *coupler* connecting *locomotive* to *tender*.
Dump car Freight car that tips over to discharge cargo.
Dynamo Machine composed of rotating coils of copper wire in a magnetic field to produce a *direct current*. Used for lighting, etc.
Dynamometer Instrument for measuring energy. Used in a dynamometer car to test the performance of a *locomotive*.

E

Embankment Man-made ridge built to raise natural ground level in order to carry railway over a valley, or protect line from river etc.
EMU Electric *multiple unit*.
Entrance-exit (NX) signaling Descriptive name for modern power signaling from large control panel in central office. Once the signalman has indicated, on the panel, the entrance to, and exit from, the route which he wishes the train to take, the operation of intermediate points and signals is performed automatically.
Expansion joint Space traditionally left between one rail and the next to allow for expansion in hot weather. New track-laying techniques are making this unnecessary.

F

Firebox Combustion chamber of a steam *boiler*.
Firebrick Material capable of withstanding great heat, used in the firebrick arch in a *firebox*.
Fishplate Metal plate used to join rail lengths.
Flange Projecting rim of wheel to hold wheels on the rails.
Fly-wheel Wheel with heavy rim on revolving shaft used to keep revolutions constant and to accumulate power.
Fog signal Detonator placed on rail giving audible signal when vehicle passes overhead.
Footplate Platform on steam *locomotive* for engineer and fireman.
Frog *Nose*. Known as a movable frog where it occurs in points.
Funicular Railway found on steep gradients with ascending and descending vehicles counterbalanced; usually cable operated.

G

Gauge (1) Distance between one rail and the other. Standard gauge is 1,435 mm (4 ft 8½ in), but several other gauges, broader and narrower, are in common use. (2) Dial indicating *boiler* pressure, etc, usually only in steam *locomotives*.
Gondola Flat, roofless car with low sides.
Grade When the railway is not traveling horizontally. It is expressed as a percentage rise or fall to the slope length, eg 2 percent down shows that the train descends 1 unit for every 50 units it travels. Two percent is steep for a main line railway.
Ground signal Secondary signal fixed at low level to aid the driver.

H

Headstock Lateral bar, part of the underframe of a freight car or coach, for the attachment of buffers or *coupler*.
High-pressure steam In locomotives, those designed to operate with a boiler pressure in excess of 14 kg/cm² (200 lb/in²).
Home signal Mandatory stop signal at entrance or exit of station, block section or junction to control movement of trains in that area.
Hopper car Freight car with opening bottom doors through which the load is discharged.
Hot box Overheated *journal box* bearing as a result of insufficient lubrication.
Hot box detector Automatic device installed in track to detect overheating in *journal box*.
Hump Artificial mound in *classification yard* over which cars are pushed before rolling down by gravity to their correct location.
Hydraulic Describes the control, usually mechanical, of water or other liquid flow through pipes, etc.

I

Induction Production of an electric current in a conductor, either by changes in the magnetic field in which it lies, or by motion of a magnet nearby.

J

Journal box Metal box, through which ends of axle pass, enclosing axle bearing and its lubrication system.

L

Light railway Branch line or short line railway, often narrow gauge, constructed cheaply. Poorly laid track and steep grades often necessitate slow speeds.
Livery Standard colors and design used for *locomotives* and cars of a particular railway company or line.
Loading gauge Maximum permitted height and width of a loaded train to ensure clearance of trackside structures.
Lock and block Refinement of the *block system* whereby it is physically impossible to signal a second train into a section of line until the first one has left it.
Locking bar Long bar along the inside of running rails and connected to the lock of mechanically operated *facing points* in order to hold the points in position while a train is passing.
Locomotive Steam, diesel or electric engine, one or more of which is used to draw a series of freight or passenger cars to form a train.
Loop, passing Short section of single-line railway which is double-tracked to allow trains going in opposite directions to pass.
Low-pressure steam (1) Pressure of exhaust steam from *compound* locomotive. (2) In a simple *locomotive*, *boiler* pressure below approximately 14 kg/cm² (200 lb/in²).

M

Manganese rail Steel rail toughened by the inclusion of more than 1% manganese.

Manual block Manually operated *block signaling* system.

Mixed traffic Steam locomotive designed to be able to work either fast passenger or heavy freight trains.

Mixed train Train which consists of both freight and passenger cars.

Monorail Railway system where only one running rail is needed. Most monorail trains run suspended beneath an elevated track.

Multiple-aspect signal System of *color light signaling* in which each signal unit can display more than two colors.

Multiple-unit train Train drawn by two or more *locomotives* (or powered vehicles) coupled together and operated by one engineer.

N

Net ton mile Commonly-used measurement of freight carried. Achieved by multiplying the *payload* of a freight train by the distance it has traveled.

Nominal rating Maximum efficient speed at which a machine may be driven without causing undue strain.

Nose Pointed part of a *crossing* or *points*, either fixed or movable. Also known as the angle.

P

Pacific Steam *locomotive* with 4-6-2 wheel arrangement.

Pallet Movable flat base used for storage or transport of goods.

Pantograph Conductor transmitting power to the circuit of an electrically operated car from an overhead contact wire.

Passenger mile Figure achieved by multiplying the number of passengers by the distance they travel. A more accurate indicator of the use made of the railways than merely counting the number of journeys undertaken.

Payload Weight of revenue-earning load of a train – ie freight, etc.

Piggyback operation Conveyance by rail of highway trailers on rail flatcars.

Poppet valve Independent, mushroom-shaped inlet and outlet valve operated by *camshaft* to ensure quick action by improving steam distribution and reducing back pressure.

Power to weight Ratio of power generated by a *locomotive* to its total weight.

Pullman car In Europe passenger car designed for luxury travel. In USA, sleeping car.

R

Rack system System used in mountainous country whereby propulsion is effected, and slipping prevented, by interaction between a cog or pinion on the *locomotive* and a cogged or rack rail laid between the running rails.

Rail, continuous welded Any rail up to $\frac{1}{4}$ mile long formed by welding together standard or short lengths of rail.

Rail, edge The early name for modern style rails, which require vehicles to have flanged wheels. Used to distinguish this style from the original L-shaped "plate rails."

Rail spike Device for fastening rail to *tie*.

Railcar Self-powered passenger carrying vehicle.

Railroad Railway (US only).

Rectifier Instrument which converts *alternating current* to *direct current*.

Regulator Valve in a steam *locomotive* which controls steam flow from the *boiler* to the cylinder.

Repeater signal Advance warning signal used when normal signal is obstructed from engineer's view.

Retarder Braking system used on a *hump* in *classification yard*.

Roundhouse Circular engine house with central turntable. Now obsolete.

Route indicator Illuminated panel attached to a junction signal to indicate which of a number of possible routes is to be taken.

Route length Overall length of route run by a particular country or railway company over which journeys are made, excluding *sidings* and *switching* areas, etc.

S

Safety valve Valve in steam *boiler* which opens automatically to release excess steam and thus relieve pressure.

Semaphore Fixed signal with one or more movable arms which, when horizontal, or "on" indicate "stop".

Servo Denotes power-assisted device.

Shinkansen Japanese high-speed line.

Shock absorber Device linked to suspension to dampen vertical oscillation.

Siding Short track alongside main line for the purpose of *switching*, storing or passing.

Slab track Experimental low maintenance track, the base of which is made up of a continuous stretch of concrete or asphalt, as opposed to *ties* and *ballast*, thus minimizing settlement and changes in alignment.

Sleeper Car on long-distance train which contains sleeping accommodation.

Slide valve Valve with sliding plate for opening and closing gap between steam chest and cylinder of a steam engine.

Smokebox Chamber in steam *boiler* located between chimney and flues.

Spark arrester Mesh or plate contained in the smokebox to prevent sparks and live coals issuing from the stack.

Spiral tunnel Tunnel built in spiral formation rather than straight in order to gain height when crossing mountains, etc.

Stephenson valve gear Commonly used *valve gear* designed in 1842 by an employee of Robert Stephenson & Company.

Streamliner Vehicle shaped so as to reduce air resistance and thus increase speed.

Supercharger Device supplying *diesel engine* with air at high pressure in order to increase efficiency.

Superelevation Amount of elevation of one rail above the other at a curve in the track.

Superheater Device used for raising temperature of steam as it leaves the *boiler* barrel in order to increase its pressure.

Switch Divert vehicles on to a subsidiary line or *siding*, or classify them into a specific order.

Switch heater Heater fitted to *switches* to prevent freezing.

Switching, gravity System of *switching* or classification carried out on a grade and relying on gravity to propel the freight cars to their correct *siding*.

Switch lock Compulsory safety device fitted to *facing switches* on passenger-carrying lines, usually comprising a bolt which slots into the bar between the points and is operated from the signal box. A link to the relevant signals ensures that the points must be fully closed and locked before a signal is cleared.

Switch Movable rails by which a train is directed from one line to another. "Facing" switches are those presenting a forward moving train with a choice of direction; "trailing" switches are those over which a train has to reverse in order to switch tracks.

Switches, interlocking Switches whose operation is linked to corresponding signals to ensure synchronized movement, thus preventing accidents.

Switch point The thinned rail at the actual place of junction in a switch.

Synchronous Applied to an electric motor, the speed of which is directly proportionate to the supply frequency.

T

TEE (Trans-Europe Express) Luxury trans-European passenger service containing first-class accommodation exclusively.

Tender Car coupled to a *locomotive* for the purpose of carrying fuel and water.

TGV (Très grande vitesse) The French equivalent of England's APT (Advanced Passenger Train).

Third rail system System of carrying electric current along a third rail for supply to electric *locomotive* or train.

Throttle *Regulator* that controls speed of locomotive.

Thyristor control Thyristors are a form of transistor used in the power regulator of modern electric and diesel-electric *locomotives* to give a smoother power control with a continuous current flow.

Tie Wooden, steel or concrete beam laid transversely on *ballast* to support rails and spread load of passing vehicles.

Tie plate Metal plate between the flat-bottomed rail and *tie* whose purpose is to spread the weight of passing vehicles.

Tire Steel band on outer edge of wheel.

Track relay Essential part of a track-circuited modern signaling system where a low voltage current is fed through the rails of each section. The presence of a train in that section short circuits the current and trips the relay, causing indicator lamps to light on the signal box control panel.

Tractive effort The nominal power capable of being developed by the cylinders of a *locomotive* at the moment of starting, calculated by multiplying the cylinder volume by the boiler pressure, and taking into consideration the diameter of the driving wheels.

Truck Undercarriage with four or more wheels attached by a pivot under each end of car to facilitate negotiation of curves.

Turbine Rotary engine driven by gas or steam flowing on to a series of vanes on a revolving disk or cylinder.

Turbotrain Train drawn by *locomotive* powered by a *turbine*.

U

UIC (International Union of Railways) Organization founded in 1922 for the purpose of standardizing and improving railway equipment and operations.

Underframe Framework or supporting structure beneath a car or *locomotive*.

Unit coal train Permanently-coupled train of hopper cars used for regular bulk traffic between mine and power station. The train may load and unload without actually stopping, while negotiating a circular loop line.

V

Valve gear Mechanism controlling steam distribution valve in the cylinder of a *locomotive*.

Valve, reducing Device whereby pressure of steam from the *boiler* is reduced to around 4 kg/cm² (60 lb/in²) to heat passenger cars.

Variable gauge Facility for operating on more than one track *gauge*. Applicable to car or *wheel* set where wheel may be moved along axle and repositioned as required.

Viaduct Bridge resting on series of narrow arches, having high supporting piers, and carrying a railway over a valley or river.

W

Wagon-lit (Fr) Luxury sleeping car run by Cie Internationale des Wagons Lits.

Waste Point immediately below window level of a car.

Walschaert's valve gear Widely used steam *locomotive valve gear* designed by Edige Walschaert in 1844.

Wheel set Pair of wheels secured to an axle.

Whyte system Classification of *locomotives* based on arrangement of wheels, eg 2-4-2 – two leading wheels, four driving wheels and two trailing wheels. The continental system refers to wheel sets, thus 1-2-1.

Working schedule Schedule featuring all trains which are run over a specified route or area.

Y

Yard limit Limit, marked by a board, beyond which switching *locomotives* may not work.

Words in italic type indicate a cross reference.

Bibliography

Historical

E. L. Ahrons, *Locomotive and train working in the latter part of the nineteenth century*, vols 1–5, Heffer, 1952.

James Buck, *Discovering Narrow Gauge Railways*, Shire, 1972.

Michael Conant, *Railroad Mergers and Abandonments*, California University Press, 1964.

Michael Darby, *Early Railway Prints*, V & A Museum Exhibition Catalogue, 1974.

W. J. K. Davies, *Light Railways: their rise and decline*, Ian Allan, 1964.

S. Kip Farrington, Jr, *Railroads at War (USA)*, Coward McCann, 1944.

Brian Haresnape, *Railway Design since 1830*, vols 1 & 2, Ian Allan, 1968 and 1969.

Paul Hastings, *Railroads: an international history*, Benn, 1972.

Edward Hungerford, *From Covered Waggon to Streamliner*, Greystones Press, 1941.

Henry Grote Lewin, *Railway Mania and its Aftermath, 1845–1852*, David & Charles, 1968.

M. J. T. Lewis, *Early Wooden Railways*, Routledge, 1970.

John Stewart Murphy and Charles Keeping, *Railways: How they were built*, Oxford University Press, 1964.

O. S. Nock, *Railways in the transition from steam 1940–1965*, Blandford, 1974.

O. S. Nock, *Railways Then and Now*, Paul Elek, 1975.

T. M. Simmons, *Railways 2: the 20th century*, HMSO, 1969.

J. B. Snell, *Early Railways*, Weidenfeld & Nicolson, 1964.

Gerard Vuillet, *Railway Reminiscences of Three Continents*, Nelson, 1968.

J. R. S. Whiting, *Coming of the Railways 1808–1892*, Evans, 1972.

Engineering and architecture

E. F. Carter, *Famous Railway Stations of the World and their Traffic*, Muller, 1958.

Terry Coleman, *The Railway Navvies*, Penguin, 1968.

Peter Haining, *Eurotunnel: an illustrated history of the Channel Tunnel scheme*, New English Library, 1973.

Alan A. Jackson, *London's Termini*, David & Charles, 1969.

Bryan Morgan, *Civil Engineering: Railways*, Longman, 1971.

John Prebble, *High Girders: the story of the Tay Bridge disaster*, Secker & Warburg, 1975 (new ed).

Jack Simmons, *St Pancras Station*, Allen & Unwin, 1968.

Technical

Cecil J. Allen, *Modern Railways*, Faber & Faber, 1959.

Philip Burtt, *Principal Factors in Freight Train Operating*, Allen & Unwin, 1924.

John R. Day and Brian G. Wilson, *Unusual Railways*, Muller, 1957.

Horace Greenleaf and G. Tyers, *Permanent Way*, Winchester Publications, 1948.

G. M. Kitchenside and Alan Williams, *British Railway Signalling*, Ian Allan, 1975.

O. S. Nock, *British Railway Signalling*, Allen & Unwin, 1969.

O. S. Nock, *50 Years of Railway Signalling*, Institution of Railway Signal Engineers, 1954.

Railway Clearing House, *Railway Junction Diagrams, 1915: a Reprint*, David & Charles, 1969.

Michael Robbins, *Points and Signals: A railway historian at work*, Allen & Unwin, 1967.

Locomotives

E. L. Ahrons, *The British Railway Steam Locomotive 1825–1925*, Ian Allan, 1963.

Peter Allen and Robert Wheeler, *Steam on the Sierra: the narrow gauge in Spain and Portugal*, Cleaver-Hume, 1960.

A Century Plus of Locomotives, New South Wales Railways 1855–1965, Australian Railway Historical Society.

William Bay, *Danmarks Damp-Lokomotiver*, Herluf Andersens Forlag, 1977.

Alfred W. Bruce, *The Steam Locomotive in America*, Allen & Unwin, 1952.

W. J. K. Davies, *Diesel Rail Traction*, Almark, 1973.

Diesel Traction: Manual for enginemen, British Railways, 1962.

A. E. Durrant, *Garrett Locomotive*, David & Charles, 1969.

A. E. Durrant, *PNKA Power Parade: Indonesian steam locomotives*, Continental Railway Circle, 1974.

Graham Glover, *French Steam Locomotives 1840–1950*, Barry Rose, 1974.

D. W. and M. Hinde, *Electric and Diesel-Electric Locomotives*, Macmillan, 1948.

Ralph P. Johnson, *The Steam Locomotive*, Simmons-Boardman, 1942.

R. W. Kidner, *Development of the Railcar* (Locomotion papers No 12), Oakwood Press, 1958.

L. G. Marshall, *Steam on the RENFE: steam locomotive stock of the Spanish National Railways*, Macmillan, 1965.

O. S. Nock, *The British Railway Steam Locomotive 1925–1965*, Ian Allan, 1966.

O. S. Nock, *British Steam Locomotives at Work*, Allen & Unwin, 1967.

O. S. Nock, *Great Western Railway Stars, Castles and Kings*, vols 1 & 2, David & Charles, 1967 and 1970.

O. S. Nock, *Great Western Railway Steam*, David & Charles, 1972.

O. S. Nock, *Gresley Pacifics*, vols 1 & 2, David & Charles, 1973 and 1974.

O. S. Nock, *Historical Steam Locomotives*, A. & C. Black, 1959.

O. S. Nock, *Locomotion*, Routledge & Kegan Paul, 1975.

O. S. Nock, *London Midland and Scottish Steam*, David & Charles, 1971.

O. S. Nock, *London and North Eastern Railway Steam*, David & Charles, 1968.

O. S. Nock, *London and North Western Railway Locomotives of C. J. Bowen Cooke*, Bradford Barton, 1977.

O. S. Nock, *London and North Western Railway Precursor Family*, David & Charles, 1966.

O. S. Nock, *Railways of the World in Colour* (series), Blandford.

O. S. Nock, *Royal Scots and Patriots of the London Midland and Scottish*, David & Charles, 1978.

O. S. Nock, *Southern Steam*, David & Charles, 1966

O. S. Nock, *Steam Locomotive*, Allen & Unwin, 1968.

A. N. Palmer and W. Stewart, *Cavalcade of New Zealand Locomotives 1863–1964*, Angus & Robertson, 1965.

P. Ransome-Wallis, *Last Steam Locomotives of British Railways*, Ian Allan, 1973.

P. Ransome-Wallis, *Last Steam Locomotives of Eastern Europe*, Ian Allan, 1974.

James G. Robins, *World Steam Locomotives*, Bartholomew, 1973

Josef Otto Slezak, *Lokomotiven der Republik Österreich*, Verlag Slezak, 1973.

J. G. H. Warren, *A Century of Locomotive Building by Robert Stephenson and Co 1823–1923*, David & Charles, 1970.

Brian Webb, *British Internal Combustion Locomotives 1894–1940*, David & Charles, 1973.

G. F. Westcott, *The British Railway Locomotive*, HMSO, 1958.

D. W. Winkworth, *Bulleid's Pacifics*, Allen & Unwin, 1974.

Great trains and train journeys

Cecil J. Allen, *Titled Trains of Great Britain*, Ian Allan, 1967.

Michael Barsley, *Orient Express*, Macdonald, 1966.

George Behrend, *Geschichte der Luxuszüge*, Orell Füssli, 1977.

George Behrend, *History of the Wagons-Lits 1875–1955*, Modern Transport, 1959.

George Behrend, *Pullman in Europe*, Ian Allan, 1962.

Geoffrey Blainey, *Across a Red World*, Macmillan, 1968.

E. F. Carter, *Famous Trains of the World*, Muller, 1959.

A. I. Dmitriev-Mamonov, *Guide to the Great Siberian Railway, 1900* (revised by John Marshall), David & Charles, 1971.

Garry Hogg, *Orient Express: Birth, life & death of a great train*, Hutchinson, 1968.

Kenneth Westcott Jones, *Exciting Journeys of the World*, Redman, 1967.

O. S. Nock, *"The Limited" – Cornish Riviera Express*, Allen & Unwin, 1978.

Martin Page, *The Lost Pleasures of the Great Trains*, Weidenfeld & Nicolson, 1975.

P. Ransome-Wallis, *On Railways at Home and Abroad*, Spring Books 1960.

Paul Theroux, *The Great Railway Bazaar*, Hamish Hamilton, 1975.

P. B. Whitehouse, *Great Trains of the World*, Hamlyn, 1975.

Railways of Great Britain

Derek H. Aldcroft, *British Railways in Transition: the economic problems of Britain's railways since 1914*, Macmillan, 1968.

Cecil J. Allen, *Salute to the London Midland and Scottish*, Ian Allan, 1972.

J. I. C. Boyd, *Narrow Gauge Railways in South Caernarvonshire*, Oakwood Press, 1972.

British Railways Board, *Reshaping of British Railways*, parts 1 & 2, HMSO, 1963.

E. F. Carter, *Historical Geography of the Railways of the British Isles*, Cassell, 1959.

E. F. Carter, *Britain's Railway Liveries, 1825–1948*, H. Starke, 1963.

M. P. L. Caton and J. M. Stanler, *Railways in the Seventies*, Railway Invigoration Society, 1973.

Rex Christiansen, *West Midlands*, Regional History of the Railways of Great Britain, vol 7, David & Charles, 1973.

Edwin Course, *London Railways*, Batsford, 1962.

George Dow, *Great Central*, vols 1–3, Ian Allan, 1962, 1962 and 1965.

C. Hamilton Ellis, *Midland Railway*, Ian Allan, 1955.

C. Hamilton Ellis, *Railway Carriages in the British Isles 1830–1914*, Allen & Unwin, 1965.

R. J. Essery, D. P. Rowland and W. O. Steel, *British Goods Wagons from 1887 to the Present Day*, David & Charles, 1970.

G. F. Fiennes, *I Tried to Run a Railway*, Ian Allan, 1973 (revised ed).

D. I. Gordon, *Eastern Counties*, Regional History of the Railways of Great Britain, vol 5, David & Charles, 1968.

J. A. B. Hamilton, *Britain's Railways in World War One*, Allen & Unwin, 1967.

Campbell Highet, *Scottish Locomotive History 1831–1923*, Allen & Unwin, 1970.

Kenneth Hoole, *North East*, Regional History of the Railways of Great Britain, vol 4, David & Charles, 1974.

E. T. MacDermot, *History of the Great Western Railway*, vols 1 & 2, revised by C. R. Clinker, Ian Allan, 1964 and 1967.

C. F. Dendry Marshall, *History of British Railways down to the year 1830*, Oxford University Press, 1971.

G. T. Moody, *Southern Electric: the history of the world's largest suburban electrified system*, Ian Allan, 1968.

O. S. Nock, *Britain's Railways at War 1939–1945*, Ian Allan, 1971.

O. S. Nock, *British Railways in Action*, Nelson, 1956.

O. S. Nock, *British Railways in Transition*, Nelson, 1963.

O. S. Nock, *British Steam Railways*, A. & C. Black, 1961.

O. S. Nock, *Caledonian Railway*, Ian Allan, 1962.

O. S. Nock, *Electric Euston to Glasgow*, Ian Allan, 1974.

O. S. Nock, *The Golden Age of Steam*, A. & C. Black, 1973.

O. S. Nock, *Great Northern Railway*, Ian Allan, 1958.

O. S. Nock, *Great Western Railway, 19th Century*, Ian Allan, 1962.

O. S. Nock, *Great Western Railway, 20th Century*, Ian Allan, 1964.

O. S. Nock, *Highland Railway*, Ian Allan, 1965.

O. S. Nock, *History of the Great Western Railway*, vol 3, Ian Allan, 1967.

O. S. Nock, *Lancashire and Yorkshire Railway*, Ian Allan, 1969.

O. S. Nock, *London and North Western Railway*, Ian Allan, 1968.

O. S. Nock, *London and South Western Railway*, Ian Allan, 1966.

O. S. Nock, *Railway Race to the North*, Ian Allan, 1958.

O. S. Nock, *Scottish Railways*, Nelson, 1961.

O. S. Nock, *South Eastern and Chatham Railway*, Ian Allan, 1961.

O. S. Nock, *Steam Railways in Retrospect*, A. & C. Black, 1966.

B. Roberts, *Railways and Mineral Tramways of Rossendale*, Locomotion Papers No 76, Oakwood Press, 1974.

L. T. C. Rolt, *Railway Adventure*, David & Charles, 1961.

D. W. Ronald and R. J. Carter, *Longmoor Military Railway*, David & Charles, 1974.

Jack Simmons (ed), *Rail 150: The Stockton & Darlington Railway and what followed*, Methuen, 1975.

Roger Spear, *British Railways System*, Open University, 1975.

A. K. Steele, *Great Western Broad Gauge Album*, Oxford Publishing, 1972.

John Thomas, *Scotland*, Forgotten Railways Series, David & Charles, 1976.

David St. John Thomas, *West Country*, Regional History of the Railways of Great Britain, vol 1, David & Charles, 1973.

Norman W. Webster, *Britain's First Trunk Line: the Grand Junction Railway*, Adams, 1972.

Henry Patrick White, *Southern England*, Regional History of the Railways of Great Britain, vol 2, David & Charles, 1969.

Railways of Europe
Cecil J. Allen, *Switzerland's Amazing Railways*, Nelson, 1965.

G. Freeman Allen, *Into the 125 m.p.h. Era on French Railways*, Ian Allan, 1972.

Michael H. C. Baker, *Irish Railways since 1916*, Ian Allan, 1972.

George Behrend, *Railway Holiday in France*, David & Charles, 1964.

H. C. Casserley, *Outline of Irish Railway History*, David & Charles, 1974.

W. J. K. Davies, *French Minor Railways*, David & Charles, 1965.

W. J. K. Davies, *Railway Holiday in Northern Germany*, Macdonald, 1965.

H. Fayle, *Narow-Gauge Railways of Ireland*, S. R. Publishers, 1970.

Claude Jeanmaire, *Elektrischen und Diesel-Triebfahrzeuge Schweizerischer Eisenbahnen*, vol 1, Basle Eisenbahn und Strassenbahnliteratur, 1970.

P. M. Kalla-Bishop, *Hungarian Railways*, David & Charles, 1973.

P. M. Kalla-Bishop, *Italian Railways*, David & Charles, 1971.

P. M. Kalla-Bishop, *Mediterranean Island Railways*, David & Charles, 1970.

Ole Winther Laursen, *Bygone Light Railways of Europe*, Oakwood Press, 1973.

John Marshall, *Metre Gauge Railways in South and East Switzerland*, David & Charles, 1974.

Franz Marti and Walter Trub, *Gotthard Railway*, Ian Allan, 1971.

O. S. Nock, *Contintental Main Lines: today and yesterday*, Allen & Unwin, 1963.

O. S. Nock, *Railway Holiday in Austria*, Macdonald, 1965.

O. S. Nock, *Railways of Western Europe*, A. & C. Black, 1977.

J. H. Price, *Railway Holiday in Bavaria*, David & Charles, 1967.

D. Trevor Rowe, *Railway Holiday in Spain*, David & Charles, 1966.

D. Trevor Rowe, *Spain and Portugal*, Ian Allan, 1970.

Ascanio Schneider, *Railways through the Mountains of Europe*, Ian Allan, 1967.

J. B. Snell, *France* (Continental Railway Handbook), Ian Allan, 1971.

H. A. Vallance, *Railway Holiday in Northern Norway and Sweden*, David & Charles, 1964.

D. W. Winkworth, *Railway Holiday in Portugal*, David & Charles, 1968.

Railways outside Europe
George Behrend and Vincent Kelly, *Yaktali Vagon: Turkish steam travel*, Spearman, 1969.

P. S. A. Berridge, *Couplings to the Khyber*, David & Charles, 1969.

George S. Brady, *Railways of South America*, parts 1 & 2, US Dept of Commerce, 1926.

E. D. Brant, *Railways of North Africa*, David & Charles, 1971.

Robert B. Carson, *Main Line to Oblivion: the disintegration of New York railroads in the 20th century*, Kennikat Press, 1971.

Antony H. Croxton, *Railways of Rhodesia*, David & Charles, 1973.

John R. Day, *Railways of Northern Africa*, Arthur Barker, 1964.

John R. Day, *Railways of Southern Africa*, Arthur Barker, 1963.

Brian Fawcett, *Railways of the Andes*, Allen & Unwin, 1963.

John Murray Gibbon, *Steel of Empire: the romantic history of the Canadian Pacific*, Rich & Cowan, 1935.

Wesley S. Griswold, *Work of Giants: building the first transcontinental railroad*, Muller, 1963.

Richard Hall and Hugh Peyman, *The Great Uhuru Railway*, Gollancz, 1976.

Richard Hill, *Sudan Transport*, Oxford University Press, 1965.

Harold A. Innis, *History of the Canadian Pacific Railroad*, David & Charles, 1972.

S. E. Katzenellenbogen, *Railways and the Copper Mines of Katanga*, Oxford University Press, 1973.

D. B. Leitch, *Railways of New Zealand*, David & Charles, 1972.

W. Long, *Railways of South America*, vol III (Chile), US Dept of Commerce, 1926.

Norman Mackillop, *Western Rail Trail*, Nelson, 1962.

M. B. K. Malik, *Hundred Years of Pakistan Railways 1861–1961*, Ministry of Railways & Communications, Karachi, 1962.

S. M. Moir and H. Crittenden, *Namib Narrow Gauge*, Oakwood Press, 1967.

O. S. Nock, *Railways of Australia*, A. & C. Black, 1971.

O. S. Nock, *Railways of Canada*, A. & C. Black, 1973.

O. S. Nock, *Railways of Southern Africa*, A. & C. Black, 1971.

O. S. Nock, *Railways in Asia and the Far East*, A. & C. Black, 1978.

David M. Pletcher, *Rails, Mines and Progress: seven American promoters in Mexico 1867–1911*, Kennikat Press, 1972.

Charles S. Small, *Rails to the Setting Sun*, Kigei, 1971.

Patsy Adam Smith, *Romance of Australian Railways*, Hale, 1974.

J. A. Stanistreet, *Keretapi Tanah Melayu: The Malayan Railway*, Oakwood Press, 1974.

Harmon Tupper, *To the Great Ocean: Siberia and the Trans-Siberian Railway*, Secker & Warburg, 1965.

H. J. von Lochow, *China's National Railways*, privately published, 1948.

J. N. Westwood, *Railways of India*, David & Charles, 1974.

J. N. Westwood, *Soviet Railways Today*, Ian Allan, 1963.

Robert and Bruce Wheatley, *Last Days of Steam on Australia's Railways*, Angus & Robertson, 1971.

Winthrop R. Wright, *British-owned Railways in Argentina: their effect on economic nationalism 1854–1948*, Texas University Press, 1974.

Biography
H. A. V. Bulleid, *Bulleid of the Southern*, Ian Allan, 1977.

Richard S. Lambert, *Railway King: a study of George Hudson and the business morals of his time*, Allen & Unwin, 1934.

Oscar Lewis, *Big Four: the story of Huntington, Stanford, Hopkins, and Crocker, and the building of the Central Pacific*, Knopf, 1938.

John Marshall, *Lives of the Engineers*, David & Charles, 1978.

O. S. Nock, *William Stanier: an engineering biography*, Ian Allan, 1963.

E. M. S. Paine, *Two James's and two Stephensons*, Phoenix House, 1961.

Sir Alfred Pugsley (ed), *The Works of Isambard Kingdom Brunel*, Institution of Civil Engineers and University of Bristol, 1976.

L. T. C. Rolt, *Brunel*, Penguin, 1970.

L. T. C. Rolt, *George and Robert Stephenson*, Longman, 1960.

Charles Walker, *Thomas Brassey: Railway builder*, Muller, 1969.

N. W. Webster, *Joseph Locke: Railway revolutionary*, Allen & Unwin, 1970.

Archibald Williams, *Brunel and After*, Stephens, 1972.

Reference
British Railways Pre-Grouping Atlas and Gazetteer, Ian Allan, 1965.

Robert C. Fisher (ed), *Fodor's Railways of the World*, Hodder & Stoughton, 1977.

Paul J. Goldsack (ed), *Jane's World Railways*, Jane's Yearbooks, annual.

John Marshall, *Guinness Book of Rail Facts and Feats*, Guinness Superlatives, 1971.

O. S. Nock (ed), *Encyclopedia of Railways*, Octopus, 1977.

O. S. Nock, *The Railway Enthusiast's Encyclopedia*, Hutchinson, 1968.

A. C. O'Dell and P. S. Richards, *Railways and Geography*, Hutchinson, 2nd ed, 1971.

J. H. Price (ed), *Thomas Cook International Timetable*, Thomas Cook Ltd, monthly.

Railway Directory and Year Book, Railway Gazette International, annual.

Miscellaneous
George Dow, *Railway Heraldry*, David & Charles, 1973.

C. Hamilton Ellis, *Beauty of Railways*, Parrish, 1960.

G. H. I. Fairchild, *The World of Tickets*, published privately, 1972.

Miles Mosrich, *Railways and the Great Pyramid* Bungalow Books, 1977.

P. B. Whitehouse (ed), *Railway Relics and Regalia*, Hamlyn for Country Life, 1975.

Index

REFERENCE

Acknowledgements

The Editor gratefully acknowledges help, advice and encouragement from the following.

Susie Ward, Paul Ekpenyong, Chris Milsome Ltd

Miss M Abbot, Dr J Davies, Birkbeck College, London
British Rail, BRB Press Office, Public Relations for Southern, London Midland, Eastern and Western Regions
British Rail Engineering Ltd, Works Manager Crewe, Public Relations Derby
Emmanuel Haussman, Carta, Jerusalem
Donald J Martin, Charles Laggan, E F Stefanovich, Conrail
J H Price, Cook's International Timetable
Messers Douglas, Ludlow, Middlehurst and Page, Crown Agents, London
Sarah Dale
Department of Trade and Industry, Export House Library
Diagram Ltd, London
Sally Foy
Railway Gazette International, Editorial Staff
J N Slater, Railway Magazine
Severn Valley Railway
Deborah Yates

Photographs

Picture research was assisted by Helen Fayers, Annie Horton and Jonathan Moore

Picture credits are by page number, additional numbers read in order from top to bottom and left to right, taken together; i.e. top left first, bottom right last.

Alco/O S Nock, 36/4
American History Picture Library, 13/1, 27/1, 38/1, 122/1, 122/2
Ann Ronan Picture Library, 30/1, 30/3, 41/3, 42/3, 43/3, 48/5
Arts Directors Library, 25/2, 86/4, 90/2, 94
ASEA, 53, 178/1
Barnabys Picture Library, 80/1, 105/2, 106
John Bennett/Chris Milsome Ltd, 25/3, 25/4, 40/2, 40/4, 42/2, 42/4, 42/5, 43/5, 45/5, 46/4, 47/3, 48/2, 68/2, 70/2, 82/2, 83, 84/1, 88/1, 182/2, 183/1, 189/1
Chris Bonington/Bruce Coleman Ltd, 112
British Rail/O S Nock, 42/1, 43/1
British Transport Films, 45/4, 45/6, 52/2, 52/3, 55/3, 55/4, 57/1, 57/4, 62, 63/2, 63/3, 64/5, 66/5, 67/4, 68/1, 116/2
Canadian National Railways, 67/4
Canadian Pacific Ltd, 126
Kenneth Cantlie, 95/1
Chicago N.W. Railway, 67/2
CIE, 180/1
Colour Library International Ltd, 61/2
Colourviews Publications, 14, P M Alexander, 117/4, J Dunn, 64/2, P J Howard, 44/1, 44/2, 45/3, 59/2, 66/4, 69/4, 69/5, 75, 127/1, C M Whitehouse, 65/1, 65/3, 206, P B Whitehouse, 35/2, 39/3, 66/2, 77/2, 115/5
Denver Rio Grande Western Railroad/O S Nock, 22/1
Derek Cross/O S Nock, 116/3
A P Dowley, 44/2, 44/3, 44/4
EBT Bahn, 32/1
Edito Service, 27/2
EMI Films Ltd, 115/4, 115/5, 115/6
Robert Estall, 45/1, 105/1, 202/2
Fox Photos Ltd, 6/1, 23/1, 54/1
Christopher Gammell, 95/2, 115/3, 125/1, 188, 189/2, 193, 203
Victor Goldberg, 115/1, 116/1
High Commissioner for New Zealand, London, 28/2
Michael Holford, 33
Ann Horton, 26/1
Alan Hutchinson, 50/2, 198
Illustrated London News, 82/3, 82/4

Intercontainer, 68/4
Italian Railways, 54/4, 54/5, 119/2
Japan Information Centre, 100/1, 100/3, 103/1, 103/2
Kiwi, 99/2
Mike Laye/Chris Milsome Ltd, 48/3, 48/4, 51/2, 58/2, 59/4, 63/1, 70/3, 71/1, 71/2, 71/3, 71/4, 73/2, 76/1, 88/2, 117/1, 117/2, 117/3, 118/1, 118/2, 119/1
R H Leach/O S Nock, 34/1
L G Marshall, 39/1, 61/1, 72/1, 128/2, 128/3
Mary Evans Picture Library, 17, 18/1, 18/2, 19, 20/2, 30/2, 40/1, 40/3, 40/5, 41/1, 41/2, 43/2, 43/4, 114
Ken Mills, 111/1
Jonathan Moore, 11/1, 109/2
National Railway Museum York, Crown Copyright, 6/2, 32/2
O S Nock, 32/3, 35/1, 100/2, 101, 128/1
Paul Forrester/Science Museum, London, 10/3, 11/3
Pictor, 60/2, 64/3, 77/1, 196
Picturepoint London/Kay Mander, 115/2
Popperfoto, 20/1, 21/1, 21/2, 21/3, 92
Roger Pring, 4, 5, 7, 48/1, 49, 81, 113, 129, 177, 209
Radio Times Hulton Picture Library, 16/1, 16/2, 22/2, 22/3, 22/4, 23/2, 36/3, 38/3, 82/2
Walter Rawlings, 36/3, 47/1, 56/2, 58/4, 59/2, 59/4, 66/6, 66/7, 67/3, 68/5, 69/2, 69/3, 80/2, 80/3
RENFE, 61/4
Rex Features, 39/2, 54/2, 54/3, 55/5
Robert Harding Associates, 127/2, 178/2, 191/2, 202/1
G R Roberts, 66/2, 96/1, 173/3
Santa Fe Railroad Company, 123
Santa Fe/J G Moore, 78/1, 78/2, 79
Science Museum, London, 10/1, 10/2, 11/4, 12, 13/2, 26/2, 43/6
Roy Sinclair, 98/1, 98/2, 99/1, 208
SNCF, 45/2, 55/1, 55/2, 91/1, 91/2, 120, 121/1, 121/2
South African Railways, Publicity and Travel Department, 60/1, 65/4, 124/1, 125/2
Spectrum Colour Library, 25/5, 37, 46/1, 46/2, 46/3, 47/4, 50/3, 51/1, 52/1, 61/3, 65/2, 67/1, 68/3, 70/1, 97, 103/3, 107/1, 108/2, 123/2, 180/2, 181/2
Brian Stephenson, 85/1, 85/2, 184/2, 185, 186/1, 186/2, 187/1, 187/2, 189/5
Tony Stone Associates, 25/1, 28/1, 31, 34/2, 102/1, 104, 108/1, 179, 192
Swiss Railways, 47/2, 84/2, 86/1
Syndication International, 36/2
P N Trotter, 39/4, 50/1, 56/1, 58/1, 58/3, 66/1
VIA Rail Canada, 127/5
J Winkley, 64/1, 64/4, 69/1, 86/3, 182
ZEFA, 51/3, 58/5, 86/2, 87, 90/1, 93, 109/1, 181/1, 183/2, 184, 204, front cover